Cambridge Studies in Early Modern British History

CHARLES I AND THE ROAD
TO PERSONAL RULE

Cambridge Studies in Early Modern British History

Series editors

ANTHONY FLETCHER

Professor of Modern History, University of Durham

JOHN GUY

Reader in British History, University of Bristol

and JOHN MORRILL

Lecturer in History, University of Cambridge, and
Fellow and Tutor of Selwyn College

This is a series of monographs and studies covering many aspects of the history of the British Isles between the late fifteenth century and the early eighteenth century. It includes the work of established scholars and pioneering work by a new generation of scholars. It includes both reviews and revisions of major topics and books which open up new historical terrain or which reveal startling new perspectives on familiar subjects. All the volumes set detailed research into broader perspectives and the books are intended for the use of students as well as of their teachers.

For a list of titles in the series, see end of book.

CHARLES I
AND THE ROAD
TO PERSONAL RULE

L. J. REEVE

Lecturer in History,
University of Hong Kong

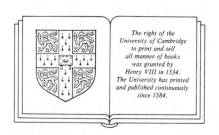

The right of the
University of Cambridge
to print and sell
all manner of books
was granted by
Henry VIII in 1534.
The University has printed
and published continuously
since 1584.

CAMBRIDGE UNIVERSITY PRESS

Cambridge
New York   Port Chester
Melbourne   Sydney

Published by the Press Syndicate of the University of Cambridge
The Pitt Building, Trumpington Street, Cambridge CB2 1RP
40 West 20th Street, New York, NY 10011, USA
10 Stamford Road, Oakleigh, Melbourne 3166, Australia

First published 1989

Printed in Great Britain at the University Press, Cambridge

British Library cataloguing in publication data
Reeve, L. J.
Charles I and the road to personal rule. – (Cambridge
studies in early modern British history).
1. Great Britain. Political events, 1625–1649
I. Title
941.06′2

Library of Congress cataloguing in publication data
Reeve, L. J.
Charles I and the road to personal rule / L. J. Reeve.
p.   cm. – (Cambridge studies in early modern British history)
Rev. version of the author's doctoral thesis, Cambridge.
Bibliography.
Includes index.
ISBN 0 521 36184 2
1. Charles I, King of England, 1600–1649. 2. Great Britain –
Politics and government – 1625–1649. I. Title. II. Series.
DA396.A2R28   1989
941.06′2′0924 – dc 19   89–723 CIP

ISBN 0 521 36184 2

WD

For Barbara, with love

CONTENTS

ACKNOWLEDGEMENTS

During the writing of this book, and of the doctoral dissertation from which it is largely derived, I have greatly appreciated the assistance, and the kindness, of many people and of a number of institutions. This list must of necessity be selective but certain names should be recorded. Professor Sir Geoffrey Elton supervised my doctoral work at Cambridge and has remained my principal academic mentor. Over the years his wise advice and friendship have been unfailing and I will always be deeply grateful to him. My examiners, Dr John Morrill and Professor Austin Woolrych, have been unstinting in their assistance, encouragement and support. John Morrill's help in his capacity as an editor of this series has been invaluable, as has that of the other editors, Professor Anthony Fletcher and Dr John Guy. Professor the Earl Russell read my dissertation, produced a most helpful commentary, and has always been very gracious in the provision of relevant information. I have enjoyed and learnt much from our discussions. Professor John Elliott kindly provided transcripts and details of documents in the Infantado and Medinaceli archives, took the time to read the typescript of this book, making a number of helpful observations, and (not least) provided the inspiration for the title. Professor John Salmon also read the typescript, giving constructive and very judicious criticism. Dr Simon Adams has always generously shared his knowledge of the English foreign policy and the European history of the period. Dr Kevin Sharpe has been a source of much useful information and good cheer. Professor George Yule has always taken a kind and supportive interest in my work. Dr Michael Bennett has been an excellent colleague. Monique Bois, Albert Llorrens and Luigi di Stadio were fine companions and helpful fellow-searchers at Simancas. Tony Camps has been a faithful friend at difficult times. His Excellency The Reverend Dr Davis McCaughey has always given me his confidence and trust. Professor John Poynter has provided important advice and support. Among the other friends and colleagues who have assisted in various ways are Gerald Aylmer, Brendan Bradshaw, Ian Breward, Mat Burrows, Tom Cogswell, Richard Cust, Colin Davis, David Dean, Damaso de Lario, Greg Dening, Richard Drayton,

Lawrie Gardiner, John Gooch, Jamie Hart, Jonathan Israel, Don Kennedy, Paul Kennedy, Karen Kupperman, Albert Loomie, Richard McCabe, Hew McLeod, Wilfred Prest, Ron Ridley, Ian Robertson, Duncan Robinson, Michael Roe, Peter Salt, Fred Shriver, Geoff Smith, Johann Sommerville, Christopher Thompson, Nicholas Tyacke, David Underdown and Stuart Woolf. Of the many librarians and archivists who have facilitated my research in a number of countries it would be remiss of me not to mention in particular Dr John Post of the Public Record Office, London, who spent much time discussing near-insoluble linguistic and palaeographical problems. William Davies and Mrs Maureen Street of Cambridge University Press have also given expert assistance. Despite the help I have received, I am solely responsible for the book and any errors it contains. The Marquis of Lothian allowed me to consult the Coke manuscripts at Melbourne Hall, and I am grateful to the Bodleian Library; the British Library; the Syndics of the Cambridge University Library; Nottingham University Library; the Keeper of the Records of Scotland; and the Controller of H.M. Stationery Office for permission to use manuscript material. Financial support for this work has been provided by Pembroke College, Cambridge; the Universities of Melbourne, Otago, and Tasmania; Yale University; Rothmans University Endowment Fund (Australia); and the Australian–American Educational Foundation in the form of a Fulbright Postdoctoral Fellowship. My typist, Ingrid Barker, has shown great skill and patience in the face of my unreasonable demands. Without the support and encouragement of my parents, Roma and the Reverend Lawrence Reeve, I would not have been able to begin an academic career. I am grateful to my parents-in-law, Dr Barbara Christen and the late Dr Robert Christen, for their friendship and good counsel. My wife Barbara has lived with this subject since before the time of our marriage and has, in innumerable ways, made possible the completion of this book. For that, and more, I cannot thank her enough.

ABBREVIATIONS

AGS, E	Archivo General de Simancas, Sección Estado
AMRE, CPA	Archives du Ministère des Relations Extérieures, Paris: Correspondance Politique, Angleterre
APC	*Acts of the Privy Council* (of England)
BIHR	*Bulletin of the Institute of Historical Research*
Birch	T. Birch (ed.), *The court and times of Charles I* (2 vols., London, 1848)
BL	British Library
Bodl. Lib.	Bodleian Library, Oxford
CD1628	M. F. Keeler, M. J. Cole and W. D. Bidwell (eds.), *The Commons debates in 1628*, 4 vols. (New Haven and London, 1977)
CD1629	W. Notestein and F. H. Relf (eds.), *The Commons debates for 1629* (Minneapolis, 1921)
CJ	*Commons' journals*
CSPCol.	*Calendar of state papers, colonial*
CSPD	*Calendar of state papers, domestic*
CSPV	*Calendar of state papers, Venetian*
CUL	Cambridge University Library
DNB	*Dictionary of national biography*
EcHR	*Economic History Review*
EHR	*The English Historical Review*
exp.	expediente (i.e. file)
fo., fos.	folio, folios
HJ	*The Historical Journal*
HLQ	*Huntington Library Quarterly*
HMC	Historical Manuscripts Commission (reports)
JBS	*The Journal of British Studies*
JEH	*The Journal of Ecclesiastical History*
JMH	*The Journal of Modern History*

LD1628	M. F. Keeler *et al.* (eds.), *Lords proceedings 1628* (New Haven, 1983)
leg.	legajo (i.e. bundle)
LJ	*Lords' journals*
membr.	membrane
NCMH, iv	*The new Cambridge modern history*, vol. iv: *The decline of Spain and the Thirty Years War 1609–48/59*, ed. J. P. Cooper (Cambridge, 1971)
NUL, Ne.C.	Nottingham University Library, Newcastle Manuscripts
n.s.	new style dating
P&P	*Past and Present*
PRO	Public Record Office, Chancery Lane, London
PRO 31/3	Baschet's French transcripts, Public Record Office
rev. art.	review article
SP	state papers, Public Record Office
SRO	Scottish Record Office
ST	W. Cobbett, T. B. Howell *et al.* (eds.), *State trials*, 34 vols. (London, 1809–28)
TLS	*The Times Literary Supplement*
TrAPS	*Transactions of the American Philosophical Society*
TRHS	*Transactions of the Royal Historical Society*
unfol.	unfoliated

NOTE ON SOURCES, QUOTATIONS AND DATES

In citing documents in the state papers, domestic series, in the Public Record Office, the article number of the document is given, being clearer, and the folio number where more precision is required. In quotations, spelling and punctuation have been modernized and abbreviations extended. All dates are given in the old style of the Julian calendar, unless otherwise indicated, with the year beginning on 1 January.

1

Introduction

The reign of Charles I saw the complete breakdown of political consensus in his three kingdoms, the reluctant resort to armed conflict and the most extensive bloodshed. While historians, it would seem, are as far as ever from agreement about the reasons for these events, the period shows no sign of losing its ability to fascinate historian and reader alike. On one level the intrinsic interest of the Caroline regime derives from the fact of its collapse. To seek to understand the causes of the civil wars is natural enough. Yet this book, while it may shed some light on those later events, is not aimed directly at explaining the history of the 1640s. It focuses, rather, on those years during the late 1620s and early 1630s when Charles's rule was becoming established and its distinct character emerged. The intention is to achieve some understanding of the nature of that regime by investigating the problem of how it came into being. Beyond this, the course and collapse of Charles's rule were largely the products of its initial creation. And in this sense the book may also help to illuminate the Caroline period as a whole.

This study is built around the intersection of two basic themes: the interaction of political and ideological developments and the two-way relationship between English and international affairs. The evidence has encouraged me to view the problems of the period in these terms. Chronologically the book extends (roughly) from early 1628 to the latter part of 1632, that is from the height of the crisis of the Buckingham era to the time when Charles's withdrawal from the Thirty Years War was completed. This space of almost five years saw a marked transformation of English politics – from government in conjunction with Parliament to government without reference to Parliament; from the administration of a royal favourite to that of the king and his circle; from government dependent upon parliamentary subsidies and rising debt to government based upon non-parliamentary taxation, customs revenues and war trade; from intervention in continental affairs to isolation; and from war to peace. The point of Charles's withdrawal from the European war is a conclusive as well as a convenient *terminus ad quem*: the king's decision in favour of non-parliamentary rule implied the necessity of peace

1

abroad, and the progressive ending of a commitment to the war allowed the rejection of parliamentary means and the continuation of religious change at home.

Conrad Russell's detailed study of the parliaments of the 1620s, published in 1979, drew a sharp contrast between the political atmosphere of the Jacobean era and that which prevailed during the early years of Charles's reign. According to Russell the Caroline period was a new age, intensely ideological and politically 'a much less safe world'.[1] While recent work has pointed to the way in which overt religious consensus was being eroded in England during the last years of James's life,[2] there can be no doubt that this conclusion of Russell's is essentially true.[3] As religious and political divisions appeared in English politics during the late 1620s they came to affect significantly the framework in which those politics were pursued. This study, as part of its account of the emergence of Charles's regime, traces the development of certain changes evident at the end of the 1620s as the king came progressively to reject parliamentary ways. I have interpreted these changes as the advent of (for want of a better term) a 'new politics'. These new politics were an uncharacteristic and in many ways an unwanted (even an unconscious) development. They were the politics of a non-parliamentary England, politics which came about with the breakdown of the traditional political and constitutional process.

Such a notion immediately begs the obvious question of what, in fact, the old politics were. It is not my purpose to paint a full-length portrait of pre-Caroline, let alone early Stuart, political society. There exists a number of very illuminating studies which already serve this need.[4] It is possible, however, to point to certain features which made English political society workable under James I, notably confidence in the monarch as the head of the social and religious order, a degree of understanding between the ruling elements within the court and the wider political leadership of the nation, a broad ideological context for constitutional and religious life which, if sometimes unstable, was not undermined by government and often allowed official agreement rather than conflict, and the innate capacity for the con-

---

[1] C. Russell, *Parliaments and English politics 1621–1629* (Oxford, 1979), pp. 366, 420.
[2] K. Fincham and P. lake, 'The ecclesiastical policy of King James I', *JBS*, xxiv, 2 (1985). See also P. G. Lake, 'Calvinism and the English Church, 1570–1635', *P&P*, cxiv (1987); H. R. Trevor-Roper, *Catholics, Anglicans and puritans* (London, 1987), p. 62.
[3] R. P. Cust, *The forced loan and English politics 1626–1628* (Oxford, 1987). Despite the importance of Dr Cust's study of this period, I am unable to agree with his view that the pattern of English politics under Charles was fully established between 1626 and 1628 (ibid., pp. 332–3), given the period of transition charted in the present book. See also R. P. Cust, 'News and politics in early seventeenth century England', *P&P*, cxii (1986).
[4] See Russell, *Parliaments*, ch. 1; R. Ashton, *The English civil war* (London, 1978), pt 1; J. S. Morrill, *The revolt of the provinces*, 2nd edn (London, 1980), introduction, pt 1; D. Hirst, 'Court, country, and politics before 1629', in K. M. Sharpe (ed.), *Faction and Parliament, essays on early Stuart history* (Oxford, 1978).

duct of an effective foreign policy based upon an official commitment to the life of the Protestant world and upon the economical and constructive application of limited resources in time of war.[5] I have discussed these features, specifically and by implication, in seeking to describe the onset of the 'new politics' which supplanted them.

How can the new politics be characterized? Briefly, they involved an increasing resort to exclusive government, conspiracy and dissent at home, certain changes in political thinking (the most important of which was the undermining of the constitutional fiction that the king could – or should – do no wrong), and the eventual breakdown of the critical relationship between the administration of domestic affairs and foreign policy. In effect these developments constituted an internal assault on the customary framework of English politics and inherently weakened Charles's rule. In seeking to describe these changes I do not wish to suggest any rigid structural defi- nitions. The idea of an emerging new politics is simply a flexible shorthand for the various changes (combined with elements of continuity) which can be detected within the period and which can, at the most basic level, be seen as a pattern of change, a pattern which should be illuminating. What caused these changes to emerge? In many ways they are inseparable from the specific policies which Charles adopted; essentially they were produced by the combination of his personality and beliefs (the effects of which were com- pounded by a grossly mismanaged war) with wider international influences. Somewhere within this book I suspect there lurks the deduction that if Charles had not succeeded to the English throne, had not been predeceased by his brother or had been assassinated like Henry IV of France (thus allowing Elizabeth of Bohemia and her children to enter the line of succession)[6] the troubles of his reign would have been avoided. While this seems a likely prop- osition, the imagined alternatives or 'ifs' of history, occasionally helpful, are not in the end a useful object of study. In terms of real events it is difficult to disagree with the conclusion reached by Clarendon in his history and by Pym in the Grand Remonstrance that Charles's accession led to increasingly serious trouble.[7] The king's character and attitudes form one of the salient themes of this book (and particularly of chapter 6). The portrait of Charles which emerges here is in many ways unflattering. Charles was an excellent connoisseur of the visual arts, but as a reigning monarch he was woefully inadequate. A major task of this book must be to explore the nature of that

---

[5] On the question of war finance see chapter 7, below.
[6] Elizabeth and her children were excluded from the immediate succession by the birth of the prince of Wales in 1630.
[7] Edward Hyde, earl of Clarendon, *History of the rebellion and civil wars in England*, ed. W. D. Macray (6 vols., Oxford, 1888), vol. i, p. 3; S. R. Gardiner (ed.), *The constitutional documents of the puritan revolution 1625–1660* (3rd edn, revised, Oxford, 1906, repr. 1979), pp. 208ff.

inadequacy: at very bottom he was an unsuccessful king because he was a weak man. But this study also contends that he was not in any sense a political man, something which his accidental involvement in public events has tended to obscure.

Within the European context the period which coincides with the span of this study was one of considerable transformation. There was a revival of Protestant fortunes and a concomitant decline in those of Spain, the reordering of the anti-Habsburg cause (previously a religious alliance in which England played a pivotal role) as a political alliance led by France, the development of an overriding conflict between France and Spain, the progress of economic warfare between Spain and the Dutch, and the great debate within the United Provinces on the possible truce with Philip IV.[8] International events had different meanings for the various interests on which they impinged. A notable example is Richelieu's consistent attempt to use the parliamentary interest in England to influence English policy, a political question for the cardinal but one which had extensive religious implications for Charles. At the international level it was ultimately England's relationship to Spain, to Spanish policy in the Low Countries and in Germany and to the Spanish war economy, which had the greatest influence upon internal English developments during this period.

To attempt to understand the interplay of political and personal forces with ideological ones is really to topple into a bottomless pit. No firm conclusions can be reached about the chemistry of individual men and women, the infinitely various mixtures of their emotions and thoughts. But since all conclusions are in varying degrees provisional there is a good case which can be made for informed speculation about human motives. The tendency to categorize the activities of individuals as basically either selfish or altruistic is a simplistic and unhelpful one based upon a false distinction: fear and ambition, for example, do not sit easily within this scheme.[9] Blair Worden has recently pointed to 'the frailty of the assumptions which historians still bring to the word "ideology", and the crudity of our approach to the relationship between self-interest and principle'.[10] Once the complexity of this problem has been recognized we are in a better position to investigate the evidence. We can remember that religious aspirations and reasons of state can co-exist in a grey area, very much the case in Europe during this period.[11] In another sense

---

[8] J. I. Israel, *The Dutch republic and the Hispanic world 1606–1661* (Oxford, 1982), ch. 4 (sections iv and v).

[9] L. B. Namier, 'Human nature in politics', in F. Stern (ed.), *The varieties of history* (London, 1970), pp. 385–6.

[10] B. Worden, rev. art., *London Review of Books*, 19 Apr.–2 May 1984, p. 15.

[11] J. H. Elliott, *Richelieu and Olivares* (Cambridge, 1984), p. 128; see also R. J. W. Evans, rev. art., *JEH*, xxxiv, 1 (1983), pp. 140–1.

personal ambition and intellectual conviction can develop, it would seem, almost as one: witness Sir John Eliot's frustrated desire for office and his belief in the prevalence of bad counsel in England, which, fused in his personality, were a major influence upon English politics during the late 1620s. And while ideological forces are by no means sovereign, their effects can be mitigated in unexpected ways. The policies which Charles adopted abroad, for example, were marginally less ideological than those he pursued at home. Emotive and irrational preferences often intrude upon and work alongside more thoughtful considerations. The initial failure of Charles's marriage came to influence his attitude to foreign policy far more than the failure of the projected Spanish match. The effect of unconscious inspiration, where it can be discerned, should not be forgotten. Clarendon understood that the English Calvinist counter-attack upon Laudianism appealed to a traditional axiom of political thought – the evil of innovation – although this was not fully applicable under the circumstances. The appeal was part of a process of coming to grips with a younger and weaker but increasingly native tradition (English Arminianism) which had achieved the patronage of the king.[12] Alert to complications such as these, we can endeavour to recognize the ways of thinking characteristic of groups and individuals, as well as to detect those points where certain ideas become independent and living forces, all the while remembering that ideological influences do not exist *in vacuo*, and seeking to point out their integration with the more human themes as best we can.

Any scholar who ventures into the pre-civil war era must acknowledge two historiographical debts. One is to Samuel Rawson Gardiner, whose masterly narrative remains the authoritative account of the events. While Gardiner's judgement upon individual episodes was often sound, his central constitutional theme remains implausibly simple and governed by an explicitly teleological approach.[13] But so assiduous was Gardiner's research and so wide his technical skill that to discover him to have been in error or to have been ignorant of certain evidence brings an almost perverse satisfaction. Understandably, the Spanish sources frequently yield information unknown to Gardiner; during the period in which he worked at Simancas the archive was apparently in an appalling state.[14] And our present knowledge is of course generally more extensive than that which Gardiner achieved. The other debt is to Conrad Russell, whose work on early Stuart parliamentary history has opened up whole new avenues of historical understanding. While

---

[12] Clarendon, *Rebellion*, vol. i, p. 123.
[13] S. R. Gardiner, *History of England from the accession of James I to the outbreak of the civil war, 1603–1642* (10 vols., London, 1883–4), vii, p. 220.
[14] *DNB* (1901–11), s.v. Gardiner, Samuel Rawson; J. P. Kenyon, *The history men* (London, 1983), p. 118.

Russell has aroused controversy and a number of scholars have striven to qualify his conclusions, the illuminating insights he has provided mean that students of the period will always benefit from his scholarship and be obliged to grapple with his views.[15]

This book is directed towards understanding the evidence for its own subject rather than taking part in the controversy surrounding Russell's work. Nevertheless it will (I hope) make some form of contribution to that debate. It may be helpful, therefore, to give an indication of my own view of the Russellian or revisionist interpretation besides what appears in the following pages. That interpretation has both a negative and a positive character. It denies the validity of Gardiner's view of a high road to constitutional conflict, civil war and parliamentary power during the early Stuart period and rejects the hindsight which facilitated this reading of the era. Speaking positively, Russell argues that Parliament existed within the wider context of early modern English society and political culture and must be understood in these (its own) terms. That culture, he maintains, was founded on assumptions of order, unity and consensus but was plagued by problems of localism, war, financial inadequacy and religious disunity. My belief is that any polarization of the debate triggered by these views is unhelpful – not because disputes are unseemly (on the contrary: they show that the field of study is alive) but because it is in the nature of the early Stuart period that it is not conducive to simple, extreme or all-embracing explanations. The Caroline period is particularly complex in this respect, a growing jungle, formed by the intertwining of the politics of power and of deeply held belief within a European context. It is also my belief that the revisionist interpretation is weakened by its attempt to describe a structure or system of politics at a time when that system was undergoing significant change, being placed under pressure and being altered in subtle ways by national and international influences. Hence this study could be read as something of an alternative interpretation on a modest scale, or in another sense as an episodic sequel to the history of the 1620s, a decade of essentially parliamentary politics which led to the establishment of a non-parliamentary regime. The book contains elements of both themes. On a different level, all those who write after Gardiner, and after Sir Geoffrey Elton's thought-provoking article of 1965, 'A high road to civil war?',[16] are in a real sense revisionists.

[15] See in particular Russell, *Parliaments*, ch. 1; C. Russell, 'The nature of a Parliament in early Stuart England', in H. Tomlinson (ed.), *Before the English civil war* (London, 1983) and C. Russell, 'Parliamentary history in perspective, 1604–1629', *History*, lxi (1976). See also T. K. Rabb and D. Hirst, 'Revisionism revised: two perspectives on early Stuart parliamentary history' and C. Hill, 'Parliament and people in seventeenth century England', *P&P*, xcii (1981); R. Zaller, 'The concept of opposition in early Stuart England', *Albion*, xii (1980).
[16] G. R. Elton, 'A high road to civil war?', in Elton, *Studies in Tudor and Stuart politics and government* (3 vols., Cambridge, 1974–83), vol. ii.

This book is a political study, rather than a specifically constitutional, theological, diplomatic or economic treatment. As with most political history it has the advantages of being eclectic in its subject matter and of dealing with the interaction of change and continuity. It concentrates on developments at a national and often at an international rather than a local level. It is really a study of English rather than of British history during this period, making brief reference to Ireland and casting but a passing glance at Scotland. Conrad Russell has recently drawn attention to the importance of the British problem in relation to the outbreak of the civil war.[17] But Russell has aptly described the kingdom of Scotland as being 'poor and despised' during the earlier years of Charles's reign.[18] The annual royal revenue in Scotland at this time was something over £16,000 sterling, less than the income of George, duke of Buckingham.[19] Charles left Scotland at the age of four, when his father became king of England, and did not return until almost thirty years later in 1633. The most significant episode in Scotland during the early years of his reign was his attempt to win a struggle with the Scottish nobility upon which his father had not even dared to enter. The Act of Revocation (1625) was intended as a re-annexation to the crown of gifts of Church property made by James as well as of grants made during Charles's minority. This enterprise was of dubious legality (it appealed to technical flaws in the ecclesiastical concessions and disregarded the fact that Charles had not succeeded as a minor) and ended in a compromise settlement in 1629.[20] But it left a legacy of mistrust among the nobility which worked dramatically against Charles when he and Laud later attempted to transform the established pattern of Scottish religious life. While Charles liked to maintain intimate relations with his Scottish relatives, particularly the duke of Lennox and the marquis of Hamilton who played important roles in England, his eventual failure in Scotland was the measure of his ignorance and neglect. The realm of Ireland had a more immediate relevance to English politics during this period. Mainly for religious reasons Ireland was clearly vulnerable to invasion during the Caroline war with Spain. It remained subject to the influences of continental politics throughout this period and was an important link between British and European affairs in a divided Europe. English Protestant perceptions of Irish Catholicism were a dynamic force. And the interregnum of the lords justices, between the departure of Falkland and the coming of Wentworth, was the occasion of a significant fightback by the Protestant interest at the

---

[17] C. Russell, 'The British problem and the English civil war', *History*, lxxii (1987).
[18] C. Russell, *The crisis of Parliaments, English history 1509–1660* (Oxford, 1971), p. 323; see also M. Lee, *The road to revolution: Scotland under Charles I, 1625–37* (Urbana, 1985).
[19] R. Mitchison, *Lordship to patronage, Scotland 1603–1745* (London, 1983), p. 29.
[20] Ibid., pp. 32–4; Gardiner, *History*, vii, pp. 276–81.

Caroline court, when Viscount Dorchester allied himself with the earl of Cork in a vigorous anti-Catholic crusade.

The loss of potential manuscript sources for the study of the early Caroline period has been extensive. Perhaps the greatest disappointment is the failure of any substantial collection of Lord Treasurer Weston's papers to survive. It is likely that his financial dealings (including those with Spain) and his Catholic leanings were considered sufficiently sensitive to warrant the premature demise of any such archive. The papers of the third earl of Pembroke were lost in a fire at Wilton in 1647. And it is possible that Providence Island Company documents were lost in government raids in 1639 and 1640.[21] This study is based on manuscript material in British and continental archives, particularly the Public Record Office in London and the Archivo General at Simancas, and on a variety of printed sources. Whatever the deficiencies of surviving evidence, this study is intended to shed fresh light on a fascinating era in British and European history.

[21] C. M. Hibbard, *Charles I and the popish plot* (Chapel Hill, 1983), p. 89.

2

Buckingham's England in crisis

The onset of the Thirty Years War after 1618 destroyed the foreign policy of James I. That policy was very much a product of the king's personality. James was a pacifist who had reacted against the violence of his Scottish background. He was also a lazy man who resented the difficulties posed by conflict and war. In addition he was ambitious. He wished to link his family to the royal line of the Spanish Habsburgs, still the virtual rulers of the world, and he sought to achieve the role of peacemaker in the Europe of his day. On becoming king of England he agreed to end the long Elizabethan war with Spain, and later played an important role in bringing about the twelve years' Truce of 1609 between Spain and the Dutch. In 1613 the marriage of his daughter Elizabeth to Frederick V, elector Palatine and the leading Calvinist prince of Germany, symbolized his commitment to the Protestant world. His aim was to combine this initiative with the marriage of his son and heir to a Spanish princess and so to fulfil both his diplomatic and dynastic ambitions. When Henry, prince of Wales, died in 1612, negotiations with Spain had come to nothing, and so from 1614 onwards James set about trying to achieve a similar marriage for his younger son Charles. But the king's pan-European diplomacy was dealt a devastating blow by the rash action of his German son-in-law. Against all sound advice, including that of James, in 1619 Frederick accepted the crown of Bohemia in an election disputed by Emperor Ferdinand II. In so doing he had issued a challenge to the whole house of Habsburg, but he had also invited a religious war in Germany. For while Frederick led the Protestant Union, Ferdinand was a zealous Catholic, determined to reverse the tide of the Protestant Reformation. James did not wish to see his family and his principal kingdom of England involved in such a conflict and he resisted English and Bohemian pressure upon him for war.[1]

In November of 1620 the Habsburgs decisively defeated Frederick's con-

---

[1] R. Lockyer, *Buckingham, the life and political career of George Villiers, first duke of Buckingham 1592–1628* (London, 1981), pp. 80–2; G. Parker, *Europe in crisis 1598–1648* (London, 1981), pp. 160–4.

federate forces in the battle of the White Mountain outside Prague. He fled with Elizabeth and their children to the Hague and his lands were overrun by the Spanish and imperial forces. The invasion of the Palatinate in 1620 created enormous difficulties for James. With a state of war in Germany, his Protestant duties and the fortunes of his family came into conflict with his desire for friendship with Spain. And with the Dutch truce about to expire, Spain's victory in the Palatinate had provided her with control of the Rhine valley, a coveted connection between Italy and the Netherlands and a strategic prize with which she would not readily part.[2] Faced with this situation, James decided to pursue the Spanish match as the basis for a settlement in Germany. But this policy finally collapsed when in 1622 Spain extinguished the last resistance in the Lower Palatinate, and when in 1623 it declared that an English marriage should be conditional upon terms to which James would not agree, namely the conversion of Charles and Frederick's heir, Frederick Henry, to membership of the Roman Church.[3] The breakdown in Anglo-Spanish relations was also generated by a personality clash between the royal favourite George, duke of Buckingham, and the count-duke of Olivares:[4] a situation compounded by Buckingham's new influence with Charles. Having rashly travelled to Spain with Buckingham, Charles took offence at the uncompromising treatment he received there, and before leaving wrote to his sister Elizabeth of his desire for revenge.[5]

The war against Spain which ensued was, for the two young men, essentially an emotional reaction to the failure of the marriage treaty. Yet English public opinion saw the conflict in more ideological terms. The Jacobean peace with Spain had brought prosperity to England, but it had also sacrificed an important source of national political unity. Elizabethan propaganda had instilled anti-Hispanic and anti-Catholic attitudes very deeply in the English mind. The idea of a Spanish marriage was unpopular, and it had led to rioting in London against Spanish diplomats and James's policy.[6] Charles and Buckingham were not opposed to Spain for religious reasons; but in Parliament in 1624 they enlisted the forces of English Protestantism, achieving considerable popularity and a grant for war of £300,000. Effectively this

---

[2] G. Parker, *The army of Flanders and the Spanish road 1567–1659* (Cambridge, 1972), p. 253.

[3] S. L. Adams, 'Spain or the Netherlands? The dilemmas of early Stuart foreign policy', in Tomlinson (ed.), *Before the English civil war*, pp. 89, 95–7; Parker, *Europe in crisis*, p. 169.

[4] Clarendon, *Rebellion*, vol. i, p. 44; H. G. R. Reade, *Sidelights on the Thirty Years War* (3 vols., London, 1924), iii, p. 260.

[5] G. Huxley, *Endymion Porter: the life of a courtier, 1587–1649* (London, 1959), p. 118.

[6] K. J. Lindley, 'Riot prevention and control in early Stuart London', *TRHS*, 5th ser., xxxiii (1983), pp. 111–12; W. S. Maltby, *The black legend: the development of anti-Spanish sentiment, 1558–1660* (Durham, N.C., 1971), pp. 100ff., 114–15, 138; Clarendon, *Rebellion*, vol. i, pp. 24, 94.

grant was conditional upon a commitment (which James was reluctant to make) to a general war against Spain and (arguably) upon the adoption of the Elizabethan strategy of war by diversion, that is of the accompaniment of Anglo-Dutch action on land by war against Spain at sea.[7] In obtaining money for war the prince and the favourite had activated powerful political and religious forces: forces which were to cause them grave trouble when hopes of an anti-Spanish crusade were disappointed.

The war was an increasingly dismal failure. James and Charles were reluctant to conclude a marriage alliance with France but Buckingham urged them on. The marriage of Charles and Henrietta Maria was popularly perceived as a threat to English Protestantism; and it did not achieve French military support for the Palatine cause. The subsidies earmarked by Parliament for a naval war were spent in the mounting of an expedition to the Palatinate under the mercenary soldier, Count Mansfeld (which failed) and in an exorbitant (and continuing) financial commitment to the war effort of Charles's uncle, Christian IV of Denmark.[8] Hostilities with Spain had not commenced when James died early in 1625, but Charles's accession accelerated the drift to war. Later that year, an attempted Anglo-Dutch naval attack on the treasure fleet and on Cadiz was a failure. To the mismanagement of the Spanish war was added the alarming prospect of war with France. The deterioration of relations between Buckingham and Richelieu stemmed from the French refusal to join the alliance of the Hague on which the duke had staked so much.[9] What was at bottom a personal quarrel appeared likely, by the beginning of 1626, to result in war.[10] For England, simultaneous conflict with France and Spain – the major continental powers – could only constitute strategic lunacy.

Charles's reign had also begun badly at home. His relations with Parliament were characterized from the beginning by misunderstanding and emerging mistrust. In 1625 the Commons had sought to grant him the customs revenues, tonnage and poundage, for one year only rather than for life as was customary. This was apparently the result of parliamentary manoeuvres for fiscal reform.[11] But Charles, it seems, took offence, and he

---

[7] S. L. Adams, 'Foreign policy and the Parliaments of 1621 and 1624', in Sharpe (ed.), *Faction and Parliament*, pp. 165, 168–9; Adams, 'Spain or the Netherlands?', p. 83; Maltby, *Black legend*, p. 109; Gardiner, *History*, vi, pp. 6–7.

[8] Lockyer, *Buckingham*, p. 279; see also *Historical collections*, ed. J. Rushworth (8 vols., n.p., 1659–1701), i, p. 474; J. Beatty, *Warwick and Holland* (Denver, 1965), p. 43; Gardiner, *History*, v, pp. 198–9; Adams, 'Spain or the Netherlands?', pp. 98–9.

[9] Adams, 'Spain or the Netherlands?', p. 98.

[10] Russell, *Parliaments*, p. 263.

[11] Ibid., pp. 227–9. Tonnage and poundage constituted the major part of the customs revenues. The desire for reform was inspired, at least partly, by fear of justifying the new Jacobean impositions during Charles's lifetime; D. Hirst, *Authority and conflict, England 1603–1658*

continued to collect the duties. When Parliament met again in 1626 a power-ful attack was made on Buckingham's conduct of affairs: an offensive led by Sir Dudley Digges and Sir John Eliot in the Commons, abetted by the French and sanctioned by the influence of William Herbert, third earl of Pembroke, in the Lords.[12] Buckingham was widely disliked for his rash and disdainful bearing, his pretensions to regality, his venality and accumulation of patron-age, as well as for his incompetence. The accelerating crisis in foreign policy gave the parliamentary proceedings an atmosphere of emergency. Charles did not share the public suspicion of the duke, and did not accept that financial supply should be dependent upon his impeachment. As Charles saw it, Parli-ament had not only attacked his favourite, but was also refusing to fund a war it had advocated.[13] He chose to defend Buckingham. As he said at the time, 'gold may be bought too dear'.[14] He dissolved the Parliament in June 1626, thus saving the duke and losing four subsidies.

The king's dealings with Parliament caused him to adopt a different attitude to the institution from that of his father. James had a clear under-standing of the political art of the possible, and despite his rhetoric about the exalted nature of kingship he had never abandoned the search for parliamen-tary co-operation. In 1610 he said there were many things he could do with-out Parliament, which he would do in Parliament.[15] Charles, however, was inclined to eliminate Parliament as a popular threat to monarchy.[16] He considered the initiation of proceedings against Buckingham an invasion of his prerogative and a reflection upon his honour. In May 1626 he had threatened both houses: 'Remember that Parliaments are altogether in my power for their calling, sitting and dissolution; therefore, as I find the fruits of them good or evil, they are to continue or not to be.'[17] After the Parliament he spoke to the bishop of Mende 'of the means used by the kings of France to rid themselves of parliament', commenting that this had been done at an opportune moment when there was no financial need.[18] While Charles's eventual resolve to govern without Parliament was a cumulative develop-ment, his antipathy to the institution grew up early in his reign. He was encouraged in this by those about him, particularly Buckingham and Bishop

(London, 1986), p. 140. The lords refused to pass a bill granting tonnage and poundage for one year only; J. P. Sommerville, *Politics and ideology in England 1603–1640* (London, 1986), p. 156.

[12] Russell, *Parliaments*, pp. 264–7.
[13] R. P. Cust, 'Charles I, the Privy Council, and the forced loan', *JBS*, xxiv, 2 (1985), p. 233.
[14] Lockyer, *Buckingham*, p. 311.
[15] S. Lambert, 'Procedure in the House of Commons in the early Stuart period', *EHR*, xcv (1980), p. 769.
[16] Cust, 'Charles I, the Privy Council, and the forced loan', pp. 211–13, 233.
[17] Gardiner, *History*, vi, p. 83; Cust, *The forced loan*, pp. 17–18.
[18] *CSPV 1626–8*, p. 508; Cust, 'Charles I, the Privy Council, and the forced loan', p. 212.

William Laud. While the duke was not an ideologue, he had modernist (as well as secular) instincts and was attuned to a milieu of high monarchy.[19] He was said to favour the government of England along French constitutional lines, and he neither understood nor wished to be troubled with popular councils.[20] Laud's hard-line attitude towards Parliament and the influence he achieved in favour of the English Arminian party indicate how Charles's resort to arbitrary measures in government was indeed the counterpart of the rise of Arminianism under his rule.[21]

In 1626 Sir Dudley Carleton warned the House of Commons of a likely change in royal policy, 'new counsels', unless Parliament ceased to encroach upon the royal prerogative. Carleton contrasted the continuing demise of representative institutions in Christian countries with the privileges of the English Parliament, still at liberty to offer financial supply voluntarily to the king. Carleton favoured concord and the sitting of Parliament and he had sought to issue a personal warning. But as Vice-Chamberlain he was also a royal spokesman, and clearly Charles wished to suggest the threat of arbitrary measures.[22] The threat had definitely not been an idle one. Carleton's speech was indeed prophetic. Following the failure of the 1626 Parliament, alternative means of funding the war were considered and pursued.

Of the financial options available to the crown at this point, a loan from the City of London proved inadequate; the king and Council rejected the traditional idea of debasing the coinage; and there was widespread refusal to contribute to a public benevolence.[23] The critical factor affecting the course of policy, however, was Charles's outright refusal to resummon Parliament. This was linked to his refusal to give up the duke. The king's attitude created an impasse which made a resort to arbitrary taxation virtually inevitable. Charles's opposition to another Parliament brought the moderates in Council to agree to a forced loan, the solution which was adopted.[24] The forced loan was entitled the 'Loan of Five Subsidies' and was a blatant substitute for the failure of parliamentary supply.[25] Like the earlier benevolence, it was justified

[19] On the duke's religious views see Lockyer, *Buckingham*, pp. 449, 474; on those of his family see Hibbard, *Popish plot*, pp. 34–6.

[20] PRO 31/3/66/fo. 123v; Clarendon, *Rebellion*, vol. i, p. 7.

[21] Cust, *The forced loan*, pp. 62ff., 78–80; Cust, 'Charles I, the Privy Council, and the forced loan', pp. 216, 235; W. Hutton, *William Laud* (1896), p. 26.

[22] L. J. Reeve, 'The secretaryship of state of Viscount Dorchester 1628–1632' (Cambridge University PhD thesis, 1984), pp. 16–18.

[23] Gardiner, *History*, vi, p. 138; Cust, 'Charles I, the Privy Council, and the forced loan', p. 210.

[24] Cust, 'Charles I, the Privy Council, and the forced loan', p. 233.

[25] R. Ashton, *The City and the court 1603–1643* (Cambridge, 1979), p. 183; Russell, *Parliaments*, p. 58.

by arguments which indicated a redirection of conventional ideas of political consensus in favour of the prerogative.[26] The loan was thus a thinly disguised form of non-parliamentary taxation which appeared dangerously new. Similar levies had occurred under the Tudors, particularly in times of emergency, but sixteenth-century taxation had never really called into question the principle that new or extraordinary taxes required the consent of Parliament.[27] The official publication of sermons preached at court, appealing to an absolute royal authority over the subject's property by divine right, could only render the loan more objectionable.[28]

The forced loan netted just over £260,000 for the crown between 1626 and 1628. The House of Commons later informed the king that 'there were never any monies demanded and paid with greater grief and general dislike of all your faithful subjects'.[29] The political cost of the loan was to prove enormous. There was considerable public awareness of the threat to parliamentary ways and resentment of the regime's aggressive political style.[30] In November 1626 the judges refused to subscribe to the legality of the loan – a most damaging blow to the crown.[31] There was also extensive resistance on the part of the gentry to collection in the counties. Conciliar opinion was divided as to how far to coerce resisters but Charles, with so much personal credit at stake, favoured a hard-line approach. Seventy-six persons, including Sir Thomas Wentworth and John Hampden, were prepared to suffer imprisonment in a remarkable example of civil disobedience which involved, for many of them, defiance of the royal authority before Council. They were supported by fifteen or sixteen peers whose rank was held to exempt them from incarceration but who nevertheless resisted.[32] The government's tactic of removing loan refusers from London led to the celebrated case of the Five Knights, whose attempt to create a test case on the loan by obtaining writs of habeas corpus focused attention on the issue of arbitrary imprisonment. Charles appealed to the notion of reason of state in having the prisoners remanded to custody, exploiting the judges' legal inability to ascertain the cause of their imprisonment. The case, with the later revelation that Charles had sought to

---

[26] Cust, *The forced loan*, p. 34; Cust, 'Charles I, the Privy Council, and the forced loan', pp. 217–20.

[27] G. R. Elton (ed.), *The Tudor constitution* (2nd edn, Cambridge, 1982), p. 44; Russell, *Parliaments*, p. 51; C. Russell, 'Parliament and the king's finances', in C. Russell (ed.), *The origins of the English civil war* (rev. edn, London, 1980), p. 94.

[28] Hutton, *Laud*, p. 32; Cust, 'Charles I, the Privy Council, and the forced loan', p. 230.

[29] *CD1628*, iv, p. 314; Russell, *Parliaments*, p. 334; C. G. A. Clay, *Economic expansion and social change: England 1500–1700* (2 vols., Cambridge, 1984), ii, p. 259.

[30] Cust, *The forced loan*, pp. 36, 39, 158ff.

[31] Gardiner, *History*, vi, pp. 149–50.

[32] The earl of Lincoln was found to be agitating against the loan and was sent to the Tower. Ibid., pp. 150, 154–6, 225; Cust, *The forced loan*, pp. 55–6, 58–9; Cust, 'Charles I, the Privy Council, and the forced loan', pp. 224ff.; Russell, *Parliaments*, p. 333.

pervert the court record, led to the House of Commons' campaign for the Petition of Right in 1628.[33]

Unquestionably the most destructive aspect of the loan was public perception of Charles's leading role. The king had overridden conciliar reservations about the loan and had sanctioned proceedings against refusers. He had also insisted on licensing sermons supporting the loan for publication (an action which indicates the direction of his thinking and his pretensions, encouraged by circumstances, to absolutism).[34] These measures, and Charles's widely publicized opposition to the summoning of another Parliament, were a crucial influence in the erosion of confidence in him among his governing classes. The peers who resisted the loan included at least five men whose social rank, when combined with their opposition to the nature of Charles's regime, was to prove critical in the years ahead: Essex, Warwick, Saye, Lincoln and Clare.[35] With the earl of Bedford they played key roles in the passing of the Petition of Right, in the political activities of the Providence Island Company and the circles connected with it, and (some of them) in the Long Parliament and during the civil war. Several possessed ancient titles and seem to have resented the station which Buckingham had achieved on the basis of such little merit.[36] For all of them the episode of the loan was a formative one in determining their attitudes towards the new king. In the autumn of 1626 Clare wrote to Saye very explicitly of his belief in Charles's design to do away with Parliament.[37] No English monarch could afford to alienate such men so seriously.

During 1627 and 1628 Charles preferred to support Buckingham's private war with Richelieu, in which his own honour was engaged, rather than to pursue the war against Spain to which Parliament had agreed. The duke encouraged Charles against the French and sought to bring down the cardinal, and even Louis XIII, by erecting a coalition comprised of French dissidents (who included Louis's brother Gaston), the dukes of Lorraine and Savoy and the Huguenots.[38] Richelieu had essentially betrayed the idea of the

---

[33] Cust, 'Charles I, the Privy Council, and the forced loan', p. 231; J. A. Guy, 'The origins of the Petition of Right reconsidered', *HJ*, xxv, 2 (1982).

[34] There are definite parallels between the situation surrounding the forced loan and the development of French absolutism during this period. There was no dramatic break with the past; there was an appeal to reason of state and divine right together with an opposition to the idea of taxation by consent; there was the link with war; and there was the same ideological rationalization of what was an *ad hoc* attempt to restore a royal authority threatened by changing circumstances. See D. Parker, *The making of French absolutism* (London, 1983), pp. 60ff., 90, 146ff.

[35] Saye in fact paid the loan by December 1626. Cust, *The forced loan*, p. 102n; Cust, 'Charles I, the Privy Council, and the forced loan', pp. 234–5; Gardiner, *History*, vi, p. 150.

[36] On criticism of Buckingham's lineage see Lockyer, *Buckingham*, p. 3.

[37] NUL, Ne.C., 15,405, pp. 170–1.

[38] Clarendon, *Rebellion*, vol. i, p. 48; Lockyer, *Buckingham*, pp. 336–7, 370; Adams, 'Spain or the Netherlands?', p. 98.

grand alliance against the Habsburgs by making peace with Spain in Italy in 1625.[39] He sought to manipulate England by engaging her in war against Spain while France suppressed the Huguenots. Charles and Buckingham had not obtained a firm French commitment before going to war against the Habsburgs, and Richelieu's strategy was thus successful, despite the Anglo-French conflict.[40] Moreover, the illogical and dangerous nature of Buckingham's war policy had exposed England to mortal threat. Simultaneous action against France and Spain created a situation in which the three powers manoeuvred for advantage with the stakes raised by war. Each power might join with another to the detriment of the third. This raised the spectre of an alliance between the two great Catholic monarchies for joint action against England. An agreement to this effect was actually concluded, at Spanish instigation, in March 1627. Buckingham may have suspected the existence of this agreement; he was aware of the possibility and of the danger of invasion.[41] That Spain was considering an agreement with the Dutch from 1627 onwards increased this threat.[42] Matters were worsened for England when Charles and Buckingham became obsessed with raising the siege of the Huguenot stronghold of La Rochelle. Their attempt in 1627 to open the sea route to the town was a disaster in which more than 3,000 Englishmen died. Charles chose to blame himself rather than Buckingham.[43] These events had serious consequences for English domestic politics. The processes of pressing and billeting and the pursuit of the French war were most unpopular. The troops were kept under arms during the winter of 1627–8, and the sum total was widespread fear and discontent in the country. It was as if new counsels might truly be at hand.[44] Added to this, the gross mismanagement of the war had created an overwhelming need for the crown to find further funds.

On 29 January 1628 the Privy Council resolved to recall Parliament.[45] The debate which led to this decision was a bitter one stretching over several months. The critical factor was the financial one. One estimate of December 1627 indicated that a sum of over half a million pounds was urgently required

---

[39] Lockyer, *Buckingham*, pp. 294–300, 349, 361–2.

[40] T. Cogswell, 'Prelude to Ré: the Anglo-French struggle over La Rochelle, 1624–1627', *History*, lxxi, 231 (1986). I am grateful to Tom Cogswell for allowing me to read this article before publication.

[41] Gardiner, *History*, vi, pp. 163–4; Lockyer, *Buckingham*, pp. 349, 361–2; Elliott, *Richelieu and Olivares*, pp. 87–8, 96.

[42] J. Alcalá-Zamora y Queipo de Llano, *España, Flandes y el mar del norte (1618–1639)* (Barcelona, 1975), p. 299.

[43] Gardiner, *History*, vi, p. 198; Russell, *Parliaments*, p. 330; Lockyer, *Buckingham*, p. 402.

[44] Rushworth, *Historical collections*, i, pp. 473, 475; SP16/95/8, SP16/95/9, SP16/95/41, SP16/101/35, SP16/102/45, SP16/106/31, SP16/107/49; Clarendon, *Rebellion*, vol. i, p. 50; Russell, *Parliaments*, pp. 335–7, 339n.

[45] William Laud, *Works*, ed. W. Scott and J. Bliss (7 vols., Oxford, 1847–60), iii, p. 207.

for the war effort. Two basic policy avenues were available: the summoning of Parliament or the imposition of further unparliamentary levies. There were several other options. Of these last, the debasement of the coinage had already been rejected, the Council decided against an excise, further loans from the City required securities (preferably future parliamentary subsidies), and the continued sale of crown lands would result in a lowering of the prices received.[46] The moderate Councillors enlisted the advice of Sir Robert Cotton, the scholar-antiquary, in countering the arguments of the anti-parliamentary hard-liners (led by the king, Laud and Buckingham). Cotton tendered his advice to the Council in a tract, *The danger wherein the kingdom now standeth and the remedy.* Cotton understood the situation in Elizabethan terms of Habsburg aggression and of England's need for self-defence. He considered that another forced loan would be refused and advocated the calling of Parliament. In Cotton's view this would restore confidence in the constitutional balance between king and subject and would maintain the social order against popular power by removing discontent. A Parliament could be used to pacify religious as well as constitutional fears and to represent Buckingham's administration as an instrument of reform. Cotton cited Burghley's supposed words to Queen Elizabeth I: 'Win hearts, and you have their hands and purses' – a motto for government by consent. Cotton predicted correctly that the next Parliament would be dominated by concern for the liberties of the subject. Clearly he saw the danger facing the nation as caused by a failure of counsel. His was the most articulate statement of a movement for political reform which grew during 1628 as the crisis of the Buckingham era reached its height.[47] While it is difficult to measure the political effect of Cotton's intervention, his arguments certainly strengthened the hand of the moderate majority: men such as Pembroke, Coventry, Manchester, Sir John Coke and Richard, Baron Weston. The decision to call Parliament constituted a major victory for this group and came about when Charles decided to forego more extreme measures.[48]

It is difficult to discern the king's thinking at this point. A proclamation he issued in February 1628 concerning a proposed levy of Ship Money (eventually abandoned) echoed his stated policy at the time of the forced loan: that the summoning of Parliament would be conditional upon his people's

---

[46] R. P. Cust, 'The forced loan and English politics 1626–1628' (London University PhD thesis, 1984), p. 100 (I am grateful to Dr Cust for allowing me to cite his thesis); Cust, *The forced loan*, pp. 72–3, 75–6; J. P. Cooper, 'The fall of the Stuart monarchy', in *NCMH*, iv, p. 555.

[47] Cust, *The forced loan*, pp. 80–2 and 'The forced loan', pp. 107–11; Rushworth, *Historical collections*, i, pp. 471–6; K. M. Sharpe, 'The earl of Arundel, his circle and the opposition to the duke of Buckingham, 1618–1628', in Sharpe (ed.), *Faction and Parliament*, p. 235 and passim.

[48] Cust, *The forced loan*, pp. 80–1; Cust, 'Charles I, the Privy Council, and the forced loan', pp. 231–3.

demonstration of their loyalty by payment of the levy at hand. In 1628, as in 1626, Charles was seeking to obtain guarantees and to have Parliament meet upon his own terms.[49] It is unlikely, therefore, that in 1628 he was really persuaded of the merits of the moderate case.[50] Understanding the extreme financial pressure upon him to act, he also, it seems, understood that to call a third Parliament was the least politically difficult of a number of unenviable choices. It held out the prospect of financial relief and might be slotted into the structure of his public statements and of his thinking thus far. Charles's decision indicated that he had not abandoned the search for parliamentary co-operation as he understood it: as the demonstration of loyalty by the satisfaction of his financial needs. On 17 March he opened the Parliament, stating that if it failed to provide him with the means to meet the common danger then 'I must, according to my conscience, take those other courses which God hath put into my hands.'[51]

The imprisoned loan resisters had been freed on 2 January, four weeks before the issuing of writs for the Parliament. The elections went strongly against the government and many loan refusers and critics of the king's policies were returned.[52] Yet the new Parliament saw no impeachment proceedings instituted against Buckingham. After the events of 1626, the duke had sought to retrieve his position by concluding a marriage alliance between his daughter and Pembroke's nephew. Thus in 1628, while Pembroke advocated a Parliament to finance the Spanish war, he did not use it to mount an attack on the duke. After the session had begun Buckingham managed to effect a reconciliation with his other enemies in the upper house, the earls of Arundel, Bristol and Essex and John Williams, bishop of Lincoln. It seems that leading members of the Commons were also included in the duke's arrangements whereby he was not to be accused of being the cause of the nation's ills.[53] The basic (and bare) success of these parliamentary manoeuvres reflected the public awareness of a political crisis: of the dangers to England from powerful enemies abroad and from serious divisions at home. In effect the duke capitalized upon the widespread desire for a successful Parliament which would work political reform and bring financial

---

[49] Cust, 'Charles I, the Privy Council, and the forced loan', pp. 219–20.
[50] Here I tend to differ with the interpretation offered by Dr Cust, who sees Charles at this point and in general as a monarch who gave great weight to Council advice. Charles could be inflexible and overbearing in Council and unheeding of unwelcome opinion on major issues of domestic and foreign policy. See Cust, *The forced loan*, pp. 41–2 and n, 56, 82–5, 87–8; and below, chapters 3, 6, 7, 8.
[51] *CD1628*, ii, p. 3; Gardiner, *History*, vi, pp. 227–8.
[52] Gardiner, *History*, vi, pp. 225–6, 229; *CSPV 1628–9*, p. 21; NUL, Ne.C., 15,404, p. 210.
[53] Russell, *Parliaments*, pp. 326–7, 342; Reeve, 'Viscount Dorchester', p. 189; Sharpe, 'The earl of Arundel', p. 235; Gardiner, *History*, vi, pp. 231–2; SP16/101/43; see also SP16/105/55.

stability. Yet Buckingham was not an able parliamentary manager. He preferred what he imagined to be his spectacular role in European high politics to the nuts and bolts of business, localism and the diligent cultivation of public opinion. His reliance upon Charles for power was virtually exclusive.[54] Only when gravely threatened, in 1626 and 1628, did he seek to build bridges to his enemies, surviving by inches and counting on Charles to protect him.

Two overriding issues preoccupied the third Parliament of the reign when it assembled in March of 1628. One was the great pressure upon it to satisfy the desperate need for money to support the war. While a substantial supply had been voted in 1624, only two subsidies had been granted in 1625 (out of suspicion of Buckingham's conduct of foreign policy) and the matter of tonnage and poundage had remained unresolved. There had been a failure of supply in 1626 when Charles refused to abandon the duke. Then the forced loan had been protested against as new and unconstitutional. Thus, despite widespread dissatisfaction with the calibre of the administration, by 1628 there was fear for the survival of Parliaments in England if the next did not fulfil the function of financing the war. Sir Benjamin Rudyerd understood this clearly in saying: 'This is the crisis of Parliaments. We shall know by this if Parliaments live or die.' He called for a large supply to be given to the king 'in proportion to his wants'.[55]

The other great concern of the Parliament was the threat (which it believed to exist) to English liberties and the desire to vindicate them. The cumulative public experience of the forced loan, the proceedings against refusers, the billeting of soldiers and the imposition of martial law had created this sense of danger. The central issue quickly became that of arbitrary imprisonment in the wake of the Five Knights' case. John Selden revealed to the Commons that Attorney-General Heath had attempted illegally to insert an actual judgement in the court record as if the issue had been decided (which it had not), and a binding precedent created, in favour of indefinite imprisonment for reason of state. This shocking revelation, and the fear that Charles's government had abandoned its commitment to the rule of law, caused the Commons to seek to define the law of imprisonment by legislation. Charles, however, forbade any bill which would encroach on his prerogative in a novel way. Yet neither did the Commons wish to trust the crown henceforth with a power which Charles appeared to have abused very seriously.[56]

The Petition of Right was Sir Edward Coke's proposed solution. This

---

[54] C. Carlton, *Charles I, the personal monarch* (London, 1983), p. 109.
[55] *CD1628*, ii, p. 58. See also Russell, *Parliaments*, pp. 224–7.
[56] Russell, *Parliaments*, p. 343; Guy, 'Origins of the Petition of Right'; L. J. Reeve, 'The legal status of the Petition of Right', *HJ*, xxix, 2 (1986).

measure was intended to achieve the aims of the Commons by explaining the law in a form traditionally used in appealing to existing rights but which was also an ancient form of legislation.[57] The Commons wished to secure their confirmation of the liberties of the subject in return for supply. They therefore voted the subsidies in principle but shelved the supply bill to await the confirmation. In effect they wished the two matters to proceed together.[58] Clare wrote to the earl of Oxford that he regretted this necessary purchasing of native liberties; but he considered the Parliament to be crucial for the future of the kingdom: an event which could save the king and his people from being driven to extremes.[59] In the circumstances, five subsidies (eventually £275,000) was an inadequate sum, but it was unprecedentedly generous and, as Clare remarked, 'a most bountiful retribution'. It was sufficient to extract concessions from Charles and to sustain his interest in the Parliament. In response to the initial vote of supply he told the Council and the lower house: 'At the first I liked Parliaments, but since [then] (I know not how) I was grown to distaste of them. But I am now where I was. I love Parliaments. I shall rejoice to meet with my people often.'[60] It is unlikely, however, that Charles had undergone such a fundamental change of heart. His earlier antipathy had gone deep, and in 1628 he did not wish to jeopardize a grant as yet inconclusive. This Parliament came to cause him great trouble. The delay to supply further undermined his war effort, and the nature of that delay, the debates culminating in the Petition of Right, were a significant constitutional threat. The parliamentary session was actually the scene of a conflict between Charles's espousal of a kind of absolutism and those who sought to defend the traditional rule of law. As Digges understood, 'We are now upon this question whether the king may be above the law, or the law above the king. It is our unhappiness but it is put upon us.'[61] The Petition of Right was the Parliament's attempt to resolve this question.

Finally, in June, Charles was faced with the need to agree to this legislation against the use by the crown of arbitrary imprisonment, unparliamentary taxation and martial law.[62] The House of Lords had rejected a proposal for including a saving clause in the Petition which would have protected a residual royal prerogative. Having already given one evasive answer to the Petition and being forced to a better by his financial need, Charles gave his definitive royal assent. When he agreed to the Petition's being enrolled as a statute and printed, a procedure which would give it legislative force, the

---

[57] Reeve, 'Petition of Right', pp. 266–7.
[58] Gardiner, *History*, vi, pp. 239–40, 250–1, 254; Russell, *Parliaments*, pp. 360–1; Birch, i, p. 341; SP16/98/52.
[59] NUL, Ne.C., 15,405, p. 168.   [60] *CD1628*, ii, p. 325.   [61] Ibid., iii, p. 98.
[62] The Petition would appear to have declared illegal the use of martial law save in armies in time of war. Reeve, 'Viscount Dorchester', p. 46n; Russell, *Parliaments*, p. 353.

Commons proceeded with the subsidy bill.[63] They considered the printing of the Petition to be politically as well as legally important, and the document was circulated in the country by leading members of the gentry. Numerous bonfires were lit to celebrate its receiving the royal assent, the number of fires apparently increased by the rumour that Buckingham was to be sent to the Tower.[64] Undoubtedly the advocates of the Petition were delighted that they had achieved the legal guarantee they sought. Charles, however, nursed a sense of injury. He was reported to have discounted the five subsidies as nothing in the light of the offence he had received. Having failed to avoid the legal implications of the Petition with an evasive answer, he endeavoured to subvert the parliamentary order for the unembroidered printing of the measure, an action exposed in Parliament in 1629.[65] He seems to have been fearful, and resentful, of what he had conceded. He would later seek strenuously to resist some of the legal implications of the Petition of Right.

The Petition, of course, had a more general constitutional significance greater than the sum of its parts. But it is the immediate legal and political implications of the measure, together with the wider ideological context of the parliamentary session, which are most important here. In legal terms, statutory revision in important areas of the royal prerogative (together with continuing royal resistance to such reform) suggested that under Charles the role of the law might be changing, that in response to his rule it might become less a vehicle of social cohesion and more an instrument of political dissent. This was, in fact, to be a salient feature of political change in England as Charles's personal rule emerged. It gives the report that Charles considered attempting to ban lawyers from the 1628 session the ring of truth.[66]

Politically, the Petition of Right was the product of a national war crisis which had led to fear over the meaning of Charles's policies. Those policies suggested constitutional change and the threat of alien ways. In 1628 Parliament challenged him to govern in traditional fashion – under the law and in co-operation with the assembled political nation. It expressed a widespread desire for reform and employed and sought to satisfy public opinion. In the Petition it also issued a warning to Charles of the lengths to which it would go to achieve such reform: to withhold badly needed supply and to resort to legislation. In the particular sense the Petition was a success. It encouraged the king to desist from forced loans and (to a lesser extent, as will be seen)

---

[63] *CD1628*, iv, pp. 220–1, 280–1, 331; Reeve, 'Petition of Right'.
[64] Hirst, 'Court, country, and politics before 1629', p. 113; Russell, *Parliaments*, p. 389; Birch, i, p. 362; Hill, 'Parliament and people', pp. 117–18; *CD1628*, iii, p. 102.
[65] AGS, E2517, fo. 79; E. R. Foster, 'Printing the Petition of Right', *HLQ*, xxxviii (1974–5). See also NUL, Ne.C., 15,405, p. 58.
[66] P. Gregg, *King Charles I* (London, 1981), p. 170.

arbitrary imprisonment. But it did not alter his instinct towards non-parliamentary rule; neither could it prevent his later use of other excuses for non-parliamentary fiscal aid – schemes such as knighthood fines and Ship Money.[67]

The successful use of supply as a bargaining tool was a remarkable aspect of the session of 1628 – the more remarkable given the moral pressure upon the Parliament to pay for the war. Financial leverage was translated into considerable political power, signifying that Parliament could influence the king and, to an extent, shape the nature of his rule. Parliament had not succeeded in this in 1624 because it was more difficult for it to influence foreign policy, but also because the crown had not yet contracted war debts. Parliamentary influence was premised upon the financial need of the king. Once that need were removed, Parliament could be powerless and could even cease to exist. Its survival depended upon a destination for its financial appropriations as well as upon its ability to appropriate.

The debates which produced the Petition of Right saw one political development with the most far-reaching implications. On 26 May Charles lost the vote in the House of Lords on the proposed saving clause protecting his prerogative. This critical vote constituted almost a test of loyalty to the crown. Charles was defeated because he could not command the support of an important group among his nobility, a group which swung the debate against him. Essentially these were the same men who had opposed the loan: Saye, Clare, Essex, Lincoln and Warwick. To these were added Bedford, who by 1628 had become an opponent of arbitrary taxation; Archbishop Abbot, whom Charles had humiliated for refusing to license the sermons justifying the loan; and three men who had suffered political exclusion (and, in the case of the last two, imprisonment) at Buckingham's hands: Bishop Williams and the earls of Arundel and Bristol. In swaying the vote these men led an alignment of what were reported to be 'the more ancient nobility'. In an hierarchical society a monarch who could lose the support of the aristocracy on such a scale was in deep trouble. Clearly those who turned the tide in the Lords had an interest, in some cases very sincere, in maintaining the rights of the subject. They were also men who in various ways had become personally alienated from Charles and his regime. In destroying the saving clause they were insisting upon legal guarantees and were showing what was, in effect, lack of trust in the king. Experience of Charles had shaped their personal and political attitudes together. The nobility were well placed to ascertain the thinking and conduct of the king. Doubtless many of them had learnt of Charles's prominent role in the proceedings concerning the forced loan. And it was in the House of Lords in 1628 that Buckingham made the amazing revelation that

[67] I am grateful to Christopher Thompson for this point.

the king had sanctioned the attempted perversion of the record in the Five Knights' case.[68] Several weeks later Clare felt able to write to his son in terms which were remarkably unsympathetic towards Charles. He reported the king's refusal to allow redefinition of the law of habeas corpus and how this would, it was expected, break the Parliament. He made it clear that he supported the efforts of the Commons to register their demands and to proceed on a course which would (Clare believed) case the responsibility for failure upon the king.[69]

All this is not to suggest that the disillusioned peers had abandoned any attempt to work with Charles. Arundel continued to do so. It was understood among the peerage that Charles was a young king, and the general resentment of Buckingham accounted for much. After the upper house had agreed to the Petition of Right without addition, one of their number, Weston, arranged for an occasion of reconciliation between Charles and the dissident peers. They were admitted to the king's presence and kissed his hand.[70] That this was seen to be necessary, however, underlines the distance which had emerged between Charles and these men. Unquestionably, the session of 1628 left a legacy of ill will (particularly on Charles's part) and of suspicion. The king rewarded Bishop Williams's advocacy of the Petition by depriving him of what had become but the nominal title of Privy Councillor.[71] By 1628, among those leading subjects who had opposed Charles, the precious store of trust was seriously diminished. This could only weaken the foundations of his rule. An attitude of confidence in and respect towards the monarch was not only the basis of the social order; it was the element which ultimately made the English constitution workable.

Despite the constitutional conflict involved in the making of the Petition of Right, such conflict was not the aim, at least not the conscious aim, of those assembled in Parliament. Their concern was not to alter things but rather, as they saw it, to solve the problem of a system which was failing to work when (they thought) it should have done.[72] The basic ideological context of early Stuart political life – the ideal of cosmic (and constitutional) harmony and its concomitant suspicion of novelty – was being forced to accommodate a political reality of tension and conflict with Charles's attempt at new counsels. In the same way that the loan had been rationalized by an appeal to divine right, Charles told Parliament in 1628 that he possessed a royal

---

[68] Guy, 'Origins of the Petition of Right', p. 300. See also Cust, 'Charles I, the Privy Council, and the forced loan', p. 230; Lockyer, *Buckingham*, p. 276; Russell, *Parliaments*, p. 374; Birch, i, pp. 346–7, 358; G. R. Elton, rev. art., *TLS*, 16 Sept. 1983, p. 991.

[69] NUL, Ne.C., 15,404, pp. 213–14.

[70] Birch, i, pp. 358–9; Lockyer, *Buckingham*, p. 440; see also SP16/529/19.

[71] H. R. Trevor-Roper, *Archbishop Laud, 1573–1645* (2nd edn, London, 1962), pp. 86–7.

[72] Russell, *Parliaments*, pp. 5, 339.

prerogative *jure divino*: a notion strongly resisted by the common lawyers who framed the Petition. Clearly the broad (if loosely defined) Jacobean constitutional consensus had been gravely weakened. Charles's rule had triggered an unwanted debate as to the true character of English government. Yet the prevailing ideal of harmony meant that the terms of that debate were on the whole unconscious or inexplicit.[73] The constitutional framework, however, was being pushed to its limits and the king himself was in the vanguard. In allowing glimpses of his absolutist predilections Charles was compassing a profound innovation. And. by indulging this provocative tolerance for the new so as to produce fierce constitutional dispute, he was offending the mental axioms as well as the established practice of English political life. This could only promote suspicion of him and dissatisfaction with his rule.

To what extent did those in the Commons harbour reservations about the king? In 1628 the lower house drew up a remonstrance or statement of grievances, eventually presented to Charles, which sheds much light upon their thinking at this time. To John Pym this document seems to have been more important than the Petition of Right.[74] The immediate inspiration for the remonstrance was the deep disappointment caused by the king's defective first answer to the Petition of Right. Yet the remonstrance debate suddenly released into the open all the fears which had pervaded the session. On 5 June, on the motion of Pym, the Commons resolved to proceed with a remonstrance which would inform the king of the real state of the kingdom.[75] From the beginning this was intended as a statement proceeding from loyalty and confidence. Such an approach was, of course, the customary mode of thought and of address; but it seems that the Commons' endeavours were essentially sincere. To their minds Buckingham was the root cause of the trouble, and the remonstrance evolved as a classical statement on the malevolent influence of

---

[73] Thus, Charles's abuse of the legitimate power of prerogative imprisonment in the Five Knights' case encouraged the Commons to believe that the crown had never possessed such a power – a power which they then proceeded to have declared illegal, all the while professing that their intentions would not prejudice the king's just prerogative. In similar fashion the accusation of constitutional innovation which came to be levelled at Charles's government was without regard to the way in which that government had built upon received notions of royal authority. Among the advocates of the crown, Laud could criticize a speech by Rudyerd on the liberties of the subject as seditious; and Charles himself could classify refusal to pay the forced loan as a failure of allegiance. I am grateful to John Morrill for discussion of these matters. See J. Daly, *Cosmic harmony and political thinking in early Stuart England* (*TrAPS*, lxix, pt 7; Philadelphia, 1979); L. J. Reeve, 'Sir Robert Heath's advice for Charles I in 1629', *BIHR*, lix, 2 (1986); Reeve, 'Petition of Right'; Cust, 'Charles I, the Privy Council, and the forced loan', p. 234; Cust, 'News and politics'; Laud, *Works*, vii, p. 631; *CD1628*, iii, pp. 94ff., 123; Russell, *Parliaments*, pp. 366–7.

[74] *CD1628*, iv, p. 140.

[75] Ibid., pp. 117, 119, 129, 133, 237–8; see also Conrad Russell's very illuminating analysis of the remonstrance debate to which I am much indebted, *Parliaments*, pp. 379–82.

evil counsel. The leading members of the house were clearly seeking to believe in the virtue of the king. Eliot was particularly insistent in his conviction that Charles could not offend. Sir Edward Coke summed up the feeling of the house: 'We must with all endeavour free the king, who hears and sees by other men's ears and eyes.'[76] Charles's response was to order that no reflection should be made upon his ministers or his government. On 11 June the Commons proceeded to disobey this order when, after four hours of debate, they resolved to name Buckingham in the remonstrance as the cause of all dangers to the king and kingdom.[77] It is difficult to avoid the conclusion that the accusations heaped upon the duke were born of the Commons' fear that the king might be suspect.[78] And, much as they sought to avoid it, the remonstrance came to read as an indirect attack upon the king himself.

What were the specific threats identified by the Commons? Initially they were listed as innovation in religion, innovation in government, and the disasters and dangers abroad and at home. These themes were woven into one indivisible pattern of fear. The forced loan was held to provide clear evidence of new counsels; and Sir Nathaniel Rich attacked those who had supposedly preached a doctrine of absolute sovereignty before the king. This constitutional threat was linked to the fear of Arminians and Catholics and to the apprehension of a general alteration in religion. The Commons held that the execution of laws against recusants and Jesuits had been lax, that the duchess of Buckingham was a great favourer of Catholics, and that open masses were held at the court of the queen: contentions which were all essentially true.

It was Christopher Sherland, on the first day of the debate, who broached the subject and the logic of a popish fifth column: 'Are not many trusted in services and employments that are known papists? What success can we expect?'[80] This idea met with immediate recognition in the Commons and it is the key to their thinking, as fully developed, in 1628. The threats to the godly commonwealth at home were one and the same with those to Protestantism abroad – and just as powerful. In this context those who allowed their religion to become corrupt would be abandoned by God. In Sir Edward Coke's words: 'God has punished us because we have not spoken plainly [against religious innovation] . . . and until we do so God will not bless us, nor go out with our armies.'[81] Phelips concluded: 'These things have made God a

---

[76] *CD1628*, iv, p. 260; and see ibid., pp. 128–9, 132, 140, 150, 160.
[77] Ibid., pp. 113, 138, 251; Birch, i, p. 237.
[78] Russell, *Parliaments*, p. 378; Lockyer, *Buckingham*, p. 469.
[79] *CD1628*, iv, pp. 143, 146, 158–9, 169–70; Hibbard, *Popish plot*, pp. 34–6.
[80] *CD1628*, iv, p. 116. See also the substance of Jeremiah Dyke's fast sermon of 5 April. J. F. Maclear, 'The influence of the puritan clergy on the House of Commons, 1625–29', *Church History*, xiv (1945), pp. 276ff.
[81] *CD1628*, iv, p. 119.

counsellor to our enemies and a general to their forces. Now fall these things at a time when our religion is almost extirpate in Christendom.'[82] God's judgement was swift and simple: in time of war corruption gave the enemy victory within and without. Sherland believed that the north of England was almost half composed of papists: 'so far as they go the king of Spain conquers already . . .'[83] Sir Edward Coke cited Homer on the fall of Troy to show that fifty men in the heart of a city could do more damage than a thousand outside: 'I fear no invasion if there be not a party within.'[84] The enemy, Coke made clear, was Spain: the same enemy who had sent the Armada, had sought to poison Queen Elizabeth, had engineered the Gunpowder Plot, and was still seeking to extend its monarchy over England.[85] For men believed that Roman religion and Spanish monarchy were allied forces. Strode pointed out that the invasion had begun when a Petition of Right was required: 'The liberties have been so invaded that we are exposed to a foreign destruction.' The remonstrance was now more important than the Petition: 'A man mending his chamber and [who] sees his house falling will not mend that but the whole.'[86] At the intersection of these religious and political threats stood Buckingham, the chief agent of destruction. Kirton voiced the fears of many in saying that the duke endeavoured to make them slaves, conspired with their enemies, and had some dangerous plot upon them.[87]

Yet Buckingham, Richard Knightley emphasized, was not only an enemy to England but to Christendom.[88] The conviction that the dangers to England were part of a wider European drama was the dominant and unifying theme of the remonstrance debate. It was the international context which appeared to prove so graphically that Arminianism was the forerunner of popery. By 1626 the king and Buckingham had committed themselves to the Arminian party in the English Church – the king more deeply out of religious sympathy and the duke somewhat cynically out of political calculation. Calvinist predestinarian doctrine was outlawed, Laud was promised the see of Canterbury (and in 1627 with Bishop Neile was admitted to Council), and ecclesiastical preferment, it seemed, was now open only to those of their persuasion.[89] The

---

[82] Ibid., p. 169.   [83] Ibid., p. 120.   [84] Ibid., p. 163.   [85] Ibid., pp. 143–4, 248.
[86] Ibid., p. 154. It was also Pym's belief that the rule of law existed to protect true religion; see C. Russell, 'The parliamentary career of John Pym, 1621–9', in P. Clark, A. G. R. Smith and N. Tyacke (eds.), *The English commonwealth 1547–1640* (Leicester, 1979), p. 164 and passim.
[87] *CD1628*, iv, p. 130.
[88] Ibid., p. 120.
[89] Trevor-Roper, *Catholics, Anglicans and puritans*, p. 66; Lockyer, *Buckingham*, pp. 307, 449; *CSPD 1627–8*, p. 400; N. Tyacke, 'Puritanism, Arminianism and counter-revolution', in Russell (ed.), *Origins of the English civil war*, pp. 132–3. The Tyacke thesis concerning the rise of English Arminianism has recently been questioned; see P. White, 'The rise of Arminianism reconsidered', *P&P*, ci (1983). This article is unconvincing in two significant respects: the failure of the anti-Arminians to register their case in Parliament is no argument

high favour shown to English Arminianism was simultaneous with the dramatic failure of English arms against the Catholic monarchies of France and Spain. When this was coupled with observation of the Dutch republic, where the Arminians were in the vanguard of the movement for peace with Spain, to English Calvinists the case against Arminianism was conclusive. Thus Sherland asked angrily: 'Why are the Arminians who have sought the ruin of the Low Countries allowed here?'[90] And Rich, reporting from the committee which drew up the remonstrance, reiterated the point, calling the Arminians the Jesuits of the Protestant religion.[91] Pym, who had attacked Arminianism in the Parliament of 1626, had been ahead of public awareness.[92] But in 1628 a link between religious change in England and the international forces of the Counter-Reformation was forged in the minds of the Commons. This explains their comparative neglect of foreign in favour of domestic religious policy during the session of 1629, which was, to their minds, no neglect at all: the enemy appeared to be the same at home and abroad.

The wider European context explains the high profile accorded to Irish affairs in the remonstrance debate. With the sense of an impending external threat it was natural to look to Ireland as the perpetual window of vulnerability for England. But to English protestants Ireland provided clear evidence that the Spanish and Roman conquest of Charles's dominions was also proceeding from within. Pym took notice of Lord Deputy Falkland's policy of tacit religious toleration, and he ensured that the condition of Ireland would feature in the preparation of the remonstrance.[93] Mention was made of the suspension of Irish recusancy fines, the holding of military commissions by Catholics, and the widespread public practice of the Catholic religion. But the Irish themselves were the cause of the greatest fear. The Commons were told how Irish troops were some of the staunchest in the army of Flanders, that most of the Irish in English service had kinsmen in the service of Spain, and that there were Irish troops in Kent, Portsmouth and the Isle of Wight 'and no powder or munition to withstand them'.[94] Anxiety about Irishmen under arms in the British Isles, in the wake of the 1627 invasion

for the emerging character of the Caroline episcopate; and White does not appreciate the link between Roman Catholicism and Arminianism in the English Calvinist mind. Yet White has usefully suggested the need not to accept Tyacke's argument uncritically and has stimulated debate. See N. Tyacke and P. White, 'Debate. The rise of Arminianism reconsidered', *P&P*, cxv (1987). See also Lake, 'Calvinism and the English Church'.

90 *CD1628*, iv, p. 120; Israel, *Dutch republic*, pp. 60–3, 76, 175, 190, 231–3, 235, 300.
91 *CD1628*,. iv, pp. 252, 269.
92 Tyacke, 'Puritanism, Arminianism', p. 134; Russell, *Parliaments*, pp. 297–9.
93 *CD1628*, iv, pp. 142, 155; Reeve, 'Viscount Dorchester', pp. 228–30.
94 *CD1628*, iv, pp. 145, 147, 151, 157. The Commons were also alarmed to discover that the crown had sought to raise cavalry in Germany.

scare, bears out that the towering structure of fear in the remonstrance debate was erected upon factual foundations. Yet fear of the Irish was another manifestation of the belief in a Catholic fifth column: a force which appeared to be making great strides towards the extinction of Protestantism in England.

Government speakers could not allay the fears triggered by the remonstrance debate. On 14 June the House voted to present the document to the king (along with a list of the extensive English losses at sea during the previous three years).[95] In effect the remonstrance was a statement of the English Calvinist view of the world in 1628.[96] It began by denying that the Commons wished to cast any aspersion on Charles or his government. According to the document most or all of the things in it were either unknown or had been misrepresented to Charles. The Church and commonwealth were in danger of ruin and destruction. The failures at Cadiz, Rhé and La Rochelle were the measure of England's decline from power to contempt. The royal assent to the Petition of Right had, stated the remonstrance, much allayed the fear of an alteration in government. But these gains were in danger of being eclipsed by a wholesale international conspiracy against free government and true religion. Observation of the European scene, where the Protestant countries and reformed Churches were under threat and in decline, provided the evidence that developments in Britain were part of the same greater design, 'some secret and strange co-operating here with the enemies of our religion abroad for the utter extirpation thereof'. This was a judgement of God, 'always bent against the neglect of his holy religion, the strokes of whose divine justice we have already felt . . . in great measure'.[97]

The remonstrance condemned Arminianism as crypto-popery which undid states and churches from within; hence James I had striven to suppress it, in neighbouring countries as well as in England. This was essentially a reference to James's intervention against Dutch Arminianism at the Synod of Dort (1619). Such an appeal to Jacobean policy was very significant in 1628. In England James had presided over a Church of moderation and breadth. But this later invocation of his policy demonstrates clearly the political importance of the late king's official commitment to orthodox Calvinism – an importance revealed in the fear produced when men believed that commitment had ended. The sense of a religious decline or a palace revolution since James's death could only encourage suspicion of Charles's rule.[98] As well as

---

[95] Ibid., pp. 120–1, 145–6, 170, 311. The Commons showed a degree of tact in sending the subsidy bill up to the Lords before seeking an arrangement for the presentation of the remonstrance to the king; ibid., pp. 331, 334–5.

[96] *CD1628*, iv, pp. 311–18.   [97] Ibid., p. 314.

[98] Reeve, 'Viscount Dorchester', p. 15; P. Collinson, *The religion of Protestants* (Oxford, 1982), pp. 79ff., 282, and passim; Russell, 'Career of John Pym', pp. 159ff.

the spread of Arminianism the remonstrance mentioned countenancing of popery, which amounted to 'no less than a toleration', the suppression of preaching and lecturing, and the practice of Catholicism and exercise of Roman jurisdiction in Ireland.[99] There were still armed soldiers in England, the kingdom's treasure was wasted, crown lands were sold, forests disafforested, trade decayed and shipping lost.[100] Events in England, Ireland and Europe were seen to merge into a single design; and in the English context 'the principal cause of which evils and dangers' was the duke, his excessive power and its abuse.[101] Hatred for Buckingham was intense; by 1628 the driving forces behind it were all-encompassing religious fear and a growing suspicion about the integrity of the monarch. The animosity towards the duke was the measure of the power of these forces – forces which Charles, in rejecting the remonstrance and again refusing to sacrifice Buckingham, would turn more and more against himself.

With a peculiar political blindness, Charles did not perceive the depth of the Commons' fears. His reply to the remonstrance came in the form of a denial, on 17 June, that the Commons had any real competence in government or religion; he also gave Buckingham his hand in the presence of both houses.[102] There was more involved here than the king's simple loyalty to his friend. Charles had come to identify his personal authority with his confidence in the duke. His sense of honour, rectitude and insecurity caused him to believe that he could not surrender Buckingham without inviting a threat to himself. Yet the opposite was actually the case. Charles may have been encouraged in his attitude by Laud. At the king's command the bishop drew up an answer to the remonstrance, and this is a most revealing document. Laud understood that the Commons had framed what was by implication an attack upon the king. It is in keeping with the exclusive and partisan nature of Laud's mind that he did not doubt this implication to be malicious.[103] Yet while not fully perceiving the agonies of the Commons, he focused accurately on the emerging gap in their thought: if the king was worthy of confidence, how had England come to this?

But if we be wise and judicious how comes it to pass we are thus ignorant of imminent dangers, as the same remonstrance would make us? – or led so easily by false shows and pretentions of our ministers? And if we be good and just, how is it that what our wisdom sees amiss in the state, or the ministers of it, is not punished or amended? . . . this remonstrance spares our office and government, the execution of it, no more than

[99] *CD1628*, iv, pp. 312–14.
[100] Ibid., pp. 148–9, 155, 161, 165, 170–2, 200ff., 314–16.
[101] Ibid., pp. 316–17.
[102] Ibid., pp. 352 and n, 354, 480; Gardiner, *History*, vi, pp. 316–17, 320.
[103] *CD1628*, iv, p. 352n, vi, pp. 52–6 and n. See also Laud, *Works*, vi, pp. 636–7; Cust, *The forced loan*, pp. 78–80. The remonstrance had accused Laud himself of unsound opinions; *CD1628*, iv, p. 313.

it does our person; for it makes not only ourself weak and apt to be led, but all our Council ciphers ... it has cast scandal upon us and our government through the whole body of it; for it makes both Church and state appear so disjointed that our loyal and dutiful subjects must needs be perplexed in their thoughts while they live in a government that neither stands right with God nor itself, if all were true that is remonstrated.[104]

The traditional notion of evil counsel had never been further than the shortest of steps from a reflection upon the monarch. In a situation such as that prevailing in 1628 this distinction could not be sustained. The basis for alarm was that, as events had shown, Charles was *susceptible* to such counsel. This was the basis for Pym's fast-growing distrust, inspired by the rise of Arminianism.[105] Belief in evil counsel and suspicion of the king were not mutually exclusive ideas, and in this case concern with one involved a necessary concern with the other. Laud had identified this link and the dangerous accusation to which the Commons were being forced. Charles chose to leave Laud's answer unpublished. He probably did not wish to advertise the threat to which it drew attention. But he failed to understand the nature of that threat, for he proceeded not to remove but to strengthen it. There is a tragic irony in his eventual speech to both houses proroguing the Parliament, which referred to the remonstrance as a document which no wise man could justify.[106] As with new counsels and the new official commitment to Arminianism, so with the doctrine of evil counsel, Charles was placing enormous pressure upon the traditional English view of monarchy. The Commons' appeal to his father's religious policy had been a significant (and perhaps an intentional) warning. After Charles rejected the remonstrance the house was reported to be discontented, and some men, despite the Petition of Right, to have regretted granting Charles the subsidies. The earl of Carlisle considered that Charles had fallen in the estimation of his subjects because of his tolerance of Buckingham.[107] The general confidence in Charles inspired by the launching of a war against Spain on his accession was, by 1628, gravely impaired. The majority of the Commons had no great experience of court politics and they harboured more illusions than the Lords about the nature of

---

[104] Ibid., *CD1628*, vi, pp. 55–6; see also Sir William Beecher's comment in the Commons, that the remonstrance could be a threat to the allegiance of the king's subjects if it fell into the hands of England's enemies; ibid., iv, p. 334.

[105] Russell, 'Career of John Pym', pp. 159–65.

[106] *CD1628*, iv, pp. 352n, 480.

[107] The exact nature of Carlisle's observation remains unclear as the evidence has been filtered. The earl made a statement to the duke of Savoy which was reported by Gerbier. The Spanish summary of his report states that Charles was disliked ('era mal quisto') by all his kingdom on account of Buckingham; AGS, E2042, unfol. relation of Gerbier's report, *c.* autumn 1628. On regret at having granted the subsidies see Birch, i, p. 366; see also P. Clark, 'Thomas Scott and the growth of urban opposition to the early Stuart regime', *HJ*, xxi, 1 (1978), pp. 18–19.

royal power. It was axiomatic, even more for the Commons than for the nobility, that the monarch should be above suspicion. What was the linchpin of Englishmen's conception of political society could not easily be disturbed.[108] But a painful and enduring tension was created when Charles encouraged men to think the almost unthinkable – a tension which could only damage the workings of national politics.

In addition to the remonstrance, the final weeks of the session created what would be a dangerous political legacy when Parliament resumed. No agreement was reached about the legality of the customs duties, duties which Charles was continuing to collect. The Commons wished to demonstrate that these revenues were enjoyed by parliamentary authority. Partly to underline this point, they intended to reform the system of rates. This complicated the bill for tonnage and poundage, which was inadvertently shelved in favour of other business, particularly the Petition of Right, until mid-June. The further technical difficulty emerged that over the years it had become difficult to distinguish between customs and impositions. On 20 June the Commons discovered that Charles and Buckingham were also investigating the rates. Since the Jacobean period, the Commons had seen royal exploitation of the customs as a threat to Parliament's control over taxation. On 21 June the king told the Commons specifically that it was he who had called upon Sir Edmund Sawyer, an auditor of the Exchequer, and Abraham Dawes, one of the customs farmers, for information. It emerged that the new book of rates was Sawyer's project; but Charles's message remained both constitutionally and financially alarming. The Commons sent to the king to ascertain how much longer he would allow them to sit. They indicated that the matter of tonnage and poundage had become difficult and intimated that a temporary act for the duties might be passed. Charles apparently rejected the suggestion on the basis that his predecessors had been granted tonnage and poundage for life. The Commons then requested that the session be not prorogued but rather adjourned. The envisaged legislation would then authorize all duties collected since the beginning of the session. An adjournment would also allow the house to work on the matter in committee during the recess. Charles refused an adjournment, announcing on 23 June that in three days he would prorogue the Parliament until 20 October. The Commons then set to work on a further remonstrance to declare the collection of tonnage and poundage without an act of Parliament illegal and against the Petition of Right. The document requested that Charles collect no duties until the next session, when the legislation would be passed, and that he take no action against those refusing to pay.

On 26 June Charles prorogued the Parliament several hours earlier than

---

[108] Russell, 'Career of John Pym', p. 159; Ashton, *The English civil war*, ch. 1.

expected in order to prevent the Commons completing work on this second remonstrance. After the session many of the merchants refused to pay the duties, claiming that these were against the Petition of Right. The Council proceeded to seize the goods of these refusers. Resistance continued and merchants began to be arrested. Some were brought before the Council: one of them, Richard Chambers, protested that nowhere were merchants more screwed and wrung than in England. Star Chamber proceedings were instituted against him. By November some thirty leading merchants were still unwilling to pay. (They offered security for any duties which might eventually be awarded to the king at law.) Four of them, including John Rolle, a member of the House of Commons, sued for their goods by writ in the Court of Exchequer. The Court, of which Weston was a member as Lord Treasurer, decided that the government's sequestration of the goods was justified. The Court also referred the main question to the next session of Parliament.

Thus the matter of the customs was to remain unresolved into the fourth year of Charles's reign. This was the result of a general desire for reform combined with a conflict of authority between Charles and the Commons. Yet the lower house had also shown a remarkable lack of foresight and political sense. They had failed to settle tonnage and poundage in 1626 and 1628. Charles could not suspend collection of the customs, which amounted to roughly half his ordinary revenue, particularly when he was labouring to meet the costs of war. As Wentworth had told the Commons on 21 June, if they did not pass the bill for tonnage and poundage Charles would be forced to levy the duties regardless of the Petition of Right. Moreover, the legal position was not as clear-cut as the Commons supposed. In 1606 the Court of Exchequer had decided in Bate's case that the king could legally levy impositions on imports and exports. Despite the Commons' appeal to the Petition of Right in 1628, in framing the Petition they had not intended it to refer to tonnage and poundage. And the customs duties, collected at the ports, were arguably not a tax accountable at Westminster and therefore might not be subject to the Petition. The most significant aspect of the 1628 dispute was the ambition of Charles and Weston to exploit the customs revenues. This was evident in the official desire to revise the Book of Rates, as well as in Weston's Exchequer judgement in favour of a parliamentary settlement of the dispute. It was the customs duties which became the financial mainstay of the personal rule.[109]

---

[109] CD1628, iii, pp. 447, 454–6; iv, pp. 392–3, 405–6, 407 and n, 408–10, 427, 447, 449n–50n, 468, 470–1, 480n, 481–3; vi, pp. 119, 198; Birch, i, pp. 433–4, 437; Russell, *Parliaments*, pp. 78, 386–7; Russell, *Crisis of Parliaments*, p. 322; M. C. Alexander, *Charles I's Lord Treasurer* (Chapel Hill, 1975), pp. 134–6; D. Thomas, 'Financial and administrative developments', in Tomlinson (ed.), *Before the English civil war*, p. 103; Gardiner, *History*, vi, pp. 323–4, 326–8; vii, pp. 3–6; Hirst, *Authority and conflict*, pp. 102–3, 110, 112, 116.

A sense of powerful underlying animosities, occasionally rising to the surface, pervaded the parliamentary session of 1628. This derived from the ill feeling created over the forced loan, from an ideological atmosphere concentrating upon threatened liberties, from public hatred of the duke, from fear of a standing army,[110] foreign powers and Catholic subversion, and from the mutual suspicion emerging between the king and leading critics of his government in both houses. Charles's opening speech had set the tone of the session by announcing the continued threat of arbitrary measures.[111] After Buckingham was attacked in the Commons, Charles favoured the duke's close associates such as Endymion Porter.[112] During the session the Commons championed the cause of loan refusal in the City.[113] On the day before the Commons' final approval of the remonstrance, Buckingham's astrologer, Doctor Lambe, was brutally murdered by a London mob who stated their desire to do the same to the duke. Charles fined the City heavily for failing to detect those responsible.[114] On rare occasions there was the clear suggestion that Charles could not be trusted. Pym said as much in rejecting a general confirmation of liberties and the king's first answer to the Petition of Right; and Clare wrote to Lord Vere that Charles in his public statements was attempting to renege upon his clear royal assent to the Petition.[115] The government's sensitivity about the question of trust in the king was probably evident in its investigation of a letter, reflecting upon Charles, which was delivered to the Commons on 11 May, and in the official suspicion that Pym was connected with the letter.[116] On the day Parliament was prorogued Charles freed the Cornish deputy lieutenants imprisoned by the Commons for acting against free elections, as well as Auditor Sawyer, imprisoned likewise for his work on the customs rates; the king paid the expenses of their imprisonment.[117] Manwaring, impeached and heavily sentenced by Parliament for preaching in favour of the loan, was pardoned by Charles and presented with a valuable church living.[118] After the Parliament was prorogued Charles secured all the powder in London; people were fearful and it was reported that citizens were beginning to acquire arms.[119] This atmosphere of tension, animosity, suspicion and foreboding did not dissolve with

---

[110] Russell, *Parliaments*, pp. 335–7, 343. [111] *CD1628*, ii, p. 3.

[112] Huxley, *Endymion Porter*, p. 156. [113] Ashton, *City and the court*, pp. 180–1.

[114] Gardiner, *History*, vi, pp. 318–20; Birch, i, pp. 364–5, 367; *Barrington family letters 1628–1632*, ed. A. Searle (Camden Society, London, 1983), p. 245.

[115] Russell, 'Career of John Pym', p. 162; NUL, Ne.C., 15,405, p. 58.

[116] Birch, i, p. 369; *CSPD 1628–9*, p. 198; *CD1628*, iv, pp. 424 and n, 428 and n, 433, 435–7, 440.

[117] Birch, i, pp. 373–4; *CSPD 1628–9*, p. 179; *CD1628*, iv, p. 404n.

[118] Manwaring had been sentenced to imprisonment at the pleasure of the House of Lords and to pay £1,000; Gardiner, *History*, vi, pp. 312–13, 330–1; *CSPD 1628–9*, p. 198.

[119] Birch, i, pp. 372, 374–5.

the ending of the parliamentary session. It remained alive, became intensified, and in a more complex form troubled the political scene well into the following year and even beyond.

After the parliamentary session Charles made several promotions in his service which were of great political consequence. On 15 July Laud was translated from the bishopric of Bath and Wells to that of London. His appointment was a significant milestone in the increasing Arminianization of the Church by means of key episcopal appointments. Laud's translation gave him control over the printing presses of the capital and was thus a great gain for the Arminian party. By 1628 he was already the most influential cleric in England. It required only the eventual death of the Calvinist (and now virtually powerless) Archbishop Abbot to take him to Canterbury in 1633.[120] On the same day on which Laud was translated, Weston was appointed Lord Treasurer. He became the principal ministerial policy-maker of the years which saw the emergence of the personal rule. He was a friend and former client of Arundel, and it is reasonable to link his appointment to Buckingham's conciliation of the earl.[121]

The recruitment of Sir Thomas Wentworth to the king's service and the circles of the court was doubly important. Wentworth was to exercise great power under Charles: in the north of England, in Ireland, and again in England in 1640. His entry into government was also the event which roused the jealousy of his rival Sir John Eliot to fever pitch. Wentworth's driving ambition and great ability were undeniable. Yet exactly when he received the critical overture is unclear. Weston was working in Wentworth's interests as early as 1625.[122] Inspired by a temporary falling out with Buckingham, and by a concern for reform, Wentworth opposed the forced loan in 1627. It has been said that he was in touch with the court while in confinement as a refuser.[123] In the Commons in 1628 he led the debates for much of the session, favouring a bill for the liberties of the subject and later supporting the Petition of Right. His advocacy of speedy supply and his desire to steer the house away from contentious constitutional issues mark him out as a designated or prospective servant of the crown.[124] At some point in early 1628 Weston

---

[120] Laud, *Works*, iii, p. 208; Tyacke, 'Puritanism, Arminianism', pp. 134, 137; AMRE, CPA, 42, fo. 379r; Trevor-Roper, *Laud*, p. 104; P. Welsby, *George Abbot: the unwanted archbishop* (London, 1962), pp. 121–2.

[121] Russell, *Parliaments*, p. 391; Alexander, *Charles I's Lord Treasurer*, p. 17.

[122] Alexander, *Charles I's Lord Treasurer*, pp. 88–9.

[123] P. Zagorin, 'Did Strafford change sides?', *EHR*, ci (1986), pp. 155–8; Cooper, 'Fall of the Stuart monarchy', p. 555.

[124] I am grateful to Sir Geoffrey Elton for this point. See *CD1628*, ii, pp. 414, 431; iii, pp. 98, 211, 216, 272, 328, 345, 406, 613; and iv, pp. 301, 333, 364; see also Wentworth's advice to the Commons to pass the bill for tonnage and poundage and the bill of arms, ibid., iv, pp. 406, 410; *The earl of Strafford's letters and despatches . . .* , ed. W. Knowler (2 vols., London, 1739), i, p. 46.

successfully recommended Wentworth to Buckingham. In July Sir Thomas was raised to the peerage, and in December he was appointed Lord President of the North. Weston's selection of Wentworth and his rejection of overtures from Eliot were largely responsible for rendering Eliot an implacable opponent of Weston and of the government during the next parliamentary session. Wentworth had effectively selected himself. He was the abler man; he had not launched explicit public attacks on Buckingham as had Eliot in 1626 and 1628; and very significantly he favoured (as did Weston) a policy of peace with Spain. By the summer of 1628 Buckingham was considering an end to the Spanish war, and peace with Spain became the cornerstone of state policy during Weston's years of power. Almost certainly he discussed this question with Wentworth before facilitating his admission to the administration.[125] Weston strengthened the pro-Spanish interest at court as the year progressed. He effected a reconciliation between Charles and Arundel and the earl was readmitted to the Council in October.[126] Weston also promoted the career of his friend Sir Francis Cottington, a definite Hispanophile, who entered the Council in November and in December became Chancellor of the Exchequer.[127]

The assassination of Buckingham was the decisive English political event of 1628. On 23 August he was stabbed to death in Portsmouth by a naval lieutenant, John Felton, with a tenpenny butcher's knife. Felton was discontented over arrears in his pay and his failure to obtain promotion. He was also inspired by the Commons' remonstrance which had named the duke as the cause of the nation's ills. Charles's refusal to give up his favourite had only fed the public animosity towards Buckingham. At the time of his death he was the most unpopular man in England and his life had long been in danger. There had been attacks on the duke and his followers over the course of the previous two years, and after the murder of Lambe, Charles had doubled the

---

[125] There may also have been reason to suspect Eliot's financial affairs. Alexander, *Charles I's Lord Treasurer*, pp. 136–7; Knowler, *Strafford letters*, i, p. 47; John Hacket, *Scrinia reserata* (2 pts, 1693), pt 2, pp. 82–3; P. Zagorin, 'Sir Edward Stanhope's advice to Thomas Wentworth . . . ', *HJ*, vii, 2 (1964), pp. 301, 305, 314; Russell, *Parliaments*, p. 79; C. V. Wedgwood, *Thomas Wentworth, first earl of Strafford 1593–1641: a revaluation* (London, 1961), p. 68.

[126] Gardiner, *History*, vi, p. 371; Hibbard, *Popish plot*, pp. 34–5; SP16/529/15. After Buckingham's death Weston made overtures of political alliance to Carlisle, abroad on a diplomatic mission. Carlisle was a 'trimmer' and despite his anti-Habsburg leanings recognized Weston's influence and decided to favour peace with Spain. R. E. Schreiber, *The first Carlisle* (*TrAPS*, lxxiv, pt 7; Philadelphia, 1984), pp. 1–2, 114, 188; SP16/123/3.

[127] SP16/529/15; Gardiner, *History*, vi, pp. 371–2; Alexander, *Charles I's Lord Treasurer* p. 138; Archivo del Duque del Infantado, Madrid, Palafox Mss, leg. 94, fo. 136v, Coloma's instructions for Necolalde, 26 May 1631 (n.s.), where Cottington's attitude to Spain is described as 'bonisamente'. I am grateful to John Elliott for this reference. See also chapter 6, below.

guard upon Buckingham. There were threats against the duke and prophecies of his death, one of which indeed predicted that he would die in August.[128] Felton came to repent of his act, but his initial belief that he had done a public service was entirely correct insofar as Buckingham was now removed from the political scene. The duke's death was the cause of celebration and relief amongst all classes. For it was believed that better days and better counsel were to come. Beyond the duke's immediate family, the one individual we know to have grieved was Charles.[129] Buckingham was the only friend he had ever had, and since James's death Charles had been emotionally dependent upon him. The public rejoicing at the assassination seems to have offended Charles very deeply and to have played a part in distancing him from his people. Charles also acquired the idea that Parliament, or at least Eliot, had murdered his friend by means of the remonstrance.[130] The king's later refusal to release Eliot's body from the Tower was for Charles almost certainly the execution of a vendetta. It is entirely reasonable to think that Charles's attitude towards Parliament was never fully dissociated from Buckingham's death.[131]

Despite the public expectation that the duke's demise would usher in a new era, what followed appeared to many a continuation of the old. Sir David Murray wrote in December to James, earl of Carlisle: 'there is no great change for the ghost doth yet walk'.[132] Charles's immediate reaction to Buckingham's death was to attempt to continue the duke's policies, particularly the war with France and the cause of the relief of La Rochelle. The king sought to demonstrate that he had not been simply the instrument of the duke.[133] He also wished to remain loyal to Buckingham's memory. His commitment was further evident in his burial of Buckingham in the Henry VII Chapel at Westminster (until then reserved for anointed kings and princes of the blood royal), in his payment of the duke's debts, and in his favour to the Villiers family which included the raising of Buckingham's sons with the royal children.[134] According to Clarendon, from 1628 almost to the time of his own death, Charles admitted few persons into any degree of trust who had been enemies of the duke or objects of his dislike.[135] Arundel is an obvious excep-

---

[128] Lockyer, *Buckingham*, pp. 453, 458, 463; SP16/107/78, SP16/114/21; Birch, i, pp. 368, 401; Lindley, 'Riot prevention', pp. 113–14.

[129] Laud and Dorchester also felt deeply the loss of a patron and ally. See Lockyer, *Buckingham*, p. 454; SP16/114/7, SP16/114/17, SP16/116/4; Laud, *Works*, vii, pp. 16, 17n–18n.

[130] Russell, *Crisis of Parliaments*, p. 308; Gardiner, *History*, vii, pp. 227–8.

[131] Clarendon, *Rebellion*, vol. i, p. 38.

[132] SP16/123/7.

[133] AGS, E2517, fo. 74; NUL, Ne.C., 15,404, p. 215; Birch, i, pp. 396–7; SP16/529/15.

[134] Lockyer, *Buckingham*, pp. 458, 460–1; Hibbard, *Popish plot*, p. 256 n. 55; Birch, i, p. 390; Laud, *Works*, vii, pp. 18–19.

[135] Clarendon, *Rebellion*, vol. i, p. 38.

tion to this rule. Yet it underlines the distance which existed during the 1630s between the court and men such as Saye, Clare, Essex and Warwick. It also helps to explain Charles's continued objection to them, beyond the fact that they were critics of the king himself.

The overriding consequence of Buckingham's death was the focusing of public attention upon Charles. This occurred at the moment when he was forced further into a political role to which he was ill-suited. The extent to which Charles governed during the Buckingham era should not be underestimated. His rare appearances in Council were highly influential in deciding in favour of a forced loan.[136] Yet Buckingham had enjoyed virtual *carte blanche* in the distribution of patronage and the direction of foreign policy; and he had made a large share of the running in the government of Church and state. Charles, by contrast, was left in 1628 with complete responsibility for the conduct of national affairs. Buckingham's death brought a solution to the political impasse which had been created by Charles's refusal to give up the duke.[137] Yet it exacerbated the problem of the extent to which men could have confidence in Charles himself. The removal of Buckingham was to bring those who doubted the king a step closer to recognizing him as the cause of their grievances. The Commons' remonstrance of 1628 had carried dangerous implications about Charles's kingship; but Buckingham had been eminently eligible for the role of evil counsellor. James I had looked upon favourites as a screen which shielded the crown.[138] Buckingham's death eliminated at a single stroke the personality who had served, in terms of political logic, to explain entirely the unhappy state of the nation. To a degree the rejoicing at Buckingham's death reflected the public desire to believe in the king. The idea was also voiced that Buckingham had influenced Charles's views in an abiding way and that the king needed the correction of good counsel. This was a significant extension of the belief that Charles was susceptible to bad advice.[139]

But it was also a statement of hope. There was a momentary release of optimism after Buckingham's death which linked the desire for political reform and constitutional harmony with the hope, and in some cases the confidence, that Charles's virtues would now emerge. William, earl of Pembroke, wrote to the earl of Carlisle in August that the duke's death 'grows every day more favourable to me', adding: 'the king our master begins to shine already and I hope this next session to see a happy agreement between

---

[136] Cust, 'Charles I, the Privy Council, and the forced loan', pp. 213–14.
[137] Trevor-Roper, *Archbishop Laud*, p. 87.
[138] Lockyer, *Buckingham*, p. 473.
[139] SP16/529/20, Sir Robert Aiton to James, earl of Carlisle, 29 Sept. 1628, and see above, pp. 30–1.

him and his people . . . '[140] Viscount Dorchester also wrote to Carlisle of the king at this time that 'by his manner of proceeding I believe he will give his subjects contentment in being the sole director of his affairs, leaving every man to the compass of his charge.'[141] Sir Francis Nethersole wrote: 'the stone of offence being removed by the hand of God, it is to be hoped that the king and his people will now come to a perfect unity . . . '[142] The combination of hopes of the king with hopes of political betterment was a powerful one which implied more serious disappointment if such expectations were not fulfilled. It also carried within it the power to widen political division: desire for reform begged the question of the kind of reform required,[143] and on this question there was to be serious disagreement.

Thus in late 1628 a very substantial section of opinion became eligible for deep disillusionment with the king. Ultimately it was that section which espoused the sitting of Parliament, an end to Arminian appointments in the Church, and war with Spain in the Protestant cause. The hopes of men such as Pembroke, Dorchester, Nethersole and Sir Thomas Roe, who represented these views at court, were in time disappointed. These men, however, seem to have preserved their optimism about the king a little longer than their non-court counterparts in the Providence Island Company and elsewhere.[144] It was at the end of 1628, with the unobscured figure of the king being seen in a fuller political role, and with renewed hopes being built upon the death of the duke of Buckingham, that Charles decided to govern in kingly fashion, in Dorchester's words as 'the sole director'. Having been cast in the role of a cipher by the Commons' remonstrance Charles wanted to vindicate his independence. Under the circumstances this made his views and responsibility unmistakable. During the 1630s Charles was to look back on the Buckingham era as a distinct period.[145] The duke's death was a watershed which, by changing Charles's position, changed the nature of his rule – as well as others' perceptions of it – irrevocably.

No minister was ever to receive Charles's confidence as Buckingham had done. As a result court politics came to reflect, to a limited extent, more of an interaction of personalities and views than was possible during the Buckingham era. The duke's death had created an immediate power vacuum. The principal beneficiaries, besides Charles, were Weston and the queen. Henrietta Maria had been in no position to influence Charles during her early years in England. She was only fifteen at the time of her marriage in 1625. The marriage was not initially a success, largely owing to the couple's difference

---

[140] SP16/529/9; see also SP16/529/19.   [141] SP99/30/fo. 127r.
[142] SP16/114/7; see also SP16/529/21, SP16/529/40.
[143] Hill, 'Parliament and people', p. 265.
[144] Hibbard, *Popish plot*, pp. 31–2; and see chapters 4, 5, 6, 7 and 8, below.
[145] AGS, E2562, unfol., consulta of 20 Nov. 1631 (n.s.).

in religion. Above all, Charles's life was dominated by the relationship with Buckingham until 1628. With the duke's death, however, the queen came into her own. She and Charles fell lastingly in love and her influence upon the king was greatly increased. The queen's conception of monarchy was more autocratic than constitutional; yet she was not a particularly political creature. Richelieu sought in vain to have her take any significant part in matters of government. But in questions of patronage and in deciding the social membership of the court she acquired considerable influence. Around the queen congregated a number of pro-French courtiers, notably the earl of Holland, and puritan sympathizers whose anti-Spanish sentiments caused them to hanker after a French alliance. Henrietta also became an active Catholic proselytizer and protector of Catholics in Britain.[146] Weston, as the most powerful political figure about Charles after 1628, was a natural rival to the queen. The rivalry was worsened since in seeking to control expenditure he clashed with her over money.[147] These two competing groups, around Weston and the queen, came to constitute opposing court interests during these years. In terms of foreign policy they corresponded with French and Spanish preferences, although English affairs were to be complicated by the division in French politics, between Richelieu and his opponents, when it was exported in 1631.

Another section of opinion survived the Buckingham era at court which is best described as the independently Protestant. The leading exponents of this view were Pembroke and Dorchester. Anti-Spanish and pro-Dutch, they were also pro-French, but not as close to the queen as the earl of Holland. Charles's affection for the Herbert family[148] and the wealth and position of the earls of Pembroke enabled the third earl to remain a strong advocate for the Protestant-parliamentary interest virtually until his death in 1630.[149] As Chancellor of Oxford he ensured the University's propagation of predestinarian Calvinism until Charles's declaration in 1628 silenced the theological counter-attack against the Arminians.[150] Viscount Dorchester, better known as Sir Dudley Carleton, was a distinguished career diplomat who rose to high office through Buckingham's favour in the 1620s. As English ambassador to

---

[146] SP16/121/34, SP16/123/3; PRO 31/3/66/fos. 125v, 213v, 255r; AGS, E2517, fo. 76; Russell, *Crisis of Parliaments*, p. 300; SRO, Hamilton Mss no. 11134; Adams, 'Spain or the Netherlands?', p. 91; *DNB*, s.v. Henrietta Maria; K. M. Sharpe, 'The personal rule of Charles I', in Tomlinson (ed.), *Before the English civil war*, p. 58; Lockyer, *Buckingham*, pp. 251–2, 293–4; R. M. Smuts, 'The puritan followers of Henrietta Maria in the 1630s', *EHR*, xciii (1978); Hibbard, *Popish plot*, pp. 41–2, 47–8, 51–8, 60, 228–9.

[147] *CSPV 1629–32*, pp. 142, 527; SP16/121/34, SP16/529/17; Birch, i, p. 419.

[148] I am grateful to Kevin Sharpe for this point.

[149] William, earl of Pembroke, was Lord Steward. See Russell, *Parliaments*, pp. 12–14; Clarendon, *Rebellion*, vol. i, pp. 71–4; Birch, i, pp. 406, 408; HMC, 11th report, Appx I, p. 165; Adams, 'Spain or the Netherlands?', p. 87.

[150] Tyacke, 'Puritanism, Arminianism', p. 133.

the Dutch republic, and as a strong anti-Arminian Calvinist, he played a key role in the success of the Synod of Dort and the Dutch Calvinist revolution. He became a Buckingham man when the duke took up arms against Spain. He was committed to the Protestant and anti-Habsburg causes and to the goal of a Palatine restoration. He was also a close confidant of Elizabeth of Bohemia. His appointment as Secretary of State in December 1628 was part of a ministerial reshuffle which served the interests of Weston by bringing Cottington into the Exchequer. But it fulfilled a former commitment by Charles and Buckingham, pleased the king's sister, and signified that the king remained interested in pursuing the war with Spain. Dorchester provided an official court contact for his friend Sir Thomas Roe, whose uncompromising commitment to the Protestant international eventually caused his exclusion from government employment. Dorchester, by contrast, was able to remain in office, combining ideological commitment with a subtle and worldly personality. In this way he continued to be an advocate for his views until his death in 1632. His was a final rearguard action against Charles's developing pro-Spanish and anti-parliamentary policies.[151]

The political divisions which came to bear upon national policy after Buckingham's death arose, as we have seen, over the related conduct of domestic and foreign affairs. These divisions were largely produced by a deeper political process. By mid-1628, with England's engagement in war, events suggested the possibility of a breakdown in the relationship between the execution of policy at home and abroad. The incompetence of Buckingham's strategy and planning, the retreat to arbitrary measures, the delays to supply caused by the parliamentary debates of 1628, and the inadequacy of that supply in the face of financial needs all combined to create a tension between domestic and foreign policy.[152] The result was military failure and a resort to peace negotiations. Just as the breakdown of diplomacy leads to war, so in England in 1628 the impending breakdown of war encouraged diplomacy. With diplomatic initiatives launched, Buckingham met his end, and during the ensuing months foreign relations formed the arena in which the surviving views of policy competed.

What were the military failures encountered by England in 1628? In 1626 Christian of Denmark had committed himself to war against the Habsburgs in alliance with England and the Dutch. The conflict went badly against the Danes. In August Christian was defeated at Lutter; he lost his German allies and was forced to retreat to Holstein as the imperial army advanced to the Baltic. At the beginning of 1628 the Danes still held the strategic fortresses

[151] Reeve, 'Viscount Dorchester', ch. 1; SP16/123/3.
[152] On the Council's efforts to extract the maximum yield from the subsidies of 1628 see NUL, Ne.C., 15,405, p. 58.

guarding the mouth of the Elbe. That on the west side, Stade, was garrisoned by English troops under Sir Charles Morgan. Stade was also important for England as an entrepôt for the cloth trade. Morgan's force, however, had been neglected by the English government, while Charles and Buckingham used every penny for the war with France. The English contingent with Denmark, originally 5,000 strong, had dwindled through mutiny and desertion to less than 4,000. In February Christian asked Morgan to hold out; but the miseries of the English troops were daily increasing and it was made clear to the government in England that unless it sent money immediately the town would be lost. The burghers of Stade would advance little credit to the English ambassador, Anstruther, and the agents of the international financier Burlamachi would offer nothing without undertakings in England. Many of the troops died of hunger. With the enemy advancing and with no help forthcoming, Morgan surrendered with his remaining 2,000 men on 24 April, writing to England that he had ever acquainted them there with the state of affairs.[153] While Christian's position east of the Elbe was deteriorating rapidly, Charles's commitment to his uncle had died of neglect.

On the French front Charles and Buckingham fared no better. By 1628 the disputed Mantuan succession was precipitating conflict between France and Spain in Italy. Despite the desire of Louis XIII to lead an army over the Alps, Richelieu concentrated French efforts on the siege of La Rochelle: Huguenot resistance was to be extinguished before the escalation of the Italian war.[154] On 1 May the English fleet, under Denbigh, arrived off La Rochelle, finding the town heavily besieged. With the town unapproachable, and with the wind blowing from the landward, the English decided to await the spring tides which would allow them to use fire ships. Denbigh weighed anchor and returned to England in confused circumstances, having achieved nothing.[155] Charles had wanted to keep the fleet at La Rochelle and to send reinforcements. He grew impatient with the Commons who had not yet passed the subsidies. In the third week of May he was angered to learn that the fleet was returning home. He and Buckingham resolved upon another expedition as soon as possible.

Denbigh's force, however, was broken and scattered. Three vessels of corn were taken by the Dunkirk privateers. The ships at Portsmouth were ill-provisioned and in disrepair, the men sick or ready to desert. It was these circumstances which forced Charles to give his assent to the Petition of Right:

---

[153] Parker, *Europe in crisis*, pp. 187–9; Gardiner, *History*, vi, pp. 290–1; Clay, *Economic expansion*, i, p. 119; SP75/9/fos. 40r, 62r, 121r–122r, 132r–v.

[154] Parker, *Europe in crisis*, p. 202; *Lettres, instructions diplomatiques et papiers d'état du Cardinal de Richelieu*, ed. D. L. M. Avenel (8 vols., Paris, 1853–77), iii, pp. 118, 121.

[155] Gardiner, *History*, vi, pp. 291–2; SP16/103/57, SP16/103/61, SP16/104/3, SP16/104/8, SP16/104/17.

an unavoidable concession if he were to avoid ignominious defeat at the hands of the French. In early July he ordered that no money be issued to any person whatsoever until the new expedition for La Rochelle was prepared. The state of the English fleet continued to deteriorate. Secretary Coke wrote from Portsmouth that all things seemed to go backwards and that his efforts were spent in vain. In June he barely appeased a general mutiny and in July he reported to Buckingham that each day's delay cost the king £300.[156] While Charles attached priority to the relief of La Rochelle there were other demands on his resources. French and Spanish shipping was a threat at sea and could attack the English coasts.[157] English ships were needed at the mouth of the Elbe to support Christian's precarious presence in Germany. The Danish king repeatedly sent to Charles during the summer of 1628, saying that he would be forced to negotiate for peace unless immediate help arrived.[158] The state of the English Exchequer, however, was near-catastrophic. Charles had not fulfilled his extravagant financial commitment to Denmark; jewels he had pawned in Amsterdam were falling due for redemption;[159] and the five subsidies voted in Parliament could not be realized immediately: the last was not due for collection until March of 1629. In financing the war Charles and Buckingham had erected an enormous structure of debt upon a foundation of income that was neither adequate nor assured. By the middle of 1628 royal bankruptcy appeared imminent.

Weston stepped into the breach and advocated a campaign of fiscal retrenchment. It was only by cutting war expenditure and by increasing revenue that disaster could be avoided. In early August Weston drew up a statement of Charles's finances and asked Buckingham to make it known to the king. He also recommended that the duke burn the document after the king had been informed of its contents, 'for it is not fit to be spoken of till your Grace be dispatched away [to La Rochelle] . . . '[160] England's financial position was a very powerful argument for peace. Buckingham, less suscep-

---

[156] SP16/103/80, SP16/104/8, SP16/104/60–1, SP16/105/28, SP16/105/73, SP16/108/18, SP16/108/22, SP16/110/10, SP16/112/45, SP16/528/75; NUL, Ne.C., 15,405, p. 58; Lockyer, *Buckingham*, pp. 437, 445; Gardiner, *History*, vi, pp. 292–3; Birch, i, p. 350; Reade, *Sidelights on the Thirty Years War*, iii, pp. 114–15; R. Ashton, *The crown and the money market 1603–1640* (London, 1960), pp. 132–41, 171.

[157] Birch, i, pp. 352, 369–70, 376, 384–5; R. J. W. Swales, 'The Ship Money levy of 1628', *BIHR*, 1, 122 (1977), p. 167.

[158] SP75/9/fos. 160r–163r; PRO, 47th Deputy Keeper's report, Appx, pp. 69–70; Gardiner, *History*, vi, pp. 346–7.

[159] SP75/9/fos. 72r, 82r, 84r–85r, 126r, 161v, 162v; SP16/108/10.

[160] SP16/112/75; one official report indicated at this time that £1,300,000 would be needed for impending war expenses and for debt repayment while the five subsidies could not be expected to yield more than £300,000; Alexander, *Charles I's Lord Treasurer*, pp. 127–8, 133–4.

tible to arguments of financial than of political or military failure, was consequently impatient with the Treasurer.[161] Weston, however, made Charles more aware of financial considerations. These were more likely to influence him in regard to the Spanish conflict, for while that conflict derived from the dispossession of his sister and the rebuff he had received in Spain, it had not become invested with the personal animosities which were keeping the French war alive. Preoccupation with the French war meant that Charles's sense of military dishonour (from failures in Germany, at La Rochelle and at sea)[162] became concentrated upon that conflict. Buckingham was completely involved in the war with France right up to the time of his death; he envisaged peace with Spain largely to prosecute it better.[163] Weston wanted peace with Spain in order to end England's participation in the wider war. This, he considered, would bring solvency and political stability. Charles, his favourite and his minister, therefore, were all inclined to place fewer obstacles in the path of peace with Spain. With a Protestant war lobby at court this could only worsen political division, which in turn came to encourage indecision in Charles.

The negotiations for a possible settlement of the Anglo-Spanish conflict had a history going back to early 1627. Buckingham had made overtures through the painter Rubens at that time. These conversations proved abortive, however, when the Franco-Spanish plan for the invasion of England became known.[164] Failure at La Rochelle and the threat of actual invasion encouraged Buckingham to reopen negotiations during the winter of 1627–8. In January Weston wrote to Brussels, to the Infanta Isabella, informing her that Charles was inclined to treat for peace with Spain. Weston's links with the Spanish Netherlands, where he had been on embassy in 1622, were to prove useful in sustaining negotiations. Rubens continued to work for peace and informed Olivares of the English overtures. Buckingham and Cottington, also in touch with the count-duke, were encouraged with favourable replies. There was apprehension in Spain at the prospect of an Anglo-French peace, and by the spring Olivares had launched his intervention in Mantua: it would be prudent to neutralize England when beginning a conflict with France in Italy.

As the English parliamentary session ran the length of its difficult course, Charles and Buckingham developed hopes of a peaceful settlement with

---

[161] Alexander, *Charles I's Lord Treasurer*, pp. 129–30.
[162] Trevor-Roper, *Archbishop Laud*, pp. 86–7.
[163] Clarendon, *Rebellion*, vol. i, p. 42; Reade, *Sidelights on the Thirty Years War*, iii, p. 105; AGS, E2517, fo. 77.
[164] Gardiner, *History*, vi, pp. 160–3, 185; *The letters of Sir Peter Paul Rubens*, ed. R. S. Magurn (Cambridge, Mass., 1955), p. 165. Buckingham broke off the talks in October 1627.

Spain. By the early summer both men were speaking of the Habsburgs with great respect. On 24 June the Spanish Council of State resolved to look into the dealings with England and to receive an ambassador.[165] At the Hague, Elizabeth and Frederick suspected that there were negotiations with Spain, but Charles sought to keep developments from them. Early in August the English envoy, Endymion Porter, left London bound for Madrid. He sailed to the Hague and saw the Palatines but did not discuss his mission. He arrived in Madrid in the last week of September and was welcomed by Olivares. Between Porter's departure from England and his arrival in Spain, Buckingham was removed from the scene. Weston wrote to Porter within days of the duke's death, stating that the instructions with which he had been furnished still held good. Porter was to return to England, having launched the Anglo-Spanish treaty, and Cottington would then leave for Spain to continue the talks.[166] Cottington also wrote to Porter giving him news of another development: Venetian diplomats were working to bring about peace between England and France.[167] To the Spanish faction in England this was a potentially sinister development which could undermine the progress made with Spain. Charles, Cottington wrote, was resisting any dialogue with France.[168] It was Buckingham, in the weeks before his death, who had sanctioned these concurrent negotiations.

Buckingham's resort to diplomacy was essentially forced upon him by England's failure in war against the two nations. Charles and Buckingham hoped to obtain a German settlement from Spain by peaceful means. They also wished to continue the French war until coming to satisfactory terms with Louis and Richelieu. Buckingham was surely aware of the fact that parallel dealings with France and Spain could well improve his leverage with each nation.[169] But his preference was clearly to end the Spanish war first. By the summer of 1628 this was a key objective for Buckingham and for his French ally Marie, the duchess of Chevreuse. Marie de Chevreuse, a woman of great ability and ambition, was by marriage a member of the house of Guise, a cadet branch of the ruling dynasty in independent Lorraine. In 1626 she had been involved in a conspiracy to assassinate Cardinal Richelieu. The cardinal saw her as the prime mover of the international coalition against him. Banished to Poitou, she escaped to Lorraine and continued to plot

---

[165] Alcalá-Zamora, *España, Flandes*, pp. 262–3; Alexander, *Charles I's Lord Treasurer*, pp. 24–7; Lockyer, *Buckingham*, pp. 421–2, 449–50; Reade, *Sidelights on the Thirty Years War*, iii, pp. xxviii, 105–6; AGS, E2517, fos. 73, 83, 86–7, 107; Magurn, *Rubens letters*, pp. 246, 248–53, 281–90; A. J. Loomie, 'Canon Henry Taylor, Spanish Habsburg diplomat', *Recusant History*, xvii, 3 (May 1985), pp. 225–6.
[166] SP16/111/44; AGS, E2517, fos. 72, 76–8, 105; Huxley, *Endymion Porter*, pp. 158–62.
[167] AGS, E2517, fo. 105.
[168] Ibid.   [169] Ibid., fo. 55.

against Richelieu and his ministers. In August 1628 she was scheming with Buckingham, and with pro-Habsburg elements in France, to achieve the goal of peace between England and Spain. This *rapprochement* might be used to bring down the cardinal by a combination of diplomatic and military pressure. The scheme was encouraged by Mirabel, the Spanish ambassador in Paris. In England, Charles and the earl of Holland were involved in the Chevreuse–Buckingham alliance. The king had a particular affection for Marie de Chevreuse, and Holland, besides being loyal to Buckingham, had been her lover.[170] Buckingham wanted the Anglo-Spanish treaty to be a personal triumph and hoped to conclude it himself in a Spanish port (while leading the fleet against La Rochelle).[171]

Peace with Spain would free England to concentrate against France, but Buckingham had a more complicated aim than this. He sought to kindle war between France and Spain over Mantua and by so doing gain further advantages for England.[172] This was an ambitious and dubious plan which necessitated freeing Spain for an Italian war. Buckingham's illogical war policy had led him to adopt a desperate diplomatic policy. For England to benefit from an Italian war would require subtle and cohesive diplomacy and the risks were considerable. The Palatines could be left with nothing and England could lose her allies. The Dutch were suspicious from the outset and considered dealings with both Spain and France duplicitous.[173] Their judgement was certainly correct if England were to remain at war. But Buckingham's death at this critical juncture left an emerging division in the English government, between those who favoured continuing the war with Spain and those who favoured a general peace. This was a contest of which only time would determine the outcome and which had implications for the wider situation from Scandinavia to Madrid. Thus, during the autumn and winter of 1628, the balance of Europe hung upon the negotiations of England with France and with Spain, and Europe awaited the outcome.[174]

England's friends and allies had long sought an end to the war between

---

[170] It seems that Charles and Buckingham were seeking to link the French and Spanish treaties by means of the duchess and her scheme, an arrangement rejected by Olivares; ibid., unfol. letter of Mirabel from Paris, 10 Oct. 1628, and fo. 52. See also ibid., fos. 54, 111; V.-L. Tapié, *France in the age of Louis XIII and Richelieu* (Cambridge, 1984), p. 157; M. Prawdin, *Marie de Rohan, duchesse de Chevreuse* (London, 1971), pp. 32, 34, 45, 49, 50–1; Elliott, *Richelieu and Olivares*, pp. 107–8, 115; B. Donagan, 'A courtier's progress: greed and consistency in the life of the earl of Holland', *HJ*, xix (1976), pp. 322–3; *CSPV 1628–9*, pp. 289, 491; BL, Harl. Ms 6988, fo. 73r–v.

[171] AGS, E2517, fo. 107.

[172] Gardiner, *History*, vi, p. 333; Lockyer, *Buckingham*, pp. 449–50; BL, Harl. Ms 1584, fos. 173r–174v.

[173] *CSPV 1628–9*, pp. 237–8.

[174] SP92/14/fos. 103r–109v; *CSPV 1628–9*, p. 440; Reade, *Sidelights on the Thirty Years War*, iii, p. 255.

Buckingham and Richelieu. The conflict was a strategic disaster for the anti-Habsburg and Protestant causes and a corresponding gift of good fortune to Spain and Austria. The Palatines, the Dutch, the Danes and the Venetians were appalled at the destructive struggle between these two western powers. Venice, in her vulnerable geographical position and fearing Habsburg encroachment, had a particular interest in ending the war of distraction. The Venetians were also horrified at Buckingham's plan to enlist Spain in making Italy a Franco-Spanish battlefield. At the beginning of 1628, Elizabeth of Bohemia had written to Buckingham of the need to end the French war in the interests of Germany and Denmark.[175] Her request had gone unheeded, and by the summer, largely as a result of the Anglo-French war, the imperial victories over the Danes and the German Protestants were virtually complete. In the councils of England, Dorchester had opposed the French war from its inception as a ruinous policy. He advocated alliance with France, considering the Anglo-French war akin to a civil war, and feared for England in a struggle with both the great Catholic powers. During the summer of 1628 he worked to influence Buckingham in favour of peace with France. Dorchester's viscountcy and prominent role in the administration reflected the duke's developing willingness to settle with Richelieu.[176] It was Buckingham's unpopularity in England and the increasing difficulties of waging the French war which caused him to contemplate peace with France in mid-1628. But he still wished to raise the siege of La Rochelle. Such a feat of arms would satisfy his honour and might bring Richelieu to negotiate upon English terms. According to Spanish sources, Buckingham disposed of his personal affairs in August, as if he intended to embark perhaps never to return.[177] He wanted to do something heroic which would settle the conflict and combine the glory of war with the need for peace. Henrietta Maria and Dorchester were responsible on the English side for launching the negotiations with France. The queen was greatly concerned to end a war between her husband and her brother.[178] This diplomacy was pursued in conjunction with the Venetian representatives who acted as mediators between the two nations.

---

[175] Parker, *Europe in crisis*, pp. 188–9, 201; SP99/33/fo. 92r; *The letters of Elizabeth queen of Bohemia*, ed. L. M. Baker (London, 1953), p. 76.

[176] Reeve, 'Viscount Dorchester', pp. 20–2; SP78/78/fos. 167r–168r; SP84/138/fos. 208r–209v; SP92/13/fo. 228r; *CJ*, i, p. 845b; *CSPV 1626–8*, pp. 60, 128; *CSPV 1628–9*, pp. 206–9, 222–5, 465–6; Gardiner, *History*, vi, p. 341.

[177] The will proved after Buckingham's death was drawn up in 1627 (Lockyer, *Buckingham*, p. 460) but there may well have been a finality about his preparations in 1628. See AGS, E2517, fos. 47, 70; AMRE, CPA, 42, fo. 280r; J. H. Barcroft, *Buckingham and the central administration 1616–1628* (University of Minnesota PhD thesis, 1963; published Ann Arbor, 1964), pp. 243–4; Reade, *Sidelights on the Thirty Years War*, iii, p. 106; *CSPV 1628–9*, p. 225.

[178] *CSPV 1628–9*, p. 310.

The first overtures for peace in the Anglo-French conflict were made by France. Richelieu's hatred for Buckingham was intense, and it was principally the threat of peace between England and Spain which moved him to deal with the duke and to attempt to foil an Anglo-Spanish agreement.[179] In August a proposal for peace between England and France was sent by Zorzi, the Venetian ambassador in France, to Contarini, his colleague in England. The desire of the Venetians for self-defence against the Habsburgs and their fear of the outbreak of wholesale war in Italy gave them a common interest with Richelieu in preventing peace between England and Spain. Contarini had recently talked with Dorchester, who objected to treating with Spain and shared the desire of the Venetians to end the war with France. Thus it was Dorchester whom the Venetians approached in England with the French overture. The negotiations were launched while Charles was absent at Portsmouth. It was proposed that honour be satisfied by a meeting between the duke and the cardinal at La Rochelle, in the presence of the besieging forces and the English fleet. Yet Buckingham suspected Richelieu, who might use the negotiation to delay the fleet, misrepresent the affair to the Rochellois and even treat with Spain. The Huguenot envoys in England spoke strongly against negotiations, and Buckingham's suspicions were deepened by a consultation with Charles. But the duke, encouraged by Dorchester, hearkened to the idea, and it was arranged that the matter would be agreed in Charles's presence on 23 August.

The meeting never took place for on the way to it Buckingham was assassinated. His death was in fact a temporary setback to peace. Charles did not trust the French and was not inclined to negotiate. He decided that the fleet should sail. He conceded that if, when it arrived off La Rochelle, Louis had been induced by the Venetians to give peace to the Huguenots and raise the siege of the town, he would be prepared to negotiate if the interests of the Huguenots were included in the treaty. Charles considered himself bound to interfere between Louis and his subjects as guarantor of the 1626 agreement between Louis and the Rochellois. He also wished to redeem his honour, and that of Buckingham, by victory, military or moral, over the French. With Buckingham dead and Richelieu delighted, the Huguenots constituted the principal obstacle to a settlement.[180] After Lindsey's fleet had sailed, Charles was won over to the idea of peace with France. This was achieved with great difficulty, by the combined efforts of Dorchester, Contarini, Henrietta Maria and probably Lord Treasurer Weston. The negotiations were revived when

[179] SP92/14/fos. 168r–169v, SP92/15/fos. 81r–83v; *CSPV 1628–9*, pp. 196–7, 388.
[180] AGS, E2517, fo. 105; SP16/118/66; SP99/30/fos. 126r–127r, 146r–149r (Birch, i, pp. 388–9, 391–4); *CSPV 1628–9*, pp. 206, 223, 230–2, 242–3, 260–1, 273–6, 305, 575–6; Gardiner, *History*, vi, pp. 345–7, 361, 363; Lockyer, *Buckingham*, pp. 296–7, 450–1.

the queen obtained a promise from Charles that he would keep any undertakings he made to her or to the Venetians. Contarini and Dorchester facilitated matters, encouraging a correspondence between the queen and her mother, Marie de' Medici, in France. In England the treaty with France went ahead.[181]

Buckingham's death had given Weston and Dorchester more influence over foreign policy. In the immediate circumstances of the assassination both men were in their element. The Treasurer, a conservative financial manager, responded to the challenge of a fiscal crisis and Dorchester, the seasoned ambassador, could operate amid the increasing diplomatic complexity. Charles understood that he needed these men. He made them jointly responsible for the peace negotiations with France: an affair in which their different views of policy coincided.[182] Weston basically approved of the treaty, being an advocate of peace; he also wished to avoid the disfavour of the queen.[183] But he did not pursue the dealings with France with any degree of vigour, not wishing to jeopardize the concurrent negotiations with Spain. Dorchester, anti-Spanish in the Elizabethan tradition, was unable to halt the Anglo-Spanish dialogue kept alive by Weston and Charles. Buckingham's death, however, changed the direction of that dialogue. The murder of the duke dealt a fatal blow to the strategy he had pursued with Marie de Chevreuse: a strategy involving the use of an Anglo-Spanish axis against Richelieu and the possible continuation of the French war. After Buckingham's death Charles and Holland wrote to Marie, stating that they wished to continue the policy and to make no peace with France before doing so with Spain.[184] However much Dorchester and Weston were aware of these communications, this was not a plan to appeal to either man. Neither wanted to pursue the French war, and Weston did not wish to complicate the treaty with Spain. There was no advantage for Holland in opposing the intentions of Dorchester and Weston, not to mention the wishes of the queen. Charles allowed the French negotiations to run a natural bilateral course. During Carlisle's mission on the continent, which included dealings in Lorraine, the earl became the mobile agent of Marie de Chevreuse's scheme, favouring a policy of peace with Spain and war with France. Had he been in England his views might have influenced

---

[181] PRO 31/3/66/fo. 114r; SP16/529/17; SP78/83/fo. 159r; Gardiner, *History*, vi, pp. 366–7; *Letters of Henrietta Maria, 1628–1666*, ed. H. Ferrero (Turin, 1881), p. 35; *CSPV 1628–9*, pp. 183, 308–13, 339–40, 362–3.

[182] Alexander, *Charles I's Lord Treasurer* pp. 128, 130; SP84/137/fo. 65r; *CSPV 1628–9*, p. 286.

[183] Reade, *Sidelights on the Thirty Years War*, iii, p. 431.

[184] Charles made the same undertaking to the abbé Scaglia (in the service of Spain) at about this time; ibid., pp. 256–7. See also Prawdin, *Marie de Rohan*, p. 51; AGS, E2517, fos. 54–5, 97, 111.

Charles. By the time of his return home in early 1629 the strategy was effectively defunct.[185]

While affairs had thus altered in England during September, the English fleet, under Lindsey, had arrived at La Rochelle. Zorzi proposed mediation but Louis was wary. The French did not know what effect Buckingham's death had had in England, and with the arrival of hostile forces the negotiations appeared to be broken off. The English attacked unsuccessfully. On 30 September Richelieu wrote from his camp before the town to Mirabel in Paris, professing his friendship for Spain. On 5 October Wat Montagu, the son of the earl of Manchester, went ashore from the fleet and had lengthy discussions with the cardinal. Two days later, he received Richelieu's proposals which he took back to England. The French desired that La Rochelle surrender to Louis and that Charles withdraw his support for the Huguenots who would be allowed freedom of worship. If Charles ended his Spanish negotiations, France would declare war against Spain for the common cause. Charles rejected these terms. He would support a grand alliance, but unless the siege were ended and the Huguenots assured of their liberties he would continue the war with France. Charles considered the French terms a scandal, and Montagu was in disgrace. Although Lindsey was ordered to persevere at La Rochelle, the town surrendered to the French in mid-October. While Charles had failed in his military endeavour, an impasse had been resolved for the peacemakers.[186]

There remained the general question of the Huguenots. For Charles this was a question of honour and he wanted their interests to be guaranteed in any Anglo-French agreement. Yet with the desire of his ministers to end a disastrous war, which was not in the interests of a logical peace or war policy for England, and with the resolve of the French that Charles should not interfere in their internal affairs, it became increasingly clear to him that he could do nothing. The leading members of the Council, wrote Contarini, would be happy with some general form of pardon granted to the Huguenots, and he added with cosmopolitan condescension: 'There is nothing in this save a trifle of honour and a little Calvinistic conscientiousness.'[187] Dorchester was the leading English advocate of a treaty with France, and his attitude towards the

---

[185] AGS E2517, fos. 62, 94; AMRE, CPA, 42, fo. 379r; *CSPV 1628–9*, pp. 238–9, 491, 505–6, 537–8, 550, 562; Gardiner, *History*, vi, p. 371; Schreiber, *The first Carlisle*, pp. 108, 110–11, 114, 116, 125; see also *Calendar of the Clarendon state papers*, ed. O. Ogle, W. H. Bliss and W. D. Macray (3 vols., Oxford, 1869–76), i, Appx I, p. 7; Reade, *Sidelights on the Thirty Years War*, iii, p. xlvi.

[186] AGS, E2517, fos. 84, 96, and unfol. letter of Mirabel from Paris, 10 Oct. 1628; AMRE, CPA, 42, fos. 356r, 361r; Gardiner, *History*, vi, pp. 363–9; SP16/118/28, SP16/118/66, SP16/118/68; SP78/83/fo. 187; SP103/10/41, 57; SP92/14/fos. 64r, 158r–159v, 164r; *CSPV 1628–9*, pp. 325–6, 441.

[187] *CSPV 1628–9*, p. 311, 489; SP92/14/fo. 164r.

Huguenots was clear. He did not consider that they should be allowed to obstruct a peace which was in the wider interests of Protestantism and European self-determination. He had been responsible, with Holland, for having the Rochellois agree to the treaty with Louis in 1626, with the intention of engaging France in the German war. Three years later he believed similarly that the common cause should not go to ruin on account of the Huguenots, who should be given no alternative by England but to make peace. Contarini, who was anxious to eliminate all flashpoints between England and France, suggested that if peace were offered to the Huguenots they might not accept it. Dorchester replied that there was no doubt they would, provided the conditions were reasonable. When the Venetian went so far as to defend Richelieu's campaign against French Calvinism as self-defence against pro-Spanish subversion, Dorchester 'who is discreet and knows all [wrote Contarini], showed by a smile that he understood me, but came to the conclusion that without this peace [between Louis and the Huguenots] all the rest was vanity, as I also believe . . . '[188]

Dorchester's attitude was a remarkable combination of religious ideology and reason of state. He knew that to assist the Huguenots was to assist the enemies of France and of Protestantism, Spain in particular, and that to obstruct the treaty with France was to allow the Spanish negotiations, now promoted by Weston, to prosper. In addition there was the fact that if the Spanish negotiations failed without an agreement with France, as Dorchester understood, England would be left without allies. To him the need to conclude the peace with France was imperative. The situation was compounded by Charles's confusion: he had inherited from Buckingham both the idea of the French alliance and the dispute with Louis over the Huguenots, and the difficulties of mending the duke's quarrel with Richelieu encouraged Charles to turn to the overtures of Spain. The king's antipathy to the French, and his commitment to the Huguenots, made more difficult what to Dorchester was a vital task.[189]

Dorchester had his own objections to the French. Not only had they failed to join the alliance of the Hague, but he resented their attempt to compete with English sea power, and what he fancied was their vain attempt to introduce popery into England.[190] Yet he continued to believe in the possibility of the French alliance. Throughout the winter and spring Dorchester worked with Contarini to turn Charles against Spain, to restore the treaties with

---

[188] *CSPV 1629–32*, p. 84 (Contarini to the Doge and Senate, 29 May 1629). See also *CSPV 1628–9*, p. 340; SP78/77/fos. 187r–188v, 286r; Lockyer, *Buckingham*, pp. 296–7.

[189] SP92/15/fos. 11r–13r; *CSPV 1628–9*, pp. 339–40, 457–8; *CSPV 1629–32*, pp. 81–2.

[190] *CSPV 1628–9*, p. 340; SP103/10/1–3, reply to France, c. January 1629, Dorchester's argument that the French war was caused by French neutrality towards Spain, as well as by the commitment to the Huguenots.

France and conclude the peace.[191] The French negotiations were hampered by mutual distrust – promoted by the Anglo-Spanish talks and by Richelieu's continuation of the civil war in France – and by French delays. The fall of La Rochelle and the prospect of peace with England had freed Richelieu to lead an army into Italy, and it was in the interests of France to occupy England with diplomacy while avoiding an explicit commitment to Germany.[192] By the spring Dorchester's belief in the French option had diminished:

In effect all proves fraud and dissimulation which comes from France, it appearing plainly there is no other end the French king aims at but the ruin of those of our religion in his kingdom . . . [193]

The hope of an alliance was, however, later to be revived.[194] In January Charles appointed six Councillors to finalize the treaty, and final articles were signed at Susa on 24 April. Former treaties, including Charles's marriage contract, were restored. Henrietta's household would be regulated by mutual consent. War prizes were to be kept. Freedom of trade was restored between the two nations and commercial disputes were to be settled by agreement. One article stated that the two kings would aid their allies. No mention was made of the Huguenots.[195] Dorchester drafted the proclamation of peace, published on 10 May. It styled the French war an interruption of amity and referred to the general state of Christendom and of public affairs which made necessary the peace between England and France.[196] When Dorchester wrote to the English ambassador in Paris that 'the articles could be wished more favourable', he doubtless regretted that the treaty was not an active alliance.[197] But it ended what was essentially a pointless war which had greatly damaged international Protestantism and been an immense boon to the Habsburgs. The Peace of Susa must have given Dorchester considerable satisfaction.

While Dorchester had not wished the Huguenots to obstruct the treaty, the French had not wanted them to be included and Contarini had laboured to keep them out.[198] After the fall of La Rochelle, Charles assured the Huguenot leader, the duc de Rohan, of his support in securing Protestant liberties in

---

[191] SP92/15/fos. 11r–13r; SP78/83/fo. 229; SP103/10, passim; SP101/10, newsletter from Paris, 4 Nov. 1628; *CSPV 1628–9*, pp. 313–15, 464–6, 487–91; *CSPV 1629–32*, pp. 44–5, 61–2; Gardiner, *History*, vi, pp. 372–3.
[192] SP81/139/fos. 60r—62r; *CSPV 1628–9*, pp. 192–5, 206–9, 465–6, 484–91, 530; Parker, *Europe in crisis*, p. 202.
[193] SP75/10/fo. 121r; see also SP84/139/fo. 60v.
[194] SP78/84/fos. 184–6, SP78/87/fo. 535r–v; SP92/18/fos. 286v–287r.
[195] *CSPV 1628–9*, p. 488; SP84/139/fos. 96r–97v; SP103/10/117.
[196] SP78/84/fos. 103r–104r; SP45/10/fo. 182r; *CSPV 1629–32*, p. 62.
[197] SP78/84/fos. 212–13.
[198] SP78/83/fos. 210–11; *CSPV 1629–32*, p. 84; AMRE, CPA, 42, fo. 388r.

France; but he also explained the need to conclude the peace.[199] Charles agreed to omit the Huguenots from the public articles of the treaty so that it could proceed. This concession was communicated to Richelieu in January 1629, by the Catholic earl of Nithsdale, who acted as a go-between seeking to build some little trust between Charles and the cardinal.[200] The Huguenots feared persecution and called on Charles for aid. When none was forthcoming they held the English in contempt.[201] When their fate became the sole obstacle to peace between England and France, Charles urged them to submit to their anointed king. England would intercede for them at the time of the treaty if they had not then received peace from Louis.[202] Dorchester, who considered their plight 'more to be pitied than (as affairs stand) to be presently helped', committed their preservation to God.[203] Richelieu continued his campaign against them. In June the Edict of Grace confirmed religious toleration for the Huguenots, but their rights under the Edict of Nantes to their own political and military organization were abolished. This agreement, the Peace of Alais, was perceived across the Channel as a calculated public affront to English honour.[204] The most important consequence of peace between England and France was a new antagonism, and near break, between France and Spain, and the development of covert French participation in the European war which led to French entry in 1635.[205]

Charles's negotiations with Spain took longer to reach an agreement than those with France, but they were dealings on which he staked far greater hopes. Buckingham's death had removed much of the drive for war within the English government. Weston and Cottington used this opportunity to raise Charles's expectations of a settlement with Spain. In early September 1628, soon after the death of the duke, Charles was seen holding long conversations with Cottington.[206] On 30 September the king announced his decision to prorogue Parliament again until January. The following day, Charles penned a letter which made clear his desire to end the war with Spain. The letter, which survives in the state archive at Simancas, was written to the abbé

---

[199] SP78/83/fo. 195r, SP78/84/fos. 3–4.
[200] AMRE, CPA, 42, fo. 375r–v, and 43, fo. 15r; *CSPV 1629–32*, p. 1 and n; Avenel, *Lettres de Richelieu*, iii, p. 149 and n; Gardiner, *History*, vii, p. 277; Hibbard, *Popish plot*, p. 43; PRO, 47th Deputy Keeper's report, Appx, pp. 49, 57; see also AGS, E2517, fo. 55.
[201] SP78/84/fos. 32r, 34–5, 40r, 56–7, 58r.
[202] SP92/16/fos. 7r–8r, 103r–v; SP78/84/fo. 59r–v.
[203] SP92/16/fos. 127r–128r.
[204] SP78/84/fos. 118–20, 123–6, 162r–v; Parker, *Europe in crisis*, p. 202; Elliott, *Richelieu and Olivares*, p. 100; *CSPV 1628–9*, pp. 83, 96.
[205] SP101/10, newsletter from Paris, 4 Nov. 1628; C. V. Wedgwood, *The Thirty Years War* (London, 1981), p. 391.
[206] AGS, E2517, fo. 76; Clarendon, *Rebellion*, vol. i, p. 83; Alcalá-Zamora, *España, Flandes*, p. 263.

Scaglia of Savoy, then in the service of Philip IV.[207] Historians have always found it difficult to discern the aims of English policy at this critical time.[208] Charles's letter is key evidence of his thinking at the commencement of the post-Buckingham era and of his intentions in meeting Parliament in 1629. Scaglia had discussions with Charles in England during the summer of 1628. The abbé sought to promote peace between England and Spain so as to prevent French aid to the duke of Nevers in Mantua.[209] In September, Endymion Porter and Scaglia left England together. While Porter travelled to Spain via Italy, Scaglia went to Brussels to make his report to the Infanta. The overtures of peace he brought from England were communicated by Isabella to Madrid.[210] Charles's letter of 1 October is one of a series he wrote to Scaglia after the abbé left England. The surviving letter states clearly that the message contained in the others was the same: Charles wished to assure Scaglia of the steadfastness of his intentions and thanked the abbé fulsomely for his role in the negotiations.[211] When Charles prorogued Parliament in October he was reacting to domestic as well as to foreign events. Meeting in the autumn, Parliament would have opposed his use of the profits of the Admiralty to liquidate Buckingham's debts.[212] It would also have met amid the bitterness which had survived the last session and the active resistance to the payment of tonnage and poundage. But Parliament would also call for the prosecution of the war. In postponing its meeting until January, Charles was seeking to see the result of his treaty with Spain. He was, moreover, hedging his bets. Parliament could make a continuing grant of the customs duties, but it might also provide further support for the Spanish war. As his pro-Spanish and anti-parliamentary sentiments developed together, Charles nevertheless waited to see what time would bring.[213]

Porter arrived in Madrid ahead of the news of Buckingham's death. He

---

[207] AGS, E2042, unfol., Charles I to Scaglia (holograph), 1 Oct. 1628. (One presumes that Charles used the old style here: internal evidence is not conclusive.)

[208] Russell, *Parliaments*, p. 392.

[209] Reade, *Sidelights on the Thirty Years War*, iii, pp. 256–7, 259–60; AGS, E2517, fo. 70.

[210] H. Lonchay and J. Cuvelier (eds.), *Correspondance de la cour d'Espagne sur les affaires des Pays-Bas au XVIIᵉ siècle* (6 vols., Brussels, 1923–7), ii, p. 409; AGS, E2517, fos. 47, 83, and unfol. letter of Mirabel from Paris, 14 Sept. 1628.

[211] AGS, E2042, unfol., Charles to Scaglia, 1 Oct. 1628. See also ibid., Scaglia to Cardinal Cueva, 21 Oct. 1628, which confirms the identity of Scaglia as the recipient of Charles's letters and the substance of their message: ' . . . de la voluntad de aquel rey, de estar en la misma determinacion que quando yo parti . . . '.

[212] AGS, E2517, fo. 76; Russell, *Parliaments*, p. 394; *Stuart royal proclamations*, ed. J. F. Larkin, ii (Oxford, 1983), pp. 206–7.

[213] The Venetian ambassador was thus half correct in believing that the next parliamentary session would decide the direction of foreign policy; *CSPV 1628–9*, pp. 431–2. It is possible that lack of news from La Rochelle also influenced Charles's prorogation of Parliament; the fleet had sailed on 7 September and word of another failure, arriving during the session, could have wrecked the Parliament; Birch, i, p. 407.

confirmed that Charles and the duke wished to negotiate. Olivares intended, as he told the Council of State, to sustain the hopes which were held in England for peace. He wrote to Charles of the good reception given to his envoy.[214] On 15 September a *junta* of the Council had resolved that the treaty with England should proceed; three days later the Council heard the spasmodic history of the opening of negotiations.[215] Olivares seized upon Charles's offer to have the treaty negotiated in Spain. Porter was instructed to write to England that Charles's ambassador would be welcomed. The view of Olivares, endorsed by the Council of State on 3 November, was that the treaty should be bilateral: no mention should be made of Frederick or Denmark until hostilities between England and Spain were ended. Clearly the count-duke's intention was to break up the Protestant alliances in the German war, but three key elements can be detected within this strategy for negotiation. Peace with England was a vital goal which needed to be achieved without delay. The English were to be allowed no leverage by war in the Palatine question. Finally, the absence of any reference to the Dutch in the Council proceedings of 3 November left room for Olivares to make a secret alliance with Charles against the republic.[216] To isolate the Dutch was always a fundamental aim of the count-duke's international strategy. And he consistently held to the notion that if he could achieve a military alliance with England then all would be well.[217] Olivares set out to make the treaty of peace the vehicle of such an alliance.

By mid-October word of Buckingham's murder had reached Madrid. The Spaniards were anxious to know how this would affect the negotiations. Porter had travelled to Spain as the personal envoy of Charles I, but he had also come with letters of credence from the duke. Buckingham's influence with his king was a fact well known in Spain, where the *privado* or favourite had an established position in government.[218] On 14 October Philip sent instructions to the Infanta at Brussels: she was to learn the direction of English policy and to sustain negotiations.[219] The dialogue encouraged by Scaglia and running through Flanders had been brought to an immediate halt by the death of the duke. A correspondence was then established between Weston and Cottington in London and Don Carlos Coloma at Brussels. As well as being a key figure in the government of the Spanish Netherlands,

---

[214] AGS, E2517, fos. 72, 81, 83, 98, 105.   [215] Ibid., fos. 83, 107.

[216] Ibid., fo. 91; see also ibid., fo. 72, and Lonchay, *Correspondance de la cour d'Espagne*, ii, pp. 416, 420.

[217] I am grateful to John Elliott for this point. See also Elliott, *Richelieu and Olivares*, p. 128.

[218] AGS, E2517, fos. 72, 107; J. H. Elliott, *Imperial Spain 1496–1716* (Harmondsworth, 1970), pp. 301–2, 324; Lonchay, *Correspondance de la cour d'Espagne*, ii, p. 410n; Reade, *Sidelights on the Thirty Years War*, iii, p. xxx.

[219] Lonchay, *Correspondance de la cour d'Espagne*, ii, p. 413.

Coloma was also a long-standing friend of Weston. The Treasurer and Cottington volunteered to Coloma that Buckingham's death had not altered England's willingness to make peace: a point which they were at pains to demonstrate to the Spaniards. Weston and Cottington were aware that they were competing with the French treaty promoted by the Venetians. Weston wrote to Brussels of the need for peace with Spain as soon as possible. Cottington sought to reassure Coloma that England was seeking no preferred agreement with France. Weston, Cottington wrote, was in a position of increasing influence with Charles; and the Treasurer assured Coloma that he (Weston) was privy to Charles's most important negotiations. Weston and Cottington emphasized that peace between England and Spain would be in the interests of the whole of Christendom. They were thus speaking the language of the *pax Hispanica* and of the universal Catholic Church.[220]

Coloma's replies to these messages were equally positive. He reported the pleasure in Brussels and Madrid at Charles's favour to Weston; and he wrote of the esteem for the Treasurer in the Spanish Netherlands. Coloma was anxious not only to keep up the Anglo-Spanish dialogue, but also to foil any settlement between England and France. He portrayed the Venetians as self-interested republicans, parasites upon monarchy, who should not be allowed to obstruct the union of the crowns of England and Spain. Since Charles desired to treat for peace the Spaniards were disposed to please him; and Cottington was awaited eagerly in Madrid.[221] Yet a single statement by Weston portended trouble for the negotiations. The treaty, he wrote, would have to make reference to Charles's friends and allies.[222] There can be no doubt that Charles himself was the inspiration here. The principal obstacle to the ending of the war was his intention of having the Palatines restored. This problem may have triggered an idea which featured in a message from Weston to Coloma of 27 November.[223] Both Charles and the Spaniards were contemplating a marriage between the young prince Palatine[224] and the daughter

---

[220] Cottington's and Weston's letters were sent in copy to Madrid; see AGS, E2517, fos. 92–3, 99–102, and E2042, unfol., Weston to Coloma, 5 Nov. 1628 (old style?); Lonchay, *Correspondance de la cour d'Espagne*, ii, pp. 410, 414–16, 420; Alcalá-Zamora, *España, Flandes*, pp. 259, 263 and n; Alexander, *Charles I's Lord Treasurer*, pp. 10, 49, 154; Parker, *Army of Flanders*, pp. 118–19; H. R. Trevor-Roper, 'Spain and Europe 1598–1621', in *NCMH*, iv, pp. 269–71.

[221] AGS, E2517, fos. 92–3, 99–102, and E2042, unfol., Coloma to Cottington, 26 Sept. and n.d., unfol., Coloma to Weston, 26 Nov., unfol., Coloma to Weston and Cottington, 22 Nov.; Alcalá-Zamora, *España, Flandes*, p. 263 and n; Lonchay, *Correspondance de la cour d'Espagne*, ii, pp. 416, 420.

[222] AGS, E2517, fo. 93, Weston to Coloma, 28 Sept. 1628.

[223] AGS, E2042, unfol., copy of letter of Weston, signed by Cottington, to Coloma, 27 Nov. 1628. See also Reade, *Sidelights on the Thirty Years War*, iii, pp. xxvi–xxvii, 259.

[224] Prince Frederick Henry, who died in 1629.

of the emperor.[225] Such a pro-Habsburg solution to the German question would have been strongly opposed in England and within the Protestant international. The scheme seems to have sunk without trace. But the London–Brussels correspondence, conducted between September and December, ensured that the Anglo-Spanish treaty of peace remained alive.

As the autumn of 1628 turned into winter, Olivares became increasingly anxious about the dealings between England and France. The fall of La Rochelle had enabled Richelieu to turn his full attention to Italy. Faced with the possibility of an Anglo-French alignment as well as the conflict in Mantua, Olivares urged Cottington to hasten his journey to Spain. The Spaniards decided that the treaty with England should proceed, whatever the success of an agreement between England and France. The Anglo-Spanish schemes of Marie de Chevreuse had the approval of the count-duke and were sanctioned officially by Philip and the Council of State.[226] Such manoeuvres in France became increasingly marginal, however, with the prospect of Cottington's arrival on Spanish soil. Peace between England and Spain would allow the resumption of trade: a prospect which appealed to Olivares no less than to Weston. In September rumours of a treaty were causing the suspension of Anglo-Spanish privateering, and by December, some English trade with the Iberian peninsula was beginning again under licence from both kings.[227] The economic advantages of peace with England were offset by a disaster for Spain in the month of September. In December news reached Madrid of the capture of the entire treasure fleet from New Spain, taken by forces of the Dutch West India Company off Cuba. The fleet was then the greatest prize ever taken from Spain. Its bullion was worth over £1,200,000 sterling: a figure representing two-thirds of the annual cost of the Dutch army. This crushing blow came in the midst of an existing crisis in fiscal time-tables, and the Spanish monarchy faced the prospect of financial collapse. The position was worst in the Netherlands where, while Spain was gravely weakened, the Dutch were now in a position to take the offensive. Spain was forced to withdraw her support for the emperor, and peace with the Dutch and with England became an urgent necessity.[228] Porter returned to London

---

[225] Maria Anna. According to Venetian intelligence, Weston was supporting the idea of a Spanish marriage; *CSPV 1629–32*, p. 141.

[226] Olivares insisted, however, that the Anglo-Spanish negotiations should not be linked to those between England and France. AGS, E2517, fo. 52; see also AGS, E2042, unfol., Scaglia to Cardinal Cueva, 19, 29 Oct. 1628, and E2517, fos. 91, 108, 111–12; Lonchay, *Correspondance de la cour d'Espagne*, ii, pp. 400–1, 417, 422; *CSPV 1628–9*, p. 388; SP16/119/5.

[227] AGS, E2517, fos. 58, 108; Birch, i, p. 453; letters of marque against Spain were being restrained in England in November; Birch, i, p. 426. See also chapter 7, below.

[228] SP84/138/fos. 172r–173r; Elliott, *Richelieu and Olivares*, p. 96; Israel, *Dutch republic*, pp. 174, 197–8; Alcalá-Zamora, *España, Flandes*, pp. 262, 526; G. Parker, *The Thirty Years War* (London, 1984), p. 102; Parker, *Army of Flanders*, p. 295; Parker, *Europe in crisis*,

in the first week of 1629 and reported that Olivares and Philip wished to negotiate. When Parliament reconvened, Charles would meet it in the knowledge that he might now be able to choose between war and peace.[229]

pp. 190–2; Elliott, *Imperial Spain*, p. 335; J. H. Elliott, *The count-duke of Olivares* (New Haven, 1986), p. 363.

[229] Huxley, *Endymion Porter*, p. 162; AGS, E2519, exp. 2–3; Magurn, *Rubens letters*, p. 296.

The death of a Parliament

The political events of 1628 had involved certain developments which had come to disturb the customary workings of English political life. These developments were even more visible during 1629 and particularly during the new parliamentary session. There was a perceptible lack of trust in the king which severely undermined the tradition of confidence in the monarch. This was linked to the increasing alienation of Charles from his own people (including his failure to attract essential aristocratic support). There was continuing debate over the character of his government, involving pressure on the customary framework of constitutional practice and thought. There was also the prospect of a breakdown in the provision of adequate war finance and therefore in the conduct of an effective foreign policy. All these elements were manifest in the session of 1629, and others would emerge in their turn with the end of the Parliament. An examination of the events surrounding the collapse of the parliamentary session suggests the elements of a new kind of politics in England.

Reports of the political scene during the weeks before Parliament reassembled confirm that Charles was leaving the principal question of policy unresolved. A Spanish agent in London wrote in the middle of December that the king seemed to favour the peace party. Another report to Spain written only nine days later, probably by the same agent, stated that Charles was thinking of continuing the war.[1] He spent much time before the opening of the session engaged in private consultation with Carlisle.[2] The earl tended to equivocate in matters of foreign policy and probably reinforced his king's indecision. There was very strong pressure on Charles to hold a successful session of Parliament. His desperate financial plight made a settlement of the customs imperative.[3] A demonstration of national unity would strengthen his position abroad. There was also the perilous situation of his uncle, Christian of Denmark, who was staking his hopes on the outcome of the English

---

[1] AGS, E2519, exp. 6, 8.
[2] Schreiber, *The first Carlisle*, p. 121. [3] *CSPV 1628–9*, pp. 503, 579.

Parliament. By late 1628 Christian had suffered serious defeat at the hands of Wallenstein and Tilly. More than half his forces had been lost and his lands lay open to the imperial armies. His own people were divided against him and opposed to the war. Spain, moreover, had ambitions for dominion in the Baltic.[4] Having made it clear to Charles that only powerful assistance could prevent his capitulation to the emperor, Christian negotiated at Lübeck, seeking to gain time. The Danish envoys in England urged the desperate position of their king and enlisted Dorchester's support. Dorchester had a personal commitment to the causes of German Protestantism and self-determination and was predisposed to help the Danes. He wrote to the English ambassador with Christian that he did not wish to see that king's affairs abjectly submitted 'to the law of a conqueror'.[5] The official English response was that aid would be sent in the spring and Dorchester reassured Christian of Charles's commitment.[6]

Sir Thomas Roe was also a moving force for the northern war. At the beginning of 1629 he returned from his diplomatic appointment in Constantinople to England. In London and at the Hague he advocated a new strategic alliance to sustain the Protestant powers of northern Europe and to fight for German liberation. On arrival he conferred with Charles and, after Parliament had reconvened, gained the support of the Council for a proposal to rearm Christian. Everything depended upon parliamentary finance. Weston worked hard against these efforts to fuel the war.[7] The simultaneous activities of the war and peace lobbies during the winter of 1628–9 both reflected and encouraged Charles's equivocal attitude to the new parliamentary session. The king had a serious interest in the prosecution of the war and in the prospects of parliamentary supply. He had made undertakings to his uncle and his own treaty with Spain might yet fail. Charles believed it was the insubordination of the previous session which had produced a poor yield from the subsidies he had been granted.[8] The careful preparations which he made for the second session reflected his desire to give it a chance of success.[9]

Charles was fully aware, as he had told the Council in November, that religious questions would preoccupy the Commons when Parliament reassembled.[10] His preparatory arrangements, begun during the previous

---

[4] SP75/10/fos. 12r–15v; Parker, *Europe in crisis*, pp. 187–9; Reeve, 'Viscount Dorchester', p. 274.

[5] SP75/10/fos. 19r–20r; see also *CSPV 1628–9*, pp. 503–4, 529; PRO 47th Deputy Keeper's report, Appx, p. 57; Reeve, 'Viscount Dorchester', pp. 75–6, 273–4.

[6] Reeve, 'Viscount Dorchester', pp. 273–4.

[7] Ibid., pp. 94–5; Gardiner, *History*, vi, p. 372; *CSPV 1628–9*, p. 537.

[8] Russell, *Parliaments*, p. 398.

[9] See also a memorandum which suggests that Charles may still have been considering non-parliamentary means of funding the war; *CSPD 1628–9*, p. 482.

[10] Birch, i, p. 439.

summer, were informed by this awareness. In July it was announced that the recusancy laws would be enforced and there was a subsequent rounding-up of recusants in London. Charles declared to Council that he intended to put all non-conformist Catholics out of office and commission. In December Archbishop Abbot was allowed to appear at court and was readmitted to his place in the Privy Council. Montagu was enjoined to renounce the Arminian tenets on salvation and in January his book, *Appello caesarem*, was suppressed by proclamation.[11] At the end of 1628 it was rumoured that Viscount Saye and the earl of Bedford, those two pillars of aristocratic puritanism, were to be made Privy Councillors.[12] This may have been government disinformation or simply popular rumour. It may have been a real possibility. In any case it reflects the nature of Charles's political precautions. While Buckingham lived, preparations for the next session were interwoven with his securing of the domestic political front prior to leaving for La Rochelle.[13] Official suggestions of religious reform involved, necessarily, conciliation of the parliamentary war lobby. Several weeks before Buckingham died, he conveyed expressions of respect and service to Horace, Lord Vere, the senior English officer serving in the Low Countries and a key figure in the puritan military connection.[14] The appointment of Dorchester as Secretary of State in December can also be seen as a significant concession to those who favoured war. The Spaniards could only interpret his appointment as an act of solidarity with the Dutch.[15]

At this time Dorchester himself was able to write: 'The Parliament is like to hold at the appointed day, the twentieth of the next month; and all things by his majesty's personal order in Council as well in church as commonwealth are provisionally disposed that he may the better hope for a fair and loving meeting with his people.'[16] He also wrote to the English ambassador with

---

[11] SP16/132/26; *CSPD 1628–9*, p. 451; Russell, *Parliaments*, p. 394; Birch, i, pp. 439, 449, 451; Larkin, *Stuart royal proclamations*, ii, pp. 199–201, 218–20. In June 1628, Manwaring's two sermons, *Religion and allegiance*, were also suppressed; Larkin, *Stuart royal proclamations*, ii, pp. 197–9; Welsby, *George Abbot*, p. 136.

[12] Birch, i, pp. 440, 447.

[13] Russell, *Parliaments*, p. 391. Lockyer argues (*Buckingham*, p. 449) that in late 1628 Buckingham was preparing to renew his alliance with the anti-Arminians. It is likely that the duke's pragmatism would have allowed him to contemplate some such reform of the Church, but in practice it could not succeed. Charles was committed to the Arminians in principle, and Buckingham's diplomatic strategy in late 1628 would have been upset by concessions to the (anti-Spanish) Calvinist war lobby.

[14] It seems that Buckingham also wished to conciliate Clare; NUL, Ne.C., 15,405, p. 2. I am grateful to Simon Adams for information concerning Vere.

[15] AGS, E2519, exp. 5; S. L. Adams, 'The Protestant cause: religious alliance with the West European Calvinist communities as a political issue in England, 1585–1630' (unpublished Oxford University D.Phil. thesis, 1973), pp. 419–20. I am grateful to Simon Adams for allowing me to cite his thesis.

[16] To James, earl of Carlisle, 19 Dec. 1628, SP92/14/fo. 225r–v.

Denmark of the 'prudent and provident care his majesty hath taken . . . to remove all such things . . . as may breed distraction betwixt him and his people'. Dorchester offered this news as an encouragement to Christian 'in holding him up from sinking under the burden of his losses, and the faint resolutions of such he hath about him . . . '[17] Such hopes that the Parliament would make possible the revival of the war were expressed by other members of the Privy Council: Pembroke, Conway and Viscount Falkland, Lord Deputy of Ireland. Falkland wrote to Dorchester of the new life a successful session would give to foreign policy, to diplomacy or to war. Falkland wanted renewal of the alliance with the Dutch, 'and [when] peace be concluded with France we shall do well enough, and best, with war with Spain . . . '[18] For Pembroke, as well as for others, the hopes held of the session were bound up with the optimism about Charles triggered off by the death of the duke.[19]

These expectations of parliamentary success and of a king no longer misguided by the favourite were tempered by a definite and contrasting sense of foreboding. Just as the possibility of a fresh start existed so too did the risk of deeper failure. It was imperative that Charles and his people demonstrate their ability to work together. In September Dorchester had written to Carlisle of the need for:

a settled and constant form of government bringing the king and state into reputation . . . it imports more than anything else I know, as well in regard of home as abroad, that the next meeting betwixt the king and [his] people should be without the late disorder . . .

And hearing of the king's decision to prorogue parliament again until January he had added: 'the aegritudo which was in men's minds requires time to take it away'.[20] Falkland, despite his hopes, was apprehensive, telling Dorchester: 'Your lordship's prognostication of a good conclusion of this parliament is a sweet voice full of comfort and delight – without it we may bid farewell to the felicity of England and the glory of our king . . . '[21] Sir George Goring wrote of the political scene in December that 'all the evil spirits are not yet laid . . . '[22]

There were indeed good reasons for such apprehension. Clearly Charles was testing the Parliament by holding out the prospect of religious reform; but he had no real intention of compromising on this issue, as subsequent events were to show. The hard core of his critics who opposed his policies in the Church were not men to be satisfied by tokenism or half measures. At the end of November 1628 the bishops and judges were ordered to execute the recusancy laws. The bishops were also charged to maintain true religion, as

[17] SP75/10/fo. 19v, Dorchester to Anstruther, 26 Jan. 1629.
[18] SP63/248/fos. 97–8; Reeve, 'Viscount Dorchester', p. 77n; see also SP75/9/fos. 330r–331r; SP16/529/9; Russell, *Parliaments*, p. 82.
[19] SP16/529/9, SP16/529/40.
[20] SP16/117/83.   [21] SP63/248/fos. 97–8; *CSPV 1628–9*, p. 503.   [22] SP16/123/8.

laid down in the Prayer Book and Thirty-Nine Articles, without innovation. Of these orders Sir Thomas Barrington wrote that they 'left us not satisfied in any measure proportionable to that expectation which was among us concerning these points'.[23] Such enthusiasts for godly religion seem to have believed that the onus was on Charles: it was the king who should make the concessions which would bring about a successful parliamentary session.[24] Desire for reform of the Church was linked to desire for the unstinting prosecution of the Spanish war. The spectacular success of the Dutch in capturing the plate fleet had a powerful influence on discussions of foreign policy in England. This and other Dutch victories contrasted sharply with Buckingham's failures as Lord Admiral. The taking of the plate fleet strengthened the hand of the war hawks in Parliament and aroused great popular feeling against the idea of peace with Spain.[25] Observers were well aware that when the houses reconvened there would be strident claims for religious reform and for war. A perceptive Spanish agent made the prediction in December that the session would therefore be brief.[26] In their different ways, both Charles and an element in Parliament were interested in continuing the war. It was their disagreement over the religious issue at home which ultimately stood in the way of a militant foreign policy. In the end Charles preferred to abandon the war rather than sacrifice religious principles at home. His personal involvement in the European conflict was not ideological and he had no sympathy with the aspirations of international Calvinism.

The token measures by which Charles was seeking to render the Commons amenable were accompanied by actions which could only betoken the king's uncompromising attitude to his national Church. Between the two sessions of Charles's third Parliament, he made a series of appointments obviously intended to ensure the dominance of Laudian Arminianism in English religious life.[27] These included the election of Richard Montagu to the see of Chichester and Francis White (who had licensed his book) to Norwich, as

---

[23] Searle, *Barrington family letters*, p. 39.

[24] Ibid., p. 49, Thomas Bourchier to Lady Joan Barrington, 26 Jan. 1629.

[25] The Dutch also took the Brazil sugar fleet at the same time as the plate fleet from New Spain; Birch, i, p. 440. See also AGS, E2519, exp. 6, 8; *CSPV 1628–9*, p. 431; Clarendon, *Rebellion*, vol. i, p. 24; Sharpe, 'The personal rule of Charles I', p. 56; Hibbard, *Popish plot*, p. 32.

[26] AGS, E2519, exp. 8; see also exp. 6: 'es cierto que engendraran una rotura entre ellos y el rey . . .'

[27] On the problem of invoking Laud's name as a descriptive term see P. Collinson, 'England and international Calvinism, 1558–1640', in M. Prestwich (ed.), *International Calvinism 1541–1715* (Oxford, 1985), pp. 220–1. I have chosen to use the words 'Laudian' and 'Laudianism' as a convenient shorthand for the characteristic features of the English religious movement over which Laud undeniably presided.

well as the translation of Laud to London.[28] These promotions can also be interpreted as a demonstration to the parliamentary interest of Charles's authority in the Church.[29] In November 1628, William Prynne and others were brought before the Court of High Commission for publishing unlicensed books against Arminianism.[30] In November, Charles also issued a declaration on religion, prefixed to a new edition of the Thirty-Nine Articles. The declaration stated that the Articles were to be read literally and it forbade theological disputation of their meaning. This royal order was arguably a conciliatory measure, an attempt at comprehension and peace. As such it might fit the pattern of preparatory measures before the parliamentary session. But in fact the declaration, which was largely the work of Laud, was a distinctly anti-Calvinist initiative. The time at which it was issued, when the Arminians were in the ascendant, clearly favoured the Laudian party. Laud was to be far from impartial in applying the ban on disputation. Finally, the edition included a sentence referring to the Church's authority over ceremonies and its right to decide controversial points of religion. (This sentence was omitted from most of the copies printed and from the manuscript copies approved by Convocation.)[31] Thus the king's declaration could be and was employed as an effective weapon against the remaining defences of English Calvinist theology.

Laud has been rightly described as a man who disliked controversy.[32] He did not consider religious argument the way to knowledge or godliness. Of the debates concerning Arminianism and free will, debates which were the immediate intellectual context of his life, he was later to write:

I am yet where I was, that something about these controversies is unmasterable in this life. Neither can I think any expression can be so happy as to settle all these difficulties. And however I do much doubt, whether the king will take any man's judgement so far as to have these controversies ever further stirred, which now, God be thanked, begin to be more at peace . . . [33]

---

[28] In addition, Manwaring, besides being pardoned and promoted, was made a royal chaplain. Samuel Harsnet had been elected to York in November 1627 and Richard Neile to Winchester in December the same year. See Trevor-Roper, *Archbishop Laud*, p. 91; Trevor-Roper, *Catholics, Anglicans and puritans*, pp. 67, 90; Russell, *Parliaments*, p. 396; *DNB*, s.v. Montagu, Harsnet and Neile.

[29] Gardiner, *History*, vi, pp. 330–1.

[30] Birch, i, pp. 431–2.

[31] Trevor-Roper, *Archbishop Laud*, pp. 90, 111–12; Hutton, *William Laud*, pp. 59–60; Cooper, 'Fall of the Stuart monarchy', p. 558. The declaration may have been a response to the Commons' remonstrance of 1628 which called for the suppression of Arminian doctrine; Welsby, *George Abbot*, pp. 135–6. On previous Jacobean and Caroline attempts to keep theological peace in England see J. T. Cliffe, *The puritan gentry* (London, 1984), pp. 148, 150.

[32] Trevor-Roper, *Archbishop Laud*, pp. 85, 112–13.

[33] Laud, *Works*, vi (1), p. 292. See also W. Haller, *The rise of puritanism* (New York, 1957), p. 234; Hutton, *William Laud*, p. 132.

As far as Laud and Charles were concerned, popular and public controversy over articles of faith was positively unseemly. They also considered it intellectually fruitless. This attitude derived from the broader conception of God's Church which united the two men. It is important to understand this wider ecclesiastical view which was subject to intensive attack in 1629. Laudianism, in more ways than one, was at the root of the spectacular collapse of Charles's third Parliament.

The transformation which began to come over the appearance of the English Church during the late 1620s was essentially the work of two men: Laud and the king. Laud, once a protégé of Bishop Neile, during the new reign increasingly superseded him as the acknowledged clerical leader of Arminianism in England.[34] Laud was recommended to Charles by Buckingham, which helps to explain the king's unflinching support for his leading cleric. Yet Charles and Laud had religious views which coincided remarkably. The two men were particularly close, and Laud's statements often reflect Charles's thinking or confidence in him. Charles had a deep commitment to his own religious principles. It was Lancelot Andrewes who predicted, before Charles ever became king, that he would one day hazard his head and crown rather than forsake his support for the English Church. Charles and Laud were united in their opposition to post-Bezan Calvinism.[35] Laud's anti-Calvinism was encouraged by his earlier tribulations at the hands of the English Calvinist establishment. That establishment had opposed his election as president of St John's College, Oxford, had attacked his preaching in the University and branded him a heretic.[36] The theology of Laud and his colleagues, with the controversy it aroused in England, was largely inspired by the contemporary Dutch movement which had developed into an international reaction against predestinarian thinking.[37] Laud recorded his rejection of the idea of an eternal degree of reprobation and election; and, breaking with the English reformed tradition, his inspiration was patristic: 'For that Christ died for all men is the universal and constant doctrine of the catholic church in all ages, and no error of Arminius . . .'[38] The anti-Calvinist

---

[34] Neile, archbishop of York from 1632, remained an influential patron of Arminianism in England. See *CD1629*, pp. 132–3 and passim; *DNB*, s.v. Neile; Tyacke, 'Puritanism, Arminianism', pp. 130–1, 134; Russell, *Parliaments*, p. 404.

[35] Clarendon, *Rebellion*, vol. i, p. 120; Laud, *Works*, ii, p. 213; Trevor-Roper, *Archbishop Laud*, p. 67; N. Tyacke, *Anti-Calvinists* (Oxford, 1987), pp. 7, 48–50, 70–1, 114, 166–7, 181, 228–9, 246–7, 266–70.

[36] Clarendon, *Rebellion*, vol. i, pp. 121, 124; R. T. Kendall, *Calvin and English Calvinism to 1649* (Oxford, 1979), pp. 28, 211 (but see Collinson, 'England and international Calvinism', p. 217); see also Hutton, *William Laud*, pp. 12–14.

[37] Clarendon, *Rebellion*, vol. i, p. 81; C. Bangs, 'The enigma of Arminian politics', *Church History*, xlii (1973), p. 16; Tyacke, *Anti-Calvinists*, pp. 4, 28, 39–40, 70–1.

[38] Laud, *Works*, iii, p. 304. See also his reply to Lord Saye and Sele: 'almost all of them say that God from all eternity reprobates by far the greater part of mankind to eternal fire, without

movement in England had been allowed to make great strides during the last years of the late king's reign. But James had definitely presided over a moderate Calvinist consensus and the Jacobean Church settlement had had an orthodox Calvinist base.[39] The alliance between Charles and Laud, however, brought an official redefinition of puritanism to include the whole mainstream of orthodox English Calvinism.[40]

Yet under Charles there was more at stake than conflicting theologies of salvation. A wider struggle crystallized around the specific issue, a struggle over the nature of English religious life.[41] It seems unlikely that many so-called Arminians in England had ever read the Dutch theologian, such was the broader significance of Laudianism within the context of the national Church.[42] English Arminianism displayed additional features which distinguished it from its Dutch sister movement.[43] Laud's programme was clericalist. He lamented the passing of the days when English churchmen were powerful and independent. Consequently, he sought to reduce the power of the laity in the Church and promoted the rights of Convocation, High Commission and ecclesiastical property, as well as the idea of episcopacy *jure divino*. In this sense Laud harked back to the days of the pre-Reformation Church.[44] Arminianism in England also took on a ceremonial and sacramental dimension. Laud did not believe in transubstantiation and held to the idea of a real (as opposed to a corporeal) presence in the Eucharist.[45] Yet his

---

an eye at all to their sin. Which opinion my very soul abominates. For it makes God, the God of all mercies, to be the most fierce and unreasonable tyrant in the world'. Ibid., vi (1), p. 133 (I am grateful to John Morrill for this reference); Lake, 'Calvinism and the English Church', p. 61n.

[39] Fincham and Lake, 'The ecclesiastical policy of King James I', pp. 202–7; Collinson, *Religion of Protestants*, pp. 81–2; Collinson, 'England and international Calvinism', p. 219; P. Collinson, 'The Jacobean religious settlement: the Hampton Court conference', in Tomlinson (ed.), *Before the English civil war*, pp. 28, 49–50; Tyacke, 'Puritanism, Arminianism', pp. 123–4; Tyacke, *Anti-Calvinists*, pp. 24–5, 41–5, 186; Lake, 'Calvinism and the English Church', pp. 49, 54.

[40] Tyacke, 'Puritanism, Arminianism', pp. 133–4, 139; Cliffe, *Puritan gentry*, pp. 30, 156; see also *Correspondence of John Cosin*, ed. G. Ornsby (2 vols., London, 1869), i, p. 42.

[41] I am grateful to Don Kennedy for reminding me of this point. See also Lake, 'Calvinism and the English Church', pp. 42–5.

[42] Clarendon, *Rebellion*, vol. i, pp. 123–4.

[43] B. Worden, rev. art., *London Review of Books*, 19 Apr.–2 May 1984, p. 14; Tyacke, 'Puritanism, Arminianism', pp. 129–30. The broader and less theological elements of Laudianism clearly had roots in the more Catholic aspects remaining in English religious life despite the progress of the Reformation; see Professor Collinson's subtle discussion, 'England and international Calvinism', pp. 218–19.

[44] Laud, *Works*, vi (1), pp. 11–12, 20; C. Cross, *Church and people 1450–1660* (3rd edn, London, 1983), pp. 179–80, 183, 185–6, 188–9; C. Hill, *Economic problems of the Church from Archbishop Whitgift to the Long Parliament* (Oxford, 1956), pp. 332–3, 340–1, 343; Hutton, *William Laud*, pp. 42, 238; Sommerville, *Politics and ideology*, pp. 208–10; Tyacke, *Anti-Calvinists*, p. 221.

[45] Hutton, *William Laud*, pp. 70–1, 150, 237

desire to demonstrate the importance of the sacraments of the Eucharist and baptism was a threat to the Calvinist theology of grace as well as an expression of a stylized piety.[46] Laud believed that reform, if taken too far, could be sacrilege: the sacraments should not be maimed and images were to be adored. Charles's liking for religious display suited Laud's aspirations completely.[47] Both men also had a particularly nationalistic view of the English Church, largely inspired by their common devotion to the piety of Andrewes. They believed in a national right to speak with the authority of historical theology, in an English Catholic tradition descending through Hooker. Thus, despite Laud's departure from the mainstream of English Church life since the time of Elizabeth, he believed himself innocent of any charge of religious innovation. Laudianism was also premised upon an English *via media*, distinguished both from Rome and from Geneva.[48] Charles and Laud wished their Church to be a model for others within a wider catholic community. Throughout his career Laud was eager to win converts from the Roman to the English Church and he regarded conversion to Rome as a form of betrayal.[49] The strong religious nationalism espoused by Charles and Laud was utterly out of sympathy with the spirit of international Calvinism. Laud was solely concerned with Charles's subjects and his dominions and sought to sever all links with the Calvinist communities of continental Europe.[50] Moreover, his pride in the English Church fuelled his hatred of disorder and non-conformity in the British Isles and in English religious, military and merchant communities overseas.[51] This obsession with conformity, when combined with the theological and pietistic principles of Laudianism, produced a series of fatal political reactions.[52]

English Arminianism, through the accident of Charles's rule, also became

---

[46] Ibid., p. 73; Tyacke, 'Puritanism, Arminianism', pp. 130, 138; Tyacke, *Anti-Calvinists*, p. 7.

[47] Laud, *Works*, ii, pp. 173–4; Cross, *Church and people*, p. 177; *CSPV 1636–9*, p. 125; Tyacke, *Anti-Calvinists*, p. 194 and n.

[48] Hutton, *William Laud*, pp. 9–10, 17, 30, 139–41, 161; Welsby, *George Abbot*, pp. 122, 148–9; *CD1628*, vi, p. 56; Laud, *Works*, iii, p. 210, vi (1), p. 9; Morrill, 'The religious context of the English civil war', *TRHS*, 5th ser., xxxiv (1984), p. 163n; Clarendon, *Rebellion*, vol. i, pp. 122–3; J. S. McGee, 'William Laud and the outward face of religion', in R. L. DeMolen (ed.), *Leaders of the Reformation* (London, 1984), p. 337.

[49] Hutton, *William Laud*, pp. 155–6.

[50] Trevor-Roper, *Archbishop Laud*, p. 231; Adams, 'The Protestant cause', pp. 423–4; Hutton, *William Laud*, p. 162. Laud did not consider that the Synod of Dort could be an authority within a different national Church; Laud, *Works*, vi (1), p. 246; Collinson, 'England and international Calvinism', p. 222; M. A. Breslow, *A mirror of England, English puritan views of foreign nations, 1618–1640* (Cambridge, Mass., 1970), pp. 38–9, 42.

[51] Laud, *Works*, vi (1), pp. 19–27; vii, pp. 12–14; Hutton, *William Laud*, pp. 63, 69; K. L. Sprunger, 'Archbishop Laud's campaign against puritanism at the Hague', *Church History*, xliv (1975), pp. 308–20.

[52] Culminating of course in the Scottish revolt. See C. Russell, 'Arguments for religious unity in England, 1530–1650', *JEH*, xviii, 2 (1967).

linked to ideas of divine right monarchy. There was no necessary connection between the Arminian position and a preference for prerogative rule.[53] The relationship between these views was complicated.[54] There is no doubt, however, of the developing link between Laudianism and Charles's inclination towards arbitrary government. Laud, unlike Abbot, endorsed the views of Sibthorpe and Manwaring on the forced loan. In this case Laud and Charles seem to have sought theological rationalization of emergency measures. It is clear, however, that Laud espoused definite ideas of divine right kingship.[55] The Laudians aspired to be pillars of a monarchy which would protect them. Laud himself believed that Church and state should be mutually dependent. The nationalism of English Arminians encouraged their desire for a godly prince to serve as a bulwark against the errors of popery and Calvinism. Charles was happy to support the Laudian bishops in return, given their recognition of the royal supremacy in the Church.[56] The alliance between Laudian and high monarchical interests was encouraged by elements of resistance theory in English Calvinist thought. Laud and particularly Charles believed in an international Calvinist conspiracy seeking to undermine the foundations of the English Church and state.[57] This belief was reflected in the increasing use of the word 'puritanism' to describe all manner of anti-authoritarian behaviour and dissent.[58]

Laudianism also shared certain features with Dutch Arminianism. The most striking was a definite sympathy for and tolerance of Roman Catholicism.[59] Native religious traditions, however, considerably strengthened this attitude in England. Clearly, more distance separated Laudianism from the Calvinist communities of Europe than from the Rome of the Counter-

---

[53] Heath is a striking illustration of this fact; see Reeve, 'Sir Robert Heath's advice'; see also Tyacke, 'Puritanism, Arminianism', p. 140.

[54] D. Mathew, *The age of Charles I* (London, 1951), pp. 304–5.

[55] Hutton, *William Laud*, p. 126; Reeve, 'Viscount Dorchester', p. 56n; Cust, *The forced loan*, pp. 62ff.; Welsby, *George Abbot*, pp. 121, 126–30.

[56] J. P. Sommerville, 'The royal supremacy and episcopacy *jure divino*, 1603–1640', *JEH*, xxxiv, 4 (1983); Ornsby, *Cosin correspondence*, i, pp. 138, 147–50, 154; Birch, i, p. 439; Welsby, *George Abbot*, pp. 148–9; Cross, *Church and people*, pp. 176–7; Hutton, *William Laud*, pp. 64, 129–30.

[57] Tyacke, 'Puritanism, Arminianism', pp. 140–1; N. Tyacke, 'Arminianism and English culture', *Britain and the Netherlands*, vii (1981), p. 101; Hibbard, *Popish plot*, pp. 228, 237, 253n; Cust, *The forced loan*, p. 90; D. Hirst, 'Revisionism revised', p. 98; Sommerville, *Politics and ideology*, p. 46.

[58] G. Yule, *Puritans in politics* (Appleford, 1981), pp. 88–9; P. Collinson, 'A comment: concerning the name Puritan', *JEH*, xxi, 4 (1980).

[59] On the Dutch situation see Israel, *Dutch republic*, pp. 231–3; C. Grayson, 'James I and the religious crisis in the United Provinces', in D. Baker (ed.), *Reform and Reformation: England and the continent c. 1500–1750* (Oxford, 1979), pp. 207–8. Light is shed on the pre-civil war English situation by D. Hoyle, 'A Commons' investigation of Arminianism and popery in Cambridge on the eve of the civil war', *HJ*, xxix, 2 (1986).

Reformation.[60] There were elements of Roman theology – including doctrines of the mass and purgatory and the concept of papal doctrinal infallibility – to which Laud did not subscribe.[61] He regarded Rome, however, as a true and sister church, errant and unreformed in its superstition. In the early 1630s Laud refused the offer of a cardinalate 'till Rome were other than it is'.[62] Protestantism for Laud meant opposition to the errors of Rome, which remained a member of the wider catholic church. Laud believed that elements of truth could be found in the thinking of the Jesuits. Laudianism in England was open to certain Tridentine values, particularly ecclesiastical ornament and clericalism. Laud did not believe that any practice should be rejected on the basis that it featured in the Roman Church.[63] Neither did he consider Roman Catholicism necessarily subversive and he believed in the toleration of English recusancy. To Laud, priests and Jesuits were not a great religious danger, but should be proceeded against for treason and rebellion.[64] Catholic hierarchical influence in England was a political threat to Laud and he was sceptical about the possibility of reunion with Rome. But he still had a temperamental opposition to schism in the church.[65]

Charles shared this general Laudian sympathy towards Rome and it is legitimate to describe him as a quasi-Catholic.[66] In Spain he wrote to Pope Gregory XV in terms of friendship and respect.[67] He wished to marry his eldest daughter to a Roman Catholic prince, despite the fact that this would jeopardize her Protestant religion.[68] There was a strong Catholic streak in the Lennox-d'Aubigny branch of his family and he supported his kinsman Ludovick Stuart d'Aubigny in his candidacy for a cardinalate.[69] Charles's cosmopolitan attitudes caused him to be interested in reunion with Rome, although not at the expense of English royal power.[70] The question of recusancy involved a conflict for Charles, between the requirements of English law and his own desire for order and conformity on the one hand, and

---

[60] Clarendon, *Rebellion*, vol. i, pp. 122–3; Collinson, 'England and international Calvinism', pp. 218–19; Tyacke, 'Puritanism, Arminianism', p. 129.

[61] Hutton, *William Laud*, p. 151; R. Mousnier, 'The exponents and critics of absolutism', in *NCMH*, iv, pp. 106–8.

[62] Quoted in Trevor-Roper, *Archbishop Laud*, p. 146; see also Sommerville, *Politics and ideology*, p. 194; *CD1629*, pp. 125–6; Hutton, *William Laud*, pp. 148–9, 154.

[63] Hutton, *William Laud*, pp. 70, 81, 87, 148–9; Laud, *Works*, vi (1), pp. 11–12.

[64] Hutton, *William Laud*, p. 160.

[65] Ibid., pp. 62, 154; Hibbard, *Popish plot*, pp. 45, 60ff.

[66] Hibbard, *Popish plot*, pp. 22, 44, 49; J. H. Elliott, 'England and Europe: a common malady?', in Russell (ed.), *Origins*, p. 249.

[67] Lockyer, *Buckingham*, p. 469; see also C. Hill, *Antichrist in seventeenth century England* (Oxford, 1971), n. 66; Sommerville, *Politics and ideology*, p. 198.

[68] Hibbard, *Popish plot*, p. 253, n. 14.

[69] Ibid., pp. 143–5, 285.

[70] Ibid., p. 22; Trevor-Roper, *Archbishop Laud*, pp. 69–70.

the loyalty of his Catholic subjects, the provisions of his marriage treaty and his basically liberal religious disposition on the other. The king's inclination was to extend legal immunity to Catholics whenever he could.[71] Charles, like Laud, aspired to a catholic ideal within the English ecclesiastical setting.[72] The English Arminians, like their Dutch counterparts the Remonstrants, were opposed to any warlike foreign policy in the Protestant cause. The Laudian view of foreign policy drew inspiration from several sources: sympathy for the Roman Catholic Church and for its allies, a belief that national religious life should be based upon peace and order, and an insular nationalism opposed to the concerns of international Calvinism.[73] Collectively, these attitudes could only serve to encourage the king's emerging interest in peace with Spain.

A fundamental paradox lay at the root of English Arminianism, which helps to explain the reaction the movement provoked. Anti-Calvinism was essentially a liberal position – in modes of thought and in beliefs – which in England took on remarkably illiberal characteristics. Arminianism was, in the broadest sense, part of the wider sceptical reaction against determinism during this period.[74] Laud's clearest statement of his view on the theology of salvation was framed, significantly, as a *rejection* of the orthodox Calvinist position.[75] In theological discourse the English Arminian appeal was consciously to reason, to criticism and to history. To English rationalists such as Laud and Montagu the enemy was the dogma, as they saw it, of Calvinism and popery.[76] Likewise Laud did not consider his own church to have a monopoly on the truth. Laud also disliked any rigid theological definition of articles of faith: a practice which he saw as divisive within the wider catholic world. His consistent attempts to dampen theological controversy in England reflect the distinct Arminian approach to religious

---

[71] Hibbard, *Popish plot*, p. 22; Russell, *Parliaments*, pp. 204ff., 229–30, 239–40, 242, 248, 263–4, 297; Birch, i, pp. 375, 377, 379, 418, and ii, pp. 67–9, 76–7, 303; M. J. Havran, 'Parliament and Catholicism in England, 1626–1629', *Catholic Historical Review*, xliv (1958), pp. 279, 282; *CD1629*, p. 78; AMRE, CPA, 43, fos. 337r, 338v; Reeve, 'Viscount Dorchester', p. 207n; Searle, *Barrington family letters*, pp. 137–8.

[72] Trevor-Roper, *Archbishop Laud*, pp. 69–70; P. Tudor-Craig, 'Charles I and Little Gidding', in R. Ollard and P. Tudor-Craig (eds.), *For Veronica Wedgwood these studies in seventeenth century history* (London, 1986).

[73] Tudor-Craig, 'Charles I and Little Gidding', p. 186. In June 1630, when the negotiation of the Treaty of Madrid was nearing conclusion, John Cosin preached tellingly on the text 'Pray for the peace of Jerusalem'; *The works of the Right Reverend father in God John Cosin, Lord Bishop of Durham*, ed. J. Samson (5 vols., Oxford, 1843–55), i, pp. 108–16. See also chapter 5, p. 169, below; Laud, *Works*, vi (1), pp. 19–20; Israel, *Dutch republic*, pp. 60–3, 76, 175, 190, 231–3, 235, 300.

[74] Tyacke, 'Arminianism and English culture'.

[75] Laud, *Works*, iii, p. 304, quoted on p. 64, n. 38.

[76] Hutton, *William Laud*, pp. 18, 29–30, 151–2, 159; Haller, *Rise of puritanism*, pp. 235–6, 242; Tyacke, *Anti-Calvinists*, p. 245.

unity, an approach which can be seen as practical and non-academic but which in many ways was intellectually sophisticated.[77] The intellectual liberalism of English Arminianism, however, contrasts sharply with the illiberal and forcibly conformist character of Laudian ecclesiastical practice.[78] The international history of Arminianism serves to explain this dichotomy. Experience in the English universities and in the Dutch republic had forced home to liberal Protestant churchmen the need to fight for their lives. The Synod of Dort made clear to English Arminians their involvement in an international theological struggle for survival. A sense of persecution and insecurity can be seen lurking behind the attitudes and activities of the Laudian ecclesiastics: the redefinition of puritanism, the wholesale effort to capture all senior appointments in the Caroline Church, the keen desire for royal protection and the fast-developing Arminian opposition to the sitting of Parliament.[79] Only an intense fear of Calvinist reaction could provoke Richard Montagu, whose writings had been critical of Rome, to write: 'Before God it will never be well till we have our inquisition.'[80] Only weeks later, he wrote to John Cosin that he was afraid that Convocation would invoke the authority of the Synod of Dort.[81] England's involvement in war against France and Spain during the 1620s was linked to a virulently anti-Catholic atmosphere at home, and this could only encourage Arminian anxieties.

The paradoxical nature of Laudianism could not have been better calculated to arouse antagonism on the part of English Calvinists. Arminianism had rejected predestination in a manner similar to the teachings of the Council of Trent.[82] In England it bred an increasingly conformist ecclesiastical order. It there acquired characteristics which appeared to be manifestations of popery. Its adherents did nothing to distance themselves from the king's autocratic pretensions. In addition, there was a definite relationship between Arminianism, pro-Spanish thinking and Catholic fellow-travelling in the Protestant world. Until Charles established his personal rule in England, this association was most visible in the Dutch republic, where the Remonstrants were working to end the war with Spain. In this light, Charles's eventual ending of the Spanish war (and the Dutch alliance) simultaneously

---

[77] Hutton, *William Laud*, pp. 58, 132; Trevor-Roper, *Archbishop Laud*, p. 85; Laud, *Works*, vi (1), pp. 11–12.

[78] Tyacke, 'Arminianism and English culture'; Hutton, *William Laud*, pp. 60–1; Bangs, 'Arminian politics', p. 16; Trevor-Roper, *Archbishop Laud*, pp. 74–5.

[79] Russell, *Parliaments*, pp. 404–5; *CD1628*, vi, pp. 52ff.; Hutton, *William Laud*, pp. 6, 9, 12–14; Collinson, *Religion of Protestants*, p. 81; Tyacke, 'Puritanism, Arminianism', pp. 130–1. I am grateful to Ian Breward for discussion of these matters.

[80] Quoted in Trevor-Roper, *Archbishop Laud*, p. 103.

[81] 8 Jan. 1625; Ornsby, *Cosin correspondence*, i, p. 42.

[82] Tyacke, 'Arminianism and English culture', p. 100.

with the development of the Laudian church could only appear sinister to English Calvinists. Collectively, these features of Laudianism set off all the alarms in the sensitive mind of established English Protestantism. Anti-Arminianism in England was inextricably bound up with the nexus of international Calvinism, English Protestant nationalism and the idea of the godly commonwealth and its government. Anti-popery was the linchpin in this structure of thinking which knew no distinctions of degree in dealing with Rome. Thus Arminianism, at bottom a liberal movement, became immediately eligible for condemnation as popery; and the religious issue in England during the early years of Charles's reign became, to the mind of the anti-Arminians, a struggle for the very life of the Reformation.[83] An understanding of Laudianism shows that this was an exaggeration; but it indicates also how the issue could be seen in these terms. Charles provided his subjects with ample evidence to justify a view that Arminianism was a popish plot. He did this by demonstrating the link between liberal Protestantism and quasi-Catholicism and by giving it a reality, with other provocative features, in the English context. By the time Parliament reconvened in 1629 there was the clearest evidence of the nature of the Laudian threat. Calvinist theology had been silenced by means of a royal declaration, the episcopate was liable to be captured from within by the anti-Calvinists, and at Durham Cathedral there were ceremonies which had already been branded as popish. There were rumours, moreover, of dealings for peace with Spain.[84]

There are already two very illuminating accounts of the 1629 parliamentary proceedings.[85] Partly as a consequence, what follows will be more of an analytical than a chronological treatment. It will also seek to relate events in Parliament to the wider political and intellectual scene. In 1629 the leadership of the lower house was divided. Two groups competed for the direction of proceedings in the Commons. Pym and Rich were deeply concerned with religion, sought a settlement with the king's government, and were prepared to vote tonnage and poundage given that Charles would abandon Arminianism. Eliot and Selden were more concerned with constitutional grievances (the punishment of the customs officers and parliamentary privilege) and adopted a confrontational attitude.[86] Yet the distinction between these two political approaches is not quite so simple. Eliot was preoccupied with the

---

[83] Yule, *Puritans in politics*, pp. 83–4; Collinson, 'England and international Calvinism', p. 219; R. P. Cust and P. Lake, 'Sir Richard Grosvenor and the rhetoric of magistracy', *BIHR*, cxxx (1981).

[84] *DNB*, s.v. John Cosin; Ornsby, *Cosin correspondence*, i, pp. 144–5, 155–7, 161–99; Adams, 'Spain or the Netherlands?', p. 101; *CSPV 1628–9*, p. 358.

[85] C. Thompson, 'The divided leadership of the House of Commons in 1629', in Sharpe (ed.), *Faction and Parliament*; Russell, *Parliaments*, ch. 7.

[86] Thompson, 'Divided leadership'. There is also Selden's apparent lack of interest in religion during the remonstrance debate of 1628; *CD1628*, iv, pp. 117, 121, 126–7, 130–1, 133.

subversion of government and religion by evil counsel, and hence the two
strategies overlapped on the central question of religious policy.[87] The session
also demonstrated the link between religion and property in Calvinist thinking. The majority of members were concerned with both the religious and
constitutional themes (the latter involving the question of unparliamentary
taxation), finding it difficult to dissociate the two.[88] The divided leadership
remains a useful distinction nevertheless, for there were differences of political style and emphasis between the two groups. While religion was the main
concern of the majority of members, the issue which at bottom produced a
deadlock between Charles and the Parliament, the approach of Eliot and
Selden and their desire to investigate the matter of the customs, temporarily
carried the house. The course of the session was also strongly influenced by
the absence of two men who had been inspirational in 1628. Wentworth's
enlistment in the service of the crown meant the loss of his conciliatory leadership in the Commons, and Sir Edward Coke's failure to participate, probably
due to age and the desire to complete his *Institutes*, deprived the lower house
of his great learning in the common law. With the Commons' increasing
involvement in the issue of tonnage and poundage, Coke's absence meant the
lack of a powerful political weapon. The house was aware of being weakened
by his absence and this may well have encouraged their vindictive attitude to
the customs officers, the main constitutional stumbling-block of the
session.[89]

When Parliament reconvened on 20 January, the proceedings in the
Commons appeared to be almost a continuation of the remonstrance debate
of 1628. It was decided that a committee of the whole house would deal with
the question of religion. One week later, after a forceful speech by Pym who
pointed to the dangers of Arminianism and popery and the need to reform the
Church, the Commons resolved that religion should take precedence over all
other business.[90] This unanimous decision reflected the attitude of the House
of Commons as a whole. Francis Nethersole wrote to Elizabeth of Bohemia
that the Commons had given priority to the settlement of religion 'whereon
the hearts of all the house are expressly set'.[91] Charles informed the Commons that he wanted precedence given to tonnage and poundage; but he did
not forbid their proceeding with religion.[92] On 2 February the Commons

---

[87] Thompson, 'Divided leadership', pp. 275–6, 281.
[88] Trevor-Roper, *Archbishop Laud*, p. 93; Russell, *Parliaments*, p. 404; Yule, *Puritans in
politics*, p. 89.
[89] CD1629, p. 138; S. D. White, *Sir Edward Coke and 'the grievances of the commonwealth'*,
1621–1628 (Chapel Hill, 1979), p. 275.
[90] *CJ*, i, pp. 920, 922; CD1629, pp. 20–1.
[91] CD1629, pp. 250–1. See also Searle, *Barrington family letters*, pp. 50–1.
[92] CD1629, pp. 21–2, 112–13, 247.

explained their decision to the king. The dangers to religion were such that they could not allay their proceedings 'until something be done to secure us in this main point, which we prefer even above our lives and all earthly things whatever'. The house acknowledged Charles's good intentions in the Church but maintained that his purposes were crossed. In attaching priority to religion, and in attempting to enlist the king, the Commons stated explicitly their intention of bargaining the customs against ecclesiastical reform.[93] Normally, Parliament could not expect to force an alteration of religious policy by withholding supply.[94] But in this case the constitutionality of the king's ordinary revenue was the matter at stake; and the increasing disaffection of the chartered companies threatened a widespread stoppage of trade.[95] In time of war, moreover, the crown was highly vulnerable to parliamentary financial pressure. The Commons having staked out their political position, government spokesmen in the house continued to make encouraging statements about the king's good disposition in religion.[96] But the fact remained that Charles was not prepared to make concessions which were more than cosmetic. His religious preferences meant that the 1629 session was doomed from the start. And given the Commons' intention of withholding tonnage and poundage until they had achieved reform, further conflict over the customs duties could be expected as a consequence of the religious issue. In fact further constitutional conflict came about when Eliot and Selden, with their different critique of misgovernment, wrested control from Pym and Rich during the session's later stages.[97] Eliot's leadership did not, however, signify any fundamental change in the political priorities of the house.

It was Pym who proposed a programme, adopted by the Commons, for the investigation of the state of religion in England. The agenda referred to failure to execute the recusancy laws, countenancing of papists, and the introduction of superstitious ceremonies. To combat Arminianism, Pym recommended a parliamentary statement of reformed articles of faith; and he called for an inquiry into Arminian promotions, preaching and pardons, as well as the licensing of books.[98] The central problem in summarizing the tenets of English Protestantism was the need for an authoritative Calvinist interpretation of the Thirty-Nine Articles. The debate in the Commons foundered on a disagreement over the sources to be used, principally because those proposed were a mixture of statutory and non-statutory authorities. This part of

---

[93] Ibid., pp. 29–30.
[94] Trevor-Roper, *Archbishop Laud*, p. 94.
[95] Ashton, *City and the court*, pp. 125–31.
[96] *CD1629*, pp. 110–11, 122, 180.
[97] Thompson, 'Divided leadership', pp. 250, 254–5, 262, 279 and passim.
[98] Speech of 27 January; *CD1629*, pp. 20–1; *CJ*, i, p. 922. See also the revealing answer drafted by Laud to the programme of the Commons, Laud, *Works*, vi (1), pp. 11–12.

Pym's programme was, in effect, laid aside.[99] The Commons also investigated the recent printing of the Articles and the suppression, on Laud's authority as bishop of London, of anti-Arminian and anti-Catholic publications.[100] Time was spent in pointing to examples of failure to proceed against recusants and to enforce the laws against Catholic priests and Jesuits. All these developments, with the practice of popery at court, were held to signal the workings of Catholic subversion throughout the land.[101]

Arminianism, however, in the eyes of the Commons, was arguably a more sinister development, claiming as it did to be the proper doctrine of the English Church.[102] In the words of Francis Rous, Arminianism was 'this Trojan horse', sent to infiltrate the citadel of English religion: 'For an Arminian is the spawn of a papist . . . '[103] The Commons' failure to agree on suitable authorities for doctrine, with their belief that Arminianism and popery were allied forces, inspired them to make inquiries into the activities of individual Arminians.[104] The house was scandalized at Montagu's episcopal appointment, at the royal pardon he had received, and at similar indemnifications granted to Manwaring, Sibthorpe and Cosin. These pardons, procured by the intercession of Bishop Neile, protected the recipients against parliamentary proceedings.[105] The Commons were told of ceremonial innovations at Durham and Winchester which were clearly the work of Cosin and of Neile. The house was also told how Dr Turner, one of Laud's chaplains, had refused to license a book denying Rome to be the true church, and how Neile had instructed one Dr Moore not to preach against popery.[106] These and other such incidents involving the promotion of Laudianism in England reinforced the Commons' belief that their religion

---

[99] There is evidence of Charles's resentment of these parliamentary efforts to define true doctrine, which reflected on the role of Convocation and, by implication, the royal supremacy in the Church, SP16/133/28 (draft in the king's hand of a message to the Commons, *c.* end January 1629). See also Thompson, 'Divided leadership', pp. 255–60; Russell, *Parliaments*, pp. 410–11; *CJ*, i, pp. 924, 928; *CSPD 1628–9*, p. 460; *CD1629*, pp. 20–1, 23, 57, 117, 119–20.

[100] *CJ*, i, pp. 926, 929; *CD1629*, pp. 58–60, 125–8, 138–40.

[101] It is possible that a warrant of High Commission for the apprehension of priests and Jesuits (29 January 1629) was intended by the crown to placate the Commons, *CSPD 1628–9*, p. 460. See also *CJ*, i, pp. 922, 930, 932; *CD1629*, pp. 64ff., 70–2, 77–80, 82–3, 144, 146, 149–50, 152–3, 205, 210, 216, 218–20, 249–50.

[102] Russell, *Parliaments*, p. 410.

[103] *CD1629*, pp. 12–13.   [104] Thompson, 'Divided leadership', p. 260.

[105] The pardons related to all offences save treason to the person of the king and witchcraft, *CD1629*, pp. 36ff. Charles may, imperceptively, have imagined that the pardons would smooth the progress of the session. See also ibid., pp. 43, 45–6, 49–51, 53–5, 123, 130, 132–5, 139, 180, 246; Birch, i, p. 335; Searle, *Barrington family letters*, p. 51; Ornsby, *Cosin correspondence*, i, p. 153n; *CSPD 1628–9*, pp. 198, 456.

[106] Robert Moore (or More), prebendary of Winchester Cathedral, as opposed to Gabriel More, Fellow of Christ's College, Cambridge, sometime chaplain to Buckingham; Tyacke, *Anti-*

was under attack from a single subversive force, the workings of which displayed a discernible pattern in national religious life. Moreover, the whole godly commonwealth was at risk. Speakers continually linked religious change with arbitrary government,[107] a theme which had pervaded the previous session.

In 1629, however, there was greater concern for the Church as the target of subversion and therefore as the proper object of reform. This was certainly the way John Pym was thinking.[108] The immediate issue appeared to be, as Sir Walter Earle pointed out, the very survival of Protestantism in England.[109] It was Parliament's role to act against the cancer in the commonwealth for, as Littleton said, 'the neglect of our duty is the cause . . . '[110] In this context, the threat to parliamentary taxation was also a threat to religion. Rous urged consideration of 'whether these [Arminians] be not the men that break in upon the goods and liberties of this commonwealth . . . ': men who sought to bring an end to Parliaments.[111] The question of tonnage and poundage thus appeared as part of the religious threat; and Eliot, with his emphasis on evil counsel and ministerial scapegoats, was able to carry the house.[112] The body of the Commons was receptive to the idea of a conspiracy at conciliar level, the key perpetrators of which, Eliot, Cotton and others believed, were Laud and the Arminian bishops.[113] Laud wrote: ' . . . some are ready to slander us as maintainers of popish superstition, and I know not what'.[114]

As with the remonstrance debate of 1628, the key to understanding the Commons' attitude in 1629 is the underlying historical framework uniting English and international affairs. In 1629, however, the religious conflict in England was further developed. Moreover, the nation's commitment to war now hung in the balance. Together these facts had profound implications for

---

Calvinists, pp. 186, 214–15; J. and J. A. Venn, *Alumni Cantabrigiensis*, part I (4 vols., Cambridge, 1922–7), iii, p. 204. See also *CJ*, i, pp. 925, 932; Searle, *Barrington family letters*, p. 53; *CD1629*, pp. 34–5, 50–1, 63–4, 116, 125–6, 192–3, 203–4.

[107] *CD1629*, pp. 52, 61, 133, 140, 198.

[108] Pym's direct interest in religion in 1629, as opposed to his preoccupation with the rule of law in 1628, represents a step forward in his thinking and political activity. His legal and religious concerns were interdependent. By 1629, however, he was seeking to concentrate on what he perceived as the fundamental threat of religious innovation; see *CD1629*, pp. 18–21. See also Russell, 'Career of John Pym', pp. 159ff. and 'Arguments for religious unity', pp. 219–22; Cust and Lake, 'Rhetoric of magistracy'.

[109] *CD1629*, pp. 18–19.

[110] Ibid., p. 57.

[111] Ibid., p. 13; *The diary of John Rous*, ed. M. A. E. Green (Camden Society, London, 1856), pp. 42–3.

[112] Thompson, 'Divided leadership', p. 281.

[113] *CD1629*, p. 149; *The letter book of Sir John Eliot, 1625–1632*, ed. A. B. Grosart (London, 1882), pp. 35–8; Russell, *Parliaments*, p. 409.

[114] Laud, *Works*, vi (1), p. 21 (Laud's speech in Star Chamber in the trial of Henry Sherfield, Feb. 1632).

the course of the session. The Parliament developed into a conflict between what were essentially national and international aspirations: between Laudianism and Weston's economic and diplomatic objectives on the one hand and the priorities of activist Calvinism on the other. This conflict ultimately destined the session to destruction. The collapse of the Parliament represented a victory for the Laudian and anti-war (and thus anti-parliamentary) interests within the court, who counselled Charles against accommodation.[115] In opposing these interests, the Calvinist forces in Parliament were just as concerned with the war as with reform of the English Church. Yet, for them, a religious settlement at home was rendered imperative, not only by the political reality of an anti-war lobby, but also by the logic of international Calvinism. The elimination of the enemies of godly religion and war finance at home would allow effective action in the Protestant cause abroad. No qualitative distinction could be made, in the minds of Pym and others, between the religious enemy within England and without. Yet they considered England's spiritual health to be of great importance for the survival of Protestantism elsewhere in Europe. Why was this so?

Herein lies the solution to what may be considered one of the major mysteries of this period of English history: why did the parliamentary advocates of war in the Protestant cause become engaged in disputes with the crown which strongly encouraged Charles to withdraw from that same war?[116] During this period, the parliamentary leaders of what has been termed 'political puritanism'[117] had a distinctly ideological view of the world. Having a Calvinist rather than a Lutheran basis, it tended to be militant and independent rather than pacifist and submissive. With the outbreak of the continental conflict, the threat of Habsburg power invoked comparison in England with the period of the 1580s and 1590s, and it summoned up Elizabethan ways of thinking. English nationalism, we know, was traditionally defined in anti-Hispanic as well as anti-Catholic terms. Moreover, in the 1620s, with the direct political application of covenant theology in English puritan circles, England was seen as the chosen nation which could offer leadership to Protestantism in Europe. Thus political puritanism did not believe that England should remain an island of peace in a sea of war; and Protestantism in England acquired a renewed interventionist imperative. The Reformed Church in Europe, political puritanism believed, was engaged in a struggle for survival with the Romish Anti-Christ; and it was incumbent

---

[115] Of this more below, but see _CSPV 1628–9_, pp. 580–1; Laud, _Works_, iii, p. 210; Birch, ii, p. 4; Trevor-Roper, _Archbishop Laud_, p. 297; L. J. Reeve, 'Sir Thomas Roe's prophecy of 1629', _BIHR_, lvi, 133 (1983), p. 120.

[116] I am grateful to Conrad Russell for this question.

[117] I believe the phrase belongs to Simon Adams; see S. L. Adams, 'The Protestant cause', Abstract.

upon England to act decisively in that struggle.[118] By 1629, however, England was clearly failing in her role, and this was held to be a sign of God's disfavour. The cause of the broken covenant was the corruption of religion at home. This had been suggested in the 1628 remonstrance debate, but the following year it gave the whole session its meaning. Francis Rous spoke for the Commons when he said:

but as religion decayed so the honour and strength of this nation decayed; when the soul of a commonwealth is dead, the body cannot long overlive it ... Wherefore now let it be ... the resolution of us all to make a vow and covenant from henceforth to hold fast [to] our God and our religion, and then we shall from henceforth certainly expect prosperity in this kingdom ... [119]

Reform of the English Church was thus not simply a practical or tactical requirement. It would return God's favour to England, to her councils and her actions.

How, in political terms, did corruption of the Church appear to lead to England's failure in war abroad? The Commons believed that Arminianism was leading the attack upon true religion in England. The popish enemy had appeared in a new and particularly subversive guise. Not only was Arminianism pseudo-Catholic in its doctrine, raising up the will of man at the expense of the grace of God.[120] It was also politically active, pro-Spanish and involved in appeasement of Catholic aggression. It sought to separate England from the other reformed churches abroad. Its main tactic appeared to be the sowing of division. This undermined the efforts of the commonwealth abroad and made way for the bringing in of popery at home. In Kirton's words, 'it hath ever been a Jesuited policy, first to work a disturbance, and after that a change ... '[121] English Protestant fears were encouraged by a domino theory of Arminianism. Sir John Maynard said, 'when a man's neighbours' houses are fired [it is] time to look to ourselves'.[122] Sir Richard Grosvenor spoke of

---

[118] Adams, 'The Protestant cause', Abstract; Adams, 'Spain or the Netherlands?', p. 87; Adams, 'Foreign policy and the Parliaments of 1621 and 1624', p. 147; *Speech of Sir Robert Heath ... in the case of Alexander Leighton in the Star Chamber, 4 June 1630*, ed. S. R. Gardiner (Camden Society Miscellany VII, London, 1875), p. 8; Hill, *Antichrist*, pp. 20, 68, 71; Parker, *Thirty Years War*, pp. 94–6, 104, 117, 258n; *CD1629*, pp. 12ff., 14, 33–4, 69–70, 77, 95–101, 145, 148, 170, 178, 204–5, 210–11, 247; Cust and Lake, 'Rhetoric of magistracy', pp. 43, 46; Searle, *Barrington family letters*, pp. 203, 226–7, 230, 233–8, 240–1; Zagorin, 'Sir Edward Stanhope's advice', p. 309 and n; Cliffe, *Puritan gentry*, pp. 207–11, 230ff.; Russell, 'Arguments for religious unity', p. 222n; Russell, *Parliaments*, pp. 169, 429; Collinson, 'England and international Calvinism', pp. 212–14; Cross, *Church and people*, p. 186; Tyacke, *Anti-Calvinists*, pp. 1, 4, 75, 104, 139. See also p. 225 below.
[119] *CD1629*, p. 13; for examples of similar speeches see also ibid., pp. 16–17, 65–7. See also Russell, *Parliaments*, pp. 406–7; Yule, *Puritans in politics*, p. 252; Cliffe, *Puritan gentry*, p. 210.
[120] *CD1629*, pp. 12–13, 16.
[121] Ibid., pp. 14–15; see also ibid., pp. 13, 15–16, 97, 193–4; NUL, Ne.C., 15,404, p. 222.
[122] *CD1629*, p. 204.

'such desperate divines, as have fired a part of Christendom, almost ruined our neighbours, kindled their firebrands, and cast their dangerous sparks abroad in our church . . . '[123] Anti-Arminianism, as a reaction to the provocative pattern of Charles's religious policies, was encouraged by the example of Dutch Arminianism and the inspiration it had given to the Laudians. It was clear that the Dutch religious controversies could only benefit Spain since they divided the republic and strengthened the movement for peace. During the debate on the truce proposals in 1629 and 1630, the Dutch Calvinist war propaganda was forced to attack the Arminian position.[124] The significance of Dutch events was not lost on English observers.[125] An England defeated and religiously divided was evidence that the disease had spread. The natural tendency was to turn and face the domestic emergency first, but the theological implications were deeper. An international mission could not be fulfilled until the patient had ministered unto himself.[126]

The Commons were surely aware that Charles was dealing in some way with Spain. Rudyerd and Pembroke's other clients in the lower house were in touch with the earl at court; and rumours of a truce with Spain were circulating in the City.[127] The Commons disapproved of the Spanish treaty and attacked the resumption of Anglo-Spanish trade. A committee inquired into shipping arrangements and Charles was asked to stay vessels carrying supplies 'to the enemy'.[128] Pym, Rich and their adherents in the Commons sought to sustain the Spanish war out of religious principle. The war, however, needed financing. Almost certainly, the more hawkish members of Parliament were unaware of the extent to which Buckingham had brought the crown into debt.[129] Their belief in the war was accompanied however, by a willingness to grant further supply. In this they were doubtless encouraged by the removal of Buckingham. On 2 March Coryton stated: 'We all came with a full purpose to give his majesty tonnage and poundage, and a further

---

[123] Ibid., p. 68; see also Rous's speech, ibid., p. 13; Cliffe, *Puritan gentry*, p. 149.

[124] Israel, *Dutch republic*, pp. 226, 232, 234–5; Parker, *Europe in crisis*, pp. 191–2.

[125] See the earl of Clare's remarks on the influence of Dutch Arminianism, NUL, Ne.C., 15,404, pp. 222, 234–6.

[126] See Rich's petition to the king for a fast (27 January 1629), *CD1629*, pp. 17, 28, 247; *LJ*, iv, p. 15.

[127] B. O'Farrell, *Politician, patron, poet: William Herbert, third earl of Pembroke, 1580–1630* (UCLA PhD thesis, 1966; published Ann Arbor, 1985), p. 174; see also the link between Eliot and Warwick: H. Hulme, *The life of Sir John Eliot* (London, 1957), pp. 157, 276; *CSPV 1628–9*, p. 358.

[128] *CJ*, i, p. 922. See also ibid., pp. 923–4; AGS, E2519, exp. 8; *CD1629*, pp. 12, 23, 115, 118; *CSPV 1628–9*, p. 358. The king's desire to collect the customs was linked to the revival of Iberian trade. There was all the more reason for the Commons therefore, in terms of their own religious thinking, to bargain tonnage and poundage against religious reform.

[129] The large extent of that debt is still unclear: see Russell, *Parliaments*, p. 390; Reeve, 'Viscount Dorchester', p. 221n.

supply also, if it should be needfull: (at which words, the greatest part of the house cried, All, All).'[130] The Venetian ambassador considered that reform of the Church would purchase Charles the customs duties, as well as further subsidies.[131] The attitude of the Commons was reflected in the fact that the crown sought to represent tonnage and poundage as a war measure.[132] Charles's attitude to the session was surely bound up with his promise to help his beleaguered uncle. He did not hesitate to encourage the Commons to consider the demands of the war.[133] Extraordinary supply could not be voted before March, when the last of the subsidies granted in 1628 was due to be collected.[134] This, along with the delay over tonnage and poundage, explains Charles's patience with debates on religion and his willingness to keep Parliament in session.[135] Despite the Commons' apparent willingness to vote supply in 1629, there was probably some residual opposition to the continuing cost of the war.[136] And despite the natural English (and parliamentary) interest in the security of the Baltic, the arming of Denmark, a crippling expense, had had no place in the parliamentary war plan of 1624.[137]

The parliamentary war strategy in 1629 never fully emerged. The war lobby may well have supported the sending of reinforcements to Denmark, but clearly they favoured the traditional war of diversion by sea against Spain. An English West India company was their solution to the financial and strategic problems of foreign policy. The Dutch West India Company was the creation of the orthodox Calvinist war party. The establishment of such a company in England, as a joint-stock venture and regulated by act of Parliament, had been proposed in the Commons in 1626.[138] Since then the Dutch had had spectacular success in taking the plate fleet, which had inspired the revival of the English project in 1629. An English West India company, to harness the wealth of the gentry and perhaps co-operate with the Dutch, could, it was believed, conduct a godly and profitable war against the Spanish treasure fleets. Such a union of Anglo-Dutch sea power was the greatest fear of the Spaniards, for properly executed it could well mean the end of Spanish power. Charles, however, refused to sanction the creation of an English company. The scheme posed a threat to his royal control of foreign policy and would probably involve a reduction in Admiralty profits and in impositions. Charles, moreover, did not share the ideological stance of the parliamentary

---

[130] *CD1629*, p. 261; see also the Commons' earlier petition to the king for a fast, *LJ*, iv, p. 15.
[131] *CSPV 1628–9*, p. 537. [132] *CD1629*, pp. 31–2, 108, 201.
[133] Ibid., p. 247; *LJ*, iv, p. 15. [134] Russell, *Parliaments*, p. 400.
[135] *CD1629*, p. 32. [136] Russell, *Parliaments*, p. 426.
[137] *CD1629*, p. 108; *CSPV 1628–9*, p. 529; Adams, 'Foreign policy and the Parliaments of 1621 and 1624', pp. 165ff.
[138] Russell, *Parliaments*, pp. 262, 293–4, 299–300; C. Thompson, 'The origins of the politics of the parliamentary middle-group, 1625–1629', *TRHS*, 5th ser., xxii (1972), p. 80.

war lobby; he disliked the Dutch and was developing an interest in peace. The establishment of an English West India company could well prolong the Spanish war indefinitely.[139]

The House of Commons was the focus of political attention during the 1629 session. It was here that royal policies were attacked and where, it could be argued, the Parliament failed to work. Appearances, however, can be deceptive. The comparative silence in the Lords in 1629 is suspicious. There is strong evidence to suggest that much of the intense activity in the Commons was made possible, and was at least encouraged, by the tacit approval of important elements in the Lords. The attack on Buckingham in 1626 had clearly been sanctioned by Pembroke. In 1628, the Petition of Right had been preserved as a legislative measure when a powerful group in the Lords – Saye, Warwick and others – had brought about the exclusion of the saving clause. It is unlikely that these men were without a similar influence during the second session of the same Parliament, only six months later. An examination of key political connections and aristocratic policies in 1629 suggests that this analysis holds good. In terms of politics in the Commons in 1629, the important figures in the Lords were Pembroke and Warwick. Eliot was working with both men and spent the Christmas period, on the eve of the session, in Essex with Warwick. Rich was the earl's cousin and loyal businessman. Pym had become connected with Warwick and his family in 1626. Rudyerd was traditionally the leading spokesman for the Pembroke connection in the Commons.[140] These men were the critical focus of non-government activity in the Commons in 1629. Pym, Rich and Rudyerd consistently advocated reform of the Church, war with Spain and the avoidance of constitutional conflict.[141] Eliot's colleagues were unable to keep him in line and he adopted an increasingly divergent political approach. He did, however, make what was almost certainly a public acknowledgement of the efforts of certain peers to restrain him from investigating the customs.[142]

That particular members of the Lords – Warwick, Pembroke and probably Saye – were seeking to use the Commons to achieve religious reform is

---

[139] *CSPV 1628–9*, pp. 516, 518–19, 557, 590; AGS, E2519, exp. 6, 8; Thompson, 'Origins of the politics of the parliamentary middle-group', pp. 80–1; Magurn, *Rubens letters*, pp. 333–5, 342–5; Birch, i, pp. 369–70; Hibbard, *Popish plot*, p. 32; Adams, 'Spain or the Netherlands?', p. 83; Adams, 'Foreign policy and the Parliaments of 1621 and 1624', p. 151; Cooper, 'Fall of the Stuart monarchy', p. 556; E. H. Kossman, 'The Low Countries', in *NCMH*, iv, p. 368; Searle, *Barrington family letters*, p. 40; J. C. Appleby, 'An association for the West Indies? English plans for a West India Company, 1621–1629', *Journal of Imperial and Commonwealth History*, xv (1987).

[140] Russell, *Parliaments*, p. 13; Hulme, *Life of Sir John Eliot*, pp. 112n, 157, 276, 305; Thompson, 'Origins of the politics of the parliamentary middle-group', pp. 76–7, 81.

[141] *CD1629*, pp. 17, 167, 235; Thompson, 'Divided leadership', p. 250 and passim.

[142] ' . . . but now some raise up difficulties . . . of breach of Parliament and other fears. I meet with this here and elsewhere'; *CD1629*, p. 94.

entirely logical given their failure to combat Laud's influence at court.[143] In the sphere of foreign policy, Warwick was building a large financial stake in the continuation of the Spanish war. He was the prime mover behind the West India company scheme. A Spanish agent reported that he had readied his fleet and was awaiting the outcome of the session.[144] Why, given their deep concern for religious and foreign policy, did these men allow the Commons to make the running in calling for reform? The most likely explanation is that they did not wish to antagonize Charles unnecessarily after the events of the previous session. Moreover, the preservation of their standing with the crown was critical if they were to cap constitutional with religious reform. They would certainly have supported reforming legislation sent up from the Commons, but a comprehensive programme never got off the ground. In this situation, the peers in question did not wish to be implicated directly if the Parliament ended in fruitless constitutional collapse. In dissolving the Parliament, Charles would draw a sharp contrast between the behaviour of the upper and lower houses.

The session was to finish disastrously for all who were seeking a settlement which would alter the direction of religious and foreign policy. There can be no doubt that hostile elements at court were largely responsible for the outcome. Powerful evidence points towards Weston and Laud as the key figures involved. They had the strongest motives – religious, financial, personal and political – to wreck the session as Northampton may have sought to wreck the Addled Parliament of 1614.[145] Constitutional conflict, in this case over the collection of tonnage and poundage, created the perfect atmosphere in which to counsel the dissolution of the Parliament. In promoting such conflict, Laud and Weston found fertile ground in the attitudes of the king. Charles had strong views on the troublesome nature of Parliaments and on the need to protect his servants (such as the customs officers) when they were attacked. He was utterly opposed to the religious position adopted by the

---

[143] Thompson, 'Origins of the politics of the parliamentary middle-group', pp. 77ff.; Russell, *Parliaments*, p. 13; Beatty, *Warwick and Holland*, ch. 7; Cliffe, *Puritan gentry*, pp. 78–9; Yule, *Puritans in politics*, pp. 79–80, 82, 87; *LJ*, iv, pp. 6–7, 9–10, 31, 34.

[144] He was having difficulty obtaining his commission. His enterprise may have depended on the establishment of the company; AGS, E2519, exp. 6, 8. On Saye's advocacy of a naval war against Spain see Thompson, 'Origins of the politics of the parliamentary middle-group', pp. 72, 77–80. On 20 February, the House of Lords appointed a large committee (which included Warwick, Saye, Essex, Clare and Bedford) to investigate the shipping, arms and defence of the kingdom; *LJ*, iv, p. 37. See also Beatty, *Warwick and Holland*, p. 100; A. P. Newton, *The colonising activities of the English puritans* (New Haven, 1914), p. 58; W. F. Craven, 'The earl of Warwick, a speculator in piracy', *Hispanic American Historical Review*, x (1930), pp. 457–79; Appleby, 'Association for the West Indies?', pp. 225, 230.

[145] L. L. Peck, *Northampton: patronage and policy at the court of James I* (London, 1982), pp. 205ff.

Commons. Finally, it appeared that events were presenting him with the possibility of a peace settlement with Spain.

What were the anti-parliamentary motives of Weston and of Laud? An end to the Parliament and withdrawal from the war would give Laud the chance to pursue his policies in the Church without interference. To Laud, Parliament could only appear as a powerful assembly of laymen, opposed to his religious designs and view of the world, who could well bring about his downfall and the revival of Abbot's influence. Laud was opposed in principle to such public discussion of doctrine as was taking place in 1629.[146] His ecclesiastical nationalism also rendered him unsympathetic to the foreign complications beloved of international Calvinism.[147] He was, moreover, a decided opponent of Parliaments, considering them a threat to the royal power. Laud's attitude to Parliament, and particularly towards this session, was shared by his clerical colleagues and dependents. Montagu confided in Cosin his fears of parliamentary action against the Arminians and his relief in being awarded a royal pardon. Of the Parliament of 1628–9 he wrote: 'I know no man I can build upon in that assembly . . . '[148] Laud's attitude to Parliament was thus encouraged by the faction he led. Weston had played a part in referring the case of tonnage and poundage from Exchequer jurisdiction to the 1629 session; no doubt he wanted a settlement of the customs for financial reasons. As the session developed, however, he had stronger reasons for wishing to see it ended. The Commons had complicated the granting of tonnage and poundage, making the grant conditional upon religious reform; the parliamentary movement for war threatened to destroy the Treasurer's diplomatic and financial strategy; and Eliot eventually swore that he would impeach Weston if given the opportunity.[149] Faced with all of this, Weston could only counsel dissolution and seek to discourage Charles's hopes of an agreement. Weston may have considered that tonnage and poundage could be collected with relative impunity after Parliament had failed to settle it. In their counselling of Charles the motives of Weston and Laud overlapped. The Treasurer was, in Laud's words, 'very noble to the Church' for the same reason that James I had extended limited favour to the English Arminians: the latter approved of a policy of peace with Spain.[150] Likewise Laud inclined to the foreign policy of the Spanish faction because he wished, essentially for religious reasons, to avoid Parliaments.[151]

---

[146] Trevor-Roper, *Archbishop Laud*, pp. 87, 89, 94–5.
[147] Hutton, *William Laud*, pp. 162–3.
[148] Ornsby, *Cosin correspondence*, i, pp. 100, 141, 154.
[149] On 2 March; see Thompson, 'Divided leadership', p. 272.
[150] Laud, *Works*, vi (1), p. 273; Fincham and Lake, 'Ecclesiastical policy of King James I', p. 201.
[151] Hibbard, *Popish plot*, p. 166.

The fact of a Laudian and pro-Spanish interest at court both explains and is explained by the activity of a reformist and pro-war group in the Lords. Unable to register their views with the king as effectively as they wished, Pembroke and Warwick attempted to use the Parliament as a vehicle for putting forward those same views. In seeking to prevent conflict so as to secure an alteration of policy, these peers (with their close associates) became a threat to Weston and to Laud, who thus became involved in a struggle for political survival. Contemporaries recognized this conciliar and quasi-conciliar dimension of the session. It can be glimpsed, as will be seen, in the series of events which brought about the end of the Parliament. On the last day of 1628 it was reported in London that 'it is true that there hath been great and stormy labouring to hinder it [the Parliament]'.[152] Sir Thomas Roe had a keen political interest in the session as well as the chance to observe manoeuvres at court. Roe's overriding concern was the threat posed by Spain and the Counter-Reformation. He viewed the activities of the pro-Spanish faction as an extension of those of the Habsburgs: a judgement which was, in this instance, a great part of the truth. After the session Roe wrote to Lord Vere of the endeavours, which he had witnessed, to scuttle the Parliament and hamstring the English war effort, 'the enemy did like the devil, prophesy before hand of that, which himself hoped to bring to pass . . . '[153] The more perceptive speakers in the Commons made clear that they recognized the same deliberate design: to employ constitutional conflict to distract them from religion and to break the Parliament. In Phelips's words, 'I conceive this to be a bone thrown in by them that seek to draw a cloud over our sun, our religion, to divert or interrupt us in the prosecution of them [the Arminians] . . . '[154] The Commons were more willing to adopt this view because it coincided with two established notions: that Arminians were constitutionally subversive and that Arminians conquered by division. But this overall pattern of thought was built upon political reality: in this instance the roles of Weston and of Laud. Clearly the leaders in the Commons were receiving information from their colleagues in the Lords, as well as from those at court, particularly Roe, who sympathized with their views. Roe was significantly involved in the movement for war against Spain in the Caribbean.[155] The strength of the Commons' political analysis was, however, largely self-defeating, for it worked against the urge to deal with specifically religious questions. That is to say, the belief that Arminians and their countenancers were involved in the customs dispute reinforced the sense of an attack on the

[152] Birch, ii, p. 4.
[153] Reeve, 'Sir Thomas Roe's prophecy', p. 120.
[154] CD1629, p. 55, and see ibid., pp. 12–13, 17, 167, 186, 188, 236, 241; Russell, Parliaments, pp. 404–5; Gardiner, History, vii, p. 223.
[155] SP81/35/fo.157r–v.

commonwealth as a whole: its religion, government and property. Thus, rather ironically, it assisted Eliot in promoting constitutional issues.[156]

As the priorities of Eliot and Selden came to dominate proceedings in the Commons, the gulf between Charles and the Parliament, created by religion, was further widened. Charles believed that since the crown was in financial need the solution to the failure of ordinary supply was to vote it. When the Commons linked supply to the issue of religion, Charles was faced with further delay as well as religious criticism.[157] When the house became preoccupied with the seizure of the merchants' goods, not only was the bill for tonnage and poundage further complicated, but the king's servants were also attacked.[158] Finally, since one of the merchants in question, John Rolle, was also a member of the house, the issue of the customs led to a dispute with the king over privilege.[159] In this context, Eliot and Pym disagreed about the constitutional status of the liberties of the House of Commons. Pym, emphasizing the need to settle tonnage and poundage and opposing the punishment of the customs officers, maintained that the liberties of the house were inferior to those of the whole kingdom. Eliot, however, saw parliamentary privilege as the supreme consideration.[160] This reflected his belief that Parliament was the highest council in the realm.[161] Eliot's approach led to bitter conflict with the king. The house insisted upon punishing his servants and Charles refused to allow it.[162]

On 25 February Charles adjourned the Parliament for five days. Sir Thomas Barrington recorded the atmosphere of political failure. There was 'a face of general sadness for this probability of dissolving us, all men that wish well to church or commonwealth mourning for this threatening evil . . . '[163] As an objective assessment, the report of Contarini, the Venetian ambassador, cannot be bettered:

---

[156] *CD1629*, pp. 13, 95–101, 186; Russell, *Parliaments*, p. 405.
[157] Searle, *Barrington family letters*, p. 49; *CD1629*, p. 245; *CSPD 1628–9*, p. 461; *APC 1628–9*, p. 331; *LJ*, iv, p. 12.
[158] *CJ*, i, pp. 928–9, 931–2.   [159] Russell, *Parliaments*, pp. 402–3.
[160] There was a traditional distinction between parliamentary privilege and liberties; see the important discussion in Elton, *Tudor constitution*, pp. 260ff. Technically, Eliot was claiming privilege (freedom from arrest) for Rolle (for his goods as well as for his person). Yet Eliot's use of the term 'liberties' seems to have represented his conflation of these two spheres of parliamentary rights. This is consistent with his emphasis on the conciliar function of the Commons particularly, in the tradition of sixteenth-century 'liberties'; *CD1629*, pp. 156–7, 222–3.
[161] As opposed to Selden's belief that it was the highest court; Thompson, 'Divided leadership', p. 278.
[162] *CD1629*, pp. 61, 178, 238, 247, 250.
[163] Searle, *Barrington family letters*, pp. 58–9; *CSPV 1628–9*, p. 568; Russell, *Parliaments*, p. 414.

These affronts generate very great rancour, and there is great fear of a rupture, as the king and Parliament are brought to such close quarters that neither can give way without forfeiting their word and authority. If this happens, your Excellencies may imagine in what a miserable condition this kingdom and the north of Europe will be.[164]

During the four days' interval before Parliament was due to reassemble, Eliot and his associates planned the impeachment of Weston and Bishop Neile.[165] Bishop John Williams apparently heard of the scheme and sought to arrange an accommodation between Eliot and Weston. His efforts were unsuccessful. The evidence suggests that Weston encouraged Charles in his stand over the customs officers.[166] Charles and Weston also decided to foil the impeachment with an immediate adjournment when Parliament reconvened.

The Eliot group may have got wind of the government's intentions; they seem to have expected a dissolution and, at all events, were determined to prevent the Parliament being immediately adjourned or dissolved. When the Commons reassembled on 2 March, the group of conspirators occupied those places, usually taken by Privy Councillors, nearest the chair.[167] After prayers were read, the Speaker, Sir John Finch, announced the royal order that the house adjourn until 10 March. From the floor there were cries of 'No'. In what became a famous scene, Eliot moved to have a declaration read, but the Speaker refused to allow it. Finch had an absolute command from the king that no man be permitted to speak. He attempted to rise so as to end the sitting but was restrained in his chair by Holles and Valentine. Finch still refused to put the question. Eliot gave a paper to the clerk in an attempt to have it read. When the serjeant at arms refused to lock the door, Sir Miles Hobart did so and pocketed the key. Finch begged to be allowed to go to the king and the house was divided in opinion as to whether they should permit it.[168] Eliot proceeded to speak. The anger and jealousy he felt towards Wentworth and Weston (Thomas Roe dubbed Eliot 'the envious man')[169] was inextricably

---

[164] Contarini to the Doge and Senate, 27 Feb. 1629, *CSPV 1628–9*, p. 566.
[165] Eliot's co-conspirators in the Commons on 2 March were John Selden, Denzil Holles, Benjamin Valentine, Walter Long, William Coryton, William Strode, Sir Miles Hobart and Sir Peter Hayman.
[166] Hacket, *Scrinia reserata* (pt 2), p. 83; Alexander, *Charles I's Lord Treasurer*, p. 142. Contarini's information was that the government sought to negotiate a settlement with the Commons' leaders at this point and that these conversations foundered over the punishment of the customs officers; *CSPV 1628–9*, pp. 579–80. This was almost certainly a garbled version of the truth. That overtures were made (presumably by Williams) to Eliot alone is consistent with the fact that the other leaders of the Commons would not have allowed the Parliament to be destroyed by the constitutional issue in this way.
[167] Hulme, *Life of Sir John Eliot*, p. 307; I. H. C. Fraser, 'The agitation in the Commons, 2 March 1629, and the interrogation of the leaders of the anti-court group', *BIHR*, xxx (1957).
[168] *CJ*, i, p. 932; *LJ*, iv, p. 143; *CD1629*, pp. 242, 252–3, 255, 257–8, 261.
[169] Reeve, 'Sir Thomas Roe's prophecy', p. 120.

bound up with his belief in evil counsel. This, in turn, fuelled his desire to make clear what he considered his essential loyalty to Charles: 'God knows I now speak with all duty to the king.'[170] Eliot was certain that the disputes which had led to the adjournment of 25 February, and the adjournment itself, were Weston's work. He accused the Lord Treasurer and Bishop Neile of being innovators in government and religion. These were men who broke Parliaments, stated Eliot, lest Parliaments should break them. Weston, however, he singled out as 'the great enemy of the commonwealth. I have traced him in all his actions.'[171] This accusation was followed by a threat of impeachment. If Eliot came again to Parliament he would 'fall upon the person of that great man'. He concluded by recommending 'that we should declare all that we suffer to be the effect of new counsels to the ruin of the government of this state: and so to make a protestation against these persons . . . '[172] Eliot wanted Finch to communicate the feeling of the house to the king.[173] Concluding his speech, Eliot surreptitiously tossed the paper containing his resolutions into a fire.

Other members spoke. Littleton supported the tenor of Eliot's speech. Valentine and Hayman called for the paper to be read. Selden drew attention to the constitutional point at issue, claiming that the Speaker was the servant of the house before being that of the king. Finch, however, knew that he was trapped between two loyalties.[174] Maxwell, the usher of the black rod, sent word through the door that the serjeant at arms had been summoned to attend the king.[175] Expressing the impatience of the alternative leaders of the Commons, Rich said that Maxwell should be admitted and the house adjourned.[176] Holles, however, proceeded to read Eliot's resolutions from another copy, encountering as he did so 'some opposition'.[177] The Three Resolutions condemned anyone who promoted religious change, popery or Arminianism in England, who counselled the collection of tonnage and poundage without parliamentary consent, or anyone who so collected it, as 'a capital enemy' to the 'kingdom and commonwealth'. The resolutions also condemned any subject paying the duties, when not granted by Parliament, as an enemy to the liberties of England.[178]

---

[170] *CD1629*, pp. 101–6, 253, 258.   [171] Ibid., p. 102n.

[172] Ibid., pp. 170, 242, 259–61; Phelips called for Weston's impeachment before Eliot did; ibid., p. 243. See also Russell, *Parliaments*, pp. 415–16; Hulme, *Life of Sir John Eliot*, pp. 310–13; Thompson, 'Divided leadership', p. 272.

[173] *CD1629*, pp. 240, 242.

[174] Selden also stated that the body of the liberties of Parliament was at stake; ibid., p. 171. See also ibid., pp. 240, 243, 256, 264–5; Russell, *Parliaments*, p. 416.

[175] Hulme, *Life of Sir John Eliot*, p. 314.

[176] Digges also called for an adjournment; *CD1629*, pp. 171–2.   [177] Ibid., p. 267.

[178] Ibid., p. 101; Gardiner, *Constitutional documents*, pp. 82–3. The use of the words 'capital enemy' derived from Eliot's reluctance to lay a charge of treason without the opportunity to establish the truth of it; Thompson, 'Divided leadership', p. 273.

The Three Resolutions anticipated, and were an abbreviated substitute for, a parliamentary settlement of the customs and an impeachment. The resolutions were also based upon classical notions of evil counsel to the king. Yet they embodied three novel and interdependent themes. One was the perceived link between arbitrary government and religious change which had emerged in the remonstrance debate of 1628: the belief in an attempt to subvert the godly commonwealth of England. In this context, the promotion of Arminianism appeared as an offence of treasonable complexion. Moreover, inspired by the idea of a threat to the commonwealth, the resolutions implied the possible breaking of new ground in the definition of treason. Traditionally treason was established under statute, common law or act of attainder. Eliot's protestation implied its definition by the House of Commons and its establishment by virtual common fame. The resolutions also implied that treason could be committed against the state, rather than against the monarch. Finally, the resolutions suggest an attempt to enshrine a general constitutional principle: that innovation in religion or in government was, necessarily, an offence of a treasonable nature.[179] The novelty of these implications seems essentially to have been unintended and in part inspired by Eliot's lack of time in which to press charges. Yet in seeking to defend the established political order, he was putting pressure upon, and enlarging, traditional maxims of constitutional thought. This, combined with the refusal to accept the royal order for adjournment and the attempt to appeal to the country over the head of the government, rendered the demonstration in the Commons potentially revolutionary.[180] The house, after approving the resolutions by general acclamation, voted to adjourn itself.

After the events of 2 March there were intensive debates within the Council, 'both day and night, the king being always present'.[181] The government's first act was to order the imprisonment of those who had staged the demonstration.[182] This was a striking (but here understandable) repetition of Charles's use of physical restraint against his critics. According to Contarini, the Council was divided as to whether the Parliament should be allowed to stay in session. 'The Lord Keeper [Coventry] with a large party was in favour of gentleness. The Treasurer, with the others, seeing themselves in danger,

---

[179] I am grateful to John Morrill for encouraging me to think about the wording of the resolutions. The government's (or at least Heath's) suspicion of Eliot's choice of words may be indicated by the evidence of Heath's questions for Selden after his arrest, which use the word 'attainted' in misquoting the resolutions; SP16/139/8, fo. 15v. (Selden dissociated himself from Eliot's views; ibid.) See also A. Woolrych, 'The English revolution: an introduction', in E. W. Ives (ed.), *The English revolution 1600–1660* (London, 1968), p. 13; H. Schwartz, 'Arminianism and the English Parliament, 1624–1629', *JBS*, xii (1973).
[180] See Russell, *Parliaments*, pp. 415–16.
[181] Contarini to the Doge and Senate, 6 March 1629, *CSPV 1628–9*, p. 580.
[182] *APC 1628–9*, pp. 351–2 (3, 4 March).

insisted on force and a rupture, the course [which was] followed.'[183] To Weston's consideration of policy was now added the threat of impeachment. He had been hoarding public money for months as if (wrote Contarini) he had been working to wreck the parliamentary session.[184] His advice against conciliation, under the circumstances, finally prevailed with Charles. A proclamation announcing the dissolution had been prepared on 2 March and was published two days later. The king dissolved the Parliament in person on 10 March, a proceeding to which the Commons were not summoned, contrary to custom. Charles remarked upon the extreme unpleasantness of the occasion, praised the conduct of the Lords, and stated that it was the seditious activity of a few in the lower house which had led to the failure of the session. Charles thus appealed to what was his and the crown's interpretation of these events.[185] Undoubtedly Laud, and probably Neile, joined Weston in counselling the dissolution. Soon afterwards Laud wrote in his diary, 'The Parliament which was broken up this March 10 laboured my ruin . . . '[186] Owing to the Council debates, Weston's leading role in bringing an end to the Parliament was soon well known to wider political society. Public opinion correctly linked his name and Laud's to the event and both men became extremely unpopular.[187] The reaction of their opponents in the Lords can be glimpsed in the rumours of impeachment circulating at the time of the dissolution.[188]

Yet responsibility for the collapse of the Parliament was not unilateral. There was a fundamental conflict between Charles and the Commons over the king's religious policy. It was this which made the session unworkable from the start. In hoping that he could somehow obtain a grant of the customs without more than superficial religious concessions, Charles was imperceptive and unrealistic. The lower house never gave the slightest indication that they would compromise their desire to reform the Church. Without their conviction that the religious and constitutional issues were joined, it is unlikely that Eliot could have guided their proceedings at all. The enthusiastic endorsement of his Three Resolutions depended upon their inclusion of Arminianism and popery and the popular belief that Weston was an Hispanophile and a crypto-Catholic. And the withholding of tonnage and poundage could be seen as a means of starving an ungodly regime.[189] Eliot, of

---

[183] *CSPV 1628–9*, p. 580; Clarendon, *Rebellion*, vol. i, pp. 6–7.
[184] *CSPV 1628–9*, p. 581.
[185] For more on this subject see chapter 4, below. See also Laud, *Works*, iii, p. 210; *LJ*, iv, p. 43; SP45/10/fo. 175r; *CSPV 1628–9*, p. 580; Gardiner, *History*, vii, p. 77.
[186] Laud, *Works*, iii, p. 210; see also Trevor-Roper, *Archbishop Laud*, pp. 94–5, 297.
[187] *CSPV 1628–9*, pp. 580–1, 589; Birch, ii, p. 12; Laud, *Works*, iii, p. 210.
[188] Birch, ii, p. 13.
[189] *CSPV 1628–9*, p. 580; Green, *Diary of John Rous*, pp. 42–3.

course, also played his role. In seeking to punish the customs officers and in announcing an attack on the Treasurer, he had made a very serious misjudgement of Charles. He was wildly optimistic about the king's likely attitude to his servants and, unlike others in the Commons, insufficiently aware of the danger that the Parliament could collapse.[190] This, combined with his strong sense of personal frustration and desire for reform, made it impossible for Pembroke or Warwick to restrain him. Charles's patience with the house was sorely tried as the session progressed.[191] Eliot's final act was therefore precipitate. Weston and Laud capitalized on it immediately and a breakdown was the result.[192]

The events of 2 March constituted a failure for Pym's priorities but these remained an integral part of what had occurred. The possibility of supply was a casualty of the conflicting attitudes to the Parliament: the need to destroy it as opposed to the desire to use it for reform which would protect the godly commonwealth of England and its international commitments. Essentially the Parliament failed as a consequence of wider political and ideological influences. It was this which made for such an utter constitutional collapse. Of course, in a narrower and more immediate sense, the Commons contributed significantly to that failure. Yet they do not appear to have been striving to augment parliamentary power. The body of the house and the Warwick–Pym–Rich axis were as much traditionalists in their view of the role of Parliament as in their desire to defend established English Protestantism.[193] Eliot, like these men concerned with the threat of innovation, tended nevertheless to place extreme emphasis on the role of the House of Commons. This was inspired by his obsession with improper and inadequate counsel. Eliot was not a major or particularly original constitutional theorist. Yet the views he developed after 1628, on the importance of Parliament and particularly of the House of Commons, were a significant legacy.[194] They are inseparable, however, from the national political crisis which he did so much to precipitate in 1629.

The dissolution of Charles's third Parliament was not as decisive an event as often has been and might be supposed. The fact that eleven years then elapsed without another Parliament should not be allowed to obscure the complexity of the developments which produced the personal rule. Yet contemporaries understood that the conclusion of the Parliament was an event of undeniable significance. There was a widespread sense of failure, particularly

---

[190] *CD1629*, p. 94.   [191] Ibid., p. 250.   [192] *CSPV 1628–9*, p. 580.
[193] On conflict between crown and Parliament over religion under the Tudors see Elton, *Tudor constitution*, pp. 310–11.
[194] Hulme, *Life of Sir John Eliot*, pp. 336–7; F. W. Maitland, *The constitutional history of England* (Cambridge, 1908, repr. 1968), pp. 320–1; Sommerville, *Politics and ideology*, p. 158; see also chapter 5, below.

amongst those who wanted war and reform of the Church. Thomas Roe wrote of 'the funeral of our Parliament', an event which he believed 'hath shipwrecked all . . . '[195] Simonds D'Ewes considered it the most gloomy, sad and dismal day for England in five hundred years.[196] Such pessimism derived not only from the high hopes held of the session. They followed upon the earlier urgent sense that it was essential that it succeed. Sir Thomas Barrington, a firm supporter of Pym's priorities, failed to see any logic in Eliot's tactics:

Princes should in policy have some time and way left to evade when point of honour is in competition; if they acknowledge their acts past illegal, and their ministers confess it and plead ignorance, I know not why it were not better to take reasonable satisfaction for the rest and declare our right to posterity by a law, and the errors past, than by labouring to punish more to let fall the end of our desires in that and all.[197]

This was an intelligent and surely justifiable condemnation of Eliot. While Charles was deeply offended by Eliot's behaviour, and while he shared the prevalent sense of failure, he does not appear to have been unduly dismayed. It was reported that he returned from dissolving the Parliament in high spirits, 'as if he had freed himself from the yoke'.[198] Clearly he was pleased to be free of a troublesome session which had profited him nothing. Yet, as will be seen, his financial need and his interest in war were slow to disappear. They would not allow sudden rejection of parliamentary ways. But the 1629 session remained a powerful disincentive for Charles in subsequent consideration of policy and of the possibility of another Parliament.

The king's decision to align himself with Weston and Laud against the Commons, together with their supporters in the Lords, was a significant event. It signalled the beginning of the kind of high politics which characterized the years of personal rule. At a decisive moment Charles had identified with an insular circle of advisers who stood for Laudian, anti-war and anti-parliamentary policies in Church and state. These men and their associates were a minority in Council and vilified by public opinion. They were fiercely opposed by peers such as Warwick, alienated from the regime, and by senior members of the government jealous of their power. The earl of Holland, as Warwick's brother, was a link between those within the court and those outside who wished to bring down Weston, Laud and their dependents. In turn, the threat of impeachment became a force for the encouragement of a non-

[195] Reeve, 'Sir Thomas Roe's prophecy', p. 120; Roe supported Pym's parliamentary strategy.
[196] Gardiner, *History*, vii, p. 223. See also *DNB*, s.v. D'Ewes; Searle, *Barrington family letters*, pp. 60–1.
[197] Barrington was writing on 25 February; Searle, *Barrington family letters*, pp. 58–9. He was later a member of the Providence Island Company, *CSPCol. 1574–1660*, p. 125.
[198] *CSPV 1628–9*, p. 589.

parliamentary regime.[199] The activities of Eliot and his colleagues suggested a resort to 'underground' politics of dissent. Such covert activity developed at this time when serious conflict over policy coincided with the increasing closure of the channels which traditionally linked the inner court to wider political society. With the failure of Pym's strategy in the Commons in 1629, such politics immediately flourished among those whom Eliot had foiled: that like-minded group which, with aristocratic leadership, institutionalized itself principally in the Providence Island Company.

One critical aspect of the session cannot be allowed to pass without examination. Between 1629 and the outbreak of civil war, changing views of Charles were probably the most important aspect of politics in England. They are also one of the most difficult to chart. Men were naturally reticent to record their impressions of the king when those impressions were, in many cases, increasingly unfavourable. Yet the enormous strain Charles placed upon the constitutional fiction, the traditional need for confidence in the monarch, can be seen running, like a nerve dangerously exposed, through the parliamentary proceedings of 1629. As the events of 1628 had shown, amongst the peerage trust in Charles was seriously diminished and in the House of Commons there was similar suspicion of the king. Moreover, by the time the Parliament reconvened, there were rumours circulating in the community at large which reflected upon Charles's ability to govern and his commitment to the established religious and constitutional order.[200] Addressing both houses of Parliament on 24 January, Charles expressed his wish that they give no credence whatever to ill reports of him, reports which we know were current.[201] Given the existing doubts about his political integrity, this speech could only move the question of his personality and principles further into the spotlight. There it remained during the session and afterwards, explicitly or implicitly the central issue unifying the highly charged matters with which the Parliament chose to deal.

The first significant item of business for the Commons in 1629 had been their investigation of Charles's corruption of the printing of the Petition of Right. Interrogation of the king's printer revealed that he had carried out the parliamentary order for the printing in 1628, but that this edition was subsequently suppressed, and a second substituted, by order of the king. The second edition was clearly an attempt to impugn the legislative standing of the measure by including what was really a propaganda case for the crown. A committee was set up to check the recording of the Petition of Right in

---

[199] Hibbard, *Popish plot*, p. 32; Reeve, 'Viscount Dorchester', pp. 147, 285.
[200] Birch, i, pp. 99 and n, 167–8, 369, 431; SP16/116/92; Russell, 'Career of John Pym', pp. 159ff.; NUL, Ne.C., 15,405, p. 58; see also *CSPD 1628–9*, p. 198; *CD1629*, p. 203; Cust, 'News and politics', p. 88n; and see p. 30, n. 107.
[201] *CD1629*, p. 11; *LJ*, iv, p. 12; Cust, 'News and politics', pp. 83–5; and see the previous note.

Parliament and the courts, and likewise a committee of the whole house to investigate violations of the Petition since the previous session. The crown's perversion of the record, together with the attempt to levy the customs without parliamentary consent, revived the fear of a threat to liberties from arbitrary power. In 1629, as had happened with the Five Knights' case, this was a threat from which Charles could not ultimately be dissociated.[202]

It was the question of tonnage and poundage, and in turn the seizure of the merchants' goods, which led to the most striking and alarming reflection upon Charles during the session. Eliot and Selden were supported by Holles and Phelips in their campaign for the punishment of the customs officers: supposedly a means to vindicate the privileges of the house and obtain restitution of Rolle's goods. The Commons, after scrutinizing the king's warrant to the customers, maintained that it did not authorize the seizure of the goods and that Rolle, as a member of Parliament, should be allowed the immunity of privilege for his possessions. Rich was opposed to this line of political action as well as the reasoning which sustained it. The matter, he argued, would ultimately involve the king if it were pursued. Like Pym he had different priorities and wanted a settlement with Charles, rather than the kind of political aggression which would render such an agreement impossible. The Privy Councillors in the Commons also followed the line of argument that action against the customers would reach to the king whose servants they were. The case made against them by the Commons was for this reason legally weak. The customs farmers examined by the house made a clear distinction between their roles as customs farmers and as royal officials, insisting that only those farmers who were also customs officers, that is authorized collectors, had taken action to distrain the goods in obedience to the king's command. Eliot's persistence thus only cut the ground from beneath his feet: the case for ministerial misconduct dissolved and the stage was set for a dramatic intervention by Charles.

The king was moved by a sense of honour in seeking to protect those under him. He could also fear that proceedings like this would dissuade other royal officials from obeying him in the future. The question was thus a complicated one. Charles's action in protecting the customs officers was not the simple result of an ignorance of the value of sacrificing his servants to protect himself. While the king was moved by rectitude, as he had been in defending Buckingham, he could also claim that the Commons were being unreasonable. On 23 February he told them that the matter concerned him 'in a high degree of honour and justice' and, moreover, that what the customs officers had done was by his special direction. The statement explicitly refuted any

---

[202] *CJ*, i, p. 920; *CD1629*, pp. 245–6; Russell, *Parliaments*, pp. 401–2; Foster, 'Printing the Petition of Right'.

separation of the role of the officials from that of the king.[203] Charles's claiming of responsibility had created a constitutional impasse and the Commons were stunned. Phelips's response was to call for prayer to God that he might 'cause us to understand truly and to direct us'.[204] Eliot clung to the view of evil counsel about the king while Selden probed the possibility that the king's command did not protect delinquents from Parliament. Phelips, however, summed up the mood of the house by saying that the occasion warranted 'a fearful silence'.[205] The Commons adjourned for two days in order to ponder the implications of the king's intervention. Charles's declaration effectively ended proceedings in the house until the dramatic events of 2 March.[206]

Religious developments also inspired doubts about Charles during the course of the session. It was revealed in the Commons that ten Jesuits apprehended at Clerkenwell had been bailed, and the execution of one stayed, by order of the king.[207] It was increasingly difficult to accommodate such evidence of Charles's indulgence of popery. Phelips and Strode maintained that the Lord Chief Justice was to blame for failing to inform the king that his command contradicted a vital principle of English justice.[208] Incidents such as this, with the rise of Arminianism, caused the Commons to invoke increasingly the religious orthodoxy of the Jacobean period. While Sir Richard Grosvenor maintained that religious decline had set in under James, the desire to hold up the previous reign as a mirror for Caroline heterodoxy can be taken as evidence of a failing confidence in Charles as a godly prince.[209] This in turn created a tension in men's thinking about the royal supremacy.

---

[203] It is conceivable that Charles was influenced by Cotton's advice in 1628 against the sacrifice of royal servants as 'no less fatal to the master, than to the ministers in the end'; Rushworth, *Historical collections*, i, p. 476. See also *CD1629*, pp. 7, 83ff., 86–7, 88ff., 94, 155, 159, 165–8, 223, 236–7; *APC 1628–9*, p. 341; *CSPD 1628–9*, p. 478; *CSPV 1628–9*, pp. 579–80; Russell, *Parliaments*, p. 403; Thompson, 'Divided leadership', pp. 267, 269; Ashton, *City and the court*, pp. 133–5.

[204] *CD1629*, p. 238.

[205] Ibid., pp. 168–9, 238.

[206] Ibid., pp. 168–9; Thompson, 'Divided leadership', p. 270. It is possible to see Eliot's demonstration of 2 March as directly inspired by the king's intervention of 23 February. The Commons' self-adjournment on that day was followed by an adjournment by royal command two days later until 2 March.

[207] *CD1629*, pp. 74ff., 78, 80–1, 148, 151, 215. See also the matters of Charles's removal of the 1628 remonstrance from the records of Parliament (ibid., pp. 246–7) and Digges's complaint about the increase of popery in Ireland (ibid., p. 145).

[208] Strode maintained that Hyde should not have carried out such an order; ibid., pp. 80–1, 151. See also ibid., p. 211.

[209] Godly, of course, in Calvinist as opposed to Laudian terms. See ibid., pp. 68–9, 121, 180, 194, 234; Russell, 'Career of John Pym', pp. 155, 159ff., 165; Hill, *Antichrist*, pp. 65ff. The situation was not helped by Charles's tendency to draw attention to his own role in religious policy as in other matters; *CD1629*, pp. 31–2, 149. See also ibid., pp. 95–101; Sommerville, *Politics and ideology*, p. 219.

They wished to defend and maintain it as a shield against Laudian clericalism, but were apprehensive lest royal power be abused by an ungodly ruler.[210]

In the Commons there were different patterns of response involved in these changing perceptions of the king. Eliot, starting with a thoroughly classical view of evil counsel, developed an ultra-loyalist critique of events. He could not be convinced that the king was the guilty party, only that parliamentary advice should prevail over less desirable influences who were standing between Charles and the conciliar benefits of Parliament.[211] While Eliot subscribed to such views in their purest form, others extended them to express their own emerging fears. Phelips, Digges and Coryton were concerned with the way in which Charles had been thoroughly misguided; there was a need to go to the king and open his eyes. There was a danger that the innovators and subversives would cause the king to adopt tyranny.[212] Selden used the assumption of evil counsel in ruthless fashion, as a legal weapon to justify vigorous action by the high court of Parliament.[213]

A real distinction can be drawn, however, between the lines of thought followed by Eliot (and to a lesser extent Selden) on the one hand and what can be discerned of the thinking of Pym and Rich on the other. Pym's deepening suspicion of Charles, shared to a degree by Rich, contrasts sharply with the importance attached to evil counsel by their tactical opponents. Eliot's manner of thinking freed him to adopt an attacking policy and enabled him to take the bulk of the Commons with him. Pym, however, was grappling with the real problem of the era: the king. He understood the constitutional paradox emerging under Charles. To attack royal servants was, traditionally, a means of protecting the political integrity of the monarch. To attack Charles's servants – Buckingham, the Arminians, Weston and the customers – was, however, to attack the king himself for, as he afterwards stated publicly, he chose to protect them.[214] Here lies the key to understanding the last days of the Parliament. Pym and Rich thus sought to avoid such attacks, seeking a settlement which would be based on a programme for reform,

---

[210] Nethersole wrote to the queen of Bohemia of 'this matter which some of them study hard out of an apprehension of the danger our religion may be in by this vast power increased to our kings, if God for answer should send us one of a contrary religion or if it be but by preferring of Arminians now'; *CD1629*, pp. 248–9; see also ibid., pp. 35ff., 131.

[211] *CD1628*, iv, pp. 128–9; *CD1629*, pp. 25–8, 32, 52, 77, 94, 112–13, 132–3, 140–2, 155, 157–8, 224; Hulme, *Life of Sir John Eliot*, pp. 370–2. Littleton's thinking was very much in this vein, *CD1629*, pp. 189, 235.

[212] *CD1629*, pp. 62, 142, 198, 200–1, 205; Russell, *Parliaments*, p. 412; and see Sherland's statement that evil counsellors cast loyal subjects in the role of opponents of the king, *CD1629*, pp. 15–16.

[213] *CD1629*, pp. 136, 143, 145, 223, 226, 232. See also R. Tuck, ' "The ancient law of freedom": John Selden and the civil war', in J. S. Morrill (ed.), *Reactions to the English civil war 1642–1649* (London, 1982), pp. 139–42.

[214] In his declaration of 10 March 1629; Gardiner, *Constitutional documents*, p. 98.

rather than the punishment of individual offenders. This was, constitutionally, a far more disturbing view, implying the need to settle or work
compromise with Charles over fundamental questions. It was an attitude
derived from an intensely religious motivation, which tended to interpret
threats as signals of overwhelming danger and which led directly to disapproval of Charles as an initiator of religious change. The desire for direct
settlement as opposed to indirect attack was the concomitant of grave ideological suspicion. The way in which Pym and Rich meant business in 1629
rendered their views more fundamentally revolutionary in the longer term,
given Charles's title to the kingdom and his intransigence. The assumption of
evil counsel which gave meaning to Eliot's resolutions belongs to a different
world from the speculations of Pym and his associates.[215] Eliot was,
inadvertently, breaking mental barriers in 1629, but the ground he staked out
was essentially that of a frustrated royal servant who protested too much.
Pym would come to believe that Charles was no longer responsible for his
actions, a monarch who prompted consideration of precedents of royal
senility and madness[216] and who justified clandestine and subversive political
activity to work a wholesale reform of Church and state. It is reasonable to
believe that Pym's views found a reception in the Providence Island Company
(see pp. 210–13, below), particularly given the membership of Clare, Saye
and Warwick. The divided leadership of the House of Commons in 1629 thus
had a shifting ideological foundation of great consequence for the development of political life under Charles.[217]

By the end of the 1629 parliamentary session, there was overwhelming
evidence to warrant the deepest suspicion of Charles among established
Protestant and parliamentary interests in England. A series of developments
pointed to the date of his accession as a crucial political and religious turning
point. In 1625 the young king had pardoned a Jesuit.[218] In 1626 he had dissolved his second Parliament to save Buckingham. In 1626 and 1627 he had
levied a forced loan and opposed the resummoning of Parliament. In 1628 it
was revealed that he had approved of an attempt to pervert the legal record
so as to fabricate a precedent for prerogative imprisonment unqualified in
any way. He had then appealed in Parliament to divine authority for his
kingship in contradiction of the established rule of law; he had rejected the

---

[215] On Eliot's political thinking see Sommerville, *Politics and ideology*, p. 158; J. H. M.
Salmon, *The French religious wars in English political thought* (Oxford, 1959, repr. 1981),
pp. 62–3.
[216] Morrill (ed.), *Reactions to the English civil war*, Introduction, pp. 6–7; Morrill, 'Religious
context', p. 171 and n.
[217] *CD1629*, pp. 85, 186, 223, 232, 236, 240, 242; Thompson, 'Divided leadership', pp. 280–1;
CSPD 1628–9, p. 198; Russell, *Parliaments*, p. 424; Russell, 'Career of John Pym', pp.
159ff.; Hibbard, *Popish plot*, p. 32.
[218] Russell, *Parliaments*, pp. 239–40 and n.

Commons' remonstrance and again protected Buckingham; and he had accepted responsibility for the investigation of the customs rates. In 1629 it had been revealed that he had subverted the parliamentary order for the proper printing and dissemination of the Petition of Right. He had protected the customs officers from proceedings initiated against them in the Commons. It was also clear that he was sanctioning the rise of English Arminianism and the countenancing of popery. He was, moreover, exploring the possibility of peace with Spain. Buckingham's death had not altered religious policy, brought about the steady prosecution of the war, nor led to an agreement between Charles and his people in Parliament. The dissolution of the Parliament was a fearful event which reinforced the growing public perception of the king as a promoter of the interests represented by Weston and by Laud.

Contarini wrote during February and March of the strong mutual distrust and animosity he considered to exist between Charles and his people (by which Contarini meant the parliamentary classes).[219] And during these same weeks Ben Jonson, composing an epigram to mark the anniversary of Charles's accession, felt forced to allude to the estrangement of his subjects from their king. Choosing as his theme the notion that Charles had been sadly misunderstood, he nevertheless acknowledged:

> 'Tis not alone the Merchant, but the Clowne,
>   Is Banke-rupt turn'd! the Cassock, Cloake and Gowne,
> Are lost upon accompt! . . . [220]

Jonson was describing a widespread lack of respect for Charles among critical sections of English political society. It was this lack of respect, in the form of a lack of trust, which tended to undermine a spirit of co-operation in Parliament. Pym was not alone in his attitude towards the king. The savagely critical assessment of Charles's rule which he would record in the Grand Remonstrance (1641) was based upon a decade of increasing alienation and mutually opposing conspiracy. But it had its roots in the failure and disillusionment of 1629.[221]

In terms of a new politics, certain developments thus stand out as critical features of the 1629 session. Charles's public standing was gravely impaired. Buckingham's dire financial and strategic legacy had combined with a fundamental conflict over religion to produce a constitutional breakdown.

---

[219] *CSPV 1628–9*, pp. 557–8, 566, 580–1; Cust, 'News and politics', pp. 75, 83–5.
[220] Charles acceded to the throne on 27 March 1625. See B. H. Newdigate (ed.), *The poems of Ben Jonson* (Oxford, 1936), pp. 173–4. I am grateful to Judith Richards for drawing my attention to this poem.
[221] A. Fletcher, *The outbreak of the English civil war* (London, 1981), p. 82; Russell, 'Career of John Pym', pp. 159ff., 165; Gardiner, *Constitutional documents*, pp. 202ff.; Clarendon, *Rebellion*, vol. i, p. 3; Hibbard, *Popish plot*, pp. 214–16.

This breakdown implied the collapse of an effective English foreign policy in a Europe at war. The climax of the session suggested a resort to subversive conspiratorial dissent among those who found themselves and their views increasingly excluded by the inner circle of the court.[222] Such political polarization was accompanied by the development of conspiracy theories. Within the government and outside it, such theories were built upon an initial foundation of fact. Weston and the Arminians, for example, had an interest in breaking the Parliament, and the Eliot group were promoting constitutional conflict and opposition. Factual beginnings like these would continue to inspire extended fears, amongst Charles, his trusted advisers and their opponents.[223]

The religious conflict underlying the session provides the most spectacular example of a fundamental and devastating consequence of Charles's rule: the discrediting of the liberal interpretation of broad traditions in national life. This essential process can be seen as the catalyst stimulating all the political changes charted in this book. In levying a forced loan against the principle of parliamentary supply and in abusing the traditional right of prerogative imprisonment, Charles had provoked rejection of such methods of rule, which were not without precedent, as being alien to England. Men were seeking to describe constitutional conflict while preserving the notion of an ideal system. In the same way, English Arminianism, which had its Jacobean antecedents, adopted a persecuting attitude towards established Calvinism and generated xenophobic hostility. This is the significance of the Laudian redefinition of puritanism, which infuriated conventional English Protestants.[224] What had been a marginal interest in Jacobean religious life was attempting to dominate the Caroline Church. In so doing it brought about a hardening of attitudes and inspired a reaction which came to take on an intellectual and political life of its own. In this way the redefinition of puritanism, which implied that Calvinism was subversive, tended to become a self-fulfilling prophecy.

In addition, the atmosphere of conflict which prevailed during the session encouraged tendencies in political debate which are worthy of note. One was the belief that subversive forces – Calvinism, Arminianism and popery – were international forces. This reflected the truism that developments in England were part of a wider European scene. But it was also a means of discrediting opposing forces as foreign to England and therefore *ipso facto* as illegitimate. Like the accusation of religious change made in the Commons in 1629, the

---

[222] Trevor-Roper, *Archbishop Laud*, p. 103, for more on this subject see chapter 6, below.
[223] For more on this subject see chapter 4, below.
[224] *CD1629*, pp. 140, 178; see also Sir Miles Fleetwood's labelling of the Arminians as sectaries; ibid., p. 193.

associated sense of a godly commonwealth was a way of dealing with an anti-Calvinism which became increasingly native with each passing year. Similarly, the Laudian appeal to English ecclesiastical tradition went hand in hand with opposition to the reality of international Calvinism.[225] Moreover, ideological and particularly religious conflict, especially when pursued with the assumption that consensus and unity were the ideal, led increasingly to accusations of insincerity of belief. It was commonly held at court that critics of Charles's policies were using the language of public interest to disguise their private ends. In Parliament those who attacked the rise of Arminianism made clear that they viewed the Laudian clerics as time-servers: men who tailored their theology to obtain promotion.[226] Such interpretations were certainly oversimplified. Eliot's belief in evil counsel, for example, remains a classic example of the way in which ideology can be bound together with personal interest. But the accusation of self-interest remained a natural concomitant of ideological conflict within the traditional context of political thought.

[225] English (and Catholic Gallican) criticism of international Calvinist practice and thought has earlier, late-sixteenth-century, roots. I am grateful to John Salmon for this point. See also J. H. M. Salmon, *Renaissance and revolt. Essays in the intellectual and social history of early modern France* (Cambridge, 1987), pp. 175–6.

[226] SP16/123/8; *CD1628*, iv, p. 313; *LD1628*, p. 636; *CD1629*, p. 15; Reeve, 'Sir Thomas Roe's prophecy', p. 120; see also SP16/117/83.

4

The aftermath

Sir Thomas Barrington, writing to his mother, captured the threatening atmosphere overhanging the end of Charles's third Parliament. No man knew what to do, he wrote, 'the distraction was so sudden and so great . . . '[1] Barrington hinted at the possibility of bloodshed which he seems to have feared as the likely outcome of the events of 2 March. He concluded: 'he whose heart bleeds not at the threat of these times is too stupid. I pray God send us better grounds of comfort, and with all to be armed for the worst that can befall us . . . '[2] The imprisonment[3] of those who had staged the demonstration in the House of Commons[4] was part of Charles's response to what was, from a royal point of view, an extremely threatening situation.[5] Contarini wrote on 6 March:

Parliament is dissolved in anger, and without deciding anything . . . The present times were not suited to disputes of this sort . . . The courtiers are very disconsolate, fore-seeing that they will remain a long time in need, without money, as they have been for many months. The kingdom is furious against the Treasurer, and bears the king very little love . . . It is bad news for Italy, and the king of Denmark also will be compelled to do what he does not wish . . . What matters is that Parliament has retained the full possession of its privileges without yielding a jot, for on the last two occasions the king has always yielded something. If he returns again he will have to do the same, and if

---

[1] Searle, *Barrington family letters*, pp. 59–60.
[2] Ibid., p. 60. See also Birch, ii, p. 12.
[3] Coryton and Hayman, although released soon after their incarceration, were still subject to the Star Chamber information filed by Heath in May; SP16/142/36; and see p. 121, below. See also *APC 1628–9*, pp. 351–2, 389; *ST*, iii, cols. 236, 252, 285; Gardiner, *History*, vii, p. 80; *DNB*, s.v. Hobart, Sir Miles; T. Rymer and R. Sanderson (eds.), *Foedera* (20 vols., 1704–32), xix, pp. 63–4; *CSPD 1628–9*, p. 540.
[4] On the story of their case and the proceedings against them see chapter 5, below.
[5] It was also part of a tradition of political imprisonment, stretching back into Tudor times, which reached very striking proportions in the 1620s. See L. J. Reeve, 'The arguments in King's Bench in 1629 concerning the imprisonment of John Selden and other members of the House of Commons', *JBS*, xxv, 3 (July 1986), p. 265, n. 10.

he does not, which many believe to be his determination in order not to lose his crown, it will be a difficult matter to find money.[6]

The Venetian had painted a portrait of events most serious in its implications. Clarendon, in looking back over this era, was to describe the same developments in almost mysterious terms. Recounting the largely unsuccessful history of the first three Caroline Parliaments, he concluded: 'in a very short time after that supply granted, that Parliament was likewise, with strange circumstances of passion on all sides, dissolved'.[7]

What were the immediate elements of this strange and grave situation created by the collapse of the parliamentary session? Eliot, by his words and actions in the Commons, had accused royal counsellors of treason and had come to threaten the very authority of the crown. He had also begun to undermine the financial foundations of the state. The immediate consequence of the events of 2 March was a widespread refusal to pay customs duties and therefore a stoppage of trade. The customs constituted the largest single element of the royal income. Moreover, the tax-strike came at a time of desperate royal financial need. War naturally caused a reduction of trade (and therefore of revenue) while placing a greater burden upon the government's financial resources. The state of the English Exchequer was, as we have seen, particularly dire at this time. For some weeks the English merchant community, together with the Dutch merchants in London, refused to trade.[8] A deputation from the company of Merchant Adventurers, which effectively controlled the cloth trade, was summoned before Council. When questioned they cited the protestation (or Three Resolutions) of the Commons which they believed to have been voted by the House. To their understanding, the Commons had resolved that any who paid the duties when collected without parliamentary consent were betrayers of the liberties of England.[9] The company subsequently decided to continue their boycott. The Dutch merchants were similarly reluctant to transgress English constitutional practice.[10] Clearly the commercial community was afraid of retaliatory action by any future Parliament. Few or none were prepared to pay the duties and those who did so employed other men's names rather than their own.[11] By refusing

---

[6] *CSPV 1628–9*, pp. 580–1, the two occasions presumably being the Petition of Right and Charles's acknowledgement in 1629 that tonnage and poundage was the free gift of his subjects.

[7] Clarendon, *Rebellion*, vol. i, p. 6.

[8] Fresh disturbances had occurred over the payment of tonnage and poundage before the 1629 parliamentary session; Gardiner, *History*, vii, p. 28; Birch, ii, pp. 5–6; see also *CSPV 1629–32*, pp. 7–8, 19, 29; *CSPD 1628–9*, pp. 506, 524; Reeve, 'Viscount Dorchester', pp. 135–6.

[9] Bodl. Lib., Tanner Ms 71, fos. 1r–2r.   [10] Gardiner, *History*, vii, p. 83.

[11] *CSPD 1628–9*, p. 524. The merchants of Colchester, in refusing to pay the duties, would only agree to pay what would be agreed upon by the king and any future Parliament, *APC*

to go about their business, the bulk of the merchants could circumvent a Council order for the imprisonment of importers and exporters who denied the king the customs.[12] Charles considered dissolving the recalcitrant trading companies and replacing the Merchant Adventurers with a co-operative body of nobility.[13] The stoppage, however, continued until mid-May, when the prospect of significant losses encouraged the resumption of the cloth trade.[14] In the same month the merchant Chambers was heavily fined by the Court of Star Chamber and imprisoned until he acknowledged the offensive nature of his statement to Council.[15]

While the merchants were striking a blow at the crown's financial stability, they were not the only group to challenge the royal authority. William Lake, writing to Sir Henry Vane, observed that an ill spirit of obstinacy was motivating the merchants but also moving through every small vein of the kingdom.[16] Sir Robert Heath wrote to the earl of Carlisle of the need to inflict exemplary punishment upon the parliamentary demonstrators, 'that the ages yet to come may be warned by their folly . . . ' He continued:

whilst the vulgar part of this our little world . . . are endeavoured to be made diffident of his majesty's religious and just government, they may find how much they have been abused, with these ill-suggested fears and jealousies . . . when the good people of the land shall clearly discern how much they have been dazzled with misgrounded reports, they will both stand the firmer in their due obedience . . . and condemn those who would have misled them.[17]

Heath had credited Eliot and his companions with initiating a general tide of political subversion. Likewise Captain William Douglas wrote to Carlisle that the ending of the Parliament had encouraged 'strange conjectures':

That these seeds may mature to bear dangerous fruit if peace, plenty, letters, in heat (the form and essence of anarchy) lose allegiance from the bond of reverence. Sovereignty is not well assured . . . where power is in continual possibility of breaking the tie of obedience and multitude pretends will for reason . . . The possibility of

1628–9, pp. 378–9. Ashton (*City and the court*, p. 130) argues for the existence of a new political alliance between the chartered companies and the parliamentary leadership during the early Caroline period. The House of Commons was apparently well representative of the outport traders; B. Supple, *Commercial crisis and change in England, 1600–1642* (Cambridge, 1959), p. 231 and n. Yet there were stronger economic reasons for the merchant community to disavow political action in support of the Commons. In 1629 such action – promoted more by fear of, rather than solidarity with, Parliament – was abandoned to curtail financial loss. There was, moreover, a gulf of interest separating the merchants from Pym and the alternative leaders of the Commons. Their war strategy implied damage to trade as well as alliance with the Dutch, the *bête noire* of the English merchant community.

[12] Gardiner, *History*, vii, p. 82.
[13] Ashton, *City and the court*, p. 132; Gardiner, *History*, vii, p. 83; Supple, *Commercial crisis*, p. 113.
[14] *CSPD 1628–9*, p. 550; Supple, *Commercial crisis*, pp. 113–14.
[15] Gardiner, *History*, vii, pp. 84–6; *ST*, iii, cols. 373ff.
[16] *CSPD 1628–9*, p. 524.   [17] SP16/138/45, 7 March 1629.

growth of popular authority may be a just object of his majesty's preventing care . . . the many circumstances of it are . . . just not to be written.[18]

Douglas had voiced the fear of 'popularity' customarily felt in the upper reaches of early Stuart society.[19] He had allowed himself to envisage the dissolution of political society in England. Yet significantly, like Heath, he had diagnosed a serious threat to the sovereign power of the crown, and traced it to what had earlier transpired in Parliament. He had endorsed Heath's belief in the workings of a conspiracy.

Such a belief was doubtless amplified by fear but also had a basis in fact. In addition to the tax-strike by the merchants, the situation in the West Country was becoming highly charged. Public support for Eliot caused a dangerous situation in places and threats to public order. Sir Barnard Grenville considered this mood directly related to the events of the parliamentary session.[20] It is difficult to ascertain to what extent such incidents were isolated ones, but there can be no doubt that these problems were real and could increase. Here, moreover, the same pattern is suggested of a conspiracy of disobedience rooted in Parliament. The parliamentary sessions of 1628–9 had seen the development of ideas concerning court conspiracy. The idea of a project, within the government, for the subversion of the English commonwealth by innovation had gained increasing currency. (As will be seen, Charles's government was sensitive to accusations of innovation and of new counsels.)[21] Eventually, in the aftermath of the Parliament, conspiracy theory of parliamentary activity was developed at court. The serious and general fears for the crown which surrounded the dissolution were thus, increasingly, mutually opposing fears.[22] In a political society which conceived of itself in terms of perfect harmony, there was a tendency to characterize unwanted conflict or dissent as illegitimate conspiracy.[23] Yet the ideas of conspiracy developed during and after Charles's third Parliament were not simply the hackneyed motifs of political discussion. On the contrary, interacting with political reality and with each other, they became individual historical forces of themselves.

With the events of 2 March and the conclusion of the Parliament, an official interpretation of its destruction quickly emerged. This interpretation

---

[18] SP16/530/39, 16 April 1629.   [19] Cust, *The forced loan*, pp. 18–20.

[20] SP16/147/14, Grenville to Sir James Bagg, 19 July 1629. The letter is quoted at length in chapter 5, p. 130, below.

[21] See Heath's interrogatories for Eliot (SP16/139/6, no. 35), Abbot's archiepiscopal letter of April 1629 (*CSPD 1628–9*, pp. 516–17), and chapter 5, below.

[22] See also Russell, 'Career of John Pym', pp. 164–5.

[23] Hibbard, *Popish plot*, pp. 235–6. See also Parker, *Thirty Years War*, pp. 47–8; P. Zagorin, *The court and the country* (London, 1969), pp. 80–3.

reflected the views of Charles and his ministers and was a reaction to Eliot's resort to conspiratorial dissent. The royal proclamation which was published on 4 March[24] gave the first indication of Charles's view of what had transpired:

> By the malevolent dispositions of some ill-affected persons of the House of Commons, we have had sundry just causes of offence . . . Yet we resolved with patience to try the uttermost which we the rather did, for that we found in that house a great number of sober and grave persons, well affected to religious government, and desirous to preserve unity and peace in all parts of our kingdom . . . It hath so happened by the disobedient and seditious carriage of these said ill-affected persons of the House of Commons, that we, and our regal authority and commandment, have been so highly condemned, as our kingly office cannot bear, nor any former age can parallel. And therefore it is our . . . resolution, to dissolve the same Parliament . . . Nevertheless, we will that they, and all others should take notice that we do, and ever will distinguish between those who have showed good affection to religion and government, and those who have given themselves over to faction, and to work disturbance to the peace and good order of our kingdom.[25]

This statement reflected Charles's sense of injury as well as his belief that Eliot had mounted a conspiracy against him. Charles's sense of threat, combined with an unctuous rectitude, was always a powerful guiding influence upon him. The king, and officially the crown, had understood the events in the Commons as unprecedentedly offensive and a threat to the peace and obedience of the realm. Such events had been perpetrated by those ill-affected to the government rather than those who were loyal. This was an exercise in public information, suggesting that it was not the whole house that was disenchanted and in opposition to the regime. It was also an attempt to induce members of the house to loyalty in the future, and to appear as if they had been loyal, with a scarcely veiled threat. The label of faction was derogatory in early modern England and implied divisive and unconstructive self-interest. Charles, it seems, harboured a particular dislike of such division as an offence against the authority of monarchy. The thrust of the proclamation was the idea that in the Commons there were two distinct elements: the loyal and the disloyal.[26] In promoting this view the document sought to dispel the notion that criticism could be loyal, or justified. Despite what had been the king's considerable patience with an aggressive house, these were unrealistic assumptions. They ignored what had been the truth: the divisions

---

[24] *CSPV 1628–9*, p. 580.

[25] SP45/10/fo. 175r (printed in Larkin, *Stuart royal proclamations*, ii, pp. 223–4).

[26] This interpretation had been anticipated in a royal declaration of 1626 in which Charles gave an account of his first two Parliaments; see Cust, 'Charles I, the Privy Council, and the forced loan', p. 212. His public statements of 1629 were, however, more intense, reflecting his belief in the unprecedented nature of events. The later statements also developed the idea of a conspiracy to subvert obedience throughout the kingdom. See also Birch, ii, p. 13n.

in the Commons had not been primarily of this sort, of loyalty and disloyalty; rather, they had been ones of political priorities, and the Commons as a whole had resented the king's religious and financial policies.[27] It was for this reason that the proclamation had avoided defining the majority. It had appealed to the idea of a substantial and uncritical loyalist group in the Commons which had not really existed in 1629 in the way the crown wished to describe it. As an optimistic and virtually deliberate misapprehension at the time, this royalist tactic could only be effective when the ideological differences within the Commons were greater and the political stakes higher, and when the house as a whole could not be led to the belief that sustained and fundamental criticism of royal policy was best for the country. Things were not as they were to be in the autumn of 1641 and the Commons in 1629 were largely united. Yet the development of official conspiracy theory remained a response to a dangerous political initiative which, originating in Parliament out of personal and ideological frustration, threatened subversion and invited retaliation.

This was by no means Charles's final public statement on the fate of the Parliament. His insecurity, his fastidiousness and his highly developed moral sense caused him to make copious statements by way of justification and explanation at difficult times. This desire for public recognition of his righteousness, together with his concern for order, meant that Charles's statements tended to be very much influenced by those he had made before. Thus it is often possible, as in 1629, to trace the development of his thinking as he wished to make it known. On 10 March when Charles formally dissolved the Parliament with a speech to the House of Lords, he maintained his conspiracy theory of the session. The fault lay with a small number of 'vipers' in the Commons who had cast 'a mist of undutifulness' over the eyes of most of the members, 'yet . . . there was a good number there that could not be infected with this contagion'.[28] This was a significant elaboration on the theme by way of an admission that the majority of the Commons had supported Eliot. Charles repeated his accusation that the demonstration had been seditious. He also threw the activities of the Commons into greater relief by praising the dutiful carriage of the Lords. Charles was certainly aware that a number of peers were opposed to his government. It is also possible that he perceived their lack of sympathy with Eliot's tactics. While castigating the Commons he was also taking the opportunity to reach out for the support of the Lords.

On the day Parliament was actually dissolved, a royal declaration was published seeking to justify the king's action further. It announced his commitment to religion without innovation, the rule of law and the Petition of Right. Such commitments by Charles were always subject to his own interpretation.

---

[27] See chapter 3, above.   [28] *LJ*, iv, p. 43.

From what we know of his views concerning Arminianism and the Petition, this was less a statement of policy than a tactical response to the attacks which had been made on his government. The declaration continued the reference to a group in the Commons who had taken advantage of the times to sway the house and to stir up jealousy, fear and subversion. Their punishment, it was stated, would be reserved to a due time. Charles was leaving his political options open in dealing with popular men whose fate could well affect the course of another Parliament. Moreover, Charles's awareness that Eliot's action had been endorsed by the Commons caused him to extend his interpretation of their behaviour a good deal:

> We are not ignorant, how much that house hath of late years endeavoured to extend their privileges, by setting up general committees for religion, for courts of justice, for trade, and the like; a course never heard of until of late . . . to the unsufferable disturbance and scandal of justice and government, which having been tolerated a while by our father, and ourself, hath daily grown to more and more height . . . and some have not doubted to maintain that the resolutions of that house must bind the judges, a thing never heard of in ages past. But in this last assembly of Parliament, they have taken on them much more than ever before.

Charles considered that 'they turned the necessities grown by that war, to enforce us to yield to conditions incompatible with monarchy'.[29]

The king had come to accuse the entire House of Commons, as an institution, of serious constitutional misconduct. Moreover, his belief in a conspiracy by a group of individuals had been transformed into a belief in a wholesale conspiracy against the authority of monarchy. Charles had also pushed his accusation back in time, beyond the events of 1629, to the period of his father's reign. There was truth, as well as paranoia, in all this. The Parliaments of 1621 and 1624 had seen the most extensive efforts by the Commons to influence foreign policy.[30] In 1626 Charles had been forced to forfeit supply or sacrifice his favourite. In 1628 his power of prerogative imprisonment had been subjected to parliamentary debate and enforced redefinition. In 1629 the Commons had indulged in much committee activity reflecting upon the government.[31] This was in addition to their investigation of efforts to collect tonnage and poundage and to their opposition to the crown's religious policy. There can be no doubt that Charles's first three Parliaments, as a consequence of their concern with the character of his government, became unwittingly involved in constitutional aggression, and clearly the 1629 session had come to disturb the peace of the kingdom. Thus far Charles's declaration contained a measure of the truth.

Yet the king's interpretation remains highly questionable. Whether James's

---

[29] Rushworth, *Historical collections*, i, Appx, pp. 7, 10.
[30] See Adams, 'Foreign policy and the Parliaments of 1621 and 1624', passim.
[31] *CJ*, i, p. 920.

last two Parliaments necessarily prefigured the later and more serious events is dubious. Charles had made the inadvertent admission that he did not share his father's skills of management. Moreover, the Parliaments of the late 1620s can be seen as using financial leverage to insist upon the traditional parliamentary function of counsel. The royalist Clarendon considered that during this period Parliament was fulfilling its proper role. He saw Parliaments as experts in seeking out national diseases, in political pathology and cure.[32] The legislative and judicial pre-eminence of Parliament was long-established, and likewise the committee procedure.[33] Charles was particularly jealous of any reflection on what he saw as the sovereign power of the crown. He had written to the earl of Carlisle a year earlier that there could be 'no other condition equal to the sovereign point nor anything more sharply opposite to a monarchy than sovereignty in any particular'.[34] Above all, Charles's declaration, formulated in anger and characteristically simple, must be understood in the light of his prevailing sense of personal threat. His own belief in a conspiracy against him had grown in the face of a national crisis which was increasingly beyond his capacity to resolve. His overriding concern at this point was to convey the impression that he could not be intimidated. Any interpretation of the Parliaments of the 1620s in terms of a milestone along a high road leading to parliamentary power must accommodate the fact that, while this was Charles's view, subsequent assessments should not be unduly affected by his overdeveloped fears.[35]

There were, among Charles's advisers, men disgusted with proceedings in the Commons but who did not consider the constitutional breakdown to be irreparable. Dorchester, as Secretary of State, became in early 1629 an important advocate of the resummoning of Parliament and the continuation of the Spanish war. With the king he drafted a crucial proclamation of 27 March which outlined the official future policy of the crown towards Parliament. Dorchester, assisted by his friend Roe, strove to counteract the increasing influence of Weston and of Laud. An investigation of Dorchester's thinking sheds light on the development of policy at this point.

---

[32] Clarendon, *Rebellion*, vol. i, p. 10.
[33] On parliamentary power see Elton, *Tudor constitution*, pp. 233ff. In pointing to claims for the judicial pre-eminence of the Commons, Charles was probably overreacting to the school of thought represented by Sir Edward Coke's statement in 1628 that no judge ever contradicted a resolution of both houses of Parliament; see *CD1628*, iii, p. 628. No doubt the king was also mindful of the Commons' efforts in 1629 to recover John Rolle's goods, seized (pursuant upon the Exchequer decision) for failing to pay tonnage and poundage although he was a member of Parliament. See Thompson, 'Divided leadership', pp. 248, 266 and passim.
[34] BL, Harl. Ms 1584, fos. 173r–174v.
[35] Gardiner (*History*, vii, pp. 78–9), in taking the declaration at face value, as evidence that the Commons were tending to seize upon sovereign power, was moved to one of his digressions on his constitutional theme.

Direct experience of the religious conflict in the United Provinces and observation of the opening decade of the Thirty Years War had encouraged in Dorchester certain beliefs about the state and political life. He considered that the state should maintain strength and unity, lest it fall victim to internal weaknesses and external enemies. The healthy political society, he believed, had its foundations in the authority of a single sovereign power, religious conformity and the unity of Church and state. The subversion of these foundations, by division and dissent, violated historically established rules of government and precipitated political and social breakdown. Dorchester had expounded these views in an address to the States General of the United Provinces in 1617 in which he had criticized Arminian influence in the republic. Dorchester also believed that in the international arena true religion formed the basis of the common cause. That common cause was one of mutual defence against the common enemy: Spain, the Habsburgs and the Counter-Reformation. This enemy alliance would prey upon the weaknesses, particularly the internal divisions, of other nations. In 1617 Dorchester had warned the Dutch against 'le schisme dans l'église et la faction dans l'état'.[36] A decade later, with the enemy at the gates, he feared they would succumb to 'faction and division in the country, at which breach the enemy will be watchful to enter'.[37] Thus might internal and external enemies become one in what Dorchester once described as 'a crisis of great mutations in Europe'.[38] While these were sophisticated views, they paralleled the thinking in the Commons during the 1628 remonstrance debate, with its emphasis on Arminianism as the subversive fifth column of Spain and of Rome. Dorchester had an essentially traditional view of the English constitution. He considered that Parliament had a right to investigate government but that it should use moderation in defining the balance between the prerogative and the liberty of the subject. He believed the sovereign power of monarchy to be the most important element in the constitution and that the king had a clear right to exercise his prerogative in the interests of the state. To Dorchester the English system depended upon harmony and balance, as well as upon ultimate respect for the authority of the king.[39]

Dorchester's correspondence in March 1629 reflects the interaction of his view of the parliamentary session, and of his desire to continue the war, with the attitude of the king. The collapse of the Parliament had been a disaster for Denmark after Charles and Dorchester had held out hopes to Christian. Dorchester wrote to General Morgan that no additional money would be

[36] Reeve, 'Viscount Dorchester', p. 13. See also pp. 11, 12, 14.
[37] SP84/140/fo. 93v, Dorchester to Dudley Carleton, 14 Oct. 1629.
[38] SP84/111/fo. 92, Carleton (later Dorchester) to Calvert, 5 Feb. 1622.
[39] Reeve, 'Viscount Dorchester', pp. 13–14.

forthcoming,

till means may be found for a more real supply and assistance of the king of Denmark. A work which upon the unhappy rupture of our Parliament (whereby his majesty's affairs are mightily put out of square) cannot so well be effected as was hoped and were to be wished. But his majesty is so careful of the general good, and the king of Denmark's preservation in particular, [that] it is the end whereof his endeavours do tend . . . [40]

Neither Charles nor Dorchester wanted Christian to make a disadvantageous peace with the emperor. Dorchester wrote to the English ambassador with Denmark that Morgan's force would be maintained and ships sent to the Elbe, but that patience was required in awaiting further assistance from England. The Secretary issued a repeated plea for time: 'you are to represent to that king his majesty's constant resolution to enlarge himself as soon as he shall have rectified these accidental disorders in his government at home . . .'[41]

Dorchester was in agreement with Charles's reaction to events and described the disorders as the work of a group of individuals, who should be punished:

the hopes which were built upon the good success of [the] Parliament are already come to nothing by the disobedient and seditious carriage of some disaffected persons in the House of Commons, which hath enforced his majesty to show his royal authority whereby to free it from contempt, and make them suffer for their presumption.[42]

Moreover, the disaster of the Parliament had caused the government (inspired by Weston) to investigate avenues of non-parliamentary financial supply. As Dorchester wrote, Charles had been forced 'to think of other ways to relieve his wants and necessities; which being so great as every man knows there will the more time be required to find the means how to rectify these distractions . . .'[43] The need for supply was linked to the desire for reform and the restoration of order. Since the king, wrote Dorchester, was 'very solicitous of what may conduce to a better settle[ment] in the manner of his government, it is to be hoped that notwithstanding this unexpected event of this last Parliament, God will bless his counsels and actions . . .' Dorchester forwarded to Anstruther a copy of the king's declaration dissolving the Parliament, 'whereof you will easily discern how desirous his majesty was of the continuance thereof, and how loath to separate the same'.[44] For Dorchester the resummoning of Parliament was the ideal financial solution.

[40] SP84/139/fo. 75r.
[41] SP75/10/fo. 139r–v. See also SP75/10/fo. 119r–v; SP84/139/fos. 149r–150v.
[42] SP75/10/fo. 119r, Dorchester to Anstruther, March 1629.
[43] SP16/139/46; Alexander, *Charles I's Lord Treasurer*, pp. 145–6, 158.
[44] SP16/139/46.

Neither had Charles abandoned all hope of repairing the constitutional breach.[45]

Dorchester's political views were intrinsically involved in the formulation of policy during these weeks. His suspicion of internal enemies (particularly in time of war) and jealousy of civil order were naturally aggravated by the behaviour of the recalcitrants. Yet his religious views would have coincided with the sentiments of the Commons and their opposition to Arminianism and popery. Likewise his belief that Parliament was the correct means by which the king might govern in consultation with his people would have allowed sympathy with concern for parliamentary counsel and privilege. He was in a position to understand that Parliament should not be dispensed with and his statements, and doubtless his counsel to Charles, echoed this belief. Yet it remained the king's prerogative to call and dissolve Parliament, as it was, Dorchester believed, to levy tonnage and poundage.[46] Subsidies were necessary but not at any price. The privilege of the many could be withheld because of the actions of a few; and the actions of the Commons' leaders had been self-defeating. It was as if Eliot had not heeded Dorchester's warning in 1626 concerning the prerogative and the life of Parliament, despite his suspicion of new counsels. Eliot's activities, and those of his associates, had precipitated a situation in which the desire for reform surrounding the death of Buckingham was thought to be an even more serious need in the face of a major threat to the royal authority. From the point of view of the king and those about him, the disastrous conclusion of the session had focused attention on the absolute necessity for financial supply as well as on the rectitude of the royal prerogative.

The royal proclamation published on 27 March was entitled 'A proclamation for the suppression of false rumours touching Parliament'.[47] This important document would eventually inspire a disapproving reference in the Grand Remonstrance.[48] The proclamation was drafted by Dorchester and the draft survives in his hand.[49] It would have been produced in consultation with, and finally approved by, the king. The alterations in Dorchester's manuscript reflect this process and the printed copy confirms the final version. The document thus gives an insight into the development of official policy. Charles's issuing of the proclamation seems to have been inspired by

---

[45] SP75/10/fos. 73r–74r, Sir John Coke to Anstruther, 5 March 1629, stating that the dissolution was an interim measure to punish the offenders, and that when Parliament met again the loyal element would conform to the king's desires.

[46] SP84/139/fos. 98r–99v. Dorchester had helped to administer the forced loan in 1627 but he much preferred the parliamentary grant of 1628 as a means of supply; Reeve, 'Viscount Dorchester', p. 20.

[47] SP45/10/fos. 178–9 (printed in Larkin, *Stuart royal proclamations*, ii, pp. 226–8).

[48] Gardiner, *Constitutional documents*, p. 210.   [49] SP16/530/23.

his anger at Eliot's influence in the wake of the Parliament. Not only was the stoppage of trade continuing, but members of the peerage were visiting Eliot in the Tower.[50] Two basic themes ran in counterpoint in the text of the proclamation. There was Charles's indignation and his accompanying sense of threat combined with Dorchester's desire to bring about the resumption of the parliamentary process without damaging the crown. It was necessary for Dorchester to exercise tact in seeking to moderate Charles's anger. Manchester, the Lord Privy Seal, and Coventry, the Lord Keeper, had already risked disfavour in counselling accommodation.[51]

The proclamation began by referring to the king's declaration of 10 March. Despite it,

some ill-disposed persons do spread false and pernicious rumours abroad, as if the scandalous and seditious proposition in the House of Commons made by an outlawed man desperate in mind and fortune, which was tumultuously taken up by some few, after . . . by our royal authority, we had commanded their adjournment, had been the vote of the whole house, whereas the contrary is the truth . . . [52]

The document then related how 'the wisest and best affected' in the Commons had at the time pointed to the evil nature of Eliot's resolutions. It also stated that those suspected to have voted for the resolutions had since, 'upon examination', disavowed them. This was a reference to the interrogation of the members who had been arrested.[53] The sum total was a contrived piece of propaganda seeking to disguise the fact that Eliot's motion had been carried on the voices. Thus the proclamation returned to the notion of a supposedly loyal element which had failed to support Eliot. This element considered the resolutions 'a thing of a most wicked and dangerous consequence to the good estate of this kingdom: which appeareth to be so, by those impressions this false rumour hath made in men's minds, whereby, out of causeless fears, the trade of the kingdom is disturbed . . . '[54] While not attempting to burden his subjects with new taxation, Charles, like his father, had a right to certain duties and intended to use them for the defence of the kingdom and for the aid of friends and allies.[55] This was clearly a tactical appeal to the Protestant cause in attempting to break down the tax strike. It also reflected Dorchester's real desire for a Protestant foreign policy. Not only would those who spread dangerous rumours be punished, but any who denied the king the duties would be disavowed as his subjects.[56] This proscription was a direct negation

---

[50] SP16/139/19.   [51] *CSPV 1629–32*, pp. 580, 589.

[52] SP45/10/fos. 178–9. The description of Eliot as 'desperate in mind and fortune' was a truthful identification of the elements working within him.

[53] On this see chapter 5, below.   [54] SP45/10/fos. 178–9.

[55] Ibid.

[56] SP45/10/fo. 179: 'but shall esteem them unworthy of our protection who shall deny the same' (the only words unique to the final printing).

of Eliot's third resolution, which condemned anyone paying tonnage and poundage when not granted by Parliament as an enemy to the liberties of England. The severity of this threat indicated the seriousness of events as understood by the government.

The proclamation also modified the official theory of conspiracy in a significant way. Having resurrected the notion that a group of disloyal individuals in the Commons could be distinguished from those who were loyal, the document juxtaposed this view with a further assertion of the sovereign power of monarchy over proceedings in Parliament:

And whereas for several ill ends, the calling again of a Parliament is divulged, howsoever we have showed by our frequent meetings with our people our love to the use of Parliaments . . . we shall account it presumption for any to prescribe any time unto us for Parliaments, the calling, continuing and dissolving of which is always in our own power . . . [57]

The document thus suggested a link which had developed in Charles's mind between the conspirators of 2 March and an attempt to substitute parliamentary for monarchical power. In seeking to isolate the instigators of the attempt to prevent the adjournment while pointing to a campaign for the augmentation of parliamentary power, the proclamation reflected the attitude of a king who had come to consider the assembly of his people in Parliament as a threat.

The proclamation concluded by defining the future policy of the crown towards Parliament. Dorchester's draft included the words, in referring to Parliament, 'more in so short a time of our reign than hath ever been formerly, yet the late abuse will now not suffering us to continue . . . ' These words were deleted and did not appear in the printing. Likewise Dorchester deleted the words 'to the summoning whereunto we shall be the more inclinable . . . when our people shall see more clearly into our intents and actions . . . ' These words appeared, however, in the printing, followed by: 'when such as have bred this interruption shall have received their condign punishment, and those who are misled by them, and [by] such ill reports as are raised upon this occasion, shall come to a better understanding of us and themselves'. Initially the document had stated that Charles had done with Parliaments. This sense was expunged, almost certainly at Dorchester's suggestion, to read finally: 'yet the late abuse having for the present driven us unwillingly out of that course, we shall account it presumption . . . ' and so on. The meaning that a Parliament might possibly occur in the right circumstances was retained. First, however, it was necessary for Charles's government to be understood, for the offenders to be punished and the conspiracy banished. Although the public atmosphere was as yet unpropitious, and while its implications were very serious, as far as the

[57] SP45/10/fos. 178–9.

king and his ministerial counsel were concerned, Parliament had not, officially, died a sudden death.[58]

One significant observer had not interpreted events in this light. Sir Thomas Roe had had a substantial stake in the outcome of the Parliament. The Council had approved of his plan for the re-arming of Denmark, contingent upon parliamentary supply. He was associated with Dorchester in pushing the war option at court. Roe, like Dorchester, was a loyal servant of Elizabeth of Bohemia, an enemy of Spain and the Habsburgs and a man of strong Calvinist faith.[59] He supported the strategy advocated by Pym and Rich in the Commons: that of 'sweetening' the king by confirming a grant of the customs in order to influence religious and foreign policy.[60] Roe saw the parliamentary session as a measure of England: 'All I will say is that we betray ourselves . . . '[61] He related to Lord Vere how the session had met with disaster. His analysis was influenced by his desire, in the face of all evidence, to keep faith in the king. After mentioning the strenuous efforts of the anti-parliamentary lobby at court he chose, like Charles, to place the greatest blame upon Eliot. Eliot was, to Roe, simply a jealous would-be courtier who had used the dispute over tonnage and poundage to revenge himself upon the government:

The zeal of the Commons was vented with more passion than wisdom. They ran ill ways to good ends, and so the envious man entered at our own breaches, and laid a bait to distemper them, which they too easily swallowed. Whereas, if they had at the first given the king the ancient benevolence, which all his ancestors had possessed, and so sweetened the first actions, they might have done what they pleased in the establishing of religion, and found a good prince to concur with them, and it was impossible for any man to have been so impudent, as to counsel a breach upon that point. But they were thrust upon a work that hath shipwrecked all, and by striving for a shadow of liberty, have lost the substance.[62]

Clearly Roe was overly optimistic about Charles's willingness to accommodate religious reform. Roe was seeking to reconcile his ideological preferences with the fact that he served a king from whom he differed in religious opinions.[63] Yet there was more involved here than his difficulty in believing in Charles. An acknowledgement of the king's susceptibility to bad

---

[58] SP16/530/23; SP45/10/fos. 178–9. The arguments for the forced loan, holding out the possibility of a future Parliament (Cust, 'Charles I, the Privy Council and the forced loan', p. 219) once the people's loyalty had been demonstrated by payment of the loan, form a contrast here. The proclamation of 27 March 1629 prescribed more difficult conditions for a resummons, reflecting the extent to which politics had become more complicated by this time and conflict more serious.

[59] SP95/3/fo. 51r; Reeve, 'Viscount Dorchester', p. 10.

[60] Reeve, 'Sir Thomas Roe's prophecy', p. 120.   [61] Ibid.   [62] Ibid.

[63] It is clear in his correspondence with Elizabeth of Bohemia how his desire to believe in the king was marked by an anxiety about Charles's policies at home and abroad; SP81/35/fos. 143r–144r, 160r–v.

counsel would have amounted to an indictment of Roe himself. There was no denying that the dissolution of the Parliament was a major victory for the Treasurer and for Laud. Yet Roe wanted no such reflection upon himself or those in the government who shared his views. Thus, while sympathizing with the movement for reform, he saw Eliot's action as the key to the session's demise. Finally, on the basis of his analysis, Roe made (as he said 'fearfully') an alarming conclusion: 'that not only all mouths are stopped, but the Parliament doors sealed for many years . . . '[64] With considerable perspicacity he had predicted the political style of the next decade: a prediction with which he was not at all at ease. He related to Vere how their hopes of ready money for the war had been dashed.[65]

The following day Roe wrote to Elizabeth of Bohemia. He described the destructive constitutional conflict in England, and again refrained from blaming the king – his master and Elizabeth's brother:

Those that have ambitiously stretched the string of prerogative have weakened it: and those that have contumaciously struggled for more than just liberty have betrayed it. These extremes have been our diseases. I pray God cure them before they be mortal.[66]

He kept his pessimism about the future and his despair of England, telling Elizabeth, 'if there be an America I can live'.[67] Roe sympathized with the Commons and regretted what he saw as the extinction of freedom of speech. Yet he believed in the justice of the king's reaction. It was essentially this belief which informed his foretelling of an indefinite period of non-parliamentary government.[68] Roe, however, had made no mention of a decision, publicly announced or privately intimated, that it would be so. His was an informed deduction, not in accord with official statements, which happened to be borne out by subsequent events.

Dorchester was an important source of political information for Roe. It was he who encouraged Roe to promote the idea of a northern alliance and who assisted him in doing so. In the summer of 1629 Roe left England on a mission to the courts of northern Europe. Its aim was to bring about peace between Poland and Sweden, to test the proposed alliance and to explain Charles's policies. It was Dorchester who signed his instructions and to whom he reported while abroad.[69] Jointly responsible for a foreign initiative intimately related to politics at home, it was practically certain that these men would discuss English affairs. The evidence of Roe's letter to Vere indicates that they did so.[70] Both Dorchester and Roe had had high hopes of the parlia-

---

[64] Reeve, 'Sir Thomas Roe's prophecy', p. 121.
[65] Ibid.   [66] SP81/35/fo. 160r–v.   [67] Ibid.
[68] Reeve, 'Sir Thomas Roe's prophecy', p. 121.
[69] SP75/10/fos. 164r–165r; SP88/5/fos. 42r–48r; SP88/5–8 passim.
[70] Reeve, 'Sir Thomas Roe's prophecy', p. 119.

mentary session, deplored the events in the Commons, believed that Eliot's supporters should have been more loyal, considered the king's position and the dissolution fully justified and felt strongly the need for another Parliament. Yet while Roe had envisaged a lengthy and indefinite period of non-parliamentary government, Dorchester had drafted a public statement deliberately avoiding this implication, and his correspondence indicated his desire that government resume its normal course.

What can account for the difference between the Dorchester and Roe views of the future, given their common interpretation of events and close association? Within Roe's analysis there was a distinction between what he believed would be the case and what he wished to happen. His was a fearful conclusion which he believed not best for the country. But, after discussion with Dorchester and others, he had taken a broader view and placed it in a longer term. By virtue of perceptive observation as well as his belief in the justice of the king's reaction, Roe had foreseen what could become a link between the government's desire to reform itself and to vindicate the royal authority generally and Charles's rejection of parliamentary means in response to the Commons' behaviour in 1629.[71] This potential association of a reform in government and non-parliamentary government had no real historical precedent in England. Neither was it inevitable. There is no evidence of a decision in 1629 by the king or his ministers to govern England without Parliament. Rather, the evidence suggests the flexibility of policy at this time and the complexity of the circumstances, in England and in Europe, amid which it was formulated. Roe's observations are significant as much for their insights as for the remarkable veracity of their conclusion. While Roe was at liberty to formulate the reflective views of a waiting ambassador, he was not involved, as was Dorchester, in the daily process of government and counsel. This, and Dorchester's full awareness of the need to settle the government, inclined him less to despair and more to positive endeavour. Despite the fate of the Parliament it was necessary to pursue prerogative government, non-parliamentary taxation, obedience to the royal authority, and if possible, Protestant diplomacy or its continuation by other means. For Charles might well be kept interested in preventing a Danish capitulation, with its consequences for Protestantism and English dynastic interests. The financial needs of foreign policy were intimately related to the parliamentary question and to the government of the country as a whole.[72]

Not all royal counsellors saw policy Dorchester's way at this time. Weston, supported by Laud as well as by Cottington, continued to counsel Charles against Parliament and war. The king hearkened increasingly to this line of

[71] Ibid., pp. 120–1; Reeve, 'Sir Robert Heath's advice'; SP16/138/63, SP16/141/80.
[72] SP16/138/63, SP16/141/80.

argument. The delay to supply in 1628 was a key ingredient in Charles's overriding belief that Parliament had done him personal injury. His declaration of 10 March 1629 made this plain. Not accepting the parliamentary criticism of his war strategy, he did not consider that Parliament had adequately financed a war it had initially encouraged.[73] The collapse of the 1629 session and the stoppage of trade could only reinforce his interest in peace with Spain. Between 17 February and 17 March 1629, the Infanta at Brussels wrote three times to Philip IV in Madrid of the great good disposition of the king of England to peace. Weston and Cottington were writing to Coloma and Scaglia in Flanders to this effect. The Spanish understanding was that Charles had decided to exchange ambassadors.[74] Despite the diplomatic nature of the optimism expressed by those working for peace, Charles was more eager than ever to explore the Spanish terms.

In England the trade stoppage continued. This was a political as well as an economic threat to the government, which considered the recalcitrance of the merchants an extension of Eliot's activities. The tax strike appeared as part of an extensive and dangerous conspiracy rather than as simple wilful disobedience. Dorchester wrote to his nephew, Dudley Carleton, an English diplomat in the Dutch republic, of the widespread influence of Eliot's Three Resolutions:

a fire of discontentment hath been kindled in this kingdom by certain proscriptions or anathemas as I may call them, which were pronounced in the House of Commons by some particular men after his majesty had adjourned the Parliament, which breeds a stop of trade . . . This we find to be nourished by some practising persons, who by scattering rumours and other devices seek to harden men's hearts even to their own hurt . . . [75]

He related how activists in the merchants' companies and societies had fostered this conspiracy, how it had come to the king's knowledge that every week 'very scandalous letters' were sent to commercial centres abroad for this purpose. Dorchester asked English representatives in the United Provinces to watch for and inform upon this conspiracy. He also wrote to Sir Robert Anstruther of what he considered a malicious correspondence, damaging to the king's reputation and affairs, of the need to hunt it out and how the English government used all diligence against it.[76] Dorchester, essentially a pro-parliamentary minister, had come to subscribe to the conspiracy theory developing at court.

English merchants were in fact directing their associates abroad not to ship

---

[73] Gardiner, *Constitutional documents*, p. 84; SP16/141/80; Lockyer, *Buckingham*, p. 471.
[74] AGS, E2519, exp. 11–13, 16.
[75] SP84/139/fos. 98r–99v. In writing to Sir Robert Anstruther, Dorchester termed them 'those proscriptions and curses pronounced in the House of Commons . . . '; SP75/10/fo. 139r.
[76] SP84/139/fos. 98r–99v; SP75/10/fo. 140v.

goods to England.[77] In the long run, however, the Merchant Adventurers, who formed the backbone of the strike, faced the prospect of increasing financial loss as they accumulated unsold textiles. On 16 May it was reported that the company had resolved, by the narrow margin of two votes, to start trading again. It took some time for English commerce to resume properly and during the summer customs receipts were still much lower than usual. On 23 June the bulk of the impounded goods was restored, the government retaining sufficient to provide security for the payment of duties.[78] The tax strike had ended but the conspiracy theory it had stimulated lived on. As Dorchester made clear, the government sensed the workings of a most serious form of revolt, with utterly unacceptable axioms of thought, which could spread from Parliament into the kingdom and even abroad. It could undermine the efforts of the crown and cripple the nation in war. It was this idea of conspiracy, shared most importantly by the king, which influenced much of government policy at this time. It would remain alive despite efforts towards conciliation and pacification.

The disaffection of the merchants, which achieved such a high political profile, took place against a background of general political unrest. Eliot's demonstration in the Commons had found an echo of disobedience in some localities sufficient to cause fear among the gentry. In London civil disturbance was to become more violent and serious. Much of the perceptible unrest derived from a developing public fear that Charles would dispense with Parliament forever. He had threatened to do so as early as 1626. The fear that he might was encouraged by the proclamation of 27 March 1629, which forbade any man even to suggest another Parliament. That year the fear of an 'alteration in government' became even stronger than it had been before.[79]

Sir Robert Heath's proposals for the reform of Charles's government, drawn up in early 1629, reflect the wider political problems facing the crown. Heath was concerned to rehabilitate the royal authority generally, to renew respect for the judiciary, to obtain better local governors and elicit decisive leadership in government from the Privy Council. He also wished to reform the king's opponents and employ Star Chamber to inflict exemplary punishments upon notorious and unregenerate dissenters. How far Heath's recommendations had the support of the king is unclear.[80] The atmosphere of

---

77 *CSPV 1629–32*, p. 29.

78 The parliamentary breach of 1629 meant that all customs revenues rested effectively on the prerogative; Cooper, 'Fall of the Stuart monarchy', p. 560. See also Supple, *Commercial crisis*, pp. 113–15; Ashton, *City and the court*, p. 132; *CSPD 1628–9*, p. 530; SP16/138/63; *CSPV 1629–32*, p. 178; Reeve, 'Viscount Dorchester', p. 135; Gardiner, *History*, vii, p. 86.

79 Clarendon, *Rebellion*, vol. i, pp. 84–5; B. Whitelocke, *Memorials of English affairs* (4 vols., Oxford, 1853), i, pp. 38–9.

80 Reeve, 'Sir Robert Heath's advice'; see also Green, *Diary of John Rous*, pp. 42–3.

crisis and disturbance which inspired them, however, could only act as a disincentive for Charles to recall Parliament.

The situation lent weight to the counsel of Weston. The Treasurer wanted to persuade the king that Parliament should not be resummoned for some years. There is no evidence to suggest that Weston was opposed to the institution in principle. He had sat in the House of Commons in most of the Jacobean and Caroline Parliaments and had adopted a moderate position over the forced loan.[81] His attitude contrasts with Laud's ideological objection to Parliament as a popular assembly damaging to monarchy. Weston combined personal interest with a coherent strategy for reform. By nature a fearful man, the Treasurer was opposed to the idea of another Parliament which could be expected to proceed with his impeachment.[82] To protect himself he was prepared to forego the constitutional (and perhaps the financial) advantage of a parliamentary grant of the customs. Avoiding meetings of Parliament during the foreseeable future, however, would also remove the public forum for cries of involvement in the war. Weston's rehabilitation of the financial position of the crown would be greatly eased by the elimination of war finance altogether.

While Weston and the prevailing political circumstances argued against resummoning Parliament, there were pressing financial reasons for Charles to consider it. Until well into the autumn of 1629 the poverty of the crown was extreme. There was insufficient money to provide for the day to day needs of the queen, the household and government.[83] In foreign affairs Charles wished to support his uncle and to uphold the cause of his displaced sister Elizabeth. In mid-1629 he had received no commitments in her favour from Spain. While he had hopes of a negotiated settlement of the Palatine question, there were powerful pressures upon him to preserve his options and work towards the resumption of parliamentary supply. Such a resumption required the settling of his government at home. This, it appeared, might be a difficult matter, for Eliot and his associates remained recalcitrant in prison.

---

[81] Alexander, *Charles I's Lord Treasurer*, pp. 145–7; Cust, *The forced loan*, pp. 67ff.; *DNB*, s.v. Weston, Richard, first earl of Portland.

[82] Clarendon, *Rebellion*, vol. i, pp. 62, 64.

[83] Birch, ii, p. 20; *CSPV 1628–9*, p. 580; *CSPV 1629–32*, pp. 67, 142, 178–80, 205.

5

Government and justice

The proceedings by Charles's government against the imprisoned members of Parliament constituted the principal public issue in England during 1629. The case was of critical importance in the development of the personal rule. Charles's failure to secure a thorough political victory over the prisoners strongly contributed to his decided rejection of Parliament and war. Directly or indirectly the case involved the questions of prerogative taxation, the standing of Parliament, the legislation of the Petition of Right and arbitrary imprisonment, religious and foreign policy, and above all the question of respect for the royal authority. Eliot and the others, by carrying their activities from Parliament to the courts, mounted a major political revolt against the crown. This revolt, as Charles and his ministers understood, was a most dangerous threat to the regime, following hard upon the constitutional collapse it had served to precipitate. It coincided with a royal financial crisis, with a trade slump and a bad harvest, with delicate and desperate initiatives in foreign policy, and with a domestic atmosphere of conflict and disorder wrought by war and the course of the last Parliament. The government was under great pressure to neutralize the threat of the revolt, given the danger it posed to the stability of the state. Charles's treatment of the prisoners, moreover, suggests that he had not abandoned the idea of calling another Parliament. Yet the king instinctively differed with those members of Council who advocated a conciliatory attitude to the prisoners. The case laid bare the fundamental nature of his approach to government. That approach was arbitrary in its disregard for law and convention and in its aim of having his subjects submit to his will. It thus reflected the weak, imperceptive and unpolitical nature of a ruler who never mastered the complexities of politics and strove to bring reality into conformity with his wishes.

Largely because it so exposed the character of Charles's government, the case of the recalcitrant parliamentarians demonstrated and promoted the workings of a new politics in England. One development is worthy of special emphasis. The law, for Charles's incarcerated opponents, was clearly

118

performing a new function at this time. Its role as the cement which held political society together was supplanted, from their point of view, by its efficacy as a weapon of dissent. This was not as sharp an alteration of perspective as such a statement might suggest. The appeal to the rule of law and the jurisdiction of Parliament, made by Eliot, Selden and the others, was a conscious appeal to established political tradition. On another, perhaps unconscious, level it became increasingly radical and remained a reaction against the emerging nature of Charles's rule. As Contarini observed in 1629, 'the king . . . desires to be absolute master, and not bound by the laws . . . '[1] Charles had an utter lack of sympathy with both the letter and spirit of the law. He assessed his actions in a moral and not a legal way. As a young man he once stated that he could not become a lawyer because he was unable to defend a bad cause nor yield a good.[2] In later life he tended to equate his legal with what he considered his moral rights[3] and this encouraged his inclination to arbitrary rule. The case of the imprisoned parliamentarians as it unfolded in King's Bench was therefore a necessary legal resolution of fundamental political, and constitutional, conflict.

The proceedings of the government following the end of the 1629 session, and its concern with subversive conspiracy, reflected the subtle changes affecting the political scene. On 3 March, in the midst of the Council debates as to whether to dissolve the Parliament, the nine members of the Commons who had attempted to resist the adjournment were summoned to appear. The evidence suggests that their continuing spirit of protest before Council on 4 March encouraged the king's decision to terminate the Parliament. The same day that they appeared, the Council ordered their arrest and the proclamation dissolving the Parliament was published.[4] It was also ordered that the studies of Eliot, Selden and Holles be sealed: their papers might provide evidence against them.[5] Each of the prisoners was interrogated at length. The Council wanted detailed information about the plans, intentions and preparations of the Eliot group, about a meeting they had had at a tavern some time between 25 February and 2 March and about visitors to and occurrences at their lodgings. Coryton, despite a remarkable lapse of memory about the events in the Commons, rashly volunteered that a meeting had

[1] To the Doge and Senate, 28 Aug. 1629, *CSPV 1629–32*, p. 177.
[2] Hutton, *William Laud*, p. 25.
[3] Gardiner was perceptive on this point; *History*, vii, p. 277.
[4] *APC 1628–9*, pp. 351–2; *CSPV 1628–9*, p. 580; see also *ST*, iii, col. 236. Strode and Long did not appear before Council when summoned but were subsequently apprehended; Larkin, *Stuart royal proclamations*, ii, pp. 228–30; PRO, C115, N2, 8534, Richard Wigmore to Viscount Scudamore.
[5] 4 March; *APC 1628–9*, p. 352. Approximately forty-eight hours were available to these men in which to remove incriminating material (Eliot had destroyed his copy of the Three Resolutions in the Commons on 2 March). No evidence from their private papers was presented against them in court.

taken place at a tavern, 'The Three Cranes', before Parliament reassembled. The government, believing that it had discovered a conspiracy, was interested only in those who had plotted with Eliot. This disregarded the fact that other members of the Commons had spoken just as offensively on 2 March.

When questioned, most of the prisoners appealed to parliamentary privilege, four (including Eliot) refusing absolutely to answer questions concerning matters in the house.[6] With a view to prosecuting the offenders in Star Chamber, Charles directed certain questions to the leaders of the judiciary and later further questions to all the judges. Their answers made clear that criminal acts or contempts against the crown committed in Parliament and not there punished were punishable elsewhere. It was also clear, however, that the judiciary had reservations about the extent of privilege, and that they thought there was a marginal area in which it might prevail. Charles was also concerned to define the nature of the supposed offences committed in the Commons. He asked the senior judges what manner of offence it was to conspire against his government and defame it so as to subvert obedience. Without the facts of the case, however, they could not define the offence despite the king's insistence: 'I must know what the nature of this offence is being fully proved.' Yet they could be no more specific than before.[7] Probably as a consequence, Charles's questions to all the judges sought to suggest the treasonable nature of the demonstration of 2 March. Both sets of questions attempted to portray the revolt in the Commons as a conspiracy.[8]

The interrogation of the prisoners and their appeal to privilege signalled the beginning of a legal duel and a major state case. Eliot's resolutions had used the accusation of treason to attack royal counsellors. Charles's response was to search for a treasonable offence on the part of Eliot and the rest. These mutual accusations point to the depth of the political conflict about to be channelled into the legal sphere. They also reflect the polarization emerging between a circle about the king – exclusive, attacked and seeking to fight back – and an organized cell of opposition. Both groups saw in the other a

---

[6] SP16/138/87–9, SP16/139/6–8, SP16/143/9; *CSPD 1628–9*, p. 540; Hulme, *Life of Sir John Eliot*, p. 316; Fraser, 'The agitation in the Commons'; see also Reeve, 'The arguments in King's Bench', p. 265, n. 5.

[7] SP16/141/44.

[8] Charles's habit of obtaining the judges' opinion in advance of legislative and judicial proceedings reflected both his difficulty in dealing with the law as it stood and his desire that it be an instrument of his will. Judge Whitelocke objected in principle to this practice; Whitelocke, *Memorials*, i, p. 36. Charles's questions to the senior judges in early 1629 apparently preceded those addressed to the whole judiciary by several weeks. See *The autobiography of Sir John Bramston of Skreens*, ed. Lord Braybrooke (Camden Society, London, 1845), pp. 49–54; Rushworth, *Historical Collections*, i, pp. 662–4; *ST*, iii, cols. 236–9; SP16/141/44. Note also Hayman's belief that he had committed treason; *CSPD 1628–9*, pp. 551–2.

conspiracy against the English commonwealth and accused each other of provoking constitutional conflict.[9] Charles's belief in Eliot's treason was also a response to the emerging lack of confidence in his kingship. For Eliot's emphasis on the wickedness of senior royal servants was a critique (and a possible solution) which Charles announced he was unable to accept. Charles was also responding to Eliot's radicalized constitutional thought, to his doctrines of treason, his trenchant appeal to privilege, and the dissenting use of the law implied by this appeal. Finally, Charles was matching Eliot in blaming his enemies for the constitutional collapse – an event which might cripple English foreign policy. The king's belief that treason had been committed was, therefore, a predictably simple but clear response to the pattern of political change being seeded by his rule. The assumption of treason would be a key element of the government's brief in proceeding against these men.

By his questions to the judges Charles had demonstrated awareness of the dangerous nature of recent events. There was a general threat to the royal authority. The invocation of privilege was a serious reflection upon the crown. Finally, the likely appeal by the prisoners to the provisions of the Petition of Right implied an unwanted and perhaps damaging discussion of the prerogative in court. Charles's government had definite aims in countering this threatening combination of politics and law. It wished to prevent conspiracy and subversion, maintain its authority and preserve the traditional right of prerogative imprisonment. It would also be advantageous to conciliate the prisoners. Otherwise the case would remain an obstacle to the calling of another Parliament which had any likelihood of success. The government's policy was, therefore, to oppose the release of the prisoners unless they submitted themselves formally to the king. This reflected Charles's sense of personal offence. He wanted the prisoners to admit their guilt and acknowledge his authority, and, in effect, to throw themselves upon his mercy.[10] This line of policy indicates the political importance of such a symbolic act. But the policy was only marginally successful. In mid-May Coryton and Hayman obtained their freedom by submission. Coryton's patron Pembroke probably interceded with Charles and induced him to submit to the king. Hayman had enlisted the favour of Secretary Dorchester.[11]

---

[9] On Charles's annotation to this effect see Braybrooke, *Autobiography of Sir John Bramston*, pp. 50–1.
[10] *ST*, iii, col. 285; Whitelocke, *Memorials*, i, p. 39.
[11] Coryton was released after 7 (perhaps after 9) May and Hayman after 19 May. Both men were free by the time Littleton addressed King's Bench on 5 June, as they did not then appear with Selden and the others. Gardiner, *History*, vii, p. 92; *ST*, iii, cols. 252, 264, 285; *CSPD 1628–9*, pp. 543, 551–2; SP16/142/36; Birch, ii, p. 15; see also p. 99, n. 3, above, and p. 122, n. 13, below. Coryton owed his continuation in the Vice-Wardenship of the Stannaries to Pembroke; Russell, *Parliaments*, p. 14.

Yet the other seven prisoners would not yield. Charles was determined to inflict exemplary punishment upon them and to vindicate his authority against parliamentary privilege. In seeking to punish the prisoners he was strongly supported by Attorney-General Heath.[12]

On 6 May, six of the prisoners (Selden, Strode, Long, Valentine, Holles and Hobart) sued for writs of habeas corpus in the Court of King's Bench, seeking bail.[13] The following day Heath filed charges against all nine prisoners in Star Chamber. Charles wished neither to be compromised nor to lose the initiative.[14] Star Chamber, with its summary style of justice, was the kind of court to recommend itself to Charles. The hearing immediately attracted great public attention. Heath's information sought to sidestep the privilege issue by emphasizing the dangerous and supposedly unparliamentary conspiracy Eliot had led. Heath maintained that Eliot, with his confederates, had attacked the crown and the customary workings of Parliament. Heath repeated the official contention that the majority of the Commons were loyal and attempted to slur the sincerity of Eliot's appeal to the public good. The prisoners maintained their appeal to privilege, entering pleas against the jurisdiction of the Court. Star Chamber referred the privilege issue to three senior judges who heard it argued before them. The hearings were still continuing in early June. Charles was impatient and wanted the judges' opinion. He summoned the whole judiciary to Greenwich. Upon questioning them he learnt that a clear majority leaned to the arguments of the defendants. By the end of the summer legal recess, Charles had decided to allow the Star Chamber proceedings to lapse.[15] Walter Long was prosecuted separately in the same Court for leaving his post as High Sheriff of Wiltshire (clearly an appointment meant to exclude him from Parliament) to attend the Commons in 1628. Proceedings were instituted against him the following year.[16]

The imprisoned members of the Commons clearly decided as a group to seek release by habeas corpus in the first week of May. The crown was obviously hesitant to bring them to trial and, under these circumstances, it is

---

[12] On Heath, see Cust, *The forced loan*, p. 60; SP16/138/45; Reeve, 'Sir Robert Heath's advice'.

[13] PRO, KB29/278, King's Bench controlment roll, Hilary term, 1629; Gardiner, *History*, vii, p. 90. Apsley's statement on 9 May that he had a writ for Coryton may have been absent-minded and remains a mystery as it accords neither with the controlment roll nor the rule book of the Court. See *CSPD 1628–9*, p. 543 and the references cited above. On Eliot see below.

[14] Gardiner failed to grasp this point; *History*, vii, p. 91; SP16/142/36.

[15] SP16/142/36, SP16/143/4–13, SP16/143/32, SP16/144/11–15, 37, SP16/149/38; Birch, ii, pp. 15–18; *CSPD 1628–9*, pp. 524, 547, 556; Whitelocke, *Memorials*, i, 39; Gardiner, *History*, vii, pp. 91–2; *The autobiography and correspondence of Sir Simonds D'Ewes during the reigns of James I and Charles I*, ed. J. O. Halliwell (2 vols., London, 1845), i, pp. 413–14.

[16] *ST*, iii, cols. 233–6. On the outcome of this case see below, p. 156.

unlikely that they wished to allow it the political advantage of their extended imprisonment. Their desire to demonstrate the principle that they were legally entitled to bail was probably heightened by a suspicion that Coryton and Hayman would defect.[17] When they were imprisoned in March the warrant of the Council had stated no cause of commitment. Now, two months later, the crown complied with the requirement of the Petition of Right that a cause be shown. The situation differed from the Five Knights' case, since there was now the possibility of statutory interpretation. Precedents could be set which were clearer than in case law, and binding at common law because made under statute. For the crown not to have shown cause would have risked judicial construction of a binding requirement.[18] The crown desired to create a form of precedent which would at least protect the prerogative under the law. Moreover, the granting of bail upon the stated cause would involve political defeat, for the advantage of discretionary imprisonment would be lost. That advantage was not only symbolic and coercive. The government was genuinely concerned to prevent what it saw as conspiracy. For the prisoners to obtain their freedom under the law, even temporarily, would be a great advantage. They also wished to have the Petition of Right and its provisions seen to operate in their favour. In seeking bail and continuing their stand, they were increasingly concerned with more than politics and constitutional principle. These concerns became bound up with the preservation of their personal credibility as the stakes were raised, with the self-propelling stubbornness of dissent. This human factor implied a gulf of understanding between the prisoners and those who supported the king. Dr Benjamin Laney (later bishop of Ely) wrote on 25 June: 'So long as subjects may have their liberty so cheap as for the asking, they were extremely to blame and unthankful to complain.'[19]

The cause of imprisonment notified by the crown on 7 May was 'notable contempt committed by them against ourself and our government and for

---

[17] It may also have been significant that they applied for writs on the day that Chambers was being sentenced in Star Chamber (Gardiner, *History*, vii, p. 90). They may have wanted the cause of their imprisonment stated before the crown developed confidence in a serious charge. They may not have wanted to allow the crown the political advantage of their imprisonment until a trial which might be precipitated by the successful prosecution of Chambers. Such consideration of Chambers' case would not have been incompatible with the reasons given in the text above.

[18] The prisoners would also have been encouraged by the fact that Chambers, committed by the Council, had obtained a stated cause of imprisonment, and bail, the previous October (Gardiner, *History*, vii, pp. 4–5). His case, however, did not have the celebrity of theirs and his offence was less serious. This, combined with the fact that the Petition of Right could still be invoked for the first time against the royal prerogative, gave the 1629 hearings greater political and constitutional importance. Chambers' case was not cited in these hearings.

[19] Birch, ii, p. 21.

stirring up sedition against us'.[20] This not only echoed the suggestion of treason in Charles's questions to the judges. Seditious behaviour so described was probably the most unspecific, non-capital offence with such treasonable undertones that could be devised by the government. The intention was to avoid bail and to characterize a high crime against the state.[21] The Petition of Right had required the showing of a cause.[22] It could not specifically legislate against such an arbitrary cause, for it was impossible to include within the specific nature of any legislative act the illegality of any given arbitrary cause. It was not an easy task for the King's Bench judges to assess the bailability of this cause as returned. The arguments in the habeas corpus hearings were lengthy, complicated, and charged with the wider political conflict. My analysis of these hearings has appeared elsewhere,[23] and it is necessary only to give a brief account here.

In May and June, during the Easter and Trinity legal terms, the Court heard the arguments on both sides. The lawyers Aske and Mason, appearing for Strode and Long, held that the cause returned was not sufficiently explicit and therefore an insufficient cause of detention. Berkeley and Davenport, for the crown, argued that the cause shown was indeed sufficient, and sought to prevent the construction of the king's prerogative under the Petition of Right. The eyes of all were on the law of the future as much as the politics of the present. The crown presented a skilfully justified yet dubious opinion based upon the letter rather than the spirit of the law. It argued that the Petition did not oblige explicit statement of a cause by writ but that its legislation related to an eventual indictment. The argument also appealed to the unspecific nature of the return to characterize treason and hence argue against bail. The crown, in framing an arbitrary cause of imprisonment – general yet substantial – thus sought to have the advantage both ways. It wished to avoid the legislation of the Petition against prerogative imprisonment, and to enjoy the usual advantage at law of a treasonable accusation – the denial of bail – without having committed itself to such an accusation. This was probably out of

---

[20] PRO, KB29/278, membr. 33, King's Bench controlment roll, Hilary term 1629, Selden's cause, and the same is repeated for the others. There is no customary reference to the *coram rege* roll, indicating the arbitrary nature of the imprisonment without information laid until Michaelmas. See also Rushworth, *Historical collections*, i, p. 664; *ST*, iii, cols. 240–2.

[21] Any offender committed for a non-capital offence (i.e. for any crime except treason or felony – save petty larceny) was automatically eligible for bail. Capital offenders were bailable only under special circumstances at the discretion of King's Bench. See Whitelocke, *Memorials*, i, p. 39; Maitland, *Constitutional history*, pp. 229–30, 271ff., 314–15; *ST*, iii, col. 266. On the nature of sedition see W. S. Holdsworth, *A history of English law* (13 vols., London, 1922–52), v, pp. 208–11. I am grateful to Conrad Russell for this reference.

[22] On the legislative nature of the Petition of Right see Reeve, 'Legal status of the Petition of Right'.

[23] See Reeve, 'The arguments in King's Bench', on which the following paragraphs are based. The arguments can be found in *ST*, iii, cols. 241–86.

belief that the Court would not find the facts of the case to constitute treason, but merely non-capital offences. Likewise this reflected a desire to avoid the political difficulties of a trial for high crimes against the state, while employing the coercive device of extended imprisonment. Such was the crown's policy, expressed in its legal brief. Attorney-General Heath, reporting the proceedings to this point, said that the judges had given no indication of their judgement either way, but seemed to be 'yet unsatisfied'.[24]

On 5 June, at Trinity term, Edward Littleton appeared for John Selden. The two men had been closely involved in the progress of the imprisonment issue since 1627 and collaborated in producing Littleton's submission to the Court. The brief was clearly the work of probably the two most able common lawyers in England.[25] In arguing for Selden's right to bail, Littleton demonstrated brilliantly how failure to award it would be against the Petition of Right. The crown had argued, in effect, that the prisoners should not be bailed because the true cause of their imprisonment was not explicitly stated: an argument for arbitrary imprisonment despite the Petition. The two men were determined to register the illegality of this proposition. Littleton did so by establishing that under both the Petition and common law practice the king was required to state the true cause of imprisonment explicitly. Moreover, the cause of imprisonment stated was to be *understood* as the true cause. The submission was a *tour de force* which inspired Hobart, Holles and Valentine, who had their counsel ready to argue for them, to rely upon Littleton's case. Heath, who was to have appeared after Littleton for the crown, found the strength of this argument so off-putting that he deferred his reply indefinitely. Littleton found himself the subject of considerable celebrity in London.[26] In court Selden complained to the judges of Heath's delay. Strode, impatient of judgement, asked them whether they would bail a seditious priest but not a seditious member of Parliament, adding that if the prisoners died in custody the judges would have blood on their hands.[27]

Heath addressed the Court on 13 June. With the right to bail now clear under the law as it stood, his response was to suggest that the Petition of Right had not changed the law. He was attempting unsuccessfully to retrieve the legal position in the Five Knights' case. With an assumption of guilt before trial and a fallacy in law, he stated that

the king intends to proceed against them in convenient time. And some that were offenders in the same kind are already delivered, to wit, Mr Coryton and Sir Peter

[24] SP16/142/85.
[25] With the obvious exception of the aged Sir Edward Coke. Selden had been a counsel in the Five Knights' case and a framer of the Petition of Right, and Littleton had played an important role in the parliamentary proceedings of 1628.
[26] Birch, ii, p. 17.   [27] Ibid., pp. 18–19.

Hayman. Therefore, if any injury be done to the prisoners, they themselves are the cause of it, for not submitting themselves to the king.[28]

Heath's submission was essentially a political reaction against the legal strength of Littleton's case. He pointed to the sedition mentioned in the return and told the judges that bail should not be awarded before they had consulted with the king. Heath's defence of an arbitrary cause of imprisonment by the king was a brief for the arbitrary government of his subjects, that is, without reference to due process of law but attempting to enlist the judges in such exercise of the royal power.[29]

Heath's submission had continued the interplay of legal and constitutional issues with political conflict, themes which in this case had become inextricably linked. Personal considerations, moreover, operated behind the legal briefs, as the participants in the hearings were forced to come to terms with the wider implications of the case.[30] Heath stated clearly the constitutional relevance of the issue, a statement partly elicited by his difficulty with the law as it stood. Berkeley and Littleton agreed that the case was essentially concerned with a specific and difficult aspect of the law. Yet both made reference to the importance of the case and the potential involvement of a constitutional issue. Each man had his reasons for offering an understated assessment. Berkeley was in the early stages of a career which brought him a knighthood and eventually appointment to King's Bench, a career which was built upon a remarkable commitment to the royal prerogative and which led ultimately to his impeachment by the Long Parliament. It is unlikely that his opinion of the 1629 hearings was given without regard to his prospects and convictions. Littleton, an advocate of the Petition of Right and an eminent common lawyer, in time became Chief Justice of the Common Pleas. His opening remarks in 1629, assessing the historical standing of the case, understated its constitutional aspect to the extent of self-contradiction.[31] He showed considerable courage in representing Selden when victory could mean the lasting disapproval of the king. Hayman found, by contrast, that his legal counsel did not dare assist him.[32] Littleton was diligent in defending the legislation of the Petition of Right for which he and Selden had worked. Yet

[28] *ST*, iii, col. 285.
[29] It would seem that Heath was acting here partly as a mouthpiece for Charles's views. I am grateful to Conrad Russell for drawing my attention to this problem. Yet the Attorney-General clearly had a personal commitment to the suppression of dissent and was inclined towards arbitrary government (Reeve, 'Sir Robert Heath's advice'; *DNB*, s.v. Heath, Sir Robert). Heath was no match for Selden and Littleton and contemporaries harboured doubts about his legal ability. Birch, i, p. 341; SP16/142/85; Knowler, *Strafford letters*, i, p. 58.
[30] On what follows, see Reeve, 'The arguments in King's Bench'.
[31] *ST*, iii, col. 252.　　　　　　　　　　　　[32] *CSPD 1628–9*, pp. 551–2.

he was aware of the danger of advertising a redefinition of an important royal prerogative (against which the king had fought) in the context of a most serious political case. We can be sure that he was mindful of Selden's eligibility for a heavy sentence and of his own career.[33] Counsel, therefore, while agreeing on the importance of the case, were guided by their individual concerns in coming to terms with a combination of difficult law, constitutional principle and high politics.

What was the outcome of the hearings and the finding of the judges? Clearly they were convinced by Littleton's argument and were decided in favour of the prisoners' right to bail. Whitelocke, whose father sat in judgement throughout the case, later wrote:

> The judges were somewhat perplexed about the habeas corpus for the Parliament men, and wrote an humble and stout letter to the king, that by their oaths [as judges] they were to bail the prisoners; but thought fit, before they did it, or published their opinions therein, to inform his majesty thereof, and humbly to advise him (as had been done by his noble progenitors in such like case) to send a direction to his judges of his bench to bail the prisoners.[34]

Charles had no intention of sanctioning bail, however, and, playing for time and seeking to raise doubts about the decision, commanded the King's Bench judges not to deliver any opinion without consulting with the rest of the judiciary. The other judges could offer no opinion on a question which had not yet been argued before them. The end of term, and the long vacation, approached.[35] The prisoners, unless soon awarded bail, would languish in jail throughout the summer. The King's Bench judges, against the king's wishes, decided that they must hand down their ruling. In seeking to fulfil his aims, Charles found himself opposed by the full measure of the law. His response was to defy it by appealing unjustifiably to the royal prerogative. The prisoners became the subject of a royal attempt to evade the course of law in the highest common law court in England.

On the day appointed (23 June) they were not brought to the King's Bench bar to which they had been summoned by the rule of the Court. They were physically prevented from appearing. This device deserves to be considered nothing less than a despicable and 'dirty' trick. The Marshal of the Court was obliged to inform it that Hobart, Long and Strode had been removed from his

---

[33] This interpretation is supported by the evidence of Littleton's draft brief, containing a clear and unqualified statement that this was a major constitutional case, which he qualified in court. It also contains a lengthy profession of loyalty to the king which presented him with considerable drafting difficulties. It is not known whether Littleton made the statement of loyalty in court; CUL, Ms Mm, 6.63.4, fo. 3v.

[34] Whitelocke, *Memorials*, i, p. 38. This opinion was known in London in June; Birch, ii, p. 22.

[35] Whitelocke, *Memorials*, i, p. 38; Gardiner, *History*, vii, p. 94. Trinity term customarily ended on the quindene of St John the Baptist (8 July).

custody and placed in the Tower by the king's own warrant. There, like the other prisoners, they found themselves in the custody of the king's Lieutenant. Counsel for the prisoners requested the decision of the Court nonetheless but the judges refused. The authority of the Court was subverted and the prisoners could not be bailed or remanded.[36] On 24 June the king addressed a letter to the judges, explaining why the prisoners had not been brought to court and stating that Selden and Valentine would appear the next day. A second and shorter letter followed several hours later stating that none of the prisoners would appear. The judges were told that King's Bench was the king's court. They were also told that it was the royal prerogative to present however many of the prisoners as Charles chose, given that all the judges had not yet resolved the main question (the issue of bail). It was held, moreover, that to allow the prisoners to attend, according to the rule of the Court, would be an act of royal favour in the light of their disrespectful conduct towards Charles and the judges. Effectively this was an appeal to the special circumstances of the case, as interpreted by the crown, that is to reason of state. The royal justification for the enforced remand of the prisoners sought to defend what was, in effect, arbitrary imprisonment. Heath's initial assumption that two of the ringleaders, if presented, would be remanded, had been qualified by discussion that very day with Chief Justice Hyde, who had obviously intimated that they would be awarded bail. This inspired the government's revision of its decision. The second letter implied that to present none of the prisoners was the king's decision alone upon 'more mature deliberation'. The king's explanation sought to dispel 'various constructions' of his action, and referred to his desire not to 'decline the course of justice' but to resolve 'this great business, so much concerning our government'. The letters were drafted by Heath and Dorchester together, the Secretary's diplomatic language prevailing over the Attorney's more polemical approach, but there is no doubt that the documents expressed the will of the king.[37]

Throughout the summer of 1629 the prisoners were denied the ruling on

---

[36] The Court had been informed that Hobart, Long and Strode would be placed in the Tower 'until by due course of law they and every [one] of them shall be thence delivered': the words of the king's warrant, PRO, KB29/278, membr. 45, King's Bench controlment roll, Trinity term 1629. This was not the first time that Charles disobeyed an order of the Court in this case. In May, Apsley at the Tower, under instructions from the Lord Keeper and the Attorney-General, had stated the cause of imprisonment only upon the second issuing of a writ and without returning the prisoners. For this he was twice fined by the Court and threatened with arrest. The prisoners having originally entered his custody by the king's warrant, he was not prepared to have them leave it save under a similar warrant; SP16/142/82, Apsley to Dorchester, 14 May 1629. See also SP16/145/32, 39, 41; Rushworth, *Historical collections*, i, pp. 679–81; *ST*, iii, cols. 286–7; Whitelocke, *Memorials*, i, p. 38; *CD1628*, iii, pp. 194–5.

[37] SP16/142/78, SP16/145/35–9, SP16/145/40–2; Rushworth, *Historical collections*, i, pp. 679–84; *ST*, iii, cols. 286–7.

bail. They remained in the Tower as close prisoners under the watchful eyes of the crown.[38] In conjunction with the emerging treaty with Spain, their fate remained the leading issue in England, both for the government and for public opinion. The case was closely involved with the problem of keeping order in the country and was intimately related to financial and foreign affairs. Its outcome was critical for the possibility of another Parliament in the foreseeable future. A letter from a Spanish agent at court at the end of June placed domestic affairs in their international context. The letter, surviving in the papers of Secretary of State Sir John Coke, was intercepted by the English authorities. It referred to the atmosphere of political conflict and described the slow breakdown of the stoppage of trade. There was no way yet found 'to pay the king's debts or to relieve his wants which peace and parsimony will hardly supply in any short time'.[39] The letter reported the Danish conclusion of peace with the emperor at Lübeck and the consequent revival of Anglo-Baltic trade. Cottington, it was decided, would go to Spain, 'which is a very great sign of our good meaning here, at least in his opinion . . . '[40] This intelligence suggests that Charles's problems at home and abroad might conceivably be solved by the promotion of commerce and peace. Yet the royal court was in immediate and dire financial need.[41] The insolvency of the crown, moreover, did not help in sustaining its authority in the public eye. Heath wrote of the need to dispel the 'unworthy opinion . . . that the king is in want . . . '[42] There was thus still pressure upon Charles to consider the resummoning of Parliament. And without another Parliament he might yet be unable to influence European affairs to the degree he wished. It was for this reason that the prisoners were the subject of international attention.[43] It was not only financial and foreign affairs, however, which implied the need for a quick and favourable solution to the problem of the prisoners.

Viscount Grandison wrote to Sir Thomas Roe, who had left for the courts of northern Europe, at the end of July. Grandison wrote with the information available to a Privy Councillor. He related how the imprisoned members of Parliament continued a menace to Charles's authority at home:

The habeas corpus men remain still where you left them, where they may feed themselves with popular applause, whereas if they did ground their opinions upon religion and the true rules of government they would not become so dangerous instruments to those that hearken after them and to themselves.[44]

---

[38] NUL, Ne.C., 15,404, p. 217; SP16/139/19, SP16/142/18, SP16/142/52, SP16/145/32, SP16/150/101; Melbourne Hall, Coke Mss, bundle 36, report on visitors to the Tower by Apsley.
[39] Melbourne Hall, Coke Mss, bundle 37, 26 June 1629.
[40] Ibid.   [41] See p. 117, n. 83, above.
[42] Reeve, 'Sir Robert Heath's advice'; see also *CSPV 1629–32*, p. 289.
[43] *CSPV 1629–32*, p. 139; NUL, Ne.C., 15,404, p. 26.   [44] SP16/147/74.

Grandison saw that the prisoners' stand was a definite threat to Charles's government. At the same time in the West Country Sir Barnard Grenville wrote of

the foulness of sundry ill dispositions poisoned by that malevolent faction of Eliot. So much as I see all is out of order. Our deputy lieutenants are either fearful to execute or unwilling to do their duties commanded from the Council board . . . The lieutenancy is grown into such contempt since the Parliament began as there be [some] that dare to countermand what we have on the Lords' commands willed to be done . . . and there doth not want some that endeavour to dissuade a great part of the country from that obedience [the musters] . . . [45]

The spirit of disorder had clearly permeated some localities and its effects had been slow to subside. Clare, writing to his son Lord Haughton, also in July, linked the imprisonment of Eliot and the others to the unsettled political atmosphere and the ill will which had developed between the king and his people.[46] The prisoners were rapidly coming to be the keystone, and the leading symbol, of Charles's difficulties in governing England.

There is evidence that Charles's regime was apprehensive of the danger of actual revolt during the summer of 1629. In July an arrest in Fleet Street by the serjeants of the Sheriff was opposed by some army officers. This triggered an extensive and violent riot. The situation became, after the militia were called out, an occasion of open rebellion. Barricades were raised by the rebels but their surrenders were obtained after the king's lieutenant had delivered a proclamation.[47] There were several deaths by the time order was restored.[48] Grandison reported to Roe that men had grown 'so bold as to give public affronts to government'.[49] The episode provoked a strong response from Charles and the Council, reflecting the depth of their fears. A proclamation called for the apprehension of all involved in 'those outrages which were committed rather in a rebellious than a riotous manner . . . '[50] It mentioned affronts to public justice and to public officers and ministers, which acts were worthy of exemplary punishment. The malefactors were to be found, and surgeons were ordered to reveal them to the authorities 'upon their allegiance to us, and the duty they owe to the public good of our state, and upon pain of such punishments as by our prerogative royal can be inflicted upon them for their neglect herein'. Even suspects were to be handed over, and anyone it might concern was 'carefully to observe the same at their uttermost perils'.

The episode was debated in Council. Secretary Coke informed Chief Justice

---

[45] SP16/147/14.   [46] NUL, Ne.C., 15,404, p. 218.   [47] SP16/148/35.
[48] Clare (a biased source) reported at least a dozen killed at the hands of the trained bands; NUL, Ne.C., 15,404, pp. 218–19. See also Birch, ii, pp. 23–6; NUL, Ne.C., 15,404, pp. 218–19, 221; Lindley, 'Riot prevention and control', pp. 114–15, 119–20, 125–6.
[49] SP16/147/74.
[50] Larkin, *Stuart royal proclamations*, ii, pp. 246–8, 18 July 1629.

Hyde that the government found it strange that the events were considered only a riot. Other laws and governments, according to Coke, would have found these capital offences. The king wanted to know whether the Lord Mayor would have been legally culpable if his forces had killed a hundred or more of the seditious persons 'wherein the law itself doth justify the shedding of so much blood'.[51] The king did not seek revenge against individuals but rather 'the preservation of government'.[52] His thinking linked the recent criticisms of his government to the street fighting. He would not prosecute such a matter in Star Chamber

and so publish to all the world, that his government may not only be condemned, but opposed in this manner without further danger or penalty than a fine: the consequence whereof may in favouring particulars ruin the whole kingdom by degrees.[53]

But if the law admitted of no other form of punishment, Charles had no intention of proceeding further, 'rather than make such a precedent to encourage rebellion, which beginneth by such actions, and to which it might have been feared that this tumult . . . might have grown, if it had not been stayed by God's favour'.[54] The Chief Justice was enjoined to take the case into more serious consideration and the king requested the opinion of the judges. Hyde replied that they would not grant the offenders any degree of favour 'for they deserve it not'.[55] Not only did Charles and his ministers fear the breakdown of government. The king was seeking legal sanction for the suppression of incipient rebellion in the most summary fashion. The reaction of Charles and the Council reflected a connection between the atmosphere of political tension and the risk of civil violence.

Besides the influence of the prisoners and the violent mood of the City, economic conditions had conspired – particularly in East Anglia – to produce potentially dangerous popular unrest. In 1628 a spectacular depression had begun to affect the cloth trade and the result was pressure on standards of living in areas of textile production. The onset of the slump coincided with a bad harvest in 1629. The result was a serious shortage of grain and in places major famine. Demobilization of unpaid troops could only have aggravated the situation. Merchants were unwilling to export grain when this might provoke a rising in the country.[56] And Privy Councillors allowing the Dutch to export wheat from England ran the risk of being stoned.[57] The flashpoint was in Essex, where the peace of the county was unstable. A riotous theft of corn at Maldon on 22 May attracted a particularly strong reaction from the

---

[51] SP16/148/35, Coke to Hyde, 9 Aug. 1629.
[52] Ibid.   [53] Ibid.   [54] Ibid.
[55] Melbourne Hall, Coke Mss, bundle 37, Hyde to Coke, 27 Aug. 1629.
[56] The merchants also feared a parliamentary inquiry; *CSPV 1629–32*, pp. 207–8.
[57] Ibid., p. 202.

Privy Council. It considered the episode a crime 'of so dangerous consequence that it amounted to little less than a rebellion . . . '[58] A strong guard was mounted, a special commission (headed by Warwick) established and four rioters hanged by way of deterrence.[59] This reaction, even in a county known for political dissent, betrayed the government's fear of wholesale rebellion. The problem of dearth was to continue during 1630–1 as a result of poor harvests coinciding with the slump.[60] With economic conditions ripe for such outbreaks of violence the problem of political dissent acquired a graver complexion. The revolt in King's Bench had fertile ground for its undoubted appeal, and Charles could not afford to ignore such a demonstration against his authority nor such articulate reflections upon the character of his government.

How did Charles's attitude to the crisis compare with his ministers' views? The king's concerns – order and authority, financial solvency and uncertainty in foreign policy – very much overlapped. They returned, all of them, to the problem of parliamentary management and dissent. During the summer of 1629, despite the fact that the houses were not sitting, Charles was acutely aware of parliamentary power. Forced to keep Eliot and others in confinement, and burdened by lack of money, Charles believed that he was the victim of persecution. He told the French ambassador Chateauneuf in August that Parliament made war on him more than the king of Spain.[61] This reveals his sense of being under attack at home, as well as the way in which dissent was altering his view of foreign policy. He remained convinced of a conspiracy rooted in Parliament for the subversion of royal power. The revolt in King's Bench could only encourage this belief. Charles told Chateauneuf that his problems derived from the activities of Parliament, whose members wished to reduce his power to nothing. The parliamentary leaders, according to Charles, were puritans, enemies of monarchs, and he did not hesitate to smear them as republicans.[62] This belief sharpened Charles's attitude towards the prisoners. Of this attitude there was now no doubt after his suspension of the due process of law by force. Clare, as Holles' father a hostile witness, nevertheless stated the fact in July: 'The king . . . is obstinate to keep those gentle-

---

[58] *APC 1629–30*, pp. 24–5.

[59] Birch, ii, p. 17; J. Walter, 'Grain riots and popular attitudes to the law: Maldon and the crisis of 1629', in J. Brewer and J. Styles (eds.), *An ungovernable people* (London, 1980). See also Larkin, *Stuart royal proclamations*, ii, pp. 230–1; Clay, *Economic expansion and social change*, i, p. 222; Supple, *Commercial crisis*, pp. 14–19, 103–4, 234; *APC 1628–9*, pp. 89, 309–10, 417, 419.

[60] Larkin, *Stuart royal proclamations*, ii, pp. 271–3, 298–304, 312–14; *APC 1629–30*, pp. 371, 373, 383–4, 404; *APC 1630–1*.

[61] PRO 31/3/66/fo. 140v.

[62] Charles actually used the word, according to Chateauneuf; ibid., fo. 132r. See also *CSPV 1629–32*, p. 204.

men close [prisoners] unless they petition; this is the height of power.'[63] He wrote again in September: 'law being laid aside, what bounds can be set to will, and power?'[64]

Charles's state of mind made him particularly susceptible to Weston's counsel. The Treasurer's immediate concern was to prevent his own impeachment. In political circles this was considered inevitable should Parliament reconvene.[65] There were two individual threats of impeachment which might become one. Eliot had made his intentions clear in the Commons on 2 March, and the earl of Holland, jealous of Weston's power, was working to bring about a Parliament and his fall.[66] The Treasurer, seeking financial solvency for the crown, and the credit, prosperity and political independence it would afford him, was opposed to the demands of the war lobby. He also favoured peace with Spain out of sympathy for the Habsburg position. Like Charles, he also wished to settle the government at home, an achievement which would render his own position more secure. Weston, therefore, while not exclusively self-seeking, nevertheless had political aims which thoroughly interlocked and which would all be served by preventing the recall of Parliament for the indefinite future. The Treasurer's interests were furthered by the king's view of Parliament and he encouraged Charles's fears for his royal authority.[67] He shared the king's desire to break the revolt led by Eliot. As Clare wrote in September, 'the hard proceedings are thought to be fruits of his [Weston's] fear . . .'[68]

The Treasurer, however, was not fully secure in the favour of the king. Charles wished to appear independent and ungoverned by any favourite.[69] Court politics therefore acquired particular importance, despite the fact that Weston was tending to hold sway.[70] The other leading Councillors (with the obvious exception of Laud) openly favoured a Parliament to extend their influence at Weston's expense. An anti-Habsburg group, Protestant and basically pro-French, consistently advocated a Parliament for the renewal of the war. Its most conspicuous members were Pembroke, Holland and Dorchester. Leading courtiers such as Holland and Carlisle, denied the remuneration of office by the penury of the crown, favoured a Parliament in their own financial interest.[71] The calling of a Parliament to satisfy these various ends would require conciliation of the imprisoned members. Coventry, Manchester and Dorchester were chiefly involved in seeking to

[63] NUL, Ne.C., 15,404, p. 217.
[64] Ibid., pp. 222–3, and see also ibid., p. 227.
[65] PRO 31/3/66/fo. 123v; *CSPV 1629–32*, p. 227; Magurn, *Rubens letters*, pp. 312–14.
[66] Ibid.
[67] PRO 31/3/66/fo. 136v; *CSPV 1629–32*, p. 177.
[68] NUL, Ne.C., 15,404, p. 227.   [69] *CSPV 1629–32*, p. 204.   [70] Ibid., p. 9.
[71] Ibid., pp. 204–5; BL, Harl. Ms 7000, fo. 273r–v; PRO 31/3/66/fos. 136v–137r, 208r.

arrive at a settlement with the prisoners. These moderates favoured conciliation in the interests of the government, of which they were members, and of
the country.[72] Such a policy was not incompatible with endorsing measures
against disorder and potential rebellion. It could well assist in lowering the
political temperature. The residual obstacle to a successful Parliament was
the religious question. Yet given a sufficiently strong political and financial
need, the pro-parliamentary Councillors were not inclined to perceive that
obstacle as utterly insuperable. Such a degree of optimism, which in retrospect appears unjustified, was the child of extremity, of the desire for reform
and of a belief that the king might yet see the error of his ways. With the
government at a crossroads of policy the conflict was so fierce that to admit
defeat was certainly to be lost. Simultaneously it was essential to employ great
diplomacy with Charles, whose attitude to Parliament verged on
irreconcilability.[73]

At the end of the summer of 1629 the national atmosphere was still
unsettled. There was a partial revival of trade but in parliamentary circles the
conviction remained that the duties collected were illegal.[74] Observers noted
the sense of division and conflict which hung over the political scene. In
October the earl of Banbury wrote to Dorchester of the need to uphold the
royal authority,

because things between the king and his people be grown to such extremities I wish
sovereignty to be maintained above all. Let all men whosoever they be smart rather
than the least point thereof should be any way lessened, and let not the king be [the]
author of severity and other men mediators of clemency as they become their creatures
but for mercy let them be wholly beholding to the king himself.[75]

This was sound advice but a disturbing estimate nonetheless. It remained to
be seen whether Charles would be sufficiently forward with his clemency.
The prisoners were the obvious candidates for pacification and were still at
the centre of the stage. One Doctor John Moseley wrote to Dorchester from
London advocating a Parliament as the only means to an accord between king
and people, 'the fire of dissension and distraction daily increasing more and
more among us . . . '[76] He advised Dorchester and Weston to move the king
to release the prisoners without insistence upon their submission. The
ensuing peace with Spain would provide the occasion for Charles to promote
peace with his subjects in this way.[77] Clare heard it rumoured at the beginning
of September that the deputy lieutenants of Devon would petition the king.

---

[72] Birch, ii, p. 18; Melbourne Hall, Coke Mss, bundle 37, Coventry to Coke, 11 Sept. 1629.
[73] *CSPV 1629–32*, pp. 204–5.
[74] NUL, Ne.C., 15,404, p. 223; *CSPV 1629–32*, p. 178; Gardiner, *History*, vii, p. 108.
[75] SP16/150/114. Banbury may well have been criticizing Charles's attitude by implication. I
am grateful to Conrad Russell for this point.
[76] SP16/175/77.   [77] SP16/175/77, SP16/176/24.

The petition, he understood, would seek an end to innovation in the commonwealth and the release of the imprisoned members.[78] Devon had an interest in the fate of two of the prisoners. Eliot had sat as knight of the shire and Strode as member for Bere Alston in the last Parliament. In September the newsletters reported that the county of Cornwall had petitioned Charles for the release of the prisoners under the Petition of Right. (Valentine had sat for a Cornish constituency.)[79] The town of Dorchester presented a silver cup to Holles for his services in the last Parliament.[80] This kind of public following for dissent could not be ignored. The sense of danger continued to be reflected in political discussion. Sir William Masham, writing to his mother-in-law, Lady Barrington, in November, argued for the authority of parliamentary privilege and ended his letter, 'I pray burn this.'[81]

During the course of 1629, as Eliot and the others maintained their stand, the menacing character of their activities increasingly emerged. The revolt was not simply a threat to Charles's conception of his personal power. The prisoners can be admired for refusing to bow down before arbitrary will. Yet in several key ways their campaign was politically destructive. It undermined the authority of the crown and encouraged disorder. It kept political tension high. It eroded the dwindling prospects of co-operation between king and Parliament by further antagonizing Charles and giving the Commons more cause for complaint. In militating against the parliamentary process, and by concentrating upon certain legal and constitutional issues, the revolt in no way promoted a settlement of religious and foreign policy. The prisoners' fusion of implacable principle with uncompromising resolve was courageous but, under the circumstances, also corrosive of the national political fabric. It was for this reason that the conciliar moderates strove to heal the breach and why the Eliot group did not have powerful aristocratic sanction. The moderates saw the prisoners as an obstacle to the parliamentary aspirations with which they sympathized. Manchester was married to the daughter of the earl of Warwick, leaned towards the 'political puritan' view of the world and had gained a reputation as a friend of the loan refusers. Coventry was a thorough lawyer, concerned for legal propriety, who had opposed both Buckingham's autocracy and the 1629 dissolution.[82] Dorchester was essentially a constitutional traditionalist and committed to the Protestant cause. Eliot, frustrat-

---

[78] NUL, Ne.C., 15,404, p. 223.
[79] Birch, ii, pp. 28–9. Valentine had sat for St Germans.
[80] Hirst, 'Revisionism revised', p. 92.
[81] Searle, *Barrington family letters*, pp. 106–7. It was reported in September that Selden had survived an attempt to kill him; Birch, ii, p. 29.
[82] *DNB*, s.v. Thomas Baron Coventry, and Henry Montagu, second earl of Manchester; Clarendon, *Rebellion*, vol. i, pp. 57–8; Birch, ii, p. 18; Cust, *The forced loan*, pp. 13, 17, 23n, 41, 44–5, 52, 55, 57, 59, 68–71, 80, 86, 103, 118, 190n; Russell, *Parliaments*, pp. 31, 415.

ing such men and without the support of peers such as Pembroke, Warwick and Saye, was pursuing, increasingly, a different kind of dissent from that practised by Pym. Yet Eliot and his fellow-prisoners had certain aristocratic connections which were revealed, as will be seen, in the concurrent proceedings against Sir Robert Cotton and his associates. The only peer we know to have positively supported the prisoners was Clare. He considered his son Denzil a martyr to arbitrary power and professed incomprehension of the charges against him.[83]

At the end of the summer recess, the crown made efforts to employ the judges in achieving its ends by the bailing of the prisoners before the Michaelmas term. This policy linked the constitutional threats to the royal authority: the Petition of Right and the claim of parliamentary privilege. The crown desired that the prisoners, in being granted bail, enter into a legitimate financial bond of good behaviour. But it also wanted their bail to be provided for under royal letters patent as an act of prerogative. In addition, the royal policy was to make a second offer of such bail conditional upon a request for pardon for refusing the first. This condition was not acceptable to the judges. Such a bail would clearly imply the justice of the imprisonment and negate any construction of the Petition of Right against it. Likewise it would render untenable any objection to the jurisdiction of King's Bench in the name of privilege. Otherwise bail would constitute legal redress for the prisoners being, necessarily, the assessment of an answerable cause of imprisonment, and would be no indication of the jurisdiction of the king's court. The rider of submission and request for pardon would vitiate any reflection upon the king's absolute discretion constituted by the first refusal, and in so doing would render the guilt and the pardon general in the case. This policy, therefore, would endorse arbitrary imprisonment as a just and exemplary demonstration of the royal authority. It might avoid the necessity of a full hearing, which would be a serious liability for the crown. It would also pursue a policy of conciliation, without compromising the royal authority, a course which appealed to Charles's moderate ministers. The policy of bailing the prisoners in this way was arrived at in a meeting between Coventry, Manchester and Dorchester in September, the judges' ruling on bail pending at the term. Almost certainly, the Councillors sought to reconcile the prisoners' legal demand that they be freed with the king's desire for their submission and the preservation of his authority. The attempt at reconciliation took place in the context of critical royal financial need and coincided with tenuous rumours that a Parliament might be called.[84]

---

[83] NUL, Ne.C., 15,404, pp. 217, 222–3; P. Crawford, *Denzil Holles, 1598–1680, a study of his political career* (London, 1979), p. 24.

[84] SP16/149/37; SP97/14/fo. 330r; SP96/3/fos. 111r–112r; Clark, 'Thomas Scott and the

To release the prisoners in this way Charles needed the co-operation of the King's Bench judges. His relations with the judiciary had had a chequered history, and his desire to enlist them in the exercise of an arbitrary prerogative had met with only marginal success. They had angered the king by refusing to subscribe to the legality of the forced loan. Sir Ranulphe Crew, the Chief Justice of King's Bench, had been removed and replaced by Sir Nicholas Hyde. Hyde's legal integrity can certainly be acknowledged, and he never sought to pre-empt the collective opinion of his colleagues. In 1628 the judges had refused to guarantee that the Petition of Right would not prune the king's prerogative.[85] In the Star Chamber proceedings against the imprisoned members of Parliament they had so far appeared to favour the argument of privilege. King's Bench had insisted (despite Charles's seeking to intervene) on attempting to rule that the prisoners were entitled to bail. The law was only circumvented by the king's use of force. Constitutional conflict had cast the judges in the role of umpires and so far they had sought to uphold the law. There was, however, another complicating factor in 1629. The fear of parliamentary reprisal was probably an encouragement, for at least some of the judiciary, to avoid conclusive judgement against Eliot and the rest.[86] This may have influenced the opinion given in favour of privilege. Yet Charles's rule had associated the judges with his style of government and a number of his actions. Hyde was a Buckingham man and had drafted the duke's defence against the 1626 articles of impeachment.[87] The political context of his appointment in King's Bench could not be ignored. In 1627 the judges were forced to remand the five knights according to law. In 1628 Charles had stated in Parliament that the judges, under the king, were the supreme interpreters of the law.[88] Finally, in 1629, King's Bench had no choice but to accept the *de facto* remand which was forced upon the prisoners. Consequently, the English judiciary was falling into disrepute. Hopes of receiving justice from the judges were being supplanted by hopes of Parliament. The judges, particularly through the case of the recalcitrant parliamentarians, were to become increasingly involved in the justification of the Caroline regime.[89]

growth of urban opposition to the Spanish match', pp. 23–4; *CSPV 1629–32*, pp. 178, 289.

In connection with the royal plan for the bailing of the prisoners, Gardiner (*History*, vii, p. 109) cites a letter from Charles to the judges of King's Bench of 9 September, for which he gives no reference. I have been unable to locate this document.

[85] *DNB*, s.v. Hyde, Sir Nicholas; Whitelocke, *Memorials*, i, p. 47; Cust, *The forced loan*, pp. 54–5; Reeve, 'Legal status of the Petition of Right'.

[86] PRO 31/3/66/fos. 195v–196r; *CSPV 1629–32*, pp. 205–6.

[87] *DNB*, s.v., Hyde, Sir Nicholas.

[88] *CD1628*, iv, p. 481.

[89] Clarendon, *Rebellion*, vol. i, pp. 88–9; Green, *Diary of John Rous*, pp. 50, 62–3; Reeve, 'Sir Robert Heath's advice'; SP16/104/51; Birch, i, p. 374; Rushworth, *Historical collections*, i, Appx, p. 7.

On 30 September 1629 a meeting took place between Charles and the judges Hyde and Whitelocke at Hampton Court.[90] The judges were summoned to discuss the bailing of the prisoners. The king deliberately spoke to them alone, at a distance from the Privy Councillors, probably seeking to insist upon his own point of view. Hyde and Whitelocke nevertheless attempted to conciliate Charles. Both judges tended to sympathize with the requirements of the prerogative but wished to uphold the law. They may also have been wary of the prisoners' determination and of parliamentary authority.[91] The judges were aware of their legal obligation to bail the prisoners at the term. Charles discussed the nature of the supposed offences. He kept to his view that treason was involved and disagreed with the judges that the offences were not capital ones which would normally preclude bail. The king stated that he was, however, content that the prisoners be bailed, notwithstanding their refusal to petition him saying 'that they were sorry he was offended with them'.[92] The judges apparently agreed to insist that the prisoners give security for good behaviour while at liberty, a procedure for which the law provided. They also agreed, however, to have bail awarded under royal letters patent. The idea of submission and pardon upon refusal of this form of bail was not decided upon and perhaps not discussed. The judges were seeking to accommodate the king without prejudicing the law. Charles also said that he had decided to end the Star Chamber prosecution and to proceed against the prisoners at common law in King's Bench.[93] His case in Star Chamber appeared to be floundering on the privilege issue, the most likely reason for his changing his line of attack. It may also have occurred to the moderates in the Council that a trial in Star Chamber, a prerogative court, would arouse even further animosity. King's Bench, as the highest court in common law, might assist in giving a more normal criminal character to the case.[94]

[90] Gardiner (*History*, vii, p. 110) dated this meeting as having occurred on 4 October. This is a significant error. Gardiner implies that the judges had accepted the pardon condition and states that they supplicated the king to withdraw it. This involves an argument from absence of evidence, the misreading of a letter from Hyde to Dorchester of 4 October (SP16/150/22) which was really a statement of intent, and the apparent ignorance of a letter from Dorchester to Hyde of 30 September (SP16/530/89) not published until 1897 as part of the *Addenda* to the state papers of the period. A copy of this published volume was presented by Gardiner to the Seeley Historical Library in Cambridge, but it seems that Gardiner was unaware of the document in question at the time of his writing. The date of 30 September also accords with the date of Michaelmas Day, being the 29th, and hence with the information of Rushworth (*Historical collections*, i, p. 682), and of Whitelocke (*Memorials*, i, p. 39). The error stems also from a misunderstanding of the way in which the judges supported the crown.

[91] *DNB*, s.v. Hyde, Sir Nicholas; SP16/150/66; *ST*, iii, col. 287; Whitelocke, *Memorials*, i, p. 39; and see p. 153, n. 169, below.

[92] *ST*, iii, col. 288.   [93] Ibid., cols. 287–8.

[94] Coventry and Manchester may have encouraged Charles in this decision; Melbourne Hall,

The decision to proceed at common law was part of the emerging realization that it was necessary to bring the prisoners to public account. Proceedings in King's Bench had been initiated by the prisoners' suing for writs of habeas corpus. This had raised the matter of bail and the crown had sought to prevent it. The subsequent attempts to achieve pardons and avoid trial indicate that the Star Chamber information laid before the long vacation was partially by way of intimidation. The king's mention of pardons at Hampton Court, with the release of Coryton and Hayman, perhaps explains the Venetian ambassador's prediction in late June that the prisoners were to be released.[95] It indicates also that the decision to proceed in King's Bench was a reaction to the failure to have the prisoners submit and request pardon in the summer, and to the approach of the Michaelmas term.[96] The policy of bail by letters patent and a request for pardon was an attempt to deal with these concerns and achieve the ends of the crown without final recourse to a trial. The latter could be avoided only if a pardon provided the same full redress for Charles. The judges were to be enjoined to achieve it in King's Bench.

The day that Hyde and Whitelocke met the king at Hampton Court, Dorchester wrote to Hyde after their departure. Obviously an agreement had been reached but one affected perhaps by misunderstanding: 'Immediately after your [Hyde's] parting ... I presented a letter to his majesty according to the concept I showed you to be directed to your lordship and the rest of the judges of the Court.' Charles did not want to sign the letters patent without being informed what the judges would do if the prisoners refused bail by them:

his majesty understood your mind and Justice Whitelocke's ... yet because he would be as well satisfied of the rest before he gave order for the prisoners' release, he hath commanded me to dispatch a messenger expressly and in all diligence ... [97]

The question was, on the face of it, that of bail or remand, and perhaps that of submission and pardons. The diplomacy of the judges may have been matched by the optimism of the king, but Charles certainly knew his own mind. To this letter Hyde replied:

Coke Mss, bundle 37, Coventry to Coke, 11 Sept. 1629. There was word in August of an information being prepared for filing in King's Bench, NUL, Ne.C., 15,404, pp. 229–31. Star Chamber did not pass sentence of death (Maitland, *Constitutional history*, p. 262) but since the judges were of the opinion that the offences were not capital it is unlikely that this fact influenced Charles in his decision to proceed at common law. At the time of the Star Chamber information the threat of capital punishment may have appealed to Charles in his efforts to break the prisoners.

[95] *CSPV 1629–32*, p. 121.
[96] Whitelocke (*Memorials*, i, p. 39) also refers to the pardons, intimated by 'good hands'. This would seem to refer to Arundel and Dorset, and perhaps to others, NUL, Ne.C., 15,404, pp. 217, 220.
[97] SP16/530/89.

... if they refuse to put in bail upon this gracious direction of his majesty ... we will remand them to prison: and if they move at the term, yet if they be bailed it shall be according to his majesty's letter, without declaring what the law is which we conceive to be according to his majesty's pleasure ... [98]

The judges had been requested to conceal the legal *ratio* of the case, out of definite concern with the Petition of Right, as well as to render their judge-ment formally sanctioned by the prerogative. Dorchester replied that the king only partially approved of their opinion. If bail by the letters were offered *in perpetuum* it would be self-defeating, giving no public display of the king's absolute discretion in imprisonment nor any public redress for the crown against sedition or privilege short of full trial. Dorchester wrote,

his majesty upon such a refusal is resolved they shall neither have their liberty by his letter nor by other means till they acknowledge their fault and demand pardon. I write the more largely to your lordship because I would be the more clearly understood.[99]

Charles and those about him knew that the issue was the public standing of the prerogative and the creation of a legal precedent which could protect or prejudice it. Yet the requirement of pardon, albeit a need of the king, was no legal obligation for the judges. It was incompatible with a judgement of bail, and an extra-legal use of the Court. Hyde replied,

they shall be sure never to be bailed by us but according to such letters and ... if they should ... refuse to put in bail according to his majesty's gracious direction, and should so desire bail without acknowledging their fault or desiring pardon ... yet bail-able they are by the law.[100]

This was unmistakable. Yet the letters patent were to go forward neverthe-less. Dorchester wrote to Hyde that the king had decided that the letters should be signed. Charles was resolved that the letters would be withdrawn if the offer were refused, and was determined that the prisoners would not be freed by any means without seeking pardon as previously stipulated. The king wished to know as soon as possible how the prisoners 'govern themselves'.[101]

This was an important letter and the end desired was clear. If the prisoners refused bail upon the king's initiative before the term, the crown did not wish them to be free until it had received public redress, that is the demonstration of the royal authority over those held to have committed offences against it. In requesting that the judges deny bail until this was achieved Dorchester was not specifically asking them to break the law. Although they might be with-drawn, the letters were signed and sent in the knowledge of the judges' view, accompanied by a reiteration of policy and a request for information. On one hand Dorchester was making an absolute assertion of the king's prerogative. He was asking that the judges act as instruments of the royal authority, of

[98] SP16/149/110.   [99] SP16/150/3.   [100] SP16/150/4.   [101] SP16/150/10.

government. On the other hand he was revealing that the crown had to reckon with the law in this matter. Events would reveal the extent of the royal authority under the law. This might be a lengthy procedure, for it was clear that if the judges would not administer an unqualified submission and pardon at the term, the prisoners having refused to offer submission, then the crown would indeed be forced to try them. The knowledge of how they reacted to the bail by letters patent would indicate the nature of that trial, and whether it would be necessary to establish jurisdiction and guilt. The desire to achieve a pardon was in fact an intention to shorten the lengths to which the crown need go to achieve the end of its policy. The reaction of the judges was a measure of the king's reckoning with the law in attempting to proceed in summary fashion.

Likewise Charles had to reckon with the prisoners, suspicious of any device to deny them bail. Apsley, the Lieutenant of the Tower, wrote to Dorchester that he had habeas corpus writs for their appearance on the first day of term. He desired the king's command, signified under the Great Seal, as to whether to obey the writs. Each of the prisoners had threatened an action of £10,000 against Apsley if they were disobeyed.[102] Eliot, Selden and the others were clearly aware that they were playing for very high stakes.[103] Between victory over the crown on one hand and imprisonment and a heavy sentence on the other the gulf was wide. The political situation, and the importance of public opinion, were grasped by the Venetian ambassador. He related how during the summer the prisoners had refused to confess and 'accept liberty at the cost of their conscience':[104]

Already, by some devices, they have postponed the case of these members for two terms. Now the king himself recognizes that the judges can legitimately settle the matter, and if they do not they will be exposed to censure whenever Parliament meets ... Many still believe that these prisoners will not accept their release upon such terms [i.e. a bond of good behaviour] ... Certain it is that affairs grow more bitter every day, and by these disputes the king has made his people see that he can do much more than they may have imagined.

Yet he concluded: 'the royal authority has been notably injured and diminished'.[105]

At the end of the long vacation the prisoners were brought before the judges, according to the king's direction, to be questioned as to their willingness to accept the good behaviour bond. On 3 October they were taken from the Tower to Serjeants' Inn and appeared before the judges in Hyde's chamber. Six refused outright to accept the bond which they saw as an impli-

---

[102] SP16/150/12, Apsley to Dorchester, 2 Oct. 1629.
[103] I am grateful to John Morrill for this point.
[104] *CSPV 1629–32*, p. 205, Soranzo to the Doge and Senate, 2 Oct. 1629.
[105] Ibid., pp. 205–6.

cation of guilt. Walter Long weakened, when interviewed alone, and agreed to be bound at the persuasion of his counsel. He afterwards tried to be readmitted to custody without success.[106] Hyde reported the proceedings to Dorchester:

some of them thought it might prejudice the goodness of their cause. We resolved then, that we would never bail them now, nor hereafter, without binding them to their good behaviour . . . And we are all of opinion that they could not anyway disadvantage their cause more than by standing upon [i.e. rejecting] these terms, therefore our humble desire to his majesty is . . . to bring them to the Court at the term, according to the writs sued out by themselves [and] granted at the end of the last term. And if they come, they shall be sure of no other terms at our hand[s] than now we offered them; which if they shall publicly refuse, they will make all men witnesses of their insolent spirits, and show themselves fitter to be where they are than abroad.[107]

Apsley reported similarly that they did not wish to prejudice their cause with an imputation of guilt.[108] Hyde had furnished Dorchester with a statement of intent and with legal and political advice. It seems that the advice was taken, for the writs were obeyed, the letters patent were not withdrawn and sub- mission and pardon were not insisted upon with the offer of bail. The crown had decided that the most practical course politically was to proceed accord- ing to the law. If the prisoners accepted bail by the letters it would advance the king's purpose, but this would not end the need to achieve a pardon or con- viction. The habeas corpus proceedings were a fundamental obstacle to Charles's policy and an undermining of the political use of arbitrary imprisonment. Yet the king still had some opportunity to obtain redress.

At the beginning of term, counsel for the prisoners requested the ruling on bail.[109] The judges stated that they were eligible but also required the bond of good behaviour. The bond asked of Selden and Holles, and probably of the others, was £3,000, reflecting the government's view of the seriousness of their offences.[110] Selden stated the case for the prisoners. They would offer sureties for their future appearance, as was customary, but not for good behaviour while on bail. Selden pointed out that such a bond, usually required of disturbers of the peace, was seldom asked even in cases of felony or treason.[111] He declared that the issue had been and should be that of bail alone and never such a bond. He desired that the issues be severed, under-

[106] Birch, ii, pp. 30–1; Gardiner, *History*, vii, p. 110.
[107] SP16/150/22, Hyde to Dorchester, 4 Oct. 1629. Sir John Bramston refers to a statement by the judges to the prisoners that 'the king had determined the question [i.e. of bail] depending in court'; Braybrooke, *Autobiography of Sir John Bramston*, p. 58.
[108] SP16/150/24, Apsley to Dorchester, 4 Oct. 1629.
[109] The prisoners appeared at the bar on 9 October. See SP16/150/12; Birch, ii, pp. 31–2.
[110] Birch, i, p. 416; NUL, Ne.C., 15,404, pp. 229–31.
[111] The offences in this case were clearly not felonious or treasonable; *ST*, iii, col. 309; Maitland, *Constitutional history*, p. 314.

standing exactly the intention of the government in having the Court sanction the exercise of the prerogative. He pointed out that to accept such terms was an implication of guilt. In this instance, such an implication would defeat the provision of the Petition of Right to have an answerable cause of imprisonment assessed for bail before trial, hopefully without prejudice, and certainly without favour. He continued, 'We demand to be bailed in point of right, and if it be not grantable of right, we do not demand it: but the finding of sureties for the good behaviour is a point of discretion merely ... '[112] This was correct. Likewise the implication reflected upon parliamentary privilege: 'and we cannot assent to it without great offence to the Parliament, where these matters which are surmised by return were enacted'.[113] Charles had linked the questions of imprisonment and privilege in seeking to use the Court as an instrument of the royal authority.

The judges disavowed any legal knowledge of privilege at this point; the return of the writs made no mention of anything done in Parliament.[114] Whitelocke's reply to Selden made the issue clear. He stated that 'the surety of good behaviour is a preventing medicine of the damage that may fall out to the commonwealth; and it is an act of government and jurisdiction, and not of law'.[115] This had been Selden's point. The judges were revealing their hand and their willingness to make the law available to the interests of the king. In the same way this was to prejudice the prisoners' concerns, the Petition of Right and privilege. The crown was reckoning with the law and simultaneously desiring justice to work in the interests of government. Since bail could not be avoided, the concern was more that the prisoners sanction this procedure than with the prevention of sedition. 'And [Attorney-General] Heath ... said, that by the command of the king, he had an information ready in his hand to deliver in the Court against them.'[116] The threat of actual indictment, immediately and without notice, was coupled with a warning from Hyde:

If now you refuse to find sureties for the good behaviour, and be for that cause remanded, perhaps we afterwards will not grant a habeas corpus for you, inasmuch as we are made acquainted with the cause of your imprisonment.[117]

The Chief Justice knew both the law and the royal policy. In following due process of law he was also seeking to further the ends of the crown as Dorchester had described them. Obliged to offer bail at the term, he was acting in accordance with what he had written to Dorchester on 4 October, that

---

[112] *ST*, iii, col. 289.   [113] Ibid.

[114] The disallowal of the appeal to privilege here was apparently based upon the technical issue of legal knowledge of the return of the writs, rather than upon a substantive judgement concerning jurisdiction; *ST*, iii, col. 289. See also Guy, 'Origins of the Petition of Right', p. 294.

[115] *ST*, iii, col. 289.   [116] Ibid.   [117] Ibid.

rejection of such bail would disadvantage the cause of the prisoners, who upon refusal would be properly in prison. Under the law he could not require of them submission, but his statement to them carried the same assumption as the pardon Charles had endeavoured to register, that such a refusal was an offence against royal justice and a proper cause of detention. In refusing bail and being remanded, the six prisoners were not in the position of the five knights in the 1627 case, completely ineligible for bail, for they had desired the full advantage of the Petition of Right in principle above the actual freedom it had made possible.

One of the prisoners eventually accepted bail on the judges' terms. Holles, after being entreated by his wife and father-in-law, Serjeant Ashley, agreed to be bound on 30 October.[118] Ashley was a king's serjeant at law and a strong supporter of the prerogative.[119] He was probably afraid that Denzil's recalcitrance would damage his career. Holles went free, but his acceptance of bail, by himself and without submission to Charles, did not save him from eventual trial as a principal actor in the events of 2 March.

By claiming a right to unconditional bail, the majority of the prisoners (and Holles until almost the end) were refusing to allow a legal precedent for arbitrary imprisonment and a denial of their claim of privilege. With the knowledge that their case was one of national importance, they were forcing the crown to travel the most embarrassing and extensive lengths possible under the law to achieve its end of demonstrating the royal authority against them. It was the prisoners who were rejecting the compromise devised by the moderates in the Council. Their dissent from the manner of Charles's rule thus promoted further political polarization. The moderates could no longer stand on the shrinking ground between Eliot and Selden and the king. The Venetian ambassador, seeing the public support for the prisoners, remarked with unwitting overstatement that they had the support 'of the whole community', support which they sought to exploit and which they hoped would lead to their compensation by Parliament.[120] For the prisoners would have to be tried – that is, the cause of their imprisonment would have to be justified and the claim of privilege invalidated. The crown, however, wished to avoid this process.

Given the need for royal redress, and the prisoners' consistent resolve, there was also the possibility that they might be 'bought'. A plan to invest the recalcitrant members of Parliament with government office can be reconstructed in part from the surviving documentation. This episode is still clouded in

---

[118] Ashley and William Noy (later Attorney-General) acted as sureties for Holles. Birch, ii, pp. 36, 40, 57; NUL, Ne.C., 15,404, p. 234; Searle, *Barrington family letters*, p. 98; Crawford, *Holles*, p. 24.
[119] *CD1628*, ii, pp. 528–9; *LJ*, iii, pp. 758–9, 764.   [120] *CSPV 1629–32*, p. 212.

obscurity and may not have got beyond the initial idea. It was an option, however, definitely explored by Heath and the king. It represents, moreover, an approach often favoured by Charles to the problem of dissent. Several days after the prisoners appeared at the bar, Heath wrote to Dorchester with Hyde's advice to

leave them as men neglected until their . . . stomachs come down, and not to proffer any information at all . . . But I dare not subscribe totally to his opinion, to forbear the information; nor could I conveniently alter his opinion with reason, lest I should thereby discover too far the king's intentions touching them, which is fit to be as counsels.[121]

Such a policy was consistent with the recruitment of Wentworth, who entered the Privy Council at this time, and of the parliamentary lawyers Noy, Mason and Littleton, as well as Sir Dudley Digges.[122] Charles was usually prepared to consider, as he did at the time of the Long Parliament, the purchasing of men's loyalty with office, as long as this did not involve any alteration in policy.[123] This idea may explain Charles's reasonable mood at Hampton Court at the end of the summer of 1629. It is conceivable that the king, his honour satisfied, might have extended his official hand to all the prisoners save Eliot, his hatred for whom was clearly unappeasable. Dorchester and the moderates were probably promoting this manoeuvre. Heath was utterly frank in discussing it with the Secretary.[124] If it worked it would greatly advance the policy of conciliation and of minimizing reflections upon the crown while renewing respect for the royal authority. The last aspect was all-important. Hyde's advice to Heath echoed the meaning of his statement at the hearing, but the same week he seems to have agreed to a different measure.

The prisoners having been remanded, Heath devised a plan to prosecute them summarily and in camera. He submitted the scheme to Dorchester for review and Charles's approval, and had Hyde agree to implement it in his chamber at the inns of court. It was directly linked to the idea of 'buying' the prisoners, and in part grew out of the idea of striking a possible bargain upon a surprise attack. The Lieutenant of the Tower also agreed to use informers to spy on the prisoners. For the in camera hearing they would have to be brought before the Court, 'because otherwise they cannot . . . be compelled to answer'.[125] This could be done in the custody of the Marshal before one of the judges, where they could be charged 'on a sudden, and in an evening . . .'[126]

---

[121] SP16/150/53. See also Reeve, 'Sir Robert Heath's advice'; NUL, Ne.C., 15,405, p. 232; Gardiner (*History*, vii, p. 111) neglected to discuss this question.
[122] Whitelocke, *Memorials*, i, pp. 38–9.
[123] B. Manning, 'The aristocracy and the downfall of Charles I', in B. Manning (ed.), *Politics, religion and the English civil war* (London, 1973), pp. 79–80.
[124] See also SP97/14/fo. 330r.
[125] SP16/150/53, Heath to Dorchester, 13 Oct. 1629.   [126] Ibid.

To this Dorchester replied that it was not clear why the prisoners could not answer as well out of the Tower as the Court of King's Bench, 'because such as are in process are bound to answer from all places . . . '[127] Nevertheless it was decided in consultation with the king 'that the information shall go on with all expedition, the nature of the business not permitting neglect . . . nor protracting of time'.[128] What was the reason for all this haste and secrecy? It is likely that the situation in the country, and certainly the need for a Parliament, were felt to be pressing.[129] One consideration was definite. As the head of the judiciary, Hyde did not enjoy the full confidence of the government. Yet he was more disposed to the needs of the crown that some of the other judges, whose favour, as the present case had shown, Charles could not take for granted.

The day that Dorchester advised Heath that the extraordinary procedure was approved, he wrote to Lord Keeper Coventry on a matter which was definitely related. He wished to know whether the chief judge of the Exchequer, Baron Walter, would accede to the wishes of the king. The Secretary wanted a categorical answer.[130] Walter had altered his opinion on this case and in so doing had greatly angered Charles. Having encouraged the king to prosecute, Walter had now decided, apparently, that prosecution could legitimately be blocked by parliamentary privilege.[131] It was suggested to Walter that he petition to be allowed to retire from the bench. He maintained his stand, however, and held to the view that he could only be dismissed for breach of the law. Charles ordered his suspension from office.[132] Desperately in need of a satisfactory solution, he was willing to lean on the judges and coerce them to obtain the ruling he required. His treatment of Walter was a reaction to the dissent of one judge. But the evidence suggests that it was also Charles's intention to stop defection amongst the judiciary and *encourager les autres*.

Walter's fate shows how Charles was failing to learn (as he usually did),[133] – in this instance about the requirements of English legality. This was largely a reaction against the use made of the law by men such as Selden, abler than himself. Charles's response to the complexities of constitutional conflict – to the oracles and riddles, as he called them[134] – was to reject those complexities

---

[127] SP16/150/55, Dorchester to Heath, 13 Oct. 1629.
[128] Ibid.   [129] *CSPV 1629–32*, pp. 199, 205.   [130] SP16/150/52.
[131] This is the most logical interpretation of Whitelocke's statement of Coventry's view; Whitelocke, *Memorials*, i, pp. 45–6. See also *DNB*, s.v. Chambers, Richard. Walter's stand was clearly uninfluenced by fear of parliamentary action against the judiciary, given his preference for the loss of judicial office. See also Gardiner, *History*, vii, p. 114.
[132] SP16/150/47, SP16/150/58; NUL, Ne.C., 15,404, pp. 230–1, 233; Birch, ii, pp. 33–4, 36; Gardiner, *History*, vii, pp. 112–14.
[133] See p. 176, below.   [134] *ST*, iii, col. 288.

and urge his judges to do the same, in the interests of royal power. His attitude to the judges was derived from a belief in his own rectitude, the concomitant of which was a belief in the guilt of those (such as the prisoners) who had given him offence. The Venetian ambassador observed how the imprisoned members of Parliament remained constant in their resolution:

it clearly appears how rigorously they maintain the principle that they cannot be adjudged guilty. The king has intimated to all the judges that it is his royal pleasure that they shall proceed to their condemnation. The judges excused themselves, thus giving his majesty particular offence. He subsequently sent a writ for the suspension of one of them . . . It is thought that he will be dismissed altogether . . . [135]

With Charles now under pressure to prosecute, and with the judges very dubious of the crown's stance against privilege, it is logical to infer that Charles was seeking to signal the other judges by suspending Walter. The prisoners, moreover, understood that message: their guilt was assumed, and inherent in any assertion of the jurisdiction of King's Bench over that of Parliament.

The in camera hearing was an attempt to avoid the difficulties facing the crown in the case and their public display. Of the six prisoners in custody,[136] it was intended to prosecute only Eliot, Holles and Valentine, the ringleaders on 2 March. The trial of fewer defendants would be less embarrassing. Punishment of them might induce the others to submit, and Selden's legal ability would have disinclined the government to proceed against him further. Heath told Dorchester of the arrangements and, the king being consulted, the plan was finally approved. This was the day following Walter's statement of his intransigence.[137] Heath explained why the prisoners had to leave the Tower. The information was filed, and it was necessary to have them answer in court. If they appeared 'by the coercion of the ordinary process of the Court', this would 'require time, and may admit many delays, if the defence pleases, and there is little doubt of their wills in this case'.[138] But if the appearance was simply in the custody of the marshal,

they are as if present in court, where by the rule or order of the Court only, without any process, they may be charged . . . which is the king's action, and if they do not answer within the time prescribed to them by the Court, which shall not be long, it shall be taken *pro confesso* . . . it can be no other way but by a habeas corpus: but I advise the manner of it to be this. They shall not appear publicly in court where they may have opportunity to vent themselves, but the Lord Chief Justice shall send for them on a sudden to Serjeants' Inn, where nothing shall be done but to commit them to the person of that court and to charge them with the information, and bailed they shall not be if they would offer it . . . I find him and left him resolved, that if any of the prisoners

[135] *CSPV 1629–32*, p. 222, Soranzo to the Doge and Senate, 23 Oct. 1629.
[136] Holles not being bailed until 30 October.
[137] 15 Oct. 1629, SP16/150/66–7. [138] SP16/150/66.

would now relent, and desire to be bailed, they shall not be received until the king be first made acquainted thereof. And whensoever it shall be done I will take care that the entry thereof upon record shall appear to be *per mandatum domini regis*, and not as if it were done *mero jure*.[139]

At one stroke, Heath intended to win the legal and political battle for the crown. He wished to establish the jurisdiction of King's Bench without having the prisoners physically and publicly come to court, and to elicit, if not an acknowledgement of jurisdiction, a tacit confession of guilt. If necessary he sought, very dubiously, to invalidate by common law record any definition of an absolute power of prerogative imprisonment made by the Petition of Right in this case. Previously the bail by letters patent had been intended to prejudice the prisoners' trial and to have the operation of the law sanctioned by favour. Bail *per mandatum* . . . would be regardless of customary notions of justice, since really at the royal discretion. The whole exercise would be a strictly arbitrary procedure in admitted contradiction of the due process of law. It relied upon the co-operation of the Chief Justice and was approved by the king and the Secretary of State.[140] Such was the desire of the crown to have the prerogative sanctioned by the name of justice despite the law. In this way the issues of jurisdiction and imprisonment had become thoroughly linked. The crown's attitude presumed the guilt of its opponents and the Venetian ambassador had been perspicacious. The resolve of the prisoners had exposed the belief of the king, and of some about him,[141] that trial of the offence, the cause of imprisonment, should be unnecessary. Yet finally it could not be unnecessary. The in camera hearing, an attempted substitute for a public trial, was never held. Heath had overstated its efficacy, but in itself it could not be a conclusive measure. For the crown could not ultimately avoid a reckoning with the law, that is the insistence of the prisoners that they be freed unconditionally upon bail or tried without delay, and the likely opinion of the judiciary as a whole that a summary hearing could be no sub-

---

[139] Ibid. Whether a bail so recorded could justify arbitrary imprisonment at law is dubious, see Selden's argument, *CD1628*, ii, pp. 348–9. It would also be only a common law record, and a distinctly irregular proceeding, in the face of a statutory requirement. Heath's plan here echoes his attempt to pervert the record in the Five Knights' case; Guy, 'Origins of the Petition of Right', p. 297.

[140] SP16/150/67, Dorchester to Heath, 15 Oct. 1629. Heath's intention to interpret refusal to answer the charge *pro confesso* probably derived from the common law principle of *nihil dicit* under which the prisoners were ultimately found guilty. Yet on that occasion King's Bench required a plea against jurisdiction to be argued, and Heath's plan for the in camera hearing appears arbitrary and illegal in every sense.

[141] Not surprisingly, there is no evidence that Coventry, with his sense of legality, approved of the initiative. Dorchester, as a non-lawyer, would probably have had fewer difficulties. Hyde's agreement to participate is extraordinary; Heath may have misrepresented the extent of his co-operation which may only have been to refuse bail without consultation with the king. Whatever Heath's misrepresentation, the king's approval remains crucial evidence.

stitute for such a trial. If the law were disregarded in the way proposed by Heath, the certain objection of the prisoners would present grave difficulties for the crown. The need to establish guilt under the law could not be avoided. As Apsley reported to Dorchester, the prisoners would neither confess of their own volition nor request pardon.[142] They were inspired by a fusion of principle, personality and overwhelming political investment. They were not, therefore, such as could be coerced or bought.

Heath's information was filed in King's Bench on 4 November, eight days after Apsley reported the unwillingness of the prisoners to petition the king. Eliot, Holles and Valentine were charged with seditious conduct and speeches in Parliament, principally Eliot's speech against the Council and the judges of 23 February and, 'by confederacy aforehand', the demonstration of 2 March. The royal authority, Heath argued, had power over the sitting of Parliament.[143] With the charges laid, the defendants refused to plead to the offences. They entered a plea against the jurisdiction of the Court, as they had in Star Chamber, maintaining that only Parliament could judge them. They knew that their guilt was assumed and their offences political such as to be adjudged true upon any hearing. A plea against jurisdiction was the only one which would not *ipso facto* involve a verdict of guilty. Heath moved that the plea be overruled but the Court desired it to be argued. The judges, however, gave a telling clue to their thinking and their relationship to the crown case. Hyde invoked the resolution of all the judges earlier in the year that an offence committed in Parliament, 'criminally or contemptuously', rested punishable in another court.[144] Hence, as Whitelocke stated, the sole remaining question was whether King's Bench could punish such an offence. Croke and Jones added that jurisdiction in such a case would be only logical: King's Bench was the highest criminal court and the king technically sat in judgement there.[145] Things were quickly becoming clear. The government was succeeding in conveying its notions of guilt and jurisdiction and in enlisting the support of at least some of the judges. The case had surely had a cumulative effect upon those sitting in King's Bench. There had been the king's questions, probing the subject of privilege and emphasizing the serious nature of the offences, the crown's insistence upon a bond of good behaviour and finally the pressing home of the charges in court. There had been, above all, the suspension of Walter. It could only have had a sobering effect upon his brethren. In response to the crown's urgings and in the light of their own opinions, the King's Bench judges were apparently ready to override all former doubts about privilege and any fear of parliamentary reprisal. This was despite the

[142] SP16/150/101, Apsley to Dorchester, 27 Oct. 1629.
[144] '("the Parliament being ended")', ibid., col. 294.
[143] *ST*, iii, cols. 293–4.
[145] Ibid., cols. 294–5.

fact that the charges in King's Bench were virtually identical with those laid earlier in Star Chamber.[146]

The hearing recommenced on 25 January, in Hilary term 1630. The previous day, Sir Thomas Barrington had written to his mother, 'the great affair of the King's Bench is tomorrow to be tried between the king and our Parliament men . . . God send such an issue as may most glorify Him and benefit king and subjects.'[147] The fact that the prisoners were allowed counsel confirms that the judges did not consider this a capital trial.[148] Eliot was involved in the preparation of the defence and the submissions to the Court reflect his thought. For the prisoners privilege was, of course, the basis for a legal defence of their behaviour. Eliot, however, in the course of opposition and under the pressure of prosecution, was evolving the view of privilege as an ideal in itself. He was concerned with the standing of Parliament in the eyes of posterity, wanting to satisfy the law insofar as it did not prejudice this end, taking the Tudor idea of parliamentary liberties – the right to counsel and legislate – to a new extreme.[149] Mason, in defending Eliot, held that the offences were in fact expressions of the proper role of Parliament: 'The Parliament is . . . the grand council of the king.'[150] He argued that despite the supposed conspiracy outside the house, 'yet the act is legal; for members of the house may advise of matters out of the house: for the house is not so much for consultations as for proposition of them'.[151]

The Court replied that the issue was not the truth of the offences, but 'admitting them to be offences, the sole question is whether this court may punish them; so that a great part of your argument is nothing to the present question'.[152] The defence proceeded to argue the rights of privilege against jurisdiction without surrendering the brief that Eliot and the others had committed no wrong. Any appeal to the supposedly curial status of the Commons (not a novel idea in the seventeenth century) was very dubious. The lower house had little claim to be a court of justice.[153] The defence, however, could

---

[146] SP16/142/36; *ST*, iii, cols. 293–4.   [147] Searle, *Barrington family letters*, p. 124.
[148] I am grateful to Wilfred Prest for advice on this point. Eliot and Holles were defended by Mason, Bramston and Holt, and Valentine by Mason and Calthorpe. Later Holt was replaced by William Lenthal. Gilbert Barrell is also mentioned as a counsel for the defendants; Hulme, *Life of Sir John Eliot*, p. 329.
[149] See the discussion of the events of 2 March in chapter 3, above, particularly p. 84, n. 160. While Eliot used the word 'liberties' in the exchange with Pym in 1629, in the early seventeenth century the word 'privilege' could be used to refer to liberties in the technical sense. Braybrooke, *Autobiography of Sir John Bramston*, pp. 49ff. See also Maitland, *Constitutional history*, pp. 320–1; Clarendon, *Rebellion*, vol. i, pp. 8–10; Grosart, *Letter book of Sir John Eliot*, pp. 89ff.; Hulme, *Life of Sir John Eliot*, p. 335; J. Forster, *Sir John Eliot: a biography* (2 vols., London, 1864), pp. 550–1.
[150] *ST*, iii, col. 295.   [151] Ibid., col. 298.   [152] Ibid., col. 299.
[153] Ibid., cols. 296, 300, 301, 303; Elton, *Tudor constitution*, pp. 234n, 263–4.

and did invoke the Commons' right to govern and punish its members as well as the legal privilege implied by the ancient tradition that Parliament was the highest court in the realm.[154] This brief interlocked with the view that 'these offences are justifiable'.[155] For counsel could argue simultaneously against the jurisdiction of the Court and in defence of the behaviour of Eliot and the rest. In Calthorpe's words, 'For any thing that appears [charged], the House of Commons had approved of these matters, therefore they ought not to be questioned in this court.'[156] And again: 'the Parliament is a transcendent court, and of transcendent jurisdiction: ... and if they be offences, this reflects upon the house, which hath not punished them'.[157] This was the point of the crown's assumption of guilt with its appeal to criminal jurisdiction. If such jurisdiction were established over the House of Commons, and Parliament, then privilege could not protect acts which were incompatible with the character of the government practised by the crown. This was the basic constitutional issue at stake in the trial. Calthorpe pointed to the absence of legal precedent for the punishment of what were (in his view) similar actions in Parliament when any plea had been entered against jurisdiction. Such an argument from absence could well be good in law, but it could break down in view of the unprecedented nature of the offences as charged. Only the case itself could provide a conclusive judgement against parliamentary privilege – and it might well.[158]

Heath's reply was an effective submission confronting the arguments of the defence head-on. He moved swiftly to refute any claim that the Commons, or indeed Parliament, was a permanent criminal court. He also attacked the link the defence wanted to forge between the liberties (and probably the curial status) of the Commons and the notion of the High Court of Parliament:

the House of Commons is not a court of justice of itself. The two houses are but one body, and they cannot proceed criminally to punish crimes, but only their members by way of imprisonment; and also they are not a court of record ... And there is no necessity that the king should expect a new Parliament. The Lords may grant commissions to determine matters after the Parliament ended; but the House of Commons cannot do so. And also a new House of Commons consists of new men, which have no cognizance of these offences.[159]

Heath's argument dwelt, of course, on the nature of those offences. He held

---

[154] *ST*, iii, cols. 295–304; Elton, *Tudor constitution*, pp. 233ff., 264–6; *CD1629*, p. 178. These principles were presented in conjunction by counsel because to do so particularly suited the defence of acts in the Commons before an extra-parliamentary court. It would also seem that there was an intention to suggest the curial status of the Commons.

[155] *ST*, iii, col. 300. [156] Ibid., col. 301. [157] Ibid., col. 303.

[158] Almost certainly Calthorpe was arguing on the basis that the supposed offences were not capital; ibid., cols. 301, 303, and see ibid., col. 299.

[159] *ST*, iii, col. 299. At least two of the judges endorsed Heath's argument that Parliament was not a permanent criminal court; ibid., cols. 306–7.

that Parliament could make complaints in a parliamentary way, but not move things 'which tend to the distraction of the king and his government'.[160] The defendants had not acted as befitted counsellors of state; their behaviour had verged upon treason.[161] Heath completed his outlining of the offences by stressing that they were the actions of individuals. He thus avoided the stronger legal defence which could have been mounted if the supposed offences had been demonstrable resolutions of the whole House of Commons: 'if the truth were so these matters might be given in evidence'.[162] He stressed, moreover, the novelty of the crime in order to argue that 'there cannot be a precedent of such a judgement'.[163] Heath had presented a brief for an arbitrary government, based upon an assumption of guilt – a brief to which his political views and style of mind were eminently suited. From this an argument in favour of the Court's jurisdiction could easily flow.

The legal question was no straightforward matter calling for a clear-cut decision. The actions of the defendants could easily be seen as seriously criminal. Heath was right, however, in portraying the offences as unprecedented. They were, above all, political offences which had inspired the wrath of the king. They had also deepened the existing constitutional conflict and ushered in a web of legal complexities. The judges, when first consulted by Charles, while acknowledging the difficulty of the issue, had generally considered the offences to be punishable outside Parliament. Then, when consulted at the time of the Star Chamber proceedings, they had appeared to favour the arguments of the defence. If the judges of King's Bench were to rule in favour of the crown, they must contradict this latter opinion and overrule any marginal claim of privilege. The four judges were to display remarkable unanimity in handing down their ruling on the defendants' plea.

Essentially two principles underlay the ruling of the Court and together made the decision on jurisdiction possible. Both were evident in the opinion given by each individual judge.[164] One was the initial pronouncement of the judiciary in 1629 that offences against the crown committed in Parliament and not there punished could legitimately be punished in another court.[165] The other was the notion of guilt which the crown had striven to communicate to the judges in this case. Here the government's conspiracy theory acquired vital legal significance as a description of events. The actions of Eliot and the rest represented a conspiracy by individuals which was unparliamentary and offensive to the crown. The application of these two principles together would confirm the union of government and justice under the Caroline regime.

---

[160] Ibid., col. 304.   [161] Ibid.   [162] Ibid., col. 305; SP16/142/36.   [163] *ST*, iii, col. 305.
[164] For the full judgements see ibid., cols. 305–9.
[165] This involved the overturning of any view that Strode's case (1513) established a general principle of privilege beyond the privacy of the act of 4 Hen. 8; ibid., col. 309.

The judges all concurred that the offences were punishable in the Court of King's Bench.[166] This ruling was made and this precedent established in the name of justice, and of the government of the country. In Judge Croke's words, 'all manner of offences which are against the crown are examinable in this court'.[167] Jones said that such offences against the state should not remain unpunished. He confessed that although the case was new, the issue had been in his mind for eighteen years.[168] Whitelocke's opinion was the most revealing as to the significance of the decision. It was also one of a series of pronouncements he had made on the question of sovereignty since the previous reign, pronouncements which had increasingly favoured the royal power:[169]

But though it be not capital, yet it is criminal, for it is sowing of sedition to the destruction of the commonwealth. The question now is not between us that are judges of this court, and the Parliament, or between the king and the Parliament, but between some private members of the House of Commons and the king himself: for here the king himself questions them for those offences, as well he may. In every commonwealth there is one super-eminent power that is not subject to be questioned by any other, and that is the king in this commonwealth ... no other within the realm hath this privilege. It is true, that that which is done in Parliament by consent of all the house, shall not be questioned elsewhere; but if any private members [no longer act as befits judges but enter into sedition] is there such sanctimony in the place, that they may not be questioned for it elsewhere?[170]

Whitelocke's was a fair conclusion on a difficult constitutional issue, an issue which would remain open to debate. The point of the ruling was that the exercise of the royal authority in government was, *ipso facto*, just. The crown had found the defendants' words and actions unacceptable. They, however, believed that they had behaved properly and were therefore innocent. The appeal to privilege was essentially a legal device forced upon them by the political nature of the issue. The ruling upon jurisdiction was the legal expression of the crown's desire to punish them for behaviour which it would not tolerate. The understanding of a conspiracy by private members was vital to the crown's case and enabled it to avoid the arguable immunity provided by the resolutions of the House of Commons. Yet it begged, and evaded, the question of what could be the unacceptable behaviour of a whole house, involving as it did an essential judgement of proper parliamentary practice.

Three days had been allotted for the hearing on jurisdiction but the judges cut short the arguments on the second day (27 January) and overrode the defence by giving their ruling. It could now be required of the defendants that they answer the information as charged. Failure to enter a satisfactory plea would render them liable to condemnation upon a *nihil dicit*, tacit confession

---

[166] Ibid., cols. 305ff. [167] Ibid., col. 309. [168] Ibid., col. 306.
[169] S. R. Gardiner (ed.), *Parliamentary debates in 1610* (Camden Society, London, 1862), pp. 103–4; *LD1628*, pp. 219–20, 224, 226; Russell, *Parliaments*, p. 364.
[170] *ST*, iii, col. 308 (material in brackets my translation from the Latin)

under the common law. In being required to plead further, thereby acknowledging the jurisdiction of the Court and enabling trial of their words and
actions *per se*, the prisoners were warned that the alternative was to be judged
guilty by the ordinary process of law, given the ruling against them on the
jurisdiction of King's Bench.[171] They were at the end of the road by which
they had sought to extend and evade the crown's efforts to publicize their
arbitrary guilt of political offence and hence the justice of their imprisonment.
The only option remaining was to seek to prevaricate and delay the
inevitable.

The prisoners tried to formulate a plea defending privilege yet satisfactory
to the Court. The legal position was hopeless, however, and their counsel were
dispirited and afraid. Time was also running out. On 1 February the Court
gave the prisoners two days to enter their pleas. They could confer with
counsel but it was, as Eliot wrote, 'a time more proper to devotion than for
law'.[172] On Monday, 2 February, a reprieve was obtained until the following
Thursday, the last day of term. There was too little time, however, and
nothing could be done. On Thursday, counsel pressed for a deferment until
next term but to no avail.[173] Jones gave the judgement. He said that the
defendants had admitted the matter of the information to be true, 'and we
think their plea to the jurisdiction insufficient . . . ' The liberties of Parliament
were not in question, 'but [rather] in this case there was a conspiracy . . . to
slander the state, and to raise sedition and discord between the king, his peers,
and people; and this was not a parliamentary course'. Jones invoked the
resolution of all the judges the previous year, that such an offence against the
crown in Parliament could be punished in another court.[174] The judgement
was a foregone conclusion with the prisoners' failure to alter their pleas,
already decidedly insufficient to the judges. The sentencing marked the goal
of the crown's intentions since the arrests a year earlier. Eliot, Holles and
Valentine were to be imprisoned at the king's pleasure, and not released without giving security for their good behaviour and making submission and
acknowledgement of their offence. They were also heavily fined. Eliot's
financial penalty was £2,000.[175] Thus the prisoners' guilt was legally
recorded.

[171] Ibid., cols. 305–6; Birch, ii, p. 56; Grosart, *Letter book of Sir John Eliot*, p. 89.
[172] Grosart, *Letter book of Sir John Eliot*, p. 91.
[173] This account of proceedings between 26 January and 5 February is based principally upon
that of Eliot, a first-hand source, in preference to that of Birch. See Grosart, *Letter book of
Sir John Eliot*, pp. 89–95; ST, iii, cols. 305–9; Searle, *Barrington family letters*, p. 132;
Hulme, *Life of Sir John Eliot*, pp. 335–6; Gardiner, *History*, vii, p. 119. See also Birch, ii,
pp. 56–7.
[174] ST, iii, cols. 309–10.
[175] Holles was fined 1,000 marks and Valentine (being of less ability to pay) £500; ibid.,
col. 310.

The judges of King's Bench had not specifically prejudiced the law but they had favoured the crown in its proceedings. Their insistence upon judgement of bail and the requirements of trial created obstacles for the government which was forced to achieve its ends under the law and in the gaze of the public eye. Yet the judges' perception of the prisoners' criminality, together with pressure from the crown, confirmed them in the notions of guilt and jurisdiction which rendered their judgement possible and ultimately made them accessories to the fusion of government and justice or arbitrary rule. The ruling on jurisdiction was the legal and constitutional key. It involved a conception of royal government as being rightly unprejudiced by independent dissent in policy, or criminal law as construed by the king's courts. It also involved a progressive commitment by the King's Bench judges which, despite their final unanimity, must have been difficult.[176]

In context the case presented a paradox. The issue of arbitrary imprisonment had led to the Petition of Right and its requirement of an answerable cause being shown upon writ of habeas corpus. In forcing the crown to proceed according to law, Eliot and his companions found that their sole resort was to avoid direct answers to the charges levelled against them which had in fact been truly indicated by the cause shown. In arguing the legitimacy of their actions in pleading against jurisdiction, they also came to argue for parliamentary rights, for the legal protection of loyal political activity as individual members understood it. In forcing the prisoners to use privilege as a defence, the crown had furthered its development as an ideal in itself. It was an objection to the predisposition and the nature of Charles's government, specifically represented in the predisposition of the Court to rule upon its jurisdiction. In arguing that they should rightly answer in Parliament, Eliot and the others were also arguing against their guilt. But the final judgement of the Court was against them. It had in truth been pre-determined, and that by the crown, forced to abide by the law, and insisting upon the justice of its government.

What was the fate of the prisoners and the subsequent history of the case? The Long Parliament condemned the entire proceedings (which featured extensively in the Grand Remonstrance) as illegal and against the privilege of Parliament, awarding compensation, and in 1667 both houses upheld these resolutions, the Lords reversing the decision in the case upon writ of error.[177] Eliot died in prison in 1632, still refusing to submit to the king and admit his guilt. What happened to Holles after the judgement is unclear. He was

---

[176] How far the remainder of the judiciary subscribed to the ruling in this case it is difficult to know. The complexity of the privilege question, with that of the evidence, suggests that the judiciary would at least have remained divided on the matter in early 1630.

[177] *ST*, iii, cols. 293, 310–15; Maitland, *Constitutional history*, pp. 242, 321; Gardiner, *Constitutional documents*, pp. 209–10.

apparently still in prison in 1631. He was seeking to petition the king for release at that time. He lived in the West Country during most of the 1630s, presumably being bound for good behaviour, and finally paid his fine. He resented his prosecution, an experience which encouraged his militancy in the Long Parliament. Valentine and Strode remained in prison until they were released in 1640, on the eve of the Short Parliament. Strode and Holles were two of the 'five members' whom Charles sought to arrest for treason in 1642. Hobart gave security and was freed in 1631, at a time of plague. Selden was freed in May 1631, at the instance of Arundel and Pembroke, who wanted his assistance at law, and was bound on security for appearance in court once a term. He abjectly petitioned the king in 1635 and was unconditionally discharged. Walter Long was fined and imprisoned by Star Chamber on the very same day that Eliot, Holles and Valentine were found guilty. He was still in prison in 1632 but his later fate is unclear. He also sat in the Long Parliament.[178] Neither the prisoners' resolve nor the king's implacability were exhausted by the crown's pyrrhic victory in the political battle of 1629 and 1630.

In the midst of the trial, Weston wrote to Cardinal Richelieu that Charles was making good progress in reducing 'the puritans' to reason.[179] His use of this word echoed Charles's statement to Chateauneuf several months earlier. Weston and Dorchester were concerned that political dissent should not impair the international standing of the government. After the judgement in the case Dorchester wrote to England's envoy in Switzerland, reporting the proceedings and estimating their significance for the regime:

time hath bred no small alteration, but (thanks be to God) all to the better, by the settling of the disquiet of men's minds after the disorders of the last Parliament. And that is done more ways than one, but chiefly by sentences in the chief judicial court against such as were the chief authors of those disorders. Three of which are fined and imprisoned by the King's Bench upon the point of refusing to answer to their accusations. Whereby the world sees that Parliament men must be responsible for their words and actions in other courts, and so they will be more moderate and circumspect hereafter.[180]

For Dorchester the point of the sentences was not only the prisoners' guilt but the effect of its public demonstration. The point was that obedience should be compelled by the popular knowledge that the king's authority was

---

[178] Not long before Eliot's death he maintained that he was not the king's prisoner but the judges', PRO, C115, M35, 8389, Pory to Slego, 31 Dec. 1631. See also Birch, ii, pp. 55–6, 59, 61–2, 64, 66, 83, 96, 103, 161–2; Clarendon, *Rebellion*, vol. i, p. 249; NUL, Ne.C., 15,404, pp. 232–3; Grosart, *Letter book of Sir John Eliot*, pp. 217–18; *ST*, iii, cols. 233–6; Fletcher, *Outbreak of the English civil war*, pp. 257, 340; Gardiner, *History*, vii, pp. 226–7; Hulme, *Life of Sir John Eliot*, p. 391; *DNB*, s.v. Selden, Hobart, Holles, Valentine and Strode; Crawford, *Denzil Holles*, pp. 25–6.
[179] AMRE, CPA, 43, fol. 338r–v.
[180] SP16/162/18.

just. Dorchester's view contradicted Eliot's idea of the central and high place of parliamentary privilege. He believed that Parliament should not provide exemption from the universal authority of the crown. But Dorchester's view also reflected his belief in the parliamentary process. The judgement, he concluded, meant that 'the king, when he finds good, may meet with his people with so much the more assurance, that they will never transgress in the point of due respect and obedience'.[181] This conclusion represented the more moderate interpretation of a reform in government, an interpretation which Charles would completely reject. Dorchester's constitutionalist view had come to accommodate the drift to prerogative rule, a phase which the Secretary saw as temporary in the history of the reign. He reported the recovery of trade and the dying down of disputes over the customs. The king, moreover, had begun to fine those who, while eligible, had failed to take up knighthood – 'So as by this and other lawful (though extraordinary) ways some good sums are likely to be raised, till his majesty shall see [in] his own time to help himself again by the usual course of subsidies.'[182] The events of the last parliamentary session had prompted a general policy for the government of the kingdom, not least out of financial necessity. It was characterized by the rejection of privilege and its claim for the place of Parliament, by objection to the consistent dissent of leading members of the political nation – within both houses and beyond, by the extraordinary use of the law in the courts and the country, by a developing financial dependence on customs revenues, and by a distinct spirit of reform.

Dorchester's report was an explicit conclusion on a critical point in the development of the personal rule. Here the emergence of the style of government which characterized those years can be detected. That beginning grew out of the collapse of the Parliament and the battle in the courts, as well as out of the desire for political improvement which surrounded Buckingham's death. It was as much the inadvertent result of recent events as of any design. It was, moreover, inextricably related, as will be seen, to the opening of Anglo-Spanish talks in Madrid during the winter of 1629–30. Yet this peculiarly Caroline style of government had an overriding and unifying quality. In proceeding against the members of Parliament and in resorting to unparliamentary taxation, Charles's government had acted in arbitrary fashion and provoked very serious conflict. It had invoked the royal prerogative to imply that the king's discretion should be unimpeachable, not subject to any legal or public review.[183] Such was the depth of the crisis that even

---

[181] Ibid.   [182] Ibid.
[183] Such an approach was anticipated by the forced loan, but Dorchester's commentary marks a very significant turning point. The political crisis had become immeasurably graver since the mid-1620s: the national policy the Secretary described was definitely new and it led to an era of real personal rule. Eliot believed that England was inexorably becoming absolutist after 1629; Sommerville, *Politics and ideology*, p. 158.

moderate counsellors were willing to administer the arbitrary measures to which the king, a weak man, was instinctively disposed. This disposition of Charles derived from his constitutional preconceptions, but these were only a part of his personal reaction to great events in the face of which he felt threatened. In proceeding this way his government only encouraged dissent. Articulate and prepared to go to extremes, such dissent was highly dangerous and arguably unprecedented. The crown used this threat in seeking to justify its actions at law. Yet Charles's government was remarkably sensitive to reflections upon its justice and this was demonstrated dramatically in the prosecution of the antiquary Sir Robert Cotton. The case of Cotton and his associates was of fundamental relevance to the debate, and the conflict, over the character and principles of Charles's government.

In the troubled English autumn of 1629, at the same time that Eliot, Holles and Valentine were charged in King's Bench, Cotton was arrested, with his librarian Richard James, Oliver St John, and the earls of Bedford, Clare and Somerset, for circulating a tract held to be a seditious libel of Charles's government. They were examined by a special committee of Council, and prosecuted with Selden (already in custody) in Star Chamber. Cotton's library was sealed, and his house searched for documents potentially damaging to the crown. Heath filed charges in Michaelmas term 1629 and the hearing of the case was fixed for May of 1630. The tract was actually written during the reign of James I, apparently by Robert Dudley, the illegitimate son of Elizabeth's favourite, Leicester. It found its way into Cotton's library where St John obtained a copy, either through Richard James or Cotton himself. It came to be circulated among Bedford, Clare and Somerset in the summer of 1629. Cotton facilitated its circulation and intended to publish and answer it. Heath's information in Star Chamber recited its evils and accused Cotton and the others of having written it. The defendants denied any conspiracy and held that the document had no relevance to the events of Charles's reign. In the light of the evidence, these disavowals are scarcely credible.[184]

---

[184] It is possible that the writing became more widely known at this time as a piece of court gossip and at the inns of court. The circulation may even have extended to the United Provinces, where Charles ordered that it, or something closely resembling it, be suppressed and those responsible punished; SP84/140/fos. 198r–199v, SP84/141/fo. 10r. According to D'Ewes, it was Wentworth who first alerted the Council to the tract but this is uncorroborated. Halliwell, *Autobiography of Sir Simonds D'Ewes*, ii, pp. 40n, 41; Wedgwood, *Strafford: a revaluation*, pp. 81, 319. Clare believed that either Manchester or Arundel made it known to Charles; NUL, Ne.C., 15,404, pp. 232–3. See also SP16/151/24, SP16/151/36, SP16/151/80, SP16/152/78; PRO 31/3/66/fo. 197r–v; PRO, PC 2/39, pp. 493–6, and PC 2/40, p. 337; SP39, Sign Manual, Car. I, xii, 15; Rymer, *Foedera*, xix, pp. 198–9; *APC 1628–9*, 13, 15 Nov. 1629; *APC 1630–1*, 24 Nov. 1630; Birch, ii, pp. 43–4, 52, 57–8; BL, Harl. Ms 7000, fos. 267r–269v; Rushworth, *Historical collections*, i, pp. 681–2, and ii, pp. 51–3; *ST*, iii, cols. 387–400; HMC Buccleuch, iii, p. 345; PRO, C115, M31, 8142, Flower to Scudamore, 30 Jan. 1630; Braybrooke, *Autobiography of Sir John Bramston*, p. 61; Laud, *Works*, vii, p. 34.

The tract was a form of advice to the king of England to 'secure your state and to bridle the impertinency of Parliament'.[185] It held that the basis of government should be force and necessity, and that authority should be solely in the hands of the prince. It advocated a regal power to legislate without Parliament, considering that Parliament, as the highest court, should be subject to the king. It pointed to the danger of parliamentary usurpation of royal power and held up the example of Louis XI of France who suppressed such a development. The tract advocated many unparliamentary and novel taxes and the fortification of the country to keep the people in subjection. Heath held this to be a libel of the crown, supposedly implying Charles's intention to do such things. He argued that the document would generate disorder in England by encouraging fears of constitutional innovation. Charles, according to Heath, had upheld the kingdom's ancient and fundamental laws. The alleged crime of the defendants was to have considered publishing the tract, failing to bring it to the knowledge of the government.[186] What use Cotton sought to make of the document, and how far his intention to answer it was malicious, or out of desire for genuine debate, is difficult to know. It is very likely that he considered it relevant to current developments and desired the opinion of like-minded associates. Circulation of the tract could only encourage discussion of the form of government in England.

It has been argued that the prosecution of Cotton and his associates is evidence of conflict between court factions, and that the arrests represented a counter-attack on Buckingham's enemies by the remnants of his followers.[187] There would certainly appear to be truth in this. Cotton believed he had sore enemies at court in Bishops Laud and Neile. There remained a residual division in political circles between those who had risen under Buckingham and those who had not.[188] Yet congruent with these elements of faction and personality, there is a wider political and ideological significance to the Cotton case as an historical event. Contemporary observers believed it was very much bound up with the revolt in King's Bench. The two cases were clearly linked in the public mind.[189] Chateauneuf reported the two prosecutions as one. He understood that the Cotton arrests could be construed as

---

[185] SP16/151/fo. 134r.
[186] SP16/151/36. On seditious libel see Holdsworth, *History of English law*, v, pp. 208–12.
[187] K. M. Sharpe, *Sir Robert Cotton, 1586–1631* (Oxford, 1979), pp. 145, 213–15. I am grateful to Kevin Sharpe for helpful discussions of this period.
[188] Dorchester, a leading Buckingham client, played a prominent role in the proceedings against Cotton; Reeve, 'Viscount Dorchester', p. 182. The Venetian ambassador reported a rumour that the Dudley tract had been found in Buckingham's papers; *CSPV 1629–32*, pp. 241–2. See also Green, *Diary of John Rous*, pp. 34, 46; Halliwell, *Autobiography of Sir Simonds D'Ewes*, ii, p. 41; SP16/139/19.
[189] BL, Add. Ms 22959, fo. 37; SP16/153/23; PRO, C115, M30, 8066, 8142, M31, 8119, Flower to Scudamore, 7 and 13 Nov. 1629, 30 Jan. 1630.

an act against Parliament.[190] The Venetian ambassador considered that 'it is all dependent upon the contest going on between the king and the people . . . [the government] proceed with special secrecy'.[191]

There are striking connections between the Cotton prosecution and the proceedings against Eliot and his fellow-members of the Commons. The legal proceedings were almost simultaneous, both indictments being filed in Michaelmas term 1629. Selden was involved in both cases. Cotton's library was searched and sealed only ten days after the studies of Eliot, Selden and Holles. The alleged offence in the Cotton case was again a form of sedition destructive of good order in the country and subversive of the king's authority. As with the other case, it was held to be a conspiracy involving secret communications. Heath's information against Cotton and the others stressed the need for their exemplary punishment, and likewise in this case, as with the other, there seems to have been a definite assumption by the crown of guilt before trial.[192] There was indeed an underlying relationship between the two cases. Both had as their principal and explicitly stated theme the nature of Charles's government. The reaction of that government to the Dudley tract revealed its fear of dissent, as well as its sensitivity to any perceived accusation of absolutism.

Moreover, the defendants in the Cotton case had a remarkable history of opposition to and criticism of Charles's regime. Of those accused with Cotton, Clare was one of the king's most notable political opponents. He had resisted the forced loan. He had been one of the influential advocates in the Lords for the Petition of Right. His son Denzil Holles was eventually sentenced with Eliot. Clare had approved of Denzil's efforts to obtain release by habeas corpus in the autumn of 1629. He believed his own prosecution in the Cotton case was due to his opposition to Charles as well as Denzil's behaviour in Parliament:

I have been opposite in Parliament, and against the loan, our brother [sic] also a refractory lower house man, which is cast to my score. I must therefore pay for it accordingly.[193]

Bedford, likewise, had supported the Petition of Right. St John would be a member of the Providence Island Company (see pp. 210–13, below). Selden had been a consistent thorn in Charles's side, in the Commons and King's

---

[190] PRO 31/3/66/fos. 195v–196r, 209r.   [191] *CSPV 1629–32*, p. 233.

[192] *APC 1629–30*, 3 and 13 Nov. 1629; SP16/151/36/fos. 134r, 137v–138r; *CSPV 1629–32*, pp. 241–2; SP78/85/fo. 122v; PRO, C115, M30, 8066, Flower to Scudamore, 13 Nov. 1629.

[193] NUL, Ne.C., 15,404, p. 233, Clare to his son, Lord Haughton, 7 Oct. 1629. Clare particularly resented the proceedings against him since they were conducted in a prerogative court; ibid., p. 234.

Bench, since the time of the Five Knights' case.[194] Cotton himself had advised the Council against maintaining a hard-line attitude against Parliament in 1628. He was also closely associated with leading activists in the Commons. Eliot was an intimate friend of both Cotton and Richard James. He made use of Cotton's library in writing speeches against the government. Cotton also supplied manuscripts cited by Littleton in defending Selden in King's Bench. Eliot and Cotton both believed that Parliament deserved a major conciliar role in the king's government.[195] They corresponded in February 1629 about plans for a parliamentary campaign against the Arminian bishops. Cotton wanted resolutions in the Commons in favour of true doctrine as established in Parliament in the time of Elizabeth, to 'prevent the plot . . . of those bishops that have fancied a way to introduce innovations by a convocation power . . . '[196] Yet the concern was not only about spiritual innovation. Richard James wrote to Eliot in prison in September 1629, telling him to read Lipsius, the neo-Stoic propagator of authoritarian political ideas. Such ideas, James believed, had a suspicious echo in Charles's urge to abandon the Dutch in favour of Spain, the paradigm of tyranny and oppression.[197]

With their pedigree of political opposition under Charles, and their obvious concern with innovation, the circulation of Dudley's pamphlet by Cotton and his friends had clear relevance to public affairs in 1629. Cotton's interest in making some form of comment upon arbitrary regimes indicates that he and others were unwilling to allow their suspicion of innovation to remain private. Clare and the rest understood that their prosecution was related to their dissent. Neither did they fail to recognize the fear which Dudley's tract had inspired within the regime.

The government's reaction underlines the real significance of the Cotton episode. The case certainly involved personal animosities, and the prosecution offered Charles a financial incentive with the prospect of a sentencing of wealthy men.[198] The overriding reason for the proceedings, however, was the Council's and particularly the king's sense of a threat. Charles told the Council that the tract reflected upon the justice and sincerity of his government. He believed that it proceeded from a pernicious design against himself and against the state.[199] The Cotton case arose just as the battle in King's

---

[194] Gregg, *King Charles I*, pp. 298–9; *CSPCol. 1574–1660*, p. 123.
[195] *DNB*, s.v. Cotton, Sir Robert; *ST*, iii, cols. 256–7; Grosart, *Letter book of Sir John Eliot*, pp. 29–30, 35–8, 66–7, 137–8; Sharpe, *Sir Robert Cotton*, pp. 142, 182–3, 213.
[196] Grosart, *Letter book of Sir John Eliot*, pp. 35–8.
[197] Ibid., pp. 66–7. On the influence of Lipsius during this period see J. H. Elliott, 'Yet another crisis?', in P. Clark (ed.), *The European crisis of the 1590s* (London, 1985), pp. 306, 310.
[198] NUL, Ne.C., 15,404, p. 233; *CSPV 1629–32*, p. 242.
[199] SP16/151/70, declaration of the king to Council, 15 Nov. 1629. For examples of conciliar thinking along the same lines see SP16/167/44 (Dorchester); SP16/151/24, SP16/151/80 (Harsnet).

Bench reached its height. This coincidence seemed to point to a nest of subversives. Charles already knew that his critics included leading noblemen; Bedford and Clare, it seemed, were persisting in dissent. The Dudley tract, moreover, was apparently promoting the very rumours of innovation which the government feared.[200] Charles lashed out. He wished to punish his enemies and to justify the principles by which he ruled. Cotton and the others became potential victims of the circumstances of the government, of Charles's wounded honour and of his belief in a conspiracy against himself.[201] The tract may well have been an old curiosity. But to the minds of the king, of those about him and those accused, it acquired an historical importance belied by its provenance. The power of the issue was reflected in the government's searching inquiry and in the fear and disavowals of the defendants.[202]

The outcome of the story can be seen as anticlimactic but the case remains important. At the end of November 1629 the original of the Dudley tract was discovered in Cotton's library. Sir David Fowlis testified that he had obtained it from Dudley in Florence and brought it to England during the previous reign. The establishment of its age and true authorship seems to have diminished but not ended the king's desire to prosecute. Just as the Star Chamber proceedings began, on 29 May 1630, Henrietta Maria gave birth to a son. Charles suspended the prosecution, professing his desire to be merciful in his happiness. He also mentioned the discovery of the authorship and the social rank of the defendants. The birth of an heir may have enabled Charles to climb down without losing face. But there is no cause to doubt his stated reasons for clemency. Except for Selden, who remained in custody in connection with the other case, those accused were allowed to go free. It was ordered that the tract be burnt.[203]

The most telling evidence of the significance of the Cotton case survives in the form of a private memorandum penned by Dorchester. It consists of personal reflections probably intended as speaking notes for Star Chamber. Dorchester's objection to the Dudley tract was to its contents and what he considered their likely effect upon the public mind. He saw the circulation

---

[200] *CSPV 1629–32*, p. 270.
[201] NUL, Ne.C., 15,404, p. 233. There is circumstantial evidence that the case was popularly understood as a general proceeding against the critics of Charles's government, especially those among the nobility. It was reported in London that the case would extend to Abbot, Essex, Warwick, Bishop Williams and others; PRO, C115, M24, 7757, Moore to Scudamore, 7 Nov. 1629. See also PRO, C115, M31, 8119, Flower to Scudamore of same date.
[202] NUL, Ne.C., 15,404, p. 233; Rushworth, *Historical collections*, ii, pp. 51–3; *ST*, iii, cols. 398–400; PRO 31/3/66/fo. 206v; *CSPV 1629–32*, pp. 241–2; SP16/151/24, SP16/151/80–1, SP16/167/44; SP78/85/fos. 97r, 122v.
[203] Rushworth, *Historical collections*, ii, pp. 51–3; Gardiner, *History*, vii, p. 140.

and intended publication of the tract as a conspiracy to stir up discord between king and people: 'an opinion of innovation of government nourished by this paper, whereby to beget the hatred of the people . . . [towards the] king and government'.[204] Moreover, to Dorchester it was inconceivable 'to change the laws and customs of the kingdom'. The implied reflection upon the government was therefore every bit as libellous as seditious. He concluded:

Being in the place of trust and secrecy that I am, I praise God I may say with a good conscience that I have seen nothing in his majesty's courses or commandments which may any ways offend a just mind.[205]

This statement of personal belief in the inherent justice of Charles's government is most revealing at such a time. The Cotton episode had, in effect, involved Dorchester and other senior servants of the crown in defence of the principles of Charles's government. The Secretary believed that a just estimation would vindicate that government against any accusation that it had transgressed the spirit of the constitution.

Yet in framing this opinion Dorchester had made a significant appeal, not to precedent or history, but to reason. This suggests strongly his suspicion that such a reflection upon the government might be justified; that some of the measures he had sanctioned and implemented were dubious and extreme; that Charles was inclined to reject the rule of law and the parliamentary process; that his kingship exhibited what could be interpreted as pretensions to absolutism. Dorchester did not view the king's government in this way, but he had felt the need to ponder the accusation. He felt able to exonerate the regime because he was subject to two interrelated influences. One was his traditional belief that the royal authority was ultimately of prime importance in national life. The other was his hatred of conspiracy and subversion, disobedience and disorder, and the destructive aspects of the political crisis from which the government was only just beginning to recover.[206] These manifestations could easily appear as a threat to English society as contemporaries understood it, endorsed by divine authority and the workings of time and represented in the person of the king. It was this commitment to royal power by Dorchester and others which had allowed Charles's resort to arbitrary measures – measures such as the proceedings against the imprisoned members of Parliament and the various forms of unparliamentary taxation. Dorchester, while he denied it, had actually become a fellow-traveller for new counsels. But his denial was born of neither ignorance nor conscious rationalization. His articulate conservatism represents an habitual way of thinking among many from whom Charles drew support. Such thinking allowed the king to maintain his position in the years to come despite bitter opposition. Charles's government was indeed vulnerable to charges of autocracy and

[204] SP16/167/44.   [205] Ibid.   [206] Reeve, 'Viscount Dorchester', pp. 11–14, 199–200.

constitutional innovation. Its manner of proceeding had triggered fierce opposition in Parliament, the courts and beyond. The conflict was deep, the mutual fears were powerful, and the predicament of the moderates in government was the measure of an increasingly dangerous polarization amongst those most intensely involved in national politics.

The two leading cases in King's Bench and Star Chamber had highlighted the emerging character of Charles's rule. During these years it was evident in other cases and also reflected in the government of the country as a whole. The case of Richard Chambers, who had denounced what he saw as overtaxation of the merchants, was tried in Star Chamber when Selden and the others were seeking freedom by habeas corpus. Chambers was sentenced to imprisonment until he would acknowledge his offence, seek the king's pardon and pay a fine of £2,000. He contested the legality of the decree by bringing an action in the Court of Exchequer, also appealing for the restoration of his goods. The Barons, by this time minus Walter, found against the argument questioning the jurisdiction of Star Chamber. The hearings on Charles's right to tonnage and poundage continued inconclusively. Chambers remained in prison until 1635, refusing to pay his fine or acknowledge his fault. His protest led to the ruin of his estate.[207] As with the other cases, his had involved a serious reflection upon the government, summary justice and the crown's intention to inflict exemplary punishment.

The same features are evident in the case of Alexander Leighton, a fanatical minister of the Scottish church arrested in February 1630 for his authorship of the tract *An appeal to parliament; or, Sion's plea against prelacy*. A copy of the tract had come to the attention of Laud. A sustained polemic against the Caroline Church and government, it was virulently anti-episcopal and held the bishops responsible for all evil in the land. They had encouraged Buckingham in his opposition to Parliaments until, by God's will, he was cut down. An 'Arminianized and Jesuitical crew', they had captured the mind of the king. Leighton criticized Charles's marriage to a Catholic and England's failure to protect the Huguenots and further the Protestant cause. He called upon the Parliament of 1628–9 to bring about reformation and to resist dissolution by the king. Leighton was prosecuted in Star Chamber for the treatise in mid-1630. Heath portrayed the work as the fundamental attack which it undoubtedly was. He held that it was seditious, anarchical and verging upon treason. He correctly identified its ideological opposition both to monarchy and to episcopacy. Leighton had spent time in the United

---

[207] Chambers was sentenced to make acknowledgement before the Council. The Long Parliament decided to compensate him for his sufferings, but the money voted was appropriated for the war. See *ST*, iii, cols. 373–84; Birch, i, pp. 416–17, 420, 432, 440, and ii, pp. 40–1, 53; Gardiner, *History*, vii, pp. 84–6, 114–15; *DNB*, s.v. Chambers, Richard.

Provinces and was clearly influenced by the model of the republic, as well as by the traditions of radical presbyterianism. He had described the English Parliament as the 'states representative' who should rescue the king from error. Heath condemned *Sion's plea* as subversive of the discipline of the Church and as a brief for 'popular government'. He called for the suppression of the recent practice of printing submissions to Parliament.[208] Leighton fell foul of the fullest severity of the Court. It held publication of the book to be a scandal against the king and queen, the peers and especially the bishops. The two Chief Justices believed that the offence warranted indictment and trial for treason. Leighton was sentenced to imprisonment at the pleasure of the king, a fine of £10,000 which he could never hope to pay, degradation from ecclesiastical orders and vicious corporal punishment. He was to lose his ears, be branded on the cheeks and whipped at the pillory at Cheapside. The government attempted unsuccessfully to discover the names of those who had approved of his appeal to Parliament.[209]

The Chambers and Leighton cases underline the Caroline attitude to dissent. The offences were eligible for punishment under any political circumstances. Charles's government was defensive and rigorous, however, and concerned to make examples. This approach came naturally to men such as Wentworth and Heath.[210] But it was also encouraged by Charles himself. His instructions to Wentworth as Lord President of the North in June 1629 used the strongest language in ordering the suppression of sedition and offences against the state. More and more there were

devised, spread abroad, reported and published many false and seditious tales, news, sayings, writings, books, letters and libels which amongst the people have wrought and hereafter may work great mischief . . . [211]

Those responsible should be apprehended and all means used to trace the originators. Such offenders were to be openly punished by fine and imprisonment. Those who endangered the king and state should be referred to the king and Council.[212] Wentworth was required to use severity against notable offenders,

so as the opinion or report of severity may work that by force which is and hath been long seen will not be obtained by favours and gentleness.[213]

---

[208] Heath, significantly, styled Star Chamber 'an epitome of a Parliament'. Gardiner, *Speech of Sir Robert Heath*, p. 9.

[209] Leighton lost only one ear since only half the punishment was inflicted; Gardiner, *History*, vii, p. 151 and n. On Leighton's case see Gardiner, *Speech of Sir Robert Heath*, pp. i–xii, 1–10; *ST*, iii, cols. 383–8; Gardiner, *History*, vii, pp. 143–52.

[210] Gardiner, *History*, vii, pp. 233, 236; Reeve, 'Sir Robert Heath's advice'.

[211] Bodl. Lib., Rawl. Ms C197, fo. 12v.

[212] Ibid., fos. 12v–13r.   [213] Ibid., fo. 26v.

The king's sense of threat, fear of subversion, and inclination to repression are clearly detectable here, as is the highly unstable political climate of 1629.

The administrative initiatives of the personal rule can be seen as pragmatic and directed towards short-term solutions.[214] Yet undoubtedly they reflected Charles's personal predilections – for order, unquestioning obedience and, increasingly, non-parliamentary rule. They also constituted a reaction, within the higher reaches of government, against the disorder and instability of the Buckingham era.[215] Their enabling authority was unashamedly the royal prerogative expressed through proclamation, royal commission and the orders of the Privy Council. As Dorchester put it, a principle emerged of remedying the lack of 'particular laws not formally established' by means of 'acts of state and the prerogative royal'.[216] As Clarendon said when criticizing the government of these years in retrospect, 'supplemental acts of state were made to supply defects of laws . . . '[217] Charles, however, came to establish no effective political or financial substitute for Parliament. He always remained constrained (albeit unwillingly) by the underlying framework of the constitution. Not surprisingly, after the opposition to the forced loan, his chief sources of revenue during the 1630s – the customs, knighthood fines and Ship Money – all rested upon clearly established, if sometimes legalistic, rights. They therefore stood a chance of evading the Petition of Right, and in turn reflected the depth and strength of the traditional notion that English taxation was by consent.

After the customs, fines for distraint of knighthood were the principal form of non-parliamentary taxation during the emergence of the personal rule.[218] Charles did possess the ancient right to fine any man worth £40 a year who failed to present himself to be knighted at the coronation. The practice of levying knighthood fines had, however, long since lapsed.[219] Charles had no desire to make more knights, having stated his belief that there were too many in England already.[220] This was distinct, however, from fining men for not becoming knights, even those ineligible by birth or income.[221] A conciliar commission was established at the end of January 1630 for the levying of the

---

[214] Hirst, *Authority and conflict*, pp. 172–3.
[215] SP81/37/fos. 110r–111r; SP77/20/fos. 150r–151r; Reeve, 'Sir Robert Heath's advice'; Sharpe, 'Personal rule of Charles I', pp. 57–8.
[216] *Lismore papers*, ed. A. B. Grosart (10 vols., London, 1886–8), 2nd ser., iii, p. 176.
[217] Clarendon, *Rebellion*, vol. i, p. 84.
[218] I.e. during the years covered by this study.
[219] Gardiner believed it had lapsed for more than a century; *History*, vii, p. 167. It was unheard of during the Elizabethan period; H. H. Leonard, 'Distraint of knighthood: the last phase, 1625–1641', *History*, lxiii (1978), p. 23.
[220] *CSPD Addenda 1625–44*, p. 79.
[221] Russell, *Crisis of Parliaments*, p. 318; Thomas, 'Financial and administrative developments', p. 119.

fines. The financial return was slow until the Court of Exchequer ruled that the exercise was legal in a series of decisions between August and the following February. As a revenue-raising effort this could not be repeated but it was relatively successful. The device raised a sum in the vicinity of £170,000, the equivalent of approximately three parliamentary subsidies.[222]

The collection of the fines relied upon the co-operation of the gentry in each locality.[223] This did not necessarily signify universal or even widespread approval of the levy. Given the legality of the commission, no objection could be made to it in principle, only special pleading in the individual case. As Dorchester wrote in March,

the business of the knights goeth roundly forward, no man disputing the legality of it in general, nor alleging other than particular excuses which are admitted or rejected by his majesty's courts according to their merit.[224]

The evidence suggests that there was significant opposition, on this basis, to the levying of the fines. It was reported in London in February 1632 that twenty-five peers had refused to pay.[225] The earl of Essex and other members of the nobility, having become refusers, appeared before Council. Essex protested that he had carried Charles's sword at the coronation and had then been ready to receive any honour from the king.[226]

Resentment of non-parliamentary revenue-raising could be tacit as well as explicit. Clarendon, in retrospect, emphasized the creeping unpopularity which arbitrary fiscalism brought upon Charles and his government. Of the knighthood fines he wrote, 'though it had a foundation in right, yet, in the circumstances of proceedings, was very grievous, and no less unjust'.[227] This sense of injustice tended to merge, in principle and in the public mind, with resentment of rigorous policing of civil and moral order by the prerogative courts. The propertied classes were chagrined at their eligibility for punishment. Sir Arthur Haselrig described these years as a time when two or three gentlemen could not go out without being liable to be charged with riot.[228] Tracing the growth of such government Clarendon continued:

---

[222] Thomas, 'Financial and administrative developments', p. 119; Sharpe, 'Personal rule of Charles I', p. 68; Gardiner, *History*, vii, p. 167; Russell, *Parliaments*, p. 399; Larkin, *Stuart royal proclamations*, ii, pp. 279–80; Searle, *Barrington family letters*, pp. 189–90; Alexander, *Charles I's Lord Treasurer*, pp. 162–3.

[223] Sharpe, 'Personal rule of Charles I', pp. 66–7.

[224] SP16/162/18.   [225] Birch, ii, pp. 170–1.

[226] Ibid., p. 163. See also ibid., pp. 96, 102; HMC 7th report, Appx, p. 545; Knowler, *Strafford letters*, i, p. 56. Even the recalcitrant Clare admitted the legality of the fines; NUL, Ne.C., 15,405, pp. 178–9.

[227] Clarendon, *Rebellion*, vol. i, p. 85.

[228] Cliffe, *Puritan gentry*, p. 194. See also Clarendon, *Rebellion*, vol. i, p. 86; Reeve, 'Viscount Dorchester', pp. 205–6; Birch, ii, pp. 79, 168.

those foundations of right by which men valued their security, to the apprehension and understanding of wise men, [were] never more in danger to be destroyed.[229]

This was the critical legacy of prerogative rule.

Economic conditions were also the subject of conciliar decree. Between 1629 and 1631 England was vulnerable to the slump in the international cloth trade. When combined with bad harvests this produced, as we have seen, a serious shortage of grain – particularly in the cloth-working districts of East Anglia. The government's Book of Orders, issued in January 1631, contained a package of measures designed to stabilize the grain market, relieve the poor and maintain social order. It relied extensively upon royal prerogative powers.[230] The Orders reflected the government's fear of unrest and incipient revolt. This fear had been activated in 1629 by the coincidence of political instability with economic hardship. On a general level, the Book of Orders, with the official explanation of dearth as the work of evil men, expressed the desire of all the landed classes that order be maintained. It is reasonable to link efforts towards social pacification with an increasing desire, particularly on Charles's part, to avoid any popular demand for another Parliament.[231] The Orders reflected the king's obsession with order and interest in reform, as well as his desire to keep the gentry in their localities.[232] His objection to the gathering of the governing classes in London was probably related to his knowledge that he had enemies among them. Finally, the Orders illustrate two important aspects of prerogative government. That government was not necessarily original in conception nor successful in execution. The notion of collective social measures in this form was arguably novel, but the provisions concerning dearth and poverty had their Tudor antecedents.[233] They exemplified, moreover, the band-aid strategy of early Stuart economic policy, which alleviated the effects of crisis without tackling its causes. A defensive strategy, lacking the initiative and administrative tools for reorganization, it failed to adjust the economy to prevent distress and dislocation.[234] This was a failure of the era, not only of the

[229] Clarendon, *Rebellion*, vol. 1, p. 86.
[230] B. W. Quintrell, 'The making of Charles I's Book of Orders', *EHR*, xcv (July 1980); P. Slack, 'Books of orders: the making of English social policy, 1577–1631', *TRHS*, 5th ser., xxx (1980); Supple, *Commercial crisis*, pp. 108–11, 116–19, 237–8, 244–6; Clay, *Economic expansion and social change*, ii, p. 246; Walter, 'Grain riots and popular attitudes', in Brewer and Styles (eds.), *An ungovernable people*; Laud, *Works*, iii, p. 212; Birch, ii, p. 99.
[231] D. G. C. Allan, 'The rising in the west, 1628–1631', *EcHR*, v (1952); Cliffe, *Puritan gentry*, pp. 120–1; Supple, *Commerical crisis*, pp. 244, 251; Birch, ii, pp. 86–7, 104–5; Hutton, *William Laud*, pp. 67–8; J. Walter and K. Wrightson, 'Dearth and the social order in early modern England', *P&P*, lxxi (May 1976).
[232] Sharpe, 'The personal rule of Charles I', pp. 59ff.; Bodl. Lib., Rawl. Ms C.197, fo. 22r–v; Larkin, *Stuart royal proclamations*, ii, pp. 350–3.
[233] Slack, 'Books of orders', pp. 1–5.
[234] Supple, *Commercial crisis and change*, pp. 233, 252–3.

personal rule. It underlines the extent to which, in socio-economic terms, Caroline government was remarkably traditional.

By late 1630, the financial and military pressures upon Charles to recall Parliament were easing. The reopening of trade with France and Spain, which accompanied the coming of peace, brought customs duties to relieve the penury of the treasury. The dialogue with Spain also gave hopes of a negotiated settlement of the German question.[235] These developments could only encourage Charles's antipathy to the idea of another Parliament. In the autumn of 1630 Dorchester wrote to the earl of Cork, Lord Justice in Ireland. He announced the passing of a significant milestone for Charles's government:

I am exceedingly glad to observe, whilst the occupations of the rest of the world [i.e. the European war] give us leisure, his majesty in all his three kingdoms doth advantage himself of the opportunity in settling all in that good order that his well-affected subjects and servants have reason to receive singular contentment. Here all goeth on without noise or clamour in the accustomed manner of a well-ordered government under a prudent, just and religious prince.[236]

Dorchester was clearly relieved that the gross disorder of the Buckingham era appeared to have receded. He was also continuing to rationalize his doubts about Charles and concern for the fate of the Protestant cause in Europe. His letter betrayed the fact that all was not well in the state of England. He praised the Parliament of Scotland in its granting immediately the supply which Charles requested, without bargaining ' . . . or distrust of his majesty's gracious intention towards them . . . '[237] To Dorchester this was the way the English Parliament should have behaved, and had not, in 1629.

The Secretary was not the only observer to see that the recession of open political strife was deceptive. John Cosin, the noted Arminian, preached in Durham in June 1630 of the need for peace at home as well as abroad:

pray for no peace, pray not against any battle, saith our puritan, directly against the text . . . they are all for contentions and brabbles, both at home and abroad, and He everywhere against them, as we also ought to be . . . [238]

Cosin's rather ironical invocation of the will of God signalled the depth of the religious conflict in England. It also underlined the enduring instability of the domestic political scene. Clarendon called these years an era of 'outward visible prosperity' marked by 'the inward disposition of the people to murmur and unquietness'.[239] It is not enough understood, as Clarendon

---

[235] For a detailed discussion of foreign policy see chapter 7, below.
[236] SP63/251/fo. 133r.   [237] Ibid.
[238] Cosin took his text from Psalm 122: 'Pray for the peace of Jerusalem'; Ornsby, *Works of John Cosin*, i, pp. 115–16. See also Collinson, *Religion of Protestants*, p. 19; *DNB*, s.v. Cosin, John.
[239] Clarendon, *Rebellion*, vol. i, p. 136.

understood in retrospect, that in contrast to the upheaval of the 1620s, the years of personal rule were too quiet. Charles, we might say, was still traversing Indian country.

The political battles in England following the collapse of Charles's third Parliament compounded a legacy of subtle and critical change. By the end of 1630, with the emergence of an explicitly arbitrary style of government, a new kind of politics was not only established but self-generating. High politics displayed a remarkable degree of alienation and polarization, repression and conspiracy, fear and threat. Considerable distance now separated Charles from his most vocal critics. There was organized dissent and a consistent desire for its exemplary punishment – a desire which only aggravated the problem.[240] The belief in and fear of conspiracy, especially conspiracy against the regime, was fed by an extensive and definite reality. The Eliot group, in taking its protest from Parliament to the courts, was inspired by a complementary sense of the threat of innovation and arbitrary rule. This translation of opposition was anticipated in the Five Knights' case but it came to be more powerful and more damaging. It could now appeal to due process legislation and to rivetted public opinion and came in the wake of a general constitutional breakdown. The growing use of arbitrary measures, particularly in the courts, affected perceptions of Charles both inside and outside the government. The doubts implied by Dorchester and the explicit criticism of Clare differed in degree rather than in kind. Eliot and his fellow prisoners, standing upon law and privilege, were surely aware of engaging in a personal battle with the king. In their refusal to submit we have a clear sense of a conscious conflict in which the moderate Councillors and the judges were the unsuccessful mediators. The prisoners were placing principle and stubborn intransigence before the requirement of obedience to the monarch. More than this it is difficult to say. Eliot held fast to the notion of evil counsel as long as he could. Selden, a ruthless advocate, with less of the stuff of which martyrs are made, was probably less inclined to see things this way. By later at least appearing to have made his peace with the circles of the court he showed a pragmatic appreciation of the political world contrasting with the behaviour of the rest of the recalcitrants. The battle in the courts completed the breakdown of the attempt to fund the war and therefore of an effective foreign policy. This destructive quality of the King's Bench case in particular was a development of the destructive quality of the 1629 session. The vacuum thus created was filled by new royal policies abroad – policies which given their genesis could only be partially successful. A circular pattern also took shape whereby dissent undermined a war policy (with the associated sitting of Parliament) and this process in turn encouraged dissent.

[240] As Clarendon concluded; ibid., pp. 89–90.

The new counsels issue was also further developed. As with the religious issue, there was a growing conservative reaction against Charles's resolve to base royal policy upon a marginal extreme of tradition and, in this instance, to stretch the royal prerogative beyond its limits. Eliot and Selden were forced into promoting a radicalized notion of privilege linked to their use of the Petition of Right against arbitrary imprisonment. There was the awareness of a general constitutional issue, articulated from the bench by Whitelocke, whose judgement signalled the legal expression of broader conflict.[241] Public opinion and popular unrest, galvanized by war, dearth and dramatic parliamentary events, could not be dissociated from the conflict in the courts. Neither could the new general policy for the government of the kingdom be divorced from that conflict and the disorder surrounding it. The new political developments, interlocking and deeply consequential as they were, amounted to a change in the context of national politics. Those politics would never work successfully again until a general solution to the failure they reflected could be found. Until then, the habits of the new Caroline era would promote instability in national political life.

---

[241] The issue had of course underlain the parliamentary debates of 1628. See Reeve, 'Legal status of the Petition of Right', p. 276, and chapter 2, above.

6

The king, his court and its enemies

The emerging character of the Caroline regime, of its policies in Church and state, was definitely discernible by 1630. That character was very much the product of Charles's personality, of his views, and of the efforts of those in government who shared them. The king was the guiding spirit, not by virtue of charisma, but because he was the legally rightful ruler of his people. Charles's title to the kingdom did not, however, mean that he shared in the necessary qualities of kingship. It is appropriate to dwell here on the character of Charles Stuart the man, before examining the circles in which he chose to move. The highly emotive circumstances of Charles's eventual death, and the dignified bearing which, amid them, he achieved, have often overshadowed the shortcomings of his rule and their role in creating the tragedies of his reign. Above all, there is a complexity – and inscrutability – about Charles which has hampered our historical understanding. These elements were reflected in the ambivalence with which those who had served him, even for years, summed up his character. Laud saw Charles as a mild and gracious prince who knew not how to be or be made great.[1] Sir Philip Warwick regretted the way in which the king, admittedly in the latter days of the civil war, could be temperamental and uncommunicative in Council.[2] Clarendon, at pains to point out Charles's merits as man and king, was forced to conclude unhappily: 'His kingly virtues had some mixture and allay that hindered them from shining in full lustre, and from producing those fruits which they should have been attended with.'[3] The historian continued:

if he was not the best king, if he was without some parts and qualities which have made some kings great and happy, no other prince was ever unhappy who was possessed of half his virtues and endowments, and so much without any kind of vice.[4]

Clarendon, in trying to exonerate Charles, appealed to the notion that divine

---

[1] Hutton, *William Laud*, p. 130.
[2] Carlton, *Charles I*, p. 277.
[3] Clarendon, *Rebellion*, vol. iv, p. 490.
[4] Ibid., p. 492.

providence had been visited upon England and that the king had fallen foul of the conspiracies of men.[5]

Charles was indeed possessed of significant virtues. High-minded, religiously devout and devoid of any form of carnal vice, he was a loving husband, father and friend.[6] His civilization was reflected in his love and connoisseurship of the visual arts.[7] Yet the ambiguity of his character could not and cannot be denied. A highly cultivated man, his education and intellectual leanings had neither the depth nor the breadth of his father's and he lacked imagination. He exhibited all the bearing and qualities of a gentleman but could not be trusted to keep his word as others understood it. Outwardly reasonable, his mind was often fixed and closed.[8] He was humane save in believing that men should die for what he considered the justice of his causes.[9] A man of peace, he hardly hesitated to take up arms to defend his damaged honour. The clue to this ambiguity may be the confusing psychological nature of his family background. Charles was the child of an unhappy marriage and apparently had not received maternal confidence. He admired a father of whom he also disapproved for the lewd and worldly nature of his court. He grew up in the shadow of an able and popular older brother whom he also lost at an early age.[10] He married an innocent girl almost ten years his junior and suffered what was for some years an unhappy marriage. Perhaps it is not surprising that as an adult Charles consistently exhibited insecurity, lack of confidence and weakness. Undoubtedly he grew personally stronger as he grew older, as is clear in his bearing under trial and sentence of death. Age, personal experience of war in the 1640s and the simplicity of the principles he believed himself to be defending made him somewhat more imposing in later life. Yet he was always fundamentally unsuited to the task of kingship. How, specifically, was this the case?

Four characteristics, above all, underpinned Charles's rule. Except perhaps in the last months of his life, he was never entirely sure of himself, of his abilities or of his standing in the minds of others. Secondly, he was moralistic and judgemental. Thirdly, he was not, by inclination or equipment, a political man. As a younger son, he was not raised from childhood to be king and, in stark contrast to his father, came to the English throne with very little political experience. Those things upon which Charles placed the greatest value – order, peace,[11] domesticity, spirituality and aesthetics – are things to which

---

[5] See, for example, ibid., pp. 491–2.   [6] Ibid., p. 492.
[7] G. Parry, *The golden age restor'd* (Manchester, 1981), pp. 266–7; Collinson, *Religion of Protestants*, p. 7.
[8] AMRE, CPA, 42, fo. 375r; R. Ollard, *The image of the king: Charles I and Charles II* (New York, 1979), pp. 27ff.
[9] This point was made by J. P. Cooper ('Fall of the Stuart monarchy', p. 559).
[10] Carlton, *Charles I*, passim, especially chapters 1–5; Laud, *Works*, vii, p. 14.
[11] PRO 31/3/66/fo. 136v.

the political world is naturally hostile or indifferent. In her own way Henrietta Maria shared this apolitical disposition,[12] which served to strengthen the eventual bond between husband and wife. Charles's marriage, being true to his basic nature, thus only served to reinforce it. Finally, as has been pointed out, Charles's thinking was influenced by a deep commitment to Renaissance principles, to uniformity and symmetry, as well as by a natural inclination to the spirit of the avant-garde.[13] Taken together, these were not qualities which suggested political success in a traditional society seeking to cope with an age of ideological pluralism. Charles was a man thoroughly ill-equipped to be king, particularly during the era in which he lived, who chose to take most seriously the duties of kingship as he saw them. This was, from the very beginning, a most inauspicious combination. It is also the key to understanding the effects of his rule.

How, precisely, did these qualities translate into handicaps in a political context? Charles's essential insecurity caused him to be strongly influenced by the ideas of those he most respected – his wife (in later years), his father (particularly after his death) and Buckingham above all – even when this was politically ill-advised. Buckingham had lobbied for a Parliament and for war in 1624 and had recommended Laud for episcopal promotion. Both were courses of which James had disapproved but which Charles had chosen to follow.[14] After Buckingham's death, Charles had a tendency to take what he understood to be his father's views to a practical (or rather an impractical) extreme. His uncompromising attitude towards Parliament, his exclusive patronage of the English Arminians and his penchant for a pro-Spanish foreign policy can all be seen in this light.[15] It would seem that Charles conceived of himself as completing his father's work.[16] His own ideological inclinations, clearly owing much to James's views, did not flourish until after

---

[12] See p. 39, n. 146, above; see also Reade, *Sidelights on the Thirty Years War*, iii, p. 446.

[13] Derek Hirst (*Authority and conflict*, p. 55) has made the point about Renaissance principles. To a significant extent the difference between James and Charles was one of generations, but Charles was definitely not conservative and embraced the new.

[14] See p. 64, n. 35, above; Collinson, 'The Jacobean religious settlement', p. 51; Fincham and Lake, 'Ecclesiastical policy of King James I', p. 184.

[15] The question of James's attitude towards Arminianism is a difficult one. He clearly professed a moderate form of Calvinism around which was built what was in the English context a theologically comprehensive Church. While James apparently considered theological disputes over the basis of salvation matters indifferent, he leaned increasingly towards the Arminian party in the last years of his life. His initial inspiration was political in his desire to keep peace in Europe. There is, however, no evidence to suggest that he had not become attracted to Arminian theology. Indeed, he approved of *Appello caesarem*, and his European policy and view was well served by the Arminian attitude to Spain and Rome. See Fincham and Lake, 'Ecclesiastical policy of King James I', pp. 183, 187, 189–90, 201–6; Collinson, 'The Jacobean religious settlement', pp. 28, 49–50; Tyacke, 'Puritanism, Arminianism', pp. 123–4; Lake, 'Calvinism and the English Church', pp. 49, 51, 60, 70–2.

[16] D. Mathew, *Scotland under Charles I* (London, 1955), p. 26.

the removal of Buckingham and the passing of his own briefly rebellious youth.[17] In the context of Charles's character, such susceptibility to others' views can be considered a weakness as much as a sign of independent admiration for those ideas.

The king's lack of confidence had other, multifarious, manifestations. He was authoritarian and paranoid about loyalty, insisting that recalcitrants such as Eliot publicly yield to him. He was fearful of opposition and conspiracy. He was defensive, externalizing his failures by totally blaming others, such as subversive elements in Parliament. He was unaccommodating, inclined to reject or suppress what he did not understand or wish to accept. His basic deafness to desperate anti-Arminianism is a case in point. This allergy to compromise was linked to a desire to impose his will upon (or escape) reality, as well as to his tendency to retreat to a closed personal world of order. Difficult to counsel against his preferences and disliking (with the exception of Buckingham) more confident and more politically able men such as Wentworth, he warmed to advice which was congruent with his own inclinations, and which was therefore distinctly limited and often bad. He had an antipathy to realistic assessments (such as his nephew Rupert's that the civil war could not be won) when these contradicted his own optimistic and sanguine attitudes.[18] He disliked and was unable to make decisions and consequently, as has often been observed, he frequently obtained the worst of all possible worlds.[19] Once decided, he tended to be obsessive and inflexible. He was not spontaneously generous, whether to express affection, inspire loyalty or reward service: no way to encourage such qualities among his subjects. He lacked a commanding presence and tended to keep men at a distance.[20] He was almost certainly devoid of a sense of humour. His lack of confidence caused him to be secretive and devious, and he had a supreme capacity to rationalize his frequent betrayal of others. There is a long list of those, including members of his own family, who placed their trust in Charles and were eventually cut adrift: the Huguenots, Christian of Denmark, the Palatines, the Dutch, the Parliament of 1628–9 which obtained his assent to the Petition of Right, and Wentworth, not to mention the various parties to the civil wars. By 1630 Charles had acquired an international reputation as a

---

[17] Blair Worden makes a similar point in *TLS*, 13 June 1986, p. 636.

[18] Hirst, *Authority and conflict*, p. 161; Mathew, *Age of Charles I*, p. 38; C. V. Wedgwood, 'The Elector Palatine and the civil war', *History Today*, iv (Jan. 1954), p. 8.

[19] A Spanish agent in London once described Charles as 'flaco y inconstante'; AGS, E2519, exp. 6.

[20] Charles's reliance upon formal royal audiences supports this notion. Mathew, *Scotland under Charles I*, p. 29; AMRE, CPA, 42, fo. 375r; Archivo del Duque del Infantado, Palafox Mss, legajo 94, fo. 136v. I am grateful to John Elliott for this reference.

man who could not be trusted.[21] Inherently weak of character, he was always the potential precipitator of political disaster.

Charles's lack of a political sense was an obvious disadvantage in government. He had no conception of the art of the possible and was unreceptive and ill at ease in the world of affairs. Consistently imperceptive, he failed to learn from his own experience,[22] never seeing, for example, the damage he did to perceptions of the monarchy or acknowledging the need to abandon Buckingham to re-enlist support for himself. Charles, in a fundamental sense, did not understand the use of power. Uncomfortable with decisions, he was ill-equipped to weigh policy options[23] and tended to make passive choices. A classic example, as will be seen, was the way in which he withdrew from the European war. He was insensitive to opposition and ideological anxiety and, most fatally, took the domestic political peace of the 1630s at face value. He did not realize the importance of communication with his subjects[24] or see the need to achieve real public understanding of his rule. He seems to have had a rather superficial conception of the loyalty and approval necessary for successful government. His public statements were in a real sense irrespective of those to whom they were addressed and consequently, as with the proclamation of March 1629 concerning Parliament, could do more harm than good.[25] Charles was not politically creative as king. He did not actively endeavour to enlist support, devise compromise or maintain consensus as his father had done.[26] He tended to intervene like a foreign object in the mechanics of the political process and he was unskilled at oiling the works. Although he sought to be diligent, he lacked interest in the everyday tasks of government: a handicap in an age of monarchical rule. The most notable and (for a time) the most successful administrative initiative which he sanctioned, Ship Money, was the brainchild of Attorney-General Noy.[27] It aroused Charles's interest as a function of foreign policy. He considered diplomacy a fitting occupation for kings.[28] Increasingly preoccupied with the arts,[29]

---

[21] In the Spanish Council of State, the count of la Puebla referred to Charles as cunning and always meriting suspicion; AGS, E2562, consulta of 11 May 1630 (n.s.). On Charles's secretive nature see ibid., E2517, fo. 105.

[22] I am grateful to Gerald Aylmer for this point.   [23] Carlton, *Charles I*, p. 109.

[24] J. Richards, '"His nowe Majestie" and the English monarchy: the kingship of Charles I before 1640', *P&P*, cxiii (1986). I am grateful to Judith Richards for allowing me to read this article before publication.

[25] The proclamation encouraged a fear that Charles had done with Parliaments. Clarendon, *Rebellion*, vol. i, pp. 5, 84, and see chapter 4, above.

[26] See, for example, James's handling of the religious issue; Fincham and Lake, 'Ecclesiastical policy of King James I', especially pp. 206–7.

[27] Reeve, 'Sir Robert Heath's advice', n. 49. See also Sharpe, 'Personal rule of Charles I', pp. 59–62, 64–5.

[28] Sharpe, 'Personal rule of Charles I', pp. 64, 69; Adams, 'Spain or the Netherlands?', pp. 84–5, 100.   [29] See below, p. 197.

domesticity and the social life of the court, he was effectively insulated from the pulse of the political nation and the international scene.

The king's moralistic disposition did not assist his political fortunes. He was always fundamentally dogmatic, opinionated and self-righteous: qualities antithetical to the art of compromise. His sense of his monarchical station and divinely ordained mission caused him to believe that he was answerable only to God. This reinforced his authoritarian instincts and served both to inspire and to rationalize his unscrupulousness. Charles does not seem to have been conscious of his dishonesty or of the fact that he could not be trusted to abide by the law or the basis of a contract or treaty. High-minded persons are frequently unconcerned with detail[30] or others' perceptions of their designs. Charles's rectitude prompted him to view criticism or opposition as persecution, insubordination or subversion. This of course handicapped his ability to look objectively at the political state of play. The fixity and depth of his principles encouraged his inhuman streak and compounded his lack of social ability. Since his deep sense of honour was unaccompanied by the ability to defend it, his behaviour was significantly affected by injured pride. The record of the 1620s was one of spectacular failure at home and abroad: the failure of the Spanish match, the failure of the French marriage alliance, ideological conflict, constitutional breakdown and largely ineffective attempts to wage war. The failures of his youth reinforced Charles's difficult qualities, inviting a continuing cycle to lessen the likelihood of future success.

Charles's deep attraction to Renaissance and avant-garde principles was encouraged by his continental experience with which it was inextricably bound up. He was the first English monarch since Henry VIII to leave England,[31] and he visited France and Spain at the impressionable age of twenty-three. Spain in particular, through the medium of great art, had a deep effect upon him. The splendid royal collections confirmed his devotion to Venetian painting. Philip IV and Olivares gave Charles a number of works including a Titian.[32] As king of England he promoted the assimilation of Renaissance values and greatly modernized native taste.[33] In constitutional practice Charles was also susceptible to new continental models. His bent towards arbitrary government had a French inspiration of which his wife and

---

[30] As Ollard points out; *Image of the king*, p. 47.
[31] Excluding of course James I's life in Scotland; Hibbard, *Popish plot*, p. 23.
[32] Huxley, *Endymion Porter*, pp. 97–8, 111, 181. Philip shared Charles's avid connoisseurship of painting; J. Brown and J. H. Elliott, *A palace for a king* (New Haven and London, 1980), p. viii and passim.
[33] Carlton, *Charles I*, pp. 143ff.

her brother, Louis XIII, were perpetual reminders for him.[34] Charles's open-
ness to Tridentine Catholic and modernist influences – in government and
diplomacy, art and religion – with his aspiration to such ideals in the English
context,[35] had quite mortal political consequences. It made him an author of
innovation against the basic instincts and particular beliefs of his subjects.
And it fed his desire for order and simplicity as against the complexity of
politics and the world. Charles often preferred the image to the reality.[36] A
vignette of late 1631 captures this element of his character beautifully. At the
height of the German crisis, when the Swedish tide of victory held out the
prospect of a Palatine restoration and all the auguries were for action,
Dorchester sought out Charles to pursue the latest negotiations. He found the
king in the picture gallery, arranging his busts of the Roman emperors (with
whom he seems to have identified) in chronological order.[37] It is difficult not
to see this scene as symbolic. Charles, as we shall see, failed to seize the unique
opportunity. At that time, the gulf between aesthetic order and the necessary
kingly role could not have been much greater.

Charles's nature had, above all, three important consequences for his rule.
Weak, disliking uncertainty and compromise, pious and obsessed with the
purity of structures, Charles always sought to define the point at issue. The
best and the most crucial example of this habit is his destruction of the
delicate Jacobean religious consensus by the effective outlawing of predestinarian Calvinism. Likewise, the working of the English constitution
depended upon avoiding the activation of the various potential conflicts contained within it.[38] Charles, moreover, would allow no distinction, spoken or
unspoken, between theory and practice. In this way the notion of monarchical divine right became a dangerous political force and Laudianism made no
concessions, as James had done in religion, to political practicality.[39] These
were the instincts of a man very sure of his convictions but unsure of himself,

---

[34] Reeve, 'Viscount Dorchester', pp. 16–18, 229; *CSPV 1626–28*, p. 508; PRO 31/3/66/
fo. 123v; Adams, 'Spain or the Netherlands?', p. 91; Russell, 'Arguments for religious unity',
p. 222; D. Mathew, *The social structure of Caroline England* (Oxford, 1948), p. 32. See also
Trevor-Roper, *Archbishop Laud*, p. 68.

[35] It is of course necessary to take care in seeking so to generalize about predilections in different spheres of human activity. Blair Worden, citing Charles's brother's love of Italian art
and apparent hatred of Italian religion, has recently posited that 'The mental world where
power and imagination meet remains elusive' (*TLS*, 13 June 1986, p. 635). Yet individuals
remain human units and it is sometimes possible to perceive very illuminating links in cases
such as that of Charles.

[36] Ollard, *Image of the king*, pp. 33–4, 36.

[37] SP81/37/fos. 167r–168r; see also Carlton, *Charles I*, p. 146.

[38] I am grateful to Sir Geoffrey Elton for discussion of this question. See also Daly, *Cosmic
harmony*, pp. 28, 30.

[39] Charles's role in the Five Knights' case is a good example of the consequences of divine right
thinking; Guy, 'Origins of the Petition of Right reconsidered', p. 300 and passim. Two
important examples of James's political astuteness and flexibility in religion are his decision

not at home like his father in the realms of ideas[40] and of affairs. Finally, Charles had a politically fatal inability to operate on a basis of trust, either to inspire it or to offer it to others. Such mutual understanding was alien to him. The lack of this dimension made him suspect to his contemporaries and has often rendered him inscrutable to historians. In sum, therefore, he made misunderstanding and conflict infinitely more likely in an age of what has been rightly termed 'sustained ideological instability'.[41] Charles, by his very nature, was a consistent agent for national and for international political destruction.

Charles's personality, with its concomitant style of kingship, was the principal determining influence upon his court. The Caroline court, in turn, was critical in the history of this period. It was also politically novel, and it is important to grasp the nature of that novelty. The Tudor court, we know, had possessed a marked political and ideological pluralism. It was there that competing interests and differing policies found support and where the political battles of the day were usually fought out.[42] 'Faction' was, as we know, a derogatory term denoting division, self-interest and disloyalty.[43] Yet the ideal of political harmony gave way in practice to the necessary fact of personal and factional strife. An understanding of the earlier period throws the landscape of early Stuart politics into clearer relief. The pre-civil war era saw court faction become more exclusive and monopolistic of power. The unfortunate consequence was that conflict tended to be forced out into the public and the parliamentary arena.[44] This occurred by stages. The Buckingham era, spanning the reigns of the first two Stuarts, can be seen as a transitional period during which opposition to the duke's monopoly of power gained momentum in Parliament. A distinction must be drawn, however, between the Jacobean and Caroline eras and simultaneously between court politics before and after Buckingham's death. Despite the complete and rather grotesque control of patronage which the duke increasingly came to exercise,

to withdraw his initial approval of Dutch Arminianism, and his promotion of English Arminianism largely in the interests of a pacific foreign policy. Reeve, 'Viscount Dorchester', p. 4; Fincham and Lake, 'Ecclesiastical policy of King James I', pp. 201ff. See also Collinson, 'The Jacobean religious settlement', pp. 50–1.

[40] Thus Charles could share Laud's dislike of religious disputation; Trevor-Roper, *Archbishop Laud*, pp. 67–8.

[41] Collinson, *Religion of Protestants*, p. 3.

[42] G. R. Elton, 'Tudor government: the points of contact, iii, the court', *TRHS*, 5th ser., xxvi (1976), pp. 227–8. Simon Adams has pointed out how, despite the customary disputes and religious differences, the Elizabethan court from the early 1570s displayed a certain political homogeneity; S. L. Adams, 'Eliza enthroned? The court and its politics', in C. Haigh (ed.), *The reign of Elizabeth* (London, 1985), pp. 67ff.

[43] L. L. Peck, ' "For a king not to be bountiful were a fault": perspectives on court patronage in early Stuart England', *JBS*, xxv (1986), p. 57n; Gardiner, *History*, vii, p. 200.

[44] Elton, 'Tudor government . . . the court', pp. 227–8; Hirst, 'Court, country and politics', pp. 111–12, 115–16; Hirst, *Authority and conflict*, pp. 31, 142.

his administration, despite its exclusiveness, retained the ideological flexibility of the Jacobean years in which he rose to power.[45] The duke, for all his
faults, knew the value of such pragmatism – a worldliness he shared with
James but not with his son. The Buckingham era at court was thus a real
continuation of the Jacobean period.

Charles, by contrast, built a court which was ideologically inflexible, in
which a variety of opinion was represented but in which only one view, his
own, could hold sway. This came about through the absence of any one
favourite and the free rein simultaneously allowed to Charles's personality.
His 'court', it is thus important to grasp, can be defined in two different ways.
There was the traditional or wider circle – those having access or some
proximity to Charles, owing to office in central government or household or
to other reasons (a group perhaps comprised of hundreds of individuals)[46] –
and what can be termed the *political* court: an inner group about the king
who shared his values, views and aspirations and whose personal interaction
with him determined high policy.[47] This circle was 'political' in the sense that
it was a source of power, not in the sense that membership necessarily
betokened any overriding interest in policy-making and government.
Charles's distinct unsuitability for kingship made this inner circle a distinctly
unsuitable fountain of political power. Increasingly impenetrable, insensitive
and defensive, it constituted one pole of that political polarization which
began to affect national affairs during the parliamentary session of 1629.[48]

The Caroline governing clique had begun to form from the moment of
Buckingham's assassination – the critical event giving Charles domination of
his immediate political surroundings. His inner court did not, however, enter
into its full inheritance overnight. There was a period of gradual reorientation during the years after 1628, when Charles's preferences asserted themselves, the prospect of peace became more appealing to him and death and

[45] Hirst, 'Court, country and politics', pp. 111–12; Peck, *Northampton*, pp. 215–16; Fincham
and Lake, 'Ecclesiastical policy of King James I', pp. 206–7; Russell, *Parliaments*, p. 9;
Reeve, 'Viscount Dorchester', pp. 18–20; SP84/111/fos. 204–5; Beatty, *Warwick and
Holland*, pp. 31–3; C. Roberts, *Schemes and undertakings* (Columbus, 1985), p. 36.
[46] The early modern English court cannot be adequately defined in terms of office-holding;
Elton, 'Tudor government . . . the court', p. 212. See also K. M. Sharpe, 'The image of virtue:
the court and household of Charles I, 1625–1642' in D. Starkey *et al.*, *The English court
from the Wars of the Roses to the civil war* (London, 1987), pp. 236, 244, 246–8.
[47] While seeking to examine matters in greater detail, I am essentially in agreement with Derek
Hirst's conclusion on the Caroline court as not 'ideologically monolithic' but allowing only
'the airing of a single viewpoint'; Hirst, *Authority and conflict*, p. 31. Likewise I find myself
unable to agree with Kevin Sharpe that Charles was less susceptible to factional influence
than his father. The absence of a monopolistic favourite does not necessarily imply equal
access for a plurality of opinion. See K. M. Sharpe, 'Crown, Parliament and locality:
government and communication in early Stuart England', *EHR*, ci, 399 (Apr. 1986),
pp. 326, 343–4.
[48] See chapter 3, above.

disillusion took their toll among those who disagreed. While attitudes within the court, the upper reaches of government and the foreign service remained divided, a large and highly important section of opinion was progressively eclipsed within the personal councils and society about the king. In short, it was that basically orthodox approach to politics which espoused the Dutch alliance, war with Spain, the Protestant cause, the sitting of Parliament and the established Calvinism of the English Church. The political court came into its own in 1630 when the Spanish war was ended and the birth of Prince Charles indisputably weakened the Palatine claim to the English throne. The internal development of the court was accompanied by a limited shifting of Protestant attention in England away from foreign and towards domestic affairs as Charles appeared to be abandoning his sister's cause.[49] The absence of a Parliament meant the lack of a national forum for criticism of innovatory government policy. This compounded the polarizing effect of the regime upon political life. The emerging ideological gulf was not one between the court (in the customary or general sense) and the country. The complex and enduring connections between the centre and the localities are well known.[50] Rather, there was an increasingly precise division between the inner court and the wider national leadership such that informed and astute observers could not but recognize it. Dorchester, struggling to keep faith in the king despite Charles's leanings to Spain, by 1631 could write of

his majesty's having so good knowledge and experience of both these countries [England and the Dutch republic] and constitution of our people and affairs, which keeps not pace with the quick and variable apprehensions of those he now lives with and whom he doth humour in their erroneous opinions.[51]

By 1632 Sir Thomas Roe, excluded from government service for too fervently supporting the Protestant cause, could write with irony: 'We cannot say there is any faction in England. All goes one way and I know not the wit of it.'[52]

Who were these men whom Charles allowed to cluster so provocatively around him? How did they think and exactly how far did they mirror his views and attitude to the world? Charles's political court was never large. Essentially it was that group which contemporaries labelled the 'Spanish faction'.[53] A favourable attitude towards Spain and what it stood for, or at least a desire for peace with the Habsburgs, was the ideological adhesive which bound the group together. The circle seems to have had seven front-

---

[49] As Simon Adams has pointed out; Adams, 'The Protestant cause', pp. 421–4, Conclusion. See also Adams, 'Spain or the Netherlands?', p. 91.

[50] Hirst, 'Court, country and politics', p. 115 and passim.

[51] SP78/89/fo. 343r, Dorchester to Sir Isaac Wake, 17 July 1631.

[52] Quoted in Gardiner, *History*, vii, p. 200.

[53] NUL, Ne.C., 15,404, p. 227; AGS, E2043, exp. 172; Alcalá-Zamora, *España, Flandes*, p. 264; A. J. Loomie, 'The Spanish faction at the court of Charles I, 1630–38', *BIHR*, lix, 139 (1986). I am grateful to Albert Loomie for allowing me to read this article before publication.

rank members: Weston, Cottington, Wentworth, Laud, Arundel, Porter and eventually Francis Windebank (who became Secretary of State in 1632).[54] Within this circle there were patron–client relationships. Weston promoted Cottington's career and Laud helped to secure Windebank's appointment.[55] There was a subsidiary level of patronage, inhabited by such as Sir Henry Vane, owing his position principally to Weston.[56] The three most important members of the circle, Weston, Cottington and Porter, had been preferred by Buckingham – a fact which undoubtedly enhanced their credibility with Charles.[57] Endymion Porter was a relative of the duke by marriage.[58] The political court eventually closed along the lines of the king's closed mind, but its thought was not strictly uniform or homogeneous. It can best be described as a pattern of thinking diametrically opposed to that which it excluded. Those favoured by Charles had varying interests and differing degrees of commitment to his various policies. They could not survive in his confidence, however, without generally approving the platform he sanctioned. That platform came to consist of Laudianism, a pro-Spanish foreign policy and a leaning towards non-parliamentary rule: an ideological nexus liberally laced with Caroline self-interest. There was thus a basic court view which brooked no dissent. In this way the members of Charles's circle tended to share his inclination to modernism – in its political and religious (and often its artistic) manifestations. The rarified ideological atmosphere of personal rule, emanating from Charles himself, was also rooted in the thinking of those he allowed about him. The political court encouraged as well as reflected Charles's preferences. The policies he favoured demonstrated its relevance and indicated its power.

The orientation of Charles's regime towards the Hispanic world was an attitude of wide significance. During this period Spain remained the greatest power on earth, a political and cultural force with which all (directly or

---

[54] Loomie, 'Spanish faction'; AGS, E2562, consulta of 25 Jan. 1631 (n.s.) and see the Spanish list of English courtiers, ibid. Windebank was knighted in 1632.

[55] *DNB*, s.v. Cottington, Francis, Lord. Cottington was conscious of the need to cultivate Wentworth to obtain a political alliance as security against Weston's death; Mathew, *Age of Charles I*, pp. 90–1. On Laud and Windebank see Laud, *Works*, iii, p. 211, and vii, pp. 36, 42; Gardiner, *History*, vii, p. 200; *DNB*, s.v. Windebank, Sir Francis.

[56] Vane was Comptroller of the king's household. On Vane see *DNB*, s.v. Vane, Sir Henry, the elder; Birch, ii, pp. 16, 25, 44, 101; SP84/139/fo. 114; *CSPD 1629–31*, p. 306; Mathew, *Age of Charles I*, p. 71; Reeve, 'Viscount Dorchester', pp. 272n, 331. See also Loomie, 'Spanish faction'.

[57] This indirect link with the deceased royal favourite may have reinforced the like-mindedness of the group. Cottington, despite falling out with the duke when his scepticism about the journey to Spain was vindicated, shared Charles's views to such an extent that this proved no handicap in later years. *DNB*, s.v. Cottington; Reade, *Sidelights on the Thirty Years War*, iii, p. 496; AGS, E2517, fo. 47; Huxley, *Endymion Porter*, pp. 63ff.

[58] Huxley, *Endymion Porter*, p. 41.

indirectly) had to reckon.[59] To describe an individual as Hispanophile is to conjure up a whole set of attitudes and values often embraced together. Spain represented legitimacy and social order as well as wealth and power: the prestige and propriety of monarchy as opposed to republicanism. The *pax Hispanica* was the example and collective establishment of the European ruling class.[60] It offered an escape from the claustrophobic Calvinism and relative cultural backwardness of northern Europe. The exciting and exotic world of Mediterranean art and culture went hand in hand with the attractions of an ancient and a mysterious religion, the religion of kings and emperors, which now possessed all the energy of the Counter-Reformation. Charles and almost all his inner circle had direct experience of the Hispanic (or, in the case of Arundel, the Italian) world.[61] It was a world to which Charles was naturally attracted. It suited his notion of monarchy, his very liberal Protestantism and his highly developed artistic sense. Charles did not fancy himself as the champion or even the moderator of Calvinist Europe. A pro-Spanish policy seemed to offer the chance to join his dynastic ambitions with his ideological preferences. Spain and the Habsburgs could restore his sister by royal authority rather than force of arms.[62] Despite the failure of the plan for a Spanish match, Charles remained interested in the idea of a Habsburg marriage alliance with the Stuart line.[63] Weston told the Spanish ambassador Coloma in 1630 that Anglo-Spanish friendship was a legacy which Charles wished to bequeath to his successors.[64] Charles had known Philip IV and Olivares in Spain.[65] He considered the Spaniards his friends upon whom he could rely.[66] His foreign policy as it developed made ample demonstration of his faith in Spain.

This faith was bound up with Charles's deep animosity towards two other nations: the French and the Dutch. He made no secret of his hatred for the French and his belief that they could not be trusted. This attitude had its roots

[59] While Spain was seriously vulnerable during the late 1620s and early 1630s, the myth of inevitable Spanish decline has been laid to rest. Elliott, *Richelieu and Olivares*, p. 5; Israel, *Dutch republic*, pp. 437–9.

[60] Adams, 'Foreign policy and the Parliaments of 1621 and 1624', p. 141; Trevor-Roper, 'Spain and Europe', pp. 270–1; Hibbard, *Popish plot*, p. 237; Russell, 'Arguments for religious unity', pp. 220, 222 and n.

[61] The exceptions were Wentworth and Windebank. See *DNB*, s.v. Weston, Sir Richard and Cottington, Francis, Lord; Hibbard, *Popish plot*, pp. 34–5; Huxley, *Endymion Porter*, pp. 18ff.; M. F. S. Hervey, *The life, correspondence and collections of Thomas Howard, earl of Arundel* (Cambridge, 1921), chs. 6 and 7.

[62] SP80/6/fos. 207–8.

[63] Hibbard, *Popish plot*, p. 253; Mathew, *Age of Charles I*, p. 52; see also p. 55, n. 223, above.

[64] A statement which Coloma reported to Olivares, AGS, E2519, exp. 71.

[65] Olivares had emerged as Philip IV's first minister during Charles's visit to Madrid; Elliott, *Richelieu and Olivares*, p. 40.

[66] Adams, 'Spain or the Netherlands?', pp. 89–90.

in the squabbles over his marriage contract and in the failure of Richelieu to join an anti-Habsburg alliance. Charles was soon toying with the idea of an offensive alliance with Spain against France. His view of French duplicity seems to have encouraged his belief that the Spaniards could be trusted.[67] Charles's Francophobia did not affect, nor was it affected by, his increasing devotion to his wife. The relationship was one of domestic harmony upon which political questions scarcely impinged. Charles was careful nonetheless. Coloma reported an audience at the end of 1630 when the king stated clearly his preference for Spain over France; Charles tactfully lowered his voice seeing Henrietta approaching, the queen asking what went on between the two men.[68] This anomaly in Charles's position was partly resolved after 1631, when the enemies of Richelieu, including Henrietta's mother – Marie de' Medici, aligned themselves with Spain.[69]

Antipathy to the Dutch went naturally with an attraction to Spain. In Charles it was also fuelled by his fear of Dutch power and by the obstacle this presented to his own commercial and naval ambitions. After the Hispano-Dutch truce of 1609, England was vulnerable to the uninhibited force of Dutch competition. English opinion was divided, and Charles sided with those who saw the republic more as an economic rival than a Protestant ally. He imbibed the Spanish view of an international Protestant conspiracy led by the Dutch. This was linked to his fear of a puritan (and even republican) attempt to subvert his authority in England. Here lies the national and international logic of his opposition to the idea of an English West India company. Charles's view could be defended in strategic terms but was unacceptable to the parliamentary war lobby. During the 1630s, he indulged his desire to command sovereignty of the seas in the context of undeclared alliance with Spain.[70] The pro-Spanish and anti-Dutch foreign policy of the personal rule expressed Charles's Hispanophilia. But it was an expression also seasoned by self-interest and encouraged by his experience of failure in war.

[67] Magurn, *Rubens letters*, pp. 306, 316, 333–5, 342–7; Adams, 'Spain or the Netherlands?', pp. 89–90; AMRE, CPA, 44, fo. 351v; SRO, Hamilton Mss, no. 160; Reade, *Sidelights on the Thirty Years War*, iii, p. 447.

[68] AGS, E2519, exp. 114.

[69] Reeve, 'Viscount Dorchester', pp. 305–6.

[70] PRO 31/3/66/fo. 239r–v; Magurn, *Rubens letters*, pp. 333–5, 342–5; Loomie, 'Spanish faction', p. 40; Archivo del Duque del Infantado, Palafox Mss, leg. 94, fo. 136v (I am grateful to John Elliott for this reference); AGS, E2519, exp. 114, 139, E2562, consultas of 8 Mar. 1630 (n.s.), Apr.(?) 1630, 31 Dec. 1630(?) (n.s.), 20 Nov. 1631 (n.s.), letter of Coloma to Olivares 13 Dec. 1630 (n.s.), voto of Olivares Nov. 1631; *The poems of Thomas Carew*, ed. R. Dunlap (Oxford, 1949), p. 75; Reade, *Sidelights on the Thirty Years War*, iii, pp. 447, 468; Birch, i, p. 381; J. H. Elliott, 'A question of reputation? Spanish foreign policy in the seventeenth century', rev. art., *JMH*, lv (1983), p. 482; Trevor-Roper, *Archbishop Laud*, p. 301; Searle, *Barrington family letters*, p. 194; K. R. Andrews, *Trade, plunder and settlement* (Cambridge, 1984), pp. 363–4; and see chapter 3, above.

The political court sympathized with this approach to international affairs. Weston was known abroad as a supporter of Spain and corresponded with Olivares. He humoured Charles's ambition to restore his sister in Germany, but was ill-disposed and at best lukewarm towards Elizabeth.[71] Of Cottington's status as an ardent and sometimes politically active Hispanophile there is no doubt. The principal friend of Spain at the Caroline court, during his embassy to Madrid he professed to speak as a servant of Philip IV. No friend of the Palatines nor of their cause, he did all he could to injure France and understood well the rising threat of the Dutch. Cottington was almost a naturalized Spaniard and, at least in the early 1630s, highly respected by Olivares.[72] Endymion Porter's family had been involved in the service of Spain for several generations. When eighteen he had entered the household of the counts of Olivares, spending three years there as a page. He established a friendship with the count's son and heir who would rise to power as the favourite of Philip IV. Porter was well-inclined to Spain in later life: an attitude which was appreciated by the Spanish government.[73] Wentworth's approach to foreign policy had always been pro-Spanish. The Spanish diplomat Necolalde praised him as someone who acted as reliably as if he had been born in old Castile.[74] Windebank and Arundel were also pro-Spanish – the latter until the failure of his mission to Vienna in 1637.[75] Laud, fearful of the Parliament which would destroy him and demolish his Church,

---

[71] Reeve, 'Viscount Dorchester', pp. 286, 319; Trevor-Roper, *Archbishop Laud*, p. 211; Wedgwood, *Strafford: a revaluation*, p. 68; AGS, E2043, letter of Spanish agent in London, 15 June 1629, E2519, exp. 8 and 26; Archivo del Duque del Infantado, Madrid, Palafox Mss, leg. 94, fo. 136v (I am grateful to John Elliott for this reference).

[72] The count-duke had decided, by 1637, that Cottington was utterly self-interested. Archivo del Duque del Infantado, Madrid, Palafox Mss, leg. 94, fo. 136v; Loomie, 'Spanish faction', pp. 39, 47; AGS, E2519, exp. 25–6 and 109, and E2562, consultas 26 July, 29 Dec. 1630 (n.s.), 'prima conferencia' 14 Feb. 1630 (n.s.), summary of letters of Scaglia to Olivares *c.* spring 1632; Magurn, *Rubens letters*, pp. 342–7; Avenel, *Lettres de Richelieu*, iii, pp. 420–1; Reade, *Sidelights on the Thirty Years War*, iii, pp. xxvii, 496; *DNB*, s.v. Vane, Sir Henry, the elder; Birch, ii, p. 103; Mathew, *Age of Charles I*, p. 90; Reeve, 'Viscount Dorchester', pp. 286, 319; Zagorin, 'Sir Edward Stanhope's advice', p. 316; *CSPV 1629–32*, p. 267.

[73] Huxley, *Endymion Porter*, pp. 18ff., 163; Hibbard, *Popish plot*, p. 105; AGS, E2517, fos. 49 and 98; Reeve, 'Viscount Dorchester', p. 319; Elliott, *Count-duke of Olivares*, p. 206.

[74] Loomie, 'Spanish faction', pp. 40, 42; Russell, *Parliaments*, p. 79; Hibbard, *Popish plot*, pp. 131, 134; Wedgwood, *Strafford: a revaluation*, p. 68; J. H. Elliott, 'The year of the three ambassadors', in H. Lloyd-Jones, V. Pearl and B. Worden (eds.), *History and imagination: essays in honour of H. R.Trevor-Roper* (London, 1981), p. 170; Loomie, 'Canon Henry Taylor', p. 227.

[75] The earl of Dorset was also named by Coloma as a friend of Spain; Archivo del Duque del Infantado, Madrid, Palafox Mss, leg. 94, fo. 136v (I am grateful to John Elliott for this reference); Hibbard, *Popish plot*, pp. 34–5; Hervey, *Life . . . of Thomas Howard, earl of Arundel*, p. 396; Sharpe, 'Earl of Arundel', p. 213; AGS, E2043, exp. 172, and E2519, exp. 8.

had little alternative but to support the Hispanophile policy. His association with the Spanish faction helped to expose him to the charge of popery levelled by the Long Parliament.

These men, with Charles, allowed England to become a satellite of Spain during the 1630s and acquired a definite personal stake in the maintenance of peace. For Weston and Cottington the pro-Spanish policy became indistinguishable from their own personal interest and political survival.[76] There was also the attraction of possible pecuniary rewards. Spanish pensions had commonly been granted to leading English political figures during the previous reign.[77] In 1628 it was suspected in parliamentary circles that this practice was continuing.[78] Large lump sums were certainly distributed to key persons for services rendered to Spain. Weston and Cottington each received £2500 sterling in Spanish silver, on the conclusion of the Treaty of Madrid.[79] There is evidence that both men considered such a sum insufficient reward for the risks they had run. Despite their leaning towards Spain, such expectation of 'danger money', for service in a hostile political environment, is entirely logical.[80] It was also the general practice for Spanish agents at Charles's court to hand out gifts and sums of money. These were intended as inducements to service or as rewards. During the delicate diplomatic manoeuvres in 1628, one apparently covert agent said he had made presentations to the six gentlemen always at Charles's side.[81] It is difficult to be precise about the distribution of such lesser bribes which were certainly not given exclusively to

---

[76] Zagorin, 'Sir Edward Stanhope's advice', p. 304; *CSPV 1629–32*, p. 178; AGS, E2562, Coloma to Infanta, 5 Dec. 1630; Magurn, *Rubens letters*, pp. 324–6, 352. Laud appeared to dally with the idea of an anti-Spanish policy after French entry into the war in 1635, but this was for political reasons, i.e. to obtain the support of the queen's party; Loomie, 'Spanish faction', pp. 43–5. There is also the fact of Laud's patronage of Windebank; see p. 182, n. 55, above.

[77] G. Mattingley, *Renaissance diplomacy* (London, 1955), pp. 259ff.; Birch, ii, p. 104; Huxley, *Endymion Porter*, p. 101.

[78] *CD1628*, iv, p. 152.

[79] Necolalde gave Weston his sum on arrival in London in June 1631. Cottington received his before leaving Spain where he had negotiated the treaty; Loomie, 'Spanish faction'. In late 1630, Coloma had written from London requesting 10,000 ducats (*c.* £2,500) for disbursement among those who had facilitated the treaty and well-disposed persons. The junta in Madrid decided to send 20,000 ducats. AGS, E2562, consulta of 4 Nov. 1630 (n.s.); Loomie, 'Spanish faction', p. 38. See also Gardiner, *History*, vii, p. 201.

[80] In the light of their Catholicism particularly (see below), it is unlikely that Weston and Cottington were purely mercenary. Loomie, 'Spanish faction', p. 39; Gardiner, *History*, vii, p. 215.

[81] These almost certainly included Weston and Porter. AGS, E2517, fo. 78. See also ibid., E2517, fo. 98, E2519, exp. 109, E2562, consultas of 6 May, 4 Nov. 1630 (n.s.) and 20 Nov. 1631 (n.s.); Birch, ii, p. 103; Loomie, 'Spanish faction'; Reade, *Sidelights on the Thirty Years War*, iii, pp. xliv–xlv.

Catholics.[82] What is certain is that Spanish service, more than any other, always held out the prospect of material reward.

The Hispanophile complexion of the king's personal circle was closely linked to its crypto-Catholicism. With the exceptions of Wentworth and Laud and most notably of the king, the denizens of the political court had a positive preference for the Church of Rome. They retained, in varying degrees, a façade of conformity in England to escape loss of office or political retribution. Unconstrained by constitutional interest, or emotional commitment (such as that felt by Charles) to the English Church, they transcended the religious nationalism espoused by Laud and the king. Catholic courtiers were in one sense spiritual aliens in England; in another they shared in the catholic ideals of Laudianism: ideas which paralleled the piety of the Counter-Reformation.[83] Likewise Charles's patience of their private religious views is very significant. While sensitive to the integrity of the English Church and the royal supremacy, he was clearly not uncomfortable with the atmosphere of continental Catholicism, an atmosphere which reflected his spiritual tastes.[84] The crypto-Catholicism of Weston, Cottington, Windebank and Porter and the virtual commitment to Rome of the earl of Arundel were one refraction of the religious character of the Caroline regime.[85] The public association of the Catholics at court with Laudianism and the fear they shared with Laud of the religious prejudices of Parliament were on one level purely pragmatic. On another, these facts reflected the real affinity between the court and its international cultural sphere.

The constitutional view prevailing at court dovetailed naturally with these approaches to foreign policy and religion. Laudianism and pro-Spanish neutrality could only hope to flourish in the absence of a Parliament. In any case, Charles's antipathy to Parliament left little room for manoeuvre. The king had imbibed his father's dislike of republicanism and parliamentary and popular power.[86] Others at court shared this prejudice in favour of high monarchy. Laud, as we have seen, exhibited it strongly. Cottington's ill-disposition towards the Dutch and the English Parliament also reflects this

---

[82] AGS, E2562, consulta of 4 Nov. 1630 (n.s.).

[83] G. L. Mosse, 'Changes in religious thought', in *NCMH*, iv, pp. 182ff.

[84] Hibbard, *Popish plot*, pp. 22, 44; see also chapter 3, above.

[85] Hirst, *Authority and conflict*, p. 161; Reeve, 'Viscount Dorchester', p. 286; Hibbard, *Popish plot*, pp. 34–6, 40, 55; SP16/529/15; Birch, i, p. 409, and ii, p. 107; Alexander, *Charles I's Lord Treasurer*, p. 218; Huxley, *Endymion Porter*, pp. 25–6; Archivo del Duque del Infantado, Madrid, Palafox Mss, leg. 94, fo. 137 (I am grateful to John Elliott for this reference); *DNB*, s.v. Cottington, Francis, Lord, and Windebank, Sir Francis; Sharpe, 'Earl of Arundel', p. 238.

[86] Adams, 'Spain or the Netherlands?', pp. 88–9; Hibbard, *Popish plot*, pp. 234, 237; PRO 31/3/66/fo. 132r; Russell, 'Arguments for religious unity', pp. 220, 222 and n; see also chapter 2, above.

view. Wentworth, despite his belief in the ideal of constitutional harmony, governed with a ruthlessness and liking for arbitrary solutions which earns him a place in the period's culture of power.[87] Anti-parliamentary feeling existed on two levels, however, and was fuelled by fear of impeachment, dispossession and even death. Weston, Cottington, Laud and eventually Wentworth were all opposed to a fourth Caroline Parliament out of self-preservation.[88] Personal interests within the inner councils of the court reinforced Charles's own inclination to non-parliamentary rule.

The thinking of the political court thus constituted a series of variations upon central themes. The powerful blend of pragmatism and interlocking ideological preferences was made more powerful by the existence of external political threats. Those threats promoted a siege mentality and kind of exclusiveness which came to insulate Charles from other influences. The process by which the Protestant and parliamentary interest was eclipsed was guided by Charles's gradual rejection of such policies. As Weston and his allies obtained the ascendancy by degrees they were assisted by the deaths of several opponents: Pembroke, Dorchester and Archbishop Abbot. The passing of Dorchester in 1632 was particularly significant. His death was a watershed which, in effect, marked the triumph of the Hispanophile and Laudian party. Their last politically active opponent, he was working at that time to turn Charles to war during the momentous Swedish victories in Germany. With Windebank's succession to his Secretaryship, the authority of the anti-war party was complete. The Protestant war lobby, increasingly out-gunned, had put up a strong rearguard action. The strength of that action signified the strength of customary English court politics. Its defeat involved their demise under Charles's rule. The control of the governing circle would survive Weston's death in 1635. It would break before nothing less than the political alliance of the Scottish army and the English Parliament – an alliance coinciding with the collapse of the Spanish monarchy and of Charles's hopes of help from that quarter.[89] The influence of the circle was built upon its willingness to serve and to service the king's preferences and will.

Of those who opposed the principles upon which the political court came to be based, William, third earl of Pembroke, had always been prominent. Staunchly supportive of orthodox Calvinism and of war with Spain, he was also aware of limitations on his capacity to act and of the need to retain royal

---

[87] Reeve, 'Viscount Dorchester', p. 286; NUL, Ne.C., 15,404, p. 257; Hirst, *Authority and conflict*, pp. 87, 182, 201; Elliott, 'Yet another crisis?', pp. 309–10; *DNB*, s.v. Cottington, Francis, Lord; Elliott, 'Year of the three ambassadors'; Hibbard, *Popish plot*, p. 34; see also p. 13, n. 21, above.

[88] On Cottington's fears at the time of the Long Parliament see *DNB*, s.v. Cottington, Francis, Lord; Fletcher, *Outbreak of the English civil war*, p. 89.

[89] Elliott, 'Year of the three ambassadors'; Hibbard, *Popish plot*, chs. 5–8.

favour. His death in April 1630 deprived the king of a close friend and adviser and the Protestant party at court of its most distinguished spokesman.[90] Dorchester of course represented a definite view of European affairs: strongly pro-Palatine,[91] pro-Dutch and anti-Spanish. As diplomats he and Roe had been professional agitators for Protestant war, considering any policy of peace with Spain a dangerous appeasement of Habsburg aggression. Their Calvinism had caused them to sympathize with the Commons' attack on Laudianism in 1629.[92] Dorchester was a bridge between the more radical views of Roe and the moderate anti-Habsburg position.[93] In an atmosphere increasingly hostile to his principles he continued, with considerable skill, to resist innovatory policies. His efforts were not confined to working for a Parliament and war. In alliance with the earl of Cork he promoted, from England, vigorously anti-Catholic policies in Ireland during the interval between Falkland's and Wentworth's administrations. Dorchester and Cork favoured planter and Protestant interests and abolished the public practice of the Roman religion. When Dorchester died, the two men were working for the enforcement of recusancy fines: a project soon scuttled by Wentworth who favoured, for tactical reasons, a policy of limited concessions to Catholics. Dorchester's approach to Irish affairs was part of a wider view of a Europe divided. That approach was made more aggressive by his despair at the rise of English Arminianism and Charles's development of negotiations with Spain. Dorchester's policy in Ireland echoed the fears of the Irish voiced in the debate on the remonstrance in the Commons in 1628.[94]

The views of Pembroke and Dorchester largely coincided with those of the earl of Holland. The earl was pro-French and anti-Spanish and to a degree shared the puritan sentiments of his brother Warwick. But his politics were not strongly ideological. He lacked firm religious conviction, which removed a potential obstacle to the favour of a Catholic queen. He also had a limited financial interest in peace with Spain. As Exchanger of the Mint he received a profit on foreign bullion struck as coin in England. Yet his general political orientation, with his rivalry with Weston and Wentworth, put him at odds with those whose advice the king preferred. With his desire for Weston's impeachment, for a Parliament and for war, he was quickly estranged from the Spanish and Laudian party. Holland stayed at court during the 1630s,

---

[90] PRO 31/3/66/fo. 208r; Adams, 'Spain or the Netherlands?', pp. 87, 91–2; Adams, 'Protestant cause', p. 419; Tyacke, *Anti-Calvinists*, p. 188.

[91] Elizabeth and Frederick considered Dorchester their main representative in England; Reeve, 'Viscount Dorchester', pp. 6–7.

[92] Ibid., ch. 1 and pp. 89–90, 94, 286, 342; Reeve, 'Sir Thomas Roe's prophecy', p. 120; AGS, E2519, exp. 5.

[93] Reeve, 'Viscount Dorchester', p. 303.

[94] Ibid., ch. 5 and pp. 24–5, 282; Birch, ii, p. 69; *CD1628*, iv, p. 147; see also chapter 2, above.

unable to abandon his personal quest for power. He came to occupy a political no man's land between those who made policy and their enemies outside the court. His decision to join the parliamentary camp in 1642 reflected the fact that he had never been qualified to rise to power under Charles. Despite his moderation and considerable self-interest, he could never ultimately pass the ideological tests for admission to what was, *inter alia*, an ideological regime.[95] Manchester and Coventry were soon in much the same position, perennially on the fringes of power. Both were constitutional moderates of puritan (or in Coventry's case, at least anti-Spanish) hue who remained, despite their misgivings about Caroline policy, fellow-travellers during the personal rule. With Holland they supported Laud's abortive coup against Weston in 1634. During the 1630s they failed to make any real impression on domestic or foreign policy.[96]

Other identifiably Protestant figures were present at court in these years. Abbot, appointed archbishop of Canterbury by James I in 1611, was an orthodox and militant Calvinist. A strong supporter of the Palatines and of war in the Protestant cause, he opposed alliance with any Catholic power. An opponent of Dutch and of English Arminianism, he could not halt the Laudian revolution sanctioned by Charles. After Laud was promoted to London in 1628, Abbot was little more than a cipher in the making of policy. His relief from disgrace and readmission to the court were intended as a sop to the Parliament of 1628–9. Abbot remained, however, a significant figure. At Lambeth he held court for the disaffected: a magnet for malcontents in Church and state. The Arminian triumph could never be fully complete until his death (in 1633) and Laud's succession to Canterbury. It was then that Arminianism was exported to the parishes with the campaign for the placing of communion tables at the east ends of churches, in the manner of altars. Abbot, nevertheless, had been the first major political casualty of the personal rule.[97] Sir John Coke, the ageing Secretary of State, was a Calvinist,

---

[95] The countess of Holland was pro-parliamentary and anti-Catholic. Hibbard, *Popish plot*, p. 146; see also ibid., pp. 32, 131, 163, 227; Beatty, *Warwick and Holland*, pp. 110–15, 124–7, 232–5, 242–4; Reeve, 'Viscount Dorchester', p. 148; PRO 31/3/66/fo. 208r; Smuts, 'Puritan followers of Henrietta Maria'; Clarendon, *Rebellion*, vol. i, p. 161; Donagan, 'A courtier's progress'; Magurn, *Rubens letters*, pp. 312–14; Gardiner, *History*, vii, p. 218; Tyacke, *Anti-Calvinists*, pp. 168–9.

[96] Alexander, *Charles I's Lord Treasurer*, pp. 191–2; *DNB*, s.v. Coventry, Sir Thomas, and Manchester, Henry, first earl of.

[97] SP105/95, letter book of Sir Dudley Carlton 1616–18, passim; Bodl. Lib., Tanner Ms 71/fo. 142r; Laud, *Works*, vii, pp. 23–4; *CSPD 1628–9*, pp. 516–17; N. Tyacke, 'Arminianism in England: religion and politics 1604–1640' (Oxford University D.Phil. thesis, 1968), p. 248 (I am grateful to Nicholas Tyacke for allowing me to cite his thesis); Tyacke, *Anti-Calvinists*, pp. 199ff.; Tyacke, 'Puritanism, Arminianism', pp. 137–8; Collinson, 'England and international Calvinism', p. 219; Collinson, *Religion of Protestants*, p. 82; Lockyer, *Buckingham*, pp. 357–8; Welsby, *George Abbot*, pp. 136–40, 145.

anti-Spanish and the brother of a Calvinist bishop. Coke was never a particularly influential figure. He lacked the social advantage of a peerage and was
more of a bureaucrat than a policy-maker. He seems to have toed the
Buckingham line in the 1620s and during the thirties was suspicious of the
merits of war.[98] Attorney-General Heath was a rather anomalous figure in
the upper reaches of Caroline government. A legal careerist appointed to the
bench in 1631, he enthusiastically supported a strong royal prerogative. He
was also an anti-Arminian: a survivor of Buckingham's 'puritan' phase of the
mid-1620s. The example of Heath makes clear how it was possible to reject
the Arminian position *and* prefer prerogative rule. Given Heath's largely
ideological approach to politics, the rise of Arminianism landed him in real
trouble. Estranged from the Laudian clerics and the pro-Laudian party at
court, he was summarily dismissed from the bench in 1634 after blocking a
suit brought by Richard Montagu, the Arminian bishop of Chichester. Laud
had brought Montagu's complaint to the ear of the king. Heath's career
suffered a serious reverse because he was trapped between Charles's political
court, at whose mercy he was, and his own religious views. Buckingham had
used the full spectrum of opinion to serve his own political ends. With the
duke now dead, Heath found himself in a new and more deadly era.[99]

Sir Thomas Roe received a cool reception at court on returning from the
Baltic in 1630. Despite the friendship of Dorchester and hopes of favour from
Holland, he was thoroughly excluded and retired, most unwillingly, to the
country. He saw clearly the way in which Weston and Laud were seizing the
helm. These were not times, he wrote, for him and his rules. He sent Holland
an eloquent lament for English foreign policy and almost despaired at the
difficulties of changing its course: 'we are not right: and to strive against a
throng, or to turn a channel, is a work of . . . labour and peril'.[100] On hearing
of Dorchester's death in early 1632 he wrote,

as he walked rightly in his life, died manly, and Christianly, and rejoiced in and recommended the king of Sweden; and so like a swan sang his own funeral. We dare not
guess at his successor . . . [101]

Roe was the war party's candidate for the vacant Secretaryship of State. The
prize went to Windebank, leaving Roe in the political wilderness.[102] Roe's

[98] M. B. Young, *Servility and service: the life and work of Sir John Coke* (Royal Historical Society, London, 1986); Russell, *Parliaments*, pp. 30, 262.
[99] Heath had been a religious opponent of Montagu since 1625. His career revived after seven years when he was appointed to King's Bench in 1641. Reeve, 'Sir Robert Heath's advice'; *CD1629*, p. 250; Knowler, *Strafford letters*, i, p. 58; *CSPD 1631–33*, p. 358. See also Sommerville, *Politics and ideology*, pp. 45–6, 224.
[100] SP16/173/49, Roe to Holland, 20 Sept. 1630. See also SP16/174/101, SP16/533/46.
[101] SP16/211/74, Roe to John Dyneley, 23 Feb. 1632.
[102] SP16/533/96; Gardiner, *History*, vii, p. 200.

style differed from Dorchester's. He spoke his mind plainly and was ill-equipped to negotiate the hazards of a hostile administration. His uncompromising views, however, were the root cause of his dismissal.[103] His approach to the European conflict was strictly confessional. He refused, like Abbot, to sanction alliance with any Roman Catholic power:

I am constantly persuaded by the observation of twenty years that all leagues and trust with any papist-blinded state are Egyptian reeds, and that all their inward counsels are directed to root out our religion and to replant their ecclesiastical tyranny . . . [104]

This attitude placed Roe on the radical wing of English Protestant opinion, more so than many members of the Providence Island Company who were patient of the notion of a French alliance.[105] Roe had the devoted friendship of Elizabeth of Bohemia and the high regard of Gustavus Adolphus. He was significantly involved in the organization of the Protestant international. There were no better qualifications for exclusion from the government of Charles I after 1632.[106]

The English advocates of a Protestant policy, those who were fast-falling or whose influence was fading during this period, were all, not surprisingly, part of the pro-parliamentary interest. Pembroke, Holland and Dorchester favoured the resummoning of Parliament in 1629.[107] The Protestant rearguard had links with those more seriously alienated and standing outside the court. Dorchester was connected to the Barringtons and through them to the earl of Warwick. The Secretary was related to Sir Thomas Barrington by marriage.[108] He was also a contact for the Holles family at court, as was the earl of Holland.[109] Holland was impeccably qualified to be perceived as a fellow-traveller for opposition. The first Governor of the Providence Island Company, he was its sole courtier of note, and the brother of Warwick who seems to have been its moving force. Holland gave the Company respectability and could be a suitor for its official needs. Carefully distancing himself from its activities (which undoubtedly included planning for the reform of Church and state), he was happy to share in any dividends, act as its official

[103] Reeve, 'Viscount Dorchester', pp. 282, 331–2; Gardiner, *History*, vii, p. 200.
[104] SP16/174/101, Roe to Sir Robert Anstruther, 29 Oct. 1630.
[105] SP16/174/101; Hibbard, *Popish plot*, pp. 31–2; Mathew, *Age of Charles I*, p. 72; Trevor-Roper, *Archbishop Laud*, p. 300. On the Providence Island Company, see pp. 210–13, below.
[106] Hibbard, *Popish plot*, pp. 31, 81; HMC, 4th report, pp. xi, 159–62, 588, 592; Mathew, *Age of Charles I*, p. 75; SP95/3/fo. 93r.
[107] PRO 31/3/66/fo. 208r.
[108] Searle, *Barrington family letters*, pp. 10, 151, 217–18; SP16/29/12; Hirst, 'Court, country, and politics', p. 125; Beatty, *Warwick and Holland*, pp. 65–6. I am grateful to Conrad Russell for drawing this connection to my attention.
[109] NUL, Ne.C., 15,404, pp. 257, 268, and 15,405, p. 64.

leader and, characteristically, have a foot in both camps after 1629.[110] The sympathy of Dorchester and Roe for the strategy of war against Spain in the Caribbean, with their militant Calvinism, made them potential supporters of the Providence Island group.[111] The links possessed by Pembroke, Sir John Coke and Sir Robert Heath would similarly have rendered them suspect to the political court.[112]

A major complicating factor in English Protestant politics during this period was the idea of the French alliance. There was a temptation, for strategic and historical reasons, for Englishmen to look upon the French almost as honorary Protestants. The potential power of an Anglo-French alliance might well be sufficient to counter the Spanish Habsburgs. During the Elizabethan period, Spain replaced France as the national enemy of England in the popular mind. Spain continued to be identified as the leader of the Counter-Reformation by European Protestants. James's decision in favour of a French marriage, Buckingham's efforts to build a military alliance upon it and the natural tendency for anti-Spanish and vaguely puritan elements to congregate about Henrietta Maria, as well as Richelieu's rivalry with the papacy, all contributed to a certain English optimism about France. Godly gentry like Sir Thomas Barrington considered France a less dangerous enemy than Spain and consequently were ambivalent towards French fortunes. The development of French participation in the European war, with the contest between Richelieu and Olivares, ensured that a section of English opinion considered a French alliance an option for England throughout the 1630s. Richelieu's tendency to woo the disaffected within rival spheres of influence led to an understated alliance between successive French ambassadors and the English parliamentary interest.

The obstacles to an Anglo-French alliance were very considerable. They included English Protestant sympathy for the Huguenots, the confessional *dévot* party at the French court (critical of Richelieu, opposed to Protestant powers and pro-Spanish) and Richelieu's commitment to French rather than

---

110 Hibbard, *Popish plot*, p. 32; *CSPCol. 1574–1660*, pp. 121–5; AGS, E2519, exp. 6; Newton, *Colonising activities*, pp. 58 and passim; Russell, *Crisis of Parliaments*, p. 321; Beatty, *Warwick and Holland*, ch. 3 and pp. 232–5, 242–4; Smuts, 'Puritan followers of Henrietta Maria'; Searle, *Barrington family letters*, p. 118.

111 SP94/34/fo. 191v; SP81/35/fo. 157r–v; *CSPV 1629–32*, pp. 516, 518–19 (I am grateful to Christopher Thompson for this reference); Newton, *Colonising activities*, pp. 236ff.

112 Lord Brooke was a patron of Sir John Coke. Pembroke was associated with the Protestant cause but also with an alienated figure such as Clare. Rudyerd, Pembroke's chief spokesman in the Commons, was a member of the Providence Island Company. Heath was linked to Clare in a proposed business venture of 1632. The connection between Holland and Roe after the latter's exclusion has been mentioned. Cust, *The forced loan*, p. 33; NUL, Ne.C., 15,405, p. 56; *CSPD 1631–33*, p. 358; Adams, 'Spain or the Netherlands?', pp. 87, 91–2; SP16/173/49, SP16/533/46; *CSPCol. 1574–1660*, p. 123.

Protestant interests in Germany. There were also naval and colonial rivalry, the problem of a France divided between Richelieu and his opponents and the cardinal's reluctance to enter open war against Spain. The conflict between confessional politics and policy based on reason of state was a theme not only of English and of French politics during this period (and of the rivalry between the two nations) but of the Thirty Years War as a whole. The radicalism of men such as Roe was largely inspired by these difficulties. Nevertheless, Dorchester, Holland and lesser figures about the queen became warm advocates of the French alliance and actively pursued it. These men had been Buckingham's recruits in the 1620s and were prepared to moderate religious objectives in the interests of reason of state. On the question of the French alliance they stood apart from uncompromising Protestants such as Abbot, Roe and Elizabeth of Bohemia.[113] The latter group were survivors of the strictly anti-Catholic circle of Charles's late brother Henry. Pembroke, who had been greatly respected by Henry, sat between the two groups; in the 1620s he was suitably ambivalent about the French alliance.[114] The fact remains that Charles and his political court increasingly ignored, excluded and alienated the full spectrum of English Protestant opinion. The loss of talent to his government which this involved was very considerable.

How did Charles's court operate as a social institution? How did that court society relate to the process of policy-making and government? The social life of the court, like the formation of the political clique, was above all the work of Charles's personality. It was an introverted world, controlled and essentially artificial, in which he could indulge his idiosyncrasies and interests. Court life became a haven for all Charles accepted and the antithesis of all he rejected. It was an illusory creation which could never banish the external reality of dissenting values. At the same time it played an important role in encouraging Charles's attitudes and the antipathy of his opponents. Charles's court was far more a social and (among its elite) an artistic than a political centre.[115] In this way it expressed his personality. The fact that he was not

---

[113] Dorchester became suspicious of the self-interest of France's German policy after 1630; Reeve, 'Viscount Dorchester', pp. 11, 303, 331, 342–3. See also Hibbard, *Popish plot*, pp. 25, 31–2; Mathew, *Age of Charles I*, pp. 71, 78; Adams, 'Spain or the Netherlands?', p. 98; Russell, *Parliaments*, pp. xvii, 13, 264–7, 280–1, 294–5; HMC, 7th report, Appx, pp. 544–5, 547–8; Searle, *Barrington family letters*, pp. 148, 238, 244; Smuts, 'Puritan followers of Henrietta Maria'; SP16/174/101; Reade, *Sidelights on the Thirty Years War*, iii, pp. 468–9; Elliott, *Richelieu and Olivares*, p. 100; PRO 31/3/63/fos. 5–6, 8, 31/3/66/ fo. 125v; SP78/87/fo. 535r; AMRE, CPA, 42, fo. 280r; Breslow, *Mirror of England*, pp. 103ff. See also chapter 7, below.

[114] *DNB*, s.v. Elizabeth, queen of Bohemia. See also ibid., s.v. Abbot, George; Adams, 'Foreign policy and the Parliaments of 1621 and 1624', p. 159n; Russell, *Parliaments*, p. 13; Parry, *The golden age restor'd*, pp. 69, 82–3; Mathew, *Age of Charles I*, p. 72.

[115] On the political importance of the Tudor court see D. Starkey, 'Court and government', in C. Coleman and D. Starkey (eds.), *Revolution reassessed* (Oxford, 1986).

primarily interested in government and policy-making meant political activity at court was increasingly low-key. This atmosphere encouraged the rather bland ideological consensus of the governing circle, and did a great deal to ensure that the latter was not political in any traditional or overriding way. Charles's clique provided no forum for the interaction of differing views nor any full focus for the political life of the nation. The apolitical atmosphere Charles favoured was inseparable from his intolerance of dissent. As England entered the 1630s and the Protestant interest at court was overrun, those remaining who were uneasy with the direction of government policy kept their heads down.

In January 1631 Charles issued new orders to regulate the life of the court. They stressed his desire for order and uniformity, propriety and decorum. They also emphasized the principle of aristocratic privilege. No man under the degree of baron was to enter the king's inner closet, with the exception of Privy Councillors, gentlemen of the bedchamber and the queen's Vice-Chamberlain. Likewise, only persons of such rank could approach the royal couple on public occasions.[116] Charles's formality and strict belief in rank and degree, with his attempt to reform the manners and morality of the court, created a world in which he was comfortable but which did not endear itself to many others. Like the king, it was distant, uninterested, humourless and cool. The courtier Will Murray had long been acquainted with Charles and remained in his intimate service. In 1631 he deftly reported to a friend, 'our court is like the earth, naturally cold, and reflects no more affection than the sunshine of our gracious master's favour beats upon it . . . '[117] Within this forbidding orbit, the immediate society about the king was introverted and exclusive. Charles did not like strangers and felt threatened by unfamiliarity.[118] This atmosphere could hardly encourage a healthy exchange of views in the making of policy. Formality, distance and ultimately lack of interest also affected the relationship between the court and society at large. In June 1632 Charles banished the gentry from the capital to the counties. Their congregation in London arguably encouraged social and economic ills. Yet their removal from London surely promoted the isolation of the court

---

[116] SP16/182/31. Charles's continued patience with Arundel, an enemy of Buckingham, was doubtless encouraged by the earl's position as a representative of the ancient nobility, as well as by his artistic interests. AGS, E2562, consulta of 25 Jan. 1631 (n.s.); Sharpe, 'The earl of Arundel'; Hibbard, *Popish plot*, p. 118.

[117] SP16/204/72, Murray to Vane, 18 Dec. 1631. See also Mathew, *Scotland under Charles I*, pp. 233–4; Clarendon, *Rebellion*, vol. iv, pp. 489–90; Cliffe, *Puritan gentry*, p. 151; Laud, *Works*, vii, p. 14; *CSPD 1631–33*, p. 182; Sharpe, 'Crown, Parliament and locality', p. 343; Sharpe, 'Personal rule of Charles I', pp. 59–61.

[118] Clarendon, *Rebellion*, vol. iv, p. 490; SP78/89/fo. 343r.

from county society.[119] Charles also withdrew from the public domain to a degree unprecedented for generations. Severe restrictions were placed upon public proximity to the court and the traditional monarchical functions such as receiving petitions, touching for the king's evil,[120] and simply being seen by the subject.[121] For the well- and low-born, the king and his court were increasingly private rather than public property.

The private and apolitical life which Charles preferred was epitomized in the person of Endymion Porter, by the early 1630s one of his most trusted personal companions. Fascinated by the arts and accomplished in the graces of the gentleman-courtier, Porter had no real interest in government.[122] To a lesser extent, both Arundel and Cottington reflected this style. Weston despaired of Cottington's taste for hawking ahead of administration. The Chancellor was quite at home on Charles's progresses, more like hunting trips, on which political news rarely featured in day to day life.[123] Porter's presence in Charles's inner circle was not incongruous. Unlike the king, he was free to avoid political duties and gave expression to a critical aspect of the king's personality.[124] He also contributed to the ideological atmosphere which produced the religious and foreign policies of the personal rule. Charles's Scottish kinsman Lennox was one of his closest confidants, a man with no discernible political interests. The marquis of Hamilton, soldier and adventurer, also fits this pattern to a large extent. This apoliticism goes far towards explaining how Charles could override the pro-French attitude of these Scottish relatives, as he did that of the queen, with virtual impunity. Those with whom Charles chose to spend the greater part of his time were not instinctively political creatures.[125] Wentworth, by contrast, with his ambition and passion for matters of state, was a man whom Charles never liked. In

---

[119] Larkin, *Stuart royal proclamations*, ii, pp. 350–3; Hirst, 'Court, country and politics', p. 123.

[120] Scrofula.   [121] Richards, '"His nowe Majestie"'.

[122] Huxley, *Endymion Porter*, pp. 63ff., 106, 118, 165, 167.

[123] Richards, '"His nowe Majestie"'; Knowler, *Strafford letters*, i, p. 59; *CSPV 1629–32*, p. 463; *CSPV 1636–39*, pp. 44–6; SP16/123/3; Melbourne Hall, Coke Mss, bundle 37, newsletter of 5 June 1629. On Arundel see Sharpe, 'Earl of Arundel', pp. 237ff.; *CSPV 1629–32*, pp. 581, 596, 601–2, 605, 637, 641.

[124] Porter was sent on a brief mission to Spain in 1628, but Cottington followed to pursue negotiations proper and Porter asked his wife to intercede for his own return, *CSPV 1628–9*, p. 378.

[125] The Spanish government understood the important place held by Lennox in Charles's world. AGS, E2562, consulta of Olivares, 22 Dec. 1631 (n.s.), report on despatch for England of same date; Mathew, *Scotland under Charles I*, p. 237. See also ibid., pp. 26–9, 234–6; Green, *Diary of John Rous*, p. 54; Alexander, *Charles I's Lord Treasurer*, p. 177; Birch, ii, p. 102; Ollard, *Image of the king*, pp. 45–6; Melbourne Hall, Coke Mss, bundle 37, newsletter of 5 June 1629; *CSPV 1629–32*, p. 592; AMRE, CPA, 43, fo. 294r.

Ireland throughout the years of personal rule, his influence upon the court was never direct.[126]

Charles's commitment to kingship as he saw it has disguised the fact that it was not a task which he could ever (or probably would ever) have embraced by choice. His real interests and abilities lay elsewhere and centred on the visual arts. Charles was unquestionably a great collector and a great connoisseur. He assembled one of the very finest collections of Renaissance works which has ever existed. Connoisseurship accounted for more of his time and attention in the 1630s than any other single activity. He was never happier than when spending hours discussing painting with Rubens or Van Dyck, both of whom he knighted. There is thus a *positive* sense in which Charles was not a political man. The arts had a certain political relevance within his court. Specific works did make obvious points. Rubens' execution of the Banqueting House ceiling at Whitehall celebrated the cult of peace. The general Mediterranean and Tridentine taste of the court was significant in terms of Charles's policies. Yet his appreciation of the arts was in no way limited by political or ideological considerations. His enthusiasm for Titian, Raphael, Correggio and Mantegna was based upon his expert knowledge of their aesthetic excellence. There was, however, one way in which the arts played a vital political role under his regime. For practical reasons, they severely restricted the range of his friends.[127] Very few individuals had the interest, knowledge and necessary financial resources to indulge in collecting. Since Charles liked to surround himself with fellow enthusiasts, the visual arts became a kind of freemasonry among the senior members of the court. Porter, Arundel, Lennox, Hamilton, Wentworth and Laud all shared Charles's artistic interests. Dorchester's knowledge of antiquities and Venetian painting (he had made acquisitions for Charles abroad) undoubtedly assisted his ability to keep his place at court.[128] The arts thus served to render Charles's social world (and the political circle with which it merged) more exclusive. In this way they contributed to its ideological sameness. They also promoted its lack of political vitality.

During the early 1630s, when the threat of another Parliament had receded, a struggle for power emerged within the regime. Weston was

[126] See p. 175, n. 18, above. [127] Parry, *The golden age restor'd*, p. 267.
[128] Huxley, *Endymion Porter*, pp. 97–8, 111, 179, 181, 310; Reeve, 'Viscount Dorchester', pp. 7–8, 24, 213; Ollard, *Image of the king*, pp. 37–8; Mathew, *Scotland under Charles I*, p. 236; Carlton, *Charles I*, pp. 143ff.; Sharpe, 'Earl of Arundel', pp. 239ff.; Gregg, *King Charles I*, pp. 166ff.; Russell, *Crisis of Parliaments*, p. 311; Hibbard, *Popish plot*, ch. 2; NUL, Ne.C., 15,404, p. 220; R. M. Smuts, *The culture of absolutism at the court of Charles I* (Princeton University PhD thesis, 1976; published Ann Arbor, 1985), chs. 1, 3, 4, 6 and 7; Fletcher, *Outbreak of the English civil war*, p. 407; O. Millar, 'Strafford and Van Dyck', in Ollard and Tudor-Craig (eds.), *For Veronica Wedgwood*; D. Howarth, *Lord Arundel and his circle* (London, 1985); SRO, Hamilton Mss nos. 158, 353.

increasingly disliked at court for his influence upon the king, his tight control of royal finances (combined with his own enrichment) and, by some, for his policies. It was Laud, supported by Wentworth *in absentia*, who came to lead the attack on Weston and Cottington. To a certain extent this was a division between crypto-Catholics and official Protestants, even between Hispano-phile materialists and nationalistic moralists. Yet such contrasts were not sufficient to light the fuse. The battle between Weston and Laud was a struggle for power. This was no factional fight in the traditional sense. It was an intramural contest, no less deadly for that, between men who both sat at the summit of influence, with vested interests in the same national policies, who had united to have Charles dissolve the Parliament of 1628–9. It was a contest made possible by the establishment of non-parliamentary rule. Its outcome would little alter the shape of the regime. Laud enlisted the support of Coventry, Manchester and Holland, and in the spring of 1634 went before Charles to accuse the Treasurer of corruption. The attack failed when the Treasurer had Lennox, the queen and the duchess of Buckingham intercede for him. (Weston had secured an alliance with the Lennoxes by his son's marriage three years earlier.)[129] Weston stood at the intersection of the political court and the king's social circle. His survival in Charles's confidence pointed to the power of that nexus over conciliar dissent.

In the making of high policy, the political court eclipsed the Council under Charles. This had been anticipated during the Jacobean and Buckingham eras when the Council's traditional policy-making role was circumvented.[130] The Caroline situation was new, however, in the ascendancy of a clique as opposed to a favourite, and likewise in the ideological nature of that clique. The dissolution of Parliament in 1629 was a milestone which marked a most critical political victory over the Council. This event was repeated (as we shall see) at equally vital points in 1630 and 1631–2.[131] Crucial diplomatic

---

[129] Weston and Cottington had favoured Wentworth's appointment to Ireland to remove him from the English political scene, where he seems to have had designs upon the Lord Treasurership. Clarendon, *Rebellion*, vol. i, pp. 62–4, 67; Laud, *Works*, iii, pp. 214–15, and vii, pp. 39–40; Alexander, *Charles I's Lord Treasurer*, p. 161 and ch. 11; BL. Harl. Ms 7000, fos. 472r–473v; Knowler, *Strafford letters*, i, pp. 57–8, 79–80; Trevor-Roper, *Archbishop Laud*, pp. 211–13; Gardiner, *History*, vii, pp. 234–5; Zagorin, 'Sir Edward Stanhope's advice', pp. 301–4, 310; Reeve, 'Viscount Dorchester', p. 253.

[130] G. R. Elton, 'Tudor government: the points of contact, ii, the Council', *TRHS*, 5th ser., xxv (1975), pp. 197, 207, 211; Sharpe, 'Crown, Parliament and locality', pp. 337, 339.

[131] See chapters 7 and 8, below. The supremacy of Charles's political court was surely encouraged by the deficiencies of Council government during the 1620s. Hirst, 'Court, country and politics', p. 127. In September 1631 the earl of Clare stated his belief that king and Council were making policy as was customary. Clare, however, had no direct knowledge of the inner workings of the government in which the king was increasingly at odds with a majority in Council whose views did not prevail. Clare's assumption, in part wishful thinking, was predicated on the fact of Buckingham's death; NUL, Ne.C., 15,404, p. 226.

initiatives, such as the opening of peace talks with Spain, were conducted without reference to the Council. Charles rarely attended Privy Council meetings. Of the ninety-nine meetings during the year ending on 31 May 1630 he was present at only nine.[132] In November 1630 new orders were promulgated for the conduct of meetings. They required that proceedings be secret with as little debate as possible. No clerks were to be present when the king attended discussion of matters of state. These orders reflected Charles's defensive style of government as well as his impatience of debate and dissent. Charles would not tolerate conciliar opposition in matters upon which he had staked his honour. During his rare appearances he addressed the board curtly and inflexibly and was difficult to advise.[133] He took counsel elsewhere from men who offered no threat to the way in which he saw the world.

The eclipse of the Council by Charles's political court was linked to Charles's lack of interest in government *per se*. Effectively he rejected the formal advisory body in favour of individuals in whom he placed his trust. Kingly lack of interest in government, as well as kingly inadequacy, had been the source of Buckingham's power. Charles's decision in 1628 to govern independently did not demand, of necessity, any high level of involvement in political activity. With the death of the duke his influence passed to a collection of individuals, who could, as they chose, relieve Charles of political duties. Their response ran the gamut from the diligence of Weston and Laud to the aristocratic idleness of Porter. In this situation Charles was vulnerable to manipulation, not least by the withholding of information. Those to whom he gave great power, however, very much shared his views.[134] Charles was freer to indulge this disinclination in the absence of a Parliament and war. Whilst he had acquired an objection to Parliaments in constitutional principle,[135] they also sat ill with his dislike of politics. Charles's developed aversion to the English constitutional process was in large part an aversion to political processes in general. The fact that he made no attempt to change the structure of government in England, despite his grave difficulties with Parliament and his absolutist pretensions, is strong evidence for the fact that his

[132] J. P. Kenyon (ed.), *The Stuart constitution* (2nd edn, Cambridge, 1986), pp. 429–30. Here I am in agreement with Professor Kenyon's view that the political (i.e. the policy-making) authority of the Council was waning. This does not necessarily run counter to Dr Sharpe's view of a revival of conciliar government; Sharpe, 'Personal rule of Charles I', pp. 64–5. The Grand Remonstrance complained of nominal Councillors without power to alter the policies of an exclusive regime; Gardiner, *Constitutional documents*, p. 215.

[133] *CSPD 1629–31*, pp. 373, 376; Cust, 'Charles I, the Privy Council and the forced loan', pp. 213–14, 225, 234.

[134] Reeve, 'Viscount Dorchester', p. 25; *CSPV 1629–32*, p. 45; Carlton, *Charles I*, pp. 107–8; SP81/37/fos. 167r–168r; Magurn, *Rubens letters*, pp. 300–301; see also AGS, E2562, summary of letter of Cottington to Olivares *c*. Feb./Mar. 1632.

[135] *CSPV 1629–32*, p. 204; Hirst, *Authority and conflict*, pp. 158–9; AGS, E2562, consulta of 2 Apr. 1630 (n.s.). See also chapter 2, above.

ideological make-up and authoritarian instincts had strong roots in an apolitical personality. He had no taste for the councils and paperwork of which continental absolutism was made, even in the age of ministerial favourites.[136] Charles, quite simply, wished to be left alone. It was as much his kingly conscience as the fact of his station which denied him the uninterrupted peace which he desired. That conscience, however, had its limits. He was eminently capable of rationalizing his failure to fulfil obligations when they significantly inconvenienced or offended him. His abandonment of the attempt to fund the Spanish war is a case in point. Charles was never much involved in political life unless he saw it as the work of necessity. His attitude to the world of affairs was at best ambivalent.

Henrietta Maria provided a domestic happiness into which Charles was delighted to retreat. His enjoyment of family life was an added incentive to avoid the distraction (and perhaps the crisis) of a further Parliament and continuation of the war. The familial circle within the court doubly insulated him from the external world.[137] Henrietta, more than any other person, decided the composition of the social orbit about the king. Such characters as Lennox and Hamilton, pro-French and little interested in politics, would naturally have appealed to her. She was a young and quite frivolous woman, in her twenties during the 1630s, whose uncomplicated concerns were her religion, her family and, by extension, her country. She told Charles in 1628 that she did not wish to meddle in matters of state but wanted him to make peace with France.[138] She had, perforce, a limited political significance at court. She attracted Francophiles and was drawn into her mother's quarrel with Richelieu. Since at first she knew no English, her companions in England were mostly French-speakers like Holland and Wat Montagu. Her personal circle being anti-Spanish by implication, it was also tinged with puritanism. Henrietta, as the daughter of Henry of Navarre, had known the great Calvinist families of France. She did not share her husband's antipathy towards the Genevan religion. In direct political terms the queen's own circle had little power. It ran counter to Charles's preferences and did not include able men. Henrietta disliked great ministers about royalty, men such as Buckingham, Wentworth, Weston and Richelieu. They were too serious for her, rivals for attention, and threatened her strong notions of family and monarchy.[139]

---

[136] Parker, *Europe in crisis*, pp. 54ff.; Elliott, *Richelieu and Olivares*, pp. 40ff.
[137] Mathew, *Age of Charles I*, pp. 34–5; Gregg, *King Charles I*, pp. 186–7, 201; HMC, 7th report, Appx, p. 548; *Letters of Queen Henrietta Maria*, ed. M. A. E. Green (London, 1857), pp. 15–16; AGS, E2562, Summary of letter of Scaglia to Olivares, 11 Feb. 1632 (n.s.).
[138] *CSPV 1628–9*, p. 310; Gardiner, *History*, vii, p. 182.
[139] As Lord High Steward of the queen's household, Holland controlled Henrietta's finances; Beatty, *Warwick and Holland*, p. 55. See also ibid., pp. 53, 56; *DNB*, s.v. Henrietta Maria; Mathew, *Age of Charles I*, pp. 59–62, 91–2; Mathew, *Social structure*, p. 32; Mathew,

Charles's court was pervaded by themes which endorsed his personal values. It reinforced social hierarchy and glorified the monarch. It was consciously modelled on the court of Spain. It was also saturated with Catholicism at the highest level. The last was a particularly feminine strain affecting, among others, the wives of Weston and Porter and Kate Buckingham and being encouraged by the queen. Many of Charles's male Scottish relatives were Catholics, including (in all probability) the duke of Lennox. Toby Mathew, a prominent court Catholic, was noted by Coloma as being zealous for Spain and for Rome and as influential with Weston and Cottington. Coloma advised Necolalde to cultivate him.[140] In addition, the Caroline court was remarkable for attracting capricious and quite bizarre characters from the world where international high politics merged with the arts and Roman religion. The abbé Scaglia and in particular Balthazar Gerbier are examples of this breed. Gerbier was an artist-diplomat, a friend of Rubens and employed by Weston, who, as English agent in Brussels in 1633, betrayed Charles's conspiracy with the revolutionary nobles of the Spanish Netherlands to the Infanta for an enormous sum of money. Among other schemes, he later pursued an abortive project to combine pawnbroking with banking in France.[141] What might be termed the Caroline 'lunatic factor' is significant.[142] Individuals such as these were but the more exotic fruit of an overall atmosphere which still distinguishes Charles's regime. That atmosphere was continental, cosmopolitan and avant-garde; it deeply offended Anglo-Saxon conservatism, cultural provincialism and xenophobia. The conspicuous cultural character of the regime, with its widespread absence of duty towards

---

Scotland under Charles I, p. 30; SP16/101/43; AGS, E2519, exp. 128–30; Birch, i, p. 417, and ii, p. 41; NUL, Ne.C., 15,404, pp. 35, 261, and 15,405, p. 166; AMRE, CPA, 44, fo. 100r; Lockyer, *Buckingham,* p. 448; Smuts, 'Puritan followers of Henrietta Maria'.

[140] Coloma referred to 'los dos mayores ministros'. This can only mean Weston and Cottington. Archivo del Duque del Infantado, Madrid, Palafox Mss, leg. 94, fo. 137 (I am grateful to John Elliott for this reference). See also ibid., fo. 136v; Hirst, *Authority and conflict,* pp. 142, 162; Hibbard, *Popish plot,* ch. 2 and pp. 95–6, 143; Huxley, *Endymion Porter,* pp. 106, 165, 167, 235–7; Smuts, 'Culture of absolutism'; Mathew, *Social structure,* p. 129; Birch, i, p. 440, and ii, pp. 24–5; G. E. Aylmer, *The king's servants: the civil service of Charles I, 1625–1642* (London and New York, 1961), p. 357; Sharpe, 'Crown, Parliament and locality', p. 343; Sharpe, 'Image of virtue', p. 227. Simancas documents suggest that Olivares was interested in the Scottish Catholics; AGS, E2517, fos. 31, 34, 38–9, 40–1, 43 and E2562, undated consulta.

[141] J. R. Jones, *Britain and Europe during the seventeenth century* (London, 1966), p. 24; Gardiner, *History,* vii, p. 346; *DNB,* s.v. Gerbier, Balthazar; AGS, E2043, exp. 172; Reeve, 'Viscount Dorchester', p. 272n; Hibbard, *Popish plot,* pp. 137, 196; Lockyer, *Buckingham,* p. 336; Howarth, *Lord Arundel,* pp. 194–5, 199. Scaglia fell out with Buckingham in 1627 when the abbé countenanced the rescue, for no apparent reason, of Lady Purbeck, the duke's sister-in-law, condemned to imprisonment and penance for adultery, when she was abducted by several of Scaglia's attendants; Lockyer, *Buckingham,* p. 408.

[142] I am grateful to Simon Adams for this point.

Protestantism, when combined with the unbridled material greed of men such as Carlisle, Holland and Weston, made the court particularly offensive to those whose religion, morality and national identity caused them to see it as popish and corrupt and, if not beyond redemption, in need of radical reform.[143]

The Laudian Church was of course an inextricable part of the Caroline regime. The personal bond between Charles and Laud, which grew up during these years, was a critical feature in the landscape of court life. Charles's unwavering confidence in his bishop and their effective working relationship were founded upon a strong rapport between the two men. Neither had any real interest in the world of ideas or concern with the intricacies of theological doctrine. Rejecting the spiritual energy and militancy of puritanism, both Charles and Laud valued an eirenic and aesthetic spirituality: the 'beauty of holiness'. They shared a belief, as we have seen, that Calvinism was religiously and politically subversive – too dangerous a force with which to compromise to any degree. Laud was similar to Charles in his authoritarian personality, the single-mindedness and insensitivity of his purpose. He rarely considered the powerful animosity which his policies generated against him. Like Charles he had little conception of the political art of the possible: a blindness epitomized by their design to unify the religious life of the British Isles under Laudianism. Laud, nonetheless, was an ambitious clerical administrator, seeking power to attempt the implementation of his schemes. In this he differed from his spiritual kinsmen, Hooker and Andrewes, who found in scholarship the expression of their dissatisfaction with Calvinism.[144] Laud's bureaucratic diligence complemented Charles's lack of interest in such labour; the king gave official sanction to the Laudian revolution. Laud's understanding with Charles gave him influence outside the Church. His protégés Windebank and Juxon achieved high office in the 1630s.[145]

[143] NUL, Ne.C., 15,404, p. 220; Smuts, 'Culture of absolutism', Conclusion; Mathew, *Age of Charles I*, p. 288; Hirst, *Authority and conflict*, pp. 30–1, 144, 150–1; Donagan, 'A courtier's progress'; Reeve, 'Viscount Dorchester', p. 338n; Birch, ii, pp. 89–90; Clarendon, *Rebellion*, vol. i, pp. 62–4; BL, Harl. Ms 7000, fo. 273r–v; Laud, *Works*, vi (1), p. 275; Beatty, *Warwick and Holland*, pp. 48–9, 104ff., 117, 130. Carlisle is a classic example of sheer pragmatism without principle. AMRE, CPA, 42, fo. 379r; AGS, E2042, unfol. decipher of relation by Gerbier; SP16/123/3; *CSPD 1628–9*, p. 469; Melbourne Hall, Coke Mss, bundle 37, newsletter of 5 June 1629; Mathew, *Age of Charles I*, pp. 59ff.; Schreiber, *The first Carlisle*, pp. 1–2; Archivo del Duque del Infantado, Madrid, Palafox Mss, leg. 94, fo. 136v (I am grateful to John Elliott for this reference).

[144] I am grateful to Ian Breward for this point. See also Tyacke, 'Puritanism, Arminianism', pp. 125, 130; *CSPV 1636–9*, p. 125; Hutton, *William Laud*, pp. 31, 46–7; Trevor-Roper, *Archbishop Laud*, pp. 67–8; Haller, *Rise of puritanism*, p. 228; Mathew, *Age of Charles I*, p. 38; Hirst, *Authority and conflict*, p. 167; Cross, *Church and people*, p. 176; Charles's and Laud's design for British religious unity has been pointed out by Conrad Russell, 'The British problem and the English civil war'.

[145] Juxon (bishop of London) succeeded Weston as Lord Treasurer in 1636.

During the years before Laud's succession to Canterbury the theological and ecclesiastical tone of his Church was set. Abbot was eclipsed at court and the Arminian capture of the episcopate proceeded apace.[146] The Calvinist bloc on the Caroline episcopal bench was essentially a rump which had survived from the previous reign. Presiding over fewer than half the parishes of England, it could only hope to moderate Laudian policy to a very limited extent.[147] Laud employed the existing constitution of the English Church – bishops, deans, archdeacons and the Court of High Commission – to alter the direction of ceremony and doctrine.[148] The road of parliamentary legislation was firmly closed.[149] In December 1629 Charles issued new instructions to the bishops for the government of the Church. This initiative was clearly Laud's work and had the aim of weakening, even emasculating, puritanism and separatism.[150] The bishops were to remain in their dioceses, conserving the limited resources of the Church and taking action against undesirable religious practices. There was to be tighter control over lecturers and non-conformist preaching and the enforcement of the Henrician statute law restricting the right to keep private chaplains.[151] Charles's declaration against religious disputation was to be strictly applied, 'so that differences and questions may cease'.[152] The injunctions provided a vehicle for Laud's campaign against non-conformity waged in the name of the peace of the Church. In this he had the wholehearted support of the king. Laud had most influence in areas where puritanism was strong: Oxford (as Chancellor of the university), his diocese of London, Essex and Middlesex.[153] He was able to censor pre-destinarian writings by control of the Oxford and London presses.[154] Authors and printers were brought before High Commission and punished. The rejection of orthodox Calvinism was in accord with Charles's wishes. In 1631

[146] Neile was translated from Winchester to York in 1632. See also chapter 3, above.

[147] Cliffe, *Puritan gentry*, p. 171.

[148] Trevor-Roper, *Archbishop Laud*, pp. 101–2.

[149] Laud was jealous of the influence of the common law in the life of the Church; Laud, *Works*, vi (1), p. 310.

[150] The episcopal injunctions of 1629 constituted a revision of the Elizabethan injunctions issued at the beginning of the queen's reign. Dorchester tried to cast doubt on their authority (seeing Laud's purposes) but Charles fully supported the project. Reeve, 'Viscount Dorchester', pp. 207–8; Welsby, *George Abbot*, pp. 136–7; Laud, *Works*, vii, pp. 23–4.

[151] The right to keep a resident chaplain was restricted to the episcopate, the peerage, the judiciary, Knights of the Garter and senior officials of the crown; Cliffe, *Puritan gentry*, pp. 158, 162ff. See also Trevor-Roper, *Archbishop Laud*, pp. 104ff., 113–16.

[152] Laud to archdeacon of London, 4 Jan. 1630. Laud, *Works*, vi (1), pp. 268–9.

[153] Gardiner, *History*, vii, p. 241; Laud, *Works*, vii, p. 26; Bodl. Lib., Tanner Ms 71, fo. 128r; Searle, *Barrington family letters*, pp. 132 and n, 245; Tyacke, *Anti-Calvinists*, pp. 188ff., 224. On the problem of the enforcement of Laudianism elsewhere see A. Hughes, 'Thomas Dugard and his circle in the 1630s – a "Parliamentary-puritan" connexion?', *HJ*, xxix, 4 (1986), pp. 783–4.

[154] Cliffe, *Puritan gentry*, pp. 156–7.

Bishop Davenant of Salisbury was reprimanded for mentioning the word 'election' in a sermon at court.[155] The drive for conformity was linked to the fear of subversion felt by Charles in particular. In the aftermath of the 1629 parliamentary session, amid political disorder and considerable fear of religious change, Charles looked upon alarmist preaching against Laudianism as little less than sedition.[156] He took steps to have the bishops preach obedience to the highest magistrate as the lieutenant of God, as well as to have them pre-empt any public accusations of religious innovation and unwanted religious dispute.[157] The regime made the error of seeing superficial peace as an antidote to dissent and ideological anxiety.

How did Charles's regime, so remarkable for its ideological and political isolation, survive financially? England's prosperity, and ultimately the financial viability of the crown, depended upon international trade. The cloth trade to northern, and increasingly to southern, Europe was the nation's largest industry. The quest for economic stability was therefore bound up with the making of foreign policy. With its trading economy, England was highly vulnerable to the vagaries of the international scene, to alterations in the demand for goods and the supply of capital and to the prices of silver and gold. The outbreak of the Thirty Years War had a disastrous effect upon England's volume of trade and her balance of payments.[158] The trade slump of 1629–31, when combined with the disastrous state in which Buckingham's wars left the Exchequer, added up to a national economic crisis. The need to regain stability and a measure of solvency was acute. Economic policy was formulated perforce within the context of the two options in foreign policy: war or peace. In addition to a decision about participation in the European war, it was difficult for England to avoid deciding whether to be a partisan in the economic warfare between Spain and the Dutch. Spanish policy was to exclude the republic's merchants from Iberian trade. Dutch commerce, moreover, was threatening to eclipse England as a trading and maritime power.[159] Given the ideological factor of English Protestantism, there were

---

[155] White, 'The rise of Arminianism reconsidered', p. 53. Clarendon was critical by implication of Charles's policy of publicly rejecting orthodox Calvinism; Clarendon, *Rebellion*, vol. i, p. 124.

[156] *CSPD 1628–9*, pp. 516–17.

[157] Ibid; Welsby, *George Abbot*, p. 136; PRO 31/3/66/fo. 132r; Bodl. Lib., Tanner Ms 71, fo. 142r.

[158] Supple, *Commercial crisis*, pp. 7–10, 12–14.

[159] During this period the Dutch increasingly monopolized the European carrying trade, the Baltic timber and grain trades and the Indonesian spice trade, and made inroads into the traditionally English herring fisheries. Their finished cloth was underselling the unfinished English white cloth in northern Europe and this, with disputes over English cloth exports to the republic, was a major threat to England's economy. D. C. Coleman, *The economy of England 1450–1750* (Oxford, 1977), pp. 67–8, 185; Clay, *Economic expansion and social change*, ii, pp. 119–20, 184ff., 222; Supple, *Commercial crisis*, pp. 115–16, 118–19. On

essentially two avenues open to English policy after 1629. One was to join the Dutch in making war on the Hispanic empire, principally seeking to plunder Spanish treasure from, and possessions in, the New World. Such godly profit, it was argued, might also elicit Habsburg concessions in Germany. This policy could conceivably be linked to the formation of a northern league, advocated by Roe, to protect the Baltic trades and nourish the power of the Dutch, Denmark and Sweden in the interests of Protestantism. This general approach, whilst ideologically satisfying to the war lobby, had (as will be seen) its economic drawbacks. The other policy was to end the war with Spain, to prosper from Iberian and Mediterranean trade and to counterbalance Dutch economic power.

Charles took his financial advice solely from Weston. The Treasurer's influence largely derived from his ability to preserve financial stability and with it the peace and limited independence valued by Charles.[160] The personal rule saw no fundamental reform of the English fiscal structure. Of the four principal sources of royal revenue during this period, parliamentary subsidies were traditionally voted for war, and the royal lands were a distinctly limited asset; most of them had been alienated by the early 1630s to liquidate debt. It was only the customs, the largest individual source of revenue, which, combined with borrowing, could enable Charles to pursue unpopular policies for any length of time.[161] His commitment to Laudianism and interest in a negotiated settlement with Spain, when combined with the essential dependence of the crown upon international trade, made the pro-Spanish neutrality of the personal rule a virtual necessity. The yield of the customs (which varied with the volume of trade and the efficiency of collection) was impressive during the 1630s. During the first half of the decade the overall sum was between £300,000 and £400,000 per annum. This seems to have risen to about £500,000 per annum during the later years. The customs thus furnished almost two-thirds of the crown's annual revenue during the personal rule.[162] It is difficult to calculate the national financial position during the early modern period, but something approaching solvency had

economic warfare between Spain and the Dutch see Israel, *Dutch republic*, pp. 204ff., and passim; G. Parker, *Spain and the Netherlands 1559–1659* (London, 1979), pp. 77–81; Parker, *Thirty Years War*, pp. 95–6.

[160] According to Clarendon, Charles twice paid Weston's enormous debts; Clarendon, *Rebellion*, vol. i, pp. 62–3.

[161] Hirst, *Authority and conflict*, p. 149; Thomas, 'Financial and administrative developments', p. 119; Clay, *Economic expansion and social change*, ii, p. 263; Coleman, *Economy of England*, pp. 188–90; Cooper, 'Fall of the Stuart monarchy', p. 561.

[162] Cooper, 'Fall of the Stuart monarchy', p. 561; Clay, *Economic expansion and social change*, ii, pp. 252, 256; Hirst, *Authority and conflict*, p. 174; Coleman, *Economy of England*, p. 190; Thomas, 'Financial and administrative developments', p. 120. All the proceeds from Ship Money went to increasing the size of the navy; ibid., p. 121.

clearly been achieved by the mid-1630s. The royal debt at that point was just over a million pounds: not far in excess of a single year's income. While future crown revenues were still being anticipated at the end of the decade, the situation of imminent royal bankruptcy had certainly been vanquished when Weston died in 1635. This was his principal achievement.[163]

Charles's dependence upon the customs meant, in effect, dependence upon the customs farmers, those who rented the right to collect the duties. The great farm of the customs, initiated in 1628, was the most sought-after of all the royal concessions. During the 1630s it was held by a syndicate dominated by powerful magnates such as Sir John Wolstenholme the younger and Sir Paul Pindar. Weston became closely allied with the customs farmers. The Treasurer's political survival was inseparable from the customers' enormous financial investment in the regime. Arundel, who was granted the farm of the duties on currants, was also part of this connection. The customs farmers had a vested interest in satisfying the king's need for credit. By accepting loans Charles doubled his dependence upon these men. He made no effort to preserve his credit in the City where it markedly declined. While the wider business community profited from the years of peace and trade, they were alienated from the court concessionaries and would not lend to a king who remained a risk. When the Scottish crisis broke Charles found himself in financial as well as political isolation. The narrow financial basis of his government reflected the unpopularity of his rule. The customs farmers shared in that unpopularity. *Inter alia*, they had been responsible for collecting tonnage and poundage without parliamentary consent after 1629. Having lent enormous sums to the king in 1640, they were condemned and crushingly fined by the Long Parliament and fell with the regime.[164]

What was the strategic context, and the material basis, of an economic policy designed to attract customs revenues? The conflict with Spain had severely hampered English trade to both northern and southern Europe. The Dunkirk privateers had continually harassed the nation's shipping and caused the virtual suspension of its Mediterranean commerce. Spain also needed freedom from English attacks at sea and was desperate for the reopening of trade. In 1629 and 1630 her government encouraged the ending of hostilities by granting passports to English merchants for unmolested passage.

[163] Hirst, *Authority and conflict*, p. 174; Coleman, *Economy of England*, p. 185; F. C. Dietz, *English public finance, 1558–1641* (London, 1932), pp. 257ff.; Alexander, *Charles I's Lord Treasurer*, pp. 133–4, 158; Thomas, 'Financial and administrative developments', p. 121.

[164] Ashton, *Crown and the money market*; Ashton, *City and the court*, pp. 32, 129, 135, 147–8, 150–1, 202–3; Alexander, *Charles I's Lord Treasurer*, pp. 164–5; Zagorin, *Court and the country*, pp. 134ff.; Supple, *Commercial crisis*, pp. 105–8; Thomas, 'Financial and administrative developments', pp. 121–2; *CSPV 1628–29*, p. 358; Hirst, *Authority and conflict*, pp. 187, 214.

The bilateral conflict was terminated by the Treaty of Madrid but the wider climate remained one of European war.[165] During the 1630s neutral England engaged in wholesale war profiteering. Dover became an international entrepôt for commerce with the great powers involved in the European conflict. English merchants traded eagerly in armaments, foodstuffs and military and naval supplies. In particular, Charles became an active participant in the Spanish war economy. English customs rates were generally lower on Spanish (as opposed to French, German and Dutch) re-exported merchandise. With the land routes to Flanders blocked by Protestant forces after 1631, the sea route or 'English road' became critical for Spain. Spanish troops and bullion – to pay the army of Flanders – often went up the Channel in neutral English hulks and could count on the protection of English ports. Charles's navy never actually went into action to protect Spanish shipping, but it connived in preserving the safety of supplies for Flanders and was occasionally deployed to ward off likely French and Dutch attacks. Large amounts of Spanish silver were coined at the English mint (a most valuable injection of specie) in return for bills of exchange.[166] Such pro-Spanish neutrality dovetailed well with the growth of English trade to Spain and Portugal, the Mediterranean and Africa. The new lighter English cloth was sent to the south and ships returned with luxuries, colonial products and even Spanish wool. With the Dutch excluded, England obtained a near-monopoly of Iberian trade. The flourishing of Anglo-Spanish commerce did not involve any lessening of English trade with the north, the traditional market for heavy English cloth. During the 1630s, English overseas trade reached unprecedented heights of prosperity.[167]

The alternative for England, a war policy, had of necessity to be based upon sea power and to address itself to a conflict which was economic as well as military and political. It was also inevitably associated with some form of commitment to the aims of the Protestant world. The classical strategy of war

---

[165] Supple, *Commercial crisis*, pp. 104, 110, 226–7; *CSPV 1628–9*, p. 358; *CSPV 1629–32*, pp. 16, 45, 57, 70, 251, 267, 280, 290, 332–3, 405–6; AGS, E2517, fo. 108; Birch, i, p. 453; Reeve, 'Viscount Dorchester', p. 284; Reade, *Sidelights on the Thirty Years War*, iii, p. 494; Clarendon, *Rebellion*, vol. i, p. 49.

[166] Parker, *Army of Flanders*, pp. 73–4, 77, 155; Birch, ii, p. 110; Alcalá-Zamora, *España, Flandes*, pp. 352–3; Clay, *Economic expansion and social change*, ii, pp. 165, 187; Supple, *Commercial crisis*, pp. 125, 226–7; Reeve, 'Viscount Dorchester', pp. 318–21; H. Taylor, 'Trade, neutrality and the "English Road" 1630–1648' and J. S. Kepler, 'Fiscal aspects of the English carrying trade during the Thirty Years War', *EcHR*, ser. 2, xxv (1972); Israel, *Dutch republic*, pp. 283–5; Loomie, 'Spanish faction'; Grosart, *Letter book of Sir John Eliot*, p. 197; SP16/203/108.

[167] Israel, *Dutch republic*, pp. 58–9, 88, 90–2, 144, 204–6, 208–9, 213, 283–5, 288–91; Coleman, *Economy of England*, p. 64; Supple, *Commercial crisis*, pp. 7, 20; Clay, *Economic expansion and social change*, ii, pp. 121, 127, 131–3, 140, 162, 187, 222; Clarendon, *Rebellion*, vol. i, pp. 95, 122.

by diversion was, as we have seen, the preferred solution here. In 1629 this required an end to the war with France and to the crippling royal subsidies to Denmark. Roe's conception of a northern Protestant league overlapped with that of war by diversion. Both strategies revolved around alliance with the Dutch against Spain. While Roe supported the idea of war with Spain in the Caribbean, Dorchester, a leading official advocate of war by diversion, assisted Roe.[168] Roe's commitment was to international Calvinism and the liberty of Germany. But while his inspiration was strongly ideological, his grasp of economic warfare was sound. The defence of the Baltic was vital to the anti-Habsburg and Protestant powers. Prussia and Poland were the principal sources of Europe's surplus grain and fed England and the Dutch in time of dearth. The timber, tar, flax and hemp of the region were essential for shipbuilding. The Habsburg defeat of Denmark at the end of the 1620s was a threat to Protestant domination of Baltic trade. The Hanse towns, as well as the Danish guns guarding the Sound, fell into the Spanish sphere of influence. The Baltic was, above all, the mainstay of the Dutch republic, increasingly the most powerful enemy of Spain. Northern commerce, as well as being the source of Dutch prosperity, was also its Achilles' heel. Roe saw the significance of Olivares' design for Spanish naval supremacy in the Baltic. He was also aware of the potential power of Sweden to sway the German war.[169] While Roe became instrumental in bringing Sweden into the war, his wider scheme had its flaws. One was implied by the growing importance of reason of state at the expense of confessional politics in Europe. The emerging struggle between Richelieu and Olivares, and Richelieu's policy of subsidizing anti-Habsburg powers (particularly the Dutch and Sweden) without ideological tests, were critical in this development.[170] The Dutch refusal to fight the Emperor was also significant. Roe's idea that Charles would lead a northern league ran up against the growth of Dutch power and the fact of Dutch self-interest. War with Spain had a tendency to make England a military satellite of the republic.[171] The sustained support of a land war in Germany could stretch English resources and would at least involve royal

---

[168] SP81/35/fo. 157r–v; SP94/34/fo. 191v; Reeve, 'Viscount Dorchester', pp. 101, 276ff., 322; Adams, 'Spain or the Netherlands?', p. 83; Newton, *Colonising activities*, pp. 236ff.

[169] SP75/10/fos. 164r–165r; Elliott, *Count-duke of Olivares*, pp. 332ff., 360–1; Israel, *Dutch republic*, pp. 207, 212; Alcalá-Zamora, *España, Flandes*, p. 526; Clay, *Economic expansion and social change*, ii, pp. 117, 221–2; Parker, *Army of Flanders*, p. 255; Supple, *Commercial crisis*, pp. 18–19, 102; Gardiner, *History*, vii, pp. 199–200; Reeve, 'Viscount Dorchester', pp. 94–5, 101, 274, 276ff., 322; J. I. Israel, 'The politics of international trade rivalry during the Thirty Years War: Gabriel de Roy and Olivares' mercantilist projects, 1621–1645', *International History Review*, viii, 4 (Nov. 1986).

[170] Elliott, *Richelieu and Olivares*, p. 116; Parker, *Thirty Years War*, pp. 219ff.

[171] Andrews, *Trade, plunder and settlement*, p. 302; M. Howard, *War in European history* (Oxford, 1976), p. 45.

debt.[172] Finally, Richelieu would increasingly make Paris, rather than England or the Hague, the centre of anti-Habsburg diplomacy. Despite his vision, Roe was doomed to remain at the marginal extreme of the war lobby in England.

The war lobby – the parliamentarians of the 1620s, the Providence Island Company and leading elements in the Long Parliament – were not, for obvious reasons, generally supported by English merchants.[173] Even in the Baltic, the latter had more to lose by Dutch competition and Spanish attack than by an Anglo-Spanish peace. A bilateral treaty with Spain could blunt the Dutch economic threat. Neutrality brought commercial opportunities and protected English shipping while leaving the Dutch still excluded from Spanish markets and open to attack.[174] The war option had its material dimension in the desire to secure commodities, profit by plunder and bleed Spain to death. Neither was it necessarily a threat to national solvency. But that option was basically an ideological one. Its economic risks and disadvantages and the uncertainty of its outcome bear witness to the confessional aspirations of its advocates. The two alternative approaches to English policy in a divided Europe were fundamentally opposed. One was nationalistic, materialistic and peaceful, the other internationalist, ideological and militant. Of the two, that followed by Weston was the sounder economic policy and offered greater immediate relief to the Exchequer. It gave Charles, moreover, superficial political immunity at home. Yet the economic and foreign policy of the personal rule could not exist in an ideological vacuum.

Charles's regime had enemies in England. Not all of them, however, chose to work actively against him. Besides simple passivity, there were really two courses open to those opposed to the regime. One was emigration, out of despair of the possibility of reform. The constitutional collapse of 1629, with the advance of Laudianism, appeared as the judgement of God on a sinful nation.[175] The years after 1629 saw large-scale emigration not only to New England but also to the United Provinces. Religious dissent was a critical driving force. The principal withdrawal was from strongly puritan areas,

---

[172] On the problem of English war finance see chapter 7, below.

[173] On the plan during the Long Parliament for a West India company and war with Spain see Kepler, 'English carrying trade', pp. 271–2; Gardiner, *Constitutional documents*, pp. 208–9, 253–4; Fletcher, *Outbreak of the English civil war*, p. 64. On the disruption of trade by war and the merchants' desire for peace, see p. 207, n. 165, above.

[174] Coleman, *Economy of England*, pp. 67–8; Clay, *Economic expansion and social change*, ii, pp. 185, 187, 222; Supple, *Commercial crisis*, pp. 18–19ff.

[175] See Thomas Bourchier's lengthy lament to Lady Joan Barrington after the collapse of the Parliament; Searle, *Barrington family letters*, pp. 60–1.

such as East Anglia, attacked by Laudianism.[176] Yet people's motives were not exclusively religious. The instinctive desire for better conditions of life and the hope of material gain naturally played their part. D'Ewes saw colonization as a remedy for overpopulation as well as a fulfilment of God's will.[177] There can be no doubt, however, of the religious significance of emigration in the context of Caroline policy. Dorchester summed up eloquently the attitude of Winthrop's generation of American settlers. In 1630 the Secretary sent his friend Elizabeth of Bohemia 'a proper new poem of our godly people, who weary of this wicked land are gone (man, woman and child) in great numbers to seek new worlds'.[178] Such sentiments continued the theme, evident in Parliament in 1629, of a broken covenant between God and the English people. There was no real difference between the ideological make-up of those emigrating out of dissent and that of those remaining in England to work for reform. The decision was often a difficult one. Pym considered emigration in about 1630.[179] Warwick, Saye and Brooke were resolved to go to the Caribbean in 1638. They were encouraged to stay by the outbreak of the Scottish revolt.[180] The critical difference lay in the sense of political possibilities which distinguished the activists, as well as the nature of their resolve.

Charles's political court was exclusive, distant and innovatory in its ways. As such it was ideologically offensive to leading members of the political nation and provoked their collective, and sometimes conspiratorial, opposition. The most important case of such conspiracy was the Providence Island Company. The Company, incorporated in December 1630, had as its official aim the colonization of the West Indian Island of Providence. Its charter, however, authorized the extension of its operations in an area from Haiti to the coast of Venezuela, to the mainland of central America, to the Cayman Islands and to Jamaica – then in Spanish hands.[181] Warwick, Saye and Brooke were the investors among the peerage. Holland received a free share for his role in procuring favours. Pym personally invested and was the Company's treasurer. Other members included key figures among the puritan gentry: Sir Thomas Barrington, Sir Benjamin Rudyerd, Sir Nathaniel Rich and Richard

---

[176] Cross, *Church and people*, p. 194; HMC, 7th report, Appx, p. 547; Sprunger, 'Archbishop Laud's campaign against puritanism at the Hague', p. 319; Hibbard, *Popish plot*, pp. 237–8.

[177] Cliffe, *Puritan gentry*, p. 205; Coleman, *Economy of England*, pp. 57–8; Andrews, *Trade, plunder and settlement*, pp. 319, 338–9. There was of course no puritan monopoly on emigration. Maryland was founded as a Catholic refuge and chartered in 1632; ibid., pp. 337–8.

[178] SP81/36/fo. 113v; see also Collinson, *Religion of Protestants*, p. 283; SP81/35/fo. 160r–v.

[179] Russell, 'Career of John Pym', p. 164. See also Hughes, 'Thomas Dugard', p. 787.

[180] Cliffe, *Puritan gentry*, pp. 204–5.

[181] W. R. Scott, *The constitution and finance of English, Scottish and Irish joint-stock companies to 1720* (3 vols., Cambridge, 1910–12), ii, pp. 328–9.

Knightley. The members usually met at Brooke House, at the corner of Gray's Inn Lane and Holborn. Other venues included Warwick House and Pym's lodgings, both nearby. The Company continued the tradition of an anti-Spanish strategy in the Caribbean, encouraged by the formation of the Dutch West India Company in 1621. Association with this strategy during the 1620s and 1630s is a good test of opposition, or of developing opposition, to Charles's rule. Hostility to Spain, hatred of Laudianism and belief in the religious mission of colonization formed an underlying ideological framework which fused the political and colonial activities of the Providence Island Company into a fully coherent whole.[182] In commercial terms, the enterprise was a failure. The policy of plantation had failed by 1635, subscriptions soon fell into arrears and there was no return on the invested capital of £120,000. In serious financial difficulties, the Company proposed the sale of the island to the Dutch West India Company in 1637, which Charles refused to allow.[183] Spanish forces took Providence Island in 1641 and the entire investment was lost. The bankrupt Company dissolved itself in 1650.[184]

It is difficult to measure precisely the Company's success in political terms. There can be no doubt, however, of its critical role. Although publicly chartered, it was clearly a vehicle (as contemporaries perceived) for covert opposition activities, for the organization and encouragement, on a personal level, of dissent. Given the necessary caution involved in such doings, and the likely loss of documents through deliberate destruction and confiscation, the thrust of the group's political activity must largely be reconstructed from external evidence.[185] The Company's records do demonstrate that Pym devoted enormous amounts of time and attention to its interests during the 1630s.[186] This fact alone – the value he placed upon the communal aspir-

---

[182] *CSPCol. 1574–1660*, pp. 123, 125; Beatty, *Warwick and Holland*, pp. 90, 94; Newton, *Colonising activities*, pp. 1–12, 58ff., 86 and passim; Birch, ii, p. 10; Searle, *Barrington family letters*, p. 148 and n; Cliffe, *Puritan gentry*, pp. 203ff.; Hibbard, *Popish plot*, p. 32; Thompson, 'Origins of the politics of the parliamentary middle-group'; Collinson, 'England and international Calvinism', pp. 208–10; Andrews, *Trade, plunder and settlement*, pp. 302, 356–7; Howard, *War in European history*, p. 43; Israel, *Dutch republic*, p. 123; *DNB*, s.v. Rich, Robert, second earl of Warwick; Gardiner, *Constitutional documents*, p. 208; Fletcher, *Outbreak of the English civil war*, p. 64.

[183] Charles's refusal almost certainly derived from his dislike of the Dutch. It may also have been connected, as Newton believed, to the momentary anti-Spanish mood of the court in 1637 and the possible value of the island as a base. Newton, *Colonising activities*, pp. 236ff., 290, 307; Beatty, *Warwick and Holland*, pp. 88, 93–4; Cliffe, *Puritan gentry*, p. 117.

[184] The members assumed responsibility for the corporate debts; Newton, *Colonising activities*, ch. 14.

[185] Ibid., p. 61; *CSPV 1636–9*, p. 125; Hibbard, *Popish plot*, p. 89; Zagorin, *Court and the country*, p. 100; Hughes, 'Thomas Dugard', pp. 773–4, 784, 787.

[186] Although he still gave time to his duties as Receiver of Crown Lands; Newton, *Colonising activities*, pp. 71, 74–5.

ations of the group – is telling. It was largely men who would form the Providence Island Company, Pym and Rich, Sherland and Knightley, who had led the way in the 1628 remonstrance debate.[187] Likewise Pym, St John and Saye, with Bedford (with whom Pym and St John were connected), would provide leadership in the Long Parliament. Warwick was a powerful patron of religious radicals during the personal rule and an opponent of innovation in government. His role in gaining the navy for Parliament was critical in the outcome of the civil war. St John was counsel to Hampden in the Ship Money case and Saye opposed the tax in principle. Gregory Gawsell, a Providence man, became treasurer of the Eastern Association during the civil war. John Gurdon, likewise, would be one of the king's judges.[188] The intimate nature of the alliances, often strengthened by blood and marriage, within the Company and the circles connected with it was clearly vital in preserving like-mindedness and political impetus.[189] With their noble and gentry status (and consequent social influence),[190] fast access to news[191] and considerable financial resources, this network of dissidents constituted a powerful battalion.

Charles came to recognize the importance of the Providence Island Company. In 1630 it would probably have appeared a respectable if not an innocuous group. It was recommended by the patronage of the earl of Holland, a favourite of the queen. It was granted a royal charter, like numerous other bodies, not least because Charles apparently considered incorporation orderly.[192] Yet his lively paranoia and fear of conspiracy, with the fact that these men had opposed him (and Buckingham) in the last Parliament, seems to have registered a warning signal. By 1633 the government was spying on members of the Company, and after the Scottish revolt broke out there were raids on its headquarters, doubtless in an effort to find evidence of collusion with the rebels.[193] Senior Providence men were in fact in touch with

---

[187] As Conrad Russell has pointed out; *Parliaments*, p. 424.

[188] Oliver St John was a member of the Providence Island Company and its legal advisor. *CSPCol. 1574–1660*, p. 123; Newton, *Colonising activities*, pp. 77–8. See also *CSPV 1636–9*, pp. 124–5; Beatty, *Warwick and Holland*, pp. 79, 97, 239–40, 246; Russell, *Crisis of Parliaments*, p. 321; Tyacke, *Anti-Calvinists*, pp. 168–9, 189; Hirst, *Authority and conflict*, pp. 77–8, 167, 193–4.

[189] Hirst, *Authority and conflict*, pp. 77, 193; Newton, *Colonising activities*, pp. 60ff.; Cliffe, *Puritan gentry*, p. 45; Russell, *Crisis of Parliaments*, p. 321.

[190] Warwick's great power in Essex is a classic example; Beatty, *Warwick and Holland*, pp. 78–9; Hirst, *Authority and conflict*, p. 56.

[191] Searle, *Barrington family letters*, p. 24.

[192] G. E. Aylmer, *Rebellion or revolution? England 1640–1660* (Oxford, 1986), p. 5. It was also government policy to favour chartered companies to keep bullion in the country; Clay, *Economic expansion and social change*, ii, p. 208.

[193] Newton, *Colonising activities*, p. 58n; Hibbard, *Popish plot*, pp. 89, 280, n. 36; Reeve, 'Sir Robert Heath's advice'.

the Scots soon after the National Covenant was signed.[194] There was, however, no pretext or specific reason to arrest these men during the 1630s. Far from committing any offence they continued to serve, some of them, in office under the crown. Warwick, with the gravest misgivings, even came to co-operate in the collection of Ship Money in Essex.[195] Unlike the attitude of Eliot, who had precipitately destroyed a Parliament and himself, the Providence Island Company style was more sophisticated, more informed, and ultimately, in terms of its goals, more effective. It addressed itself to deeper and wider issues: financial solvency under the traditional constitution, religious policy and England's international role. It had a programme for settlement and reform. It was premised upon less naivety about Charles and those he gathered around him. It saw the need to eclipse a whole exclusive faction about the king and to obtain power over him, if necessary, as a substitute for trust. It involved an influential political network, deep understanding of public opinion (and of the appeal of the religious issue) and long-term planning for the use of a Parliament to achieve reform.[196] It sought settlement before confrontation and did not, save in the last resort, descend to demagogy and dramatic effects. Above all, it kept a low profile until the arrival of its chance, and stayed within the law. The relocation of political influence from the Eliot to the Providence Island connection was a critical development in pre-war Caroline politics.

While the Providence Island Company was a key focus of opposition, it was not the only group alienated by the government of Charles I and engaged in divergent activities and dissent. There was a network of such groups, interrelated in purposes and overlapping in membership, which constituted a significant, and potentially very powerful, political front. The other chartered colonial and Caribbean companies were involved not only in searching for profit but in promoting Protestant interests, particularly in the Americas. The East India, Massachusetts Bay, Virginia, Bermuda (or Somers Island) and Saybrook Companies were dominated by wealthy puritans including a number of Providence Island men. Warwick was an important link between these interests, which came to identify with parliamentary critics of Charles's government from the late 1620s onwards.[197]

---

[194] Cliffe, *Puritan gentry*, p. 205. See also Hughes, 'Thomas Dugard', p. 788.

[195] Russell, *Parliaments*, p. 424; Hirst, *Authority and conflict*, p. 56; Beatty, *Warwick and Holland*, p. 79; *CSPV 1636–9*, pp. 124–5.

[196] Reeve, 'Viscount Dorchester', p. 341n; *CSPV 1636–9*, p. 125; Hirst, *Authority and conflict*, pp. 193–4, 196, 198, 201; Russell, 'Career of John Pym'; Russell, 'Parliament and the king's finances', pp. 106–7; Mathew, *Age of Charles I*, pp. 122–3; HMC, 7th report, Appx, p. 544; Cust, 'News and politics', pp. 82, 85–6, 89.

[197] Warwick was a key investor in the East India, Massachusetts Bay, Somers Island and Virginia Companies. Beatty, *Warwick and Holland*, ch. 3; Newton, *Colonising activities*, pp. 58ff.; Howard, *War in European history*, pp. 51–2; Hirst, 'Court, country and politics',

The Feoffees for Impropriations, a trust administered by twelve prominent London puritans, prospered between 1626 and 1633. Their strategy was to purchase impropriated tithes, Church revenues and appointments, and to bestow them upon appropriate godly ministers. The clerics they nominated were often in trouble with the government and involved in the movement for emigration. The trust had very considerable financial resources and came to exercise patronage in eighteen counties. Their objective of a lay-sponsored godly ministry ran clean counter to Laud's ecclesiastical aspirations and desire for clerical independence. They threatened to become a Church within a Church and, according to Laud's chaplain Heylyn, the trustees included not one man who wished well to Charles's government. Laud succeeded in having the enterprise dissolved in 1633.[198] The Feoffees crystallized a more wide-spread resentment of Laudianism, which became increasingly anti-episcopal during the 1630s.[199]

The political power of puritanism lay unquestionably in the support it received from within the governing classes, particularly the gentry of South-east England. Intricate ties of blood and marriage linked dozens of Barringtons, St Johns, Hampdens, Eliots, Cromwells, Riches and Russells. Of singular importance was the Warwick–Barrington connection which tied this county network to the world of Pym and the Providence Island Company. The Rich and Barrington families sat at the heart of English political puritanism.[200] The social influence and familial loyalty and communication at the

p. 113; Zagorin, *Court and the country*, pp. 99ff., 141–3; Ashton, *City and the court*, pp. 121ff., 156, 160–1, 202; Andrews, *Trade, plunder and settlement*, pp. 303, 333; *DNB*, s.v. Rich, Robert, second earl of Warwick.

[198] The Court of Exchequer found the Feoffees to be an unlawful body and not properly incorporated. The Feoffees were linked to the Providence Island Company through Harwood and Sherland. Newton, *Colonising activities*, pp. 69–70; Yule, *Puritans in politics*, p. 86; I. M. Calder, *The activities of the puritan faction of the Church of England* (London, 1957), pp. xii–xiii, xxff.; Hill, *Economic problems of the Church*, pp. 146–7, 245ff., 260ff., 307, 317ff.; Cross, *Church and people*, pp. 183–5; Zagorin, *Court and the country*, pp. 179–81; Gardiner, *History*, vii, p. 258; Trevor-Roper, *Archbishop Laud*, pp. 107–9; Searle, *Barrington family letters*, p. 244.

[199] Clearly the religious radicals consciously desired to bring down Laud during the decade before the Long Parliament. Sprunger, 'Archbishop Laud's campaign against puritanism at the Hague', p. 319; Gardiner, *History*, vii, p. 128; Green, *Diary of John Rous*, pp. 69–70; NUL, Ne.C., 15,404, p. 223; Searle, *Barrington family letters*, p. 194 and n, 195; Clarendon, *Rebellion*, vol. i, p. 124; Cross, *Church and people*, p. 195; Hirst, *Authority and conflict*, p. 167; A. Fletcher, 'Factionalism in town and countryside: the significance of puritanism and Arminianism', *Studies in Church History*, xvi (1979); Morrill, 'Religious context'; Trevor-Roper, *Archbishop Laud*, p. 103; Yule, *Puritans in politics*, pp. 83, 88, 91; Mathew, *Age of Charles I*, pp. 117, 298–9; Hill, *Economic problems of the Church*, p. 332.

[200] Both Sir Francis and Sir Thomas Barrington were electoral clients of Warwick, who was related to Sir Francis by marriage. Warwick and Nathaniel Rich acted as intermediaries in the Barrington–St John marriage negotiations in 1630. The following year Warwick was short of cash and Sir Thomas Barrington went surety for him. Searle, *Barrington family*

service of puritan values – and of puritan politics – were therefore formidable.

The puritan gentry had an important overseas connection in the form of English officers in Dutch and Swedish military service. Lord Vere and Sir Edward Harwood, two of the four colonels commanding English forces in the Low Countries, were central figures here. They linked the scene at the Hague – the Palatines, the puritan refugees, the Dutch republic itself and, above all, the fact of war – with families such as the Barringtons and groups such as the Providence Island Company (of which Harwood was a member) in England.[201] Another significant international dimension was the long-standing alignment between Richelieu, and his representatives in England, and Charles's critics in Parliament. This association survived from the mid-1620s to the 1640s. The cardinal had a major stake in bringing down the pro-Spanish party at the English court. The alliance between Pym and various French agents was a vital factor in the history of the Long Parliament. France even obtained an honourable mention in the Grand Remonstrance.[202] The parliamentary–French connection compounded the international framework of English politics which were, *inter alia*, one aspect of Habsburg and anti-Habsburg rivalry.

All these dissident groupings, together with others such as German Protestant refugees and the stranger Churches in London, tended to share values

letters, pp. 117n, 119, 127, 204–5; HMC, 7th report, Appx, pp. 544, 547; Beatty, *Warwick and Holland*, pp. 65–6, 89; Cust, *The forced loan*, p. 199; Hirst, 'Court, country and politics', p. 125; A. Fletcher, 'National and local awareness in the county communities', in Tomlinson (ed.), *Before the English civil war*, p. 166. See also Searle, *Barrington family letters*; Cliffe, *Puritan gentry*, pp. 11, 68; Beatty, *Warwick and Holland*, p. 225; Zagorin, *Court and the country*, pp. 99ff., 176; Mathew, *Age of Charles I*, p. 289; Tyacke, 'Puritanism, Arminianism', p. 123.

201 The Veres were allied to the Holles family by marriage and also connected to the Barringtons. Clare's son, Lord Haughton, and John Barrington both served under Vere in the Low Countries. Samuel Balmford, chaplain to the Veres, was pastor of the English church at the Hague from 1630 and opposed Laud's design to reshape the religious community there. Lady Vere was deputy to the godmother of Elizabeth of Bohemia's daughter. Frederick of Bohemia was godfather to one of Haughton's children. Harwood was an intimate of the Palatines. Haughton lobbied in Parliament for war and the Palatine cause in 1628. Newton, *Colonising activities*, pp. 68–9; Searle, *Barrington family letters*, pp. 79, 97, 101, 122, 133, 142, 146–8, 151–2, 253; HMC, 7th report, Appx, pp. 544–6; NUL, Ne.C., 15,404, pp. 1–2, 15, 22, 24, 26, 29, 219–20, 222, 224–6, 228, 243–4, 256, and 15,405, pp. 58–61, 66; Sprunger, 'Archbishop Laud's campaign against puritanism at the Hague', pp. 312–13; Hughes, 'Thomas Dugard', p. 776.

202 The French made details of Charles's dealings with Spain available to the parliamentary opposition. Hibbard, *Popish plot*, pp. 77, 130, 167, 215, 217–18; Reeve, 'Viscount Dorchester', pp. 145–6 and n; Russell, *Parliaments*, p. xvii; Searle, *Barrington family letters*, p. 148; HMC, 7th report, Appx, pp. 545, 547–8; Reade, *Sidelights on the Thirty Years War*, iii, pp. 468–9; L. von Ranke, *A history of England principally in the seventeenth century* (6 vols., Oxford, 1875), v, p. 447.

and aspirations. Their common denominator (save in the case of France) was international Calvinism.[203] Woven together by this ideological rapport and by personal interconnections, they formed an extended fabric of dissent permeating the English upper classes. While doubtless a numerical minority and an 'inner circle',[204] this network could be activated to effect by resolute leadership when circumstances were seen to require it.[205] Such leadership came increasingly from members of the Providence Island Company and their associates such as Bedford: a critical concentration of individuals with a high level of political awareness and commitment.

What made this kind of conspiratorial dissent significantly new? Firstly, the court was no longer the undivided centre of national politics. Pym and others were concerned with the evil influences about the king. Yet the existence of a group such as the Providence Island Company makes clear that the court no longer had a monopoly on political ability, commitment, activity and influence at a national level. As the belief in malicious counsel and corruption in government grew stronger, external political activity could appear even more creditable: the greater the desire for reform, the less the hope that the initiative would come from court. Eventually, by the autumn of 1640, Charles's circle was utterly friendless and the political initiative had passed to his opponents.[206] The emerging polarization of high politics was, by definition, marked by ideological conflict, mutual fear and deep mistrust. The stakes were high, the game was deadly and the aim became the enemy's eclipse and destruction. The situation was blurred and the problem intensified, as we have seen, by the development of conspiracy theory. This was particularly prevalent amongst the government's opponents, where lack of exact and confidential knowledge, when combined with the introspection and moral intensity of puritanism, produced what were ultimately overwhelming fears.[207]

Secondly, opposition was new in the way it became truly subversive in rejecting the entire basis and orientation of the regime, and in so doing

---

[203] Richelieu's government was uninterested in the religious aspirations of international Calvinism in anything other than a mercenary way.

[204] Collinson, 'England and international Calvinism', p. 210 and passim.

[205] The various collections for the Palatinate and the management of the Long Parliament are cases in point. Ibid., pp. 208ff.; Hirst, *Authority and conflict*, p. 193; Hughes, 'Thomas Dugard', pp. 784–7, 793 and passim.

[206] Hibbard, *Popish plot*, p. 227. Belief in the merit of objectives pursued outside government did not of course imply any design to alter the constitutional infrastructure. It did, however, look forward to a Parliament which would reverse a perceived imbalance in favour of undesirable court advisors. See p. 219, n. 214, below.

[207] Gerald Aylmer and Conrad Russell have pointed to the importance of vocal and dynamic minorities in English politics during this period; Russell, *Parliaments*, pp. 429–30 (citing Aylmer). See also Yule, *Puritans in politics*, p. 88; Mathew, *Social structure*, p. 34; Parker, *Thirty Years War*, p. 220.

becoming a powerful and dangerous political force. Essential to its subversiveness was the development of a whole ideological pattern of thought fusing constitutional and religious objections to Charles's rule. That pattern would reach its culmination in the Grand Remonstrance in 1641. Its subversive nature was, however, relative to the innovatory policies it opposed and was based upon an essentially conservative set of principles. But those principles were galvanized in the process of reaction and *in extremis* were capable of inspiring revolutionary action.[208] In such a situation, English Protestant nationalism could be a force not to unite but to divide the nation.[209] The disappointed hopes raised by war with Spain and the Petition of Right, as much as the rise of Arminianism, added fuel to the fire. The events of the late 1620s and early 1630s and the deliberations of the Providence Island Company contributed to the Long Parliament's fears even during the later stages of the apparent popish plot. The Grand Remonstrance belongs to the same intellectual world as the 1628 remonstrance debate. It was not simple hindsight that led Pym to begin his 1641 recitation of the cumulative ills of the kingdom with the year 1625. On the contrary, that recitation was directly linked to the gradual erosion of confidence in Charles which did so much to undermine his rule.[210]

Thus, thirdly, pressure upon the constitutional fiction was critical in the emergence of a new kind of opposition. It was never imagined that the monarch could do no wrong in any superhuman sense. Rather, it was commonly held that the king, being king, was and should be worthy of trust to govern as a constitutional and Protestant prince. This was the earthly linchpin in the social philosophy and mental world of pre-civil war Englishmen. Attachment to that world was quite emotive, and fear of disorder and the collapse of the system almost apocalyptic.[211] It took a great deal to undermine confidence in an anointed king and when this occurred the reaction was one of terror. We have seen that by the end of the 1620s there were serious doubts about Charles among leading members of the English political nation. There was, in fact, an emerging want of confidence in him in three related

---

[208] Nicholas Tyacke has pointed to this process in relation to the religious issue; Tyacke, 'Puritanism, Arminianism', p. 143. See also Morrill, 'Religious context', pp. 162, 170–1; Reeve, 'Legal status of the Petition of Right', pp. 276–7. I am grateful to Michael Bennett for discussion of these matters.

[209] Hibbard, *Popish plot*, pp. 227–38; Russell, *Parliaments*, p. 432.

[210] Russell, *Parliaments*, p. 380; Hibbard, *Popish plot*, pp. 213–16, 227; Reeve, 'Legal status of the Petition of Right', pp. 275–7.

[211] Daly, *Cosmic harmony*, pp. 10–11, 15–17. This is distinct from the strictly legal maxim that the king could do no wrong. *ST*, iii, col. 1201; Sommerville, *Politics and ideology*, pp. 101–2. Eliot's attachment to the classical view of evil counsel is clear (see chapter 3, above). While his activities and those of his associates prefigured and initiated the subversive dissent of these years, he remained in this sense traditional.

senses. He was suspect in terms of constitutional and religious orthodoxy, in the honesty of his dealings and in his ability (and perhaps his inclination) to govern. Disturbing doubts about Charles continued to grow after 1629 among influential dissidents and in the community at large. When compared with the Elizabethan legend, the official Calvinism of James I, the dead Prince Henry, the martyrs Elizabeth and Frederick, and the victorious Gustavus Adolphus, Charles appeared to be wanting as a godly ruler.[212] In the light of his religious and foreign policies particularly, there was an emerging conflict of contemporary values: between the value placed upon the sanctity of monarchy and that placed upon the integrity of society as a whole. Charles would eventually cause the resolution of this conflict by separation of the kingly office from the kingly person.

During the 1630s classical views of evil counsel were being replaced, among some of Charles's critics, by the general idea that he was so poisoned by bad advice that he could no longer be trusted to act responsibly. This line of thinking, followed by Pym, stopped just short of accusing him of malice. Others such as Warwick apparently harboured a personal objection. On one occasion, in the winter of 1636–7, the earl lectured Charles at length on the unacceptable nature of his whole regime, comparing it unfavourably with the mild rule of Elizabeth and James I. Warwick urged constitutional reform, war with Spain and the calling of a Parliament. The speech made no impression on Charles, who simply replied that he expected Warwick's exemplary obedience.[213]

---

[212] The Elizabethan legend reached its height under Charles I and was an element in attacks on his government. N. M. Fuidge, 'Queen Elizabeth and the Petition of Right', *BIHR*, xlviii (1975), p. 45. See also Birch, ii, pp. 82, 145; Searle, *Barrington family letters*, p. 214; Green, *Diary of John Rous*, p. 19; *CSPD 1628–9*, pp. 550–1; *CSPV 1628–9*, pp. 557, 580–1; Laud, *Works*, vii, pp. 17n to 18n; NUL, Ne.C., 15,404, p. 233; Gardiner, *Constitutional documents*, pp. 256–7; SP16/173/49; Reeve, 'Viscount Dorchester', pp. 101n, 282; Reeve, 'Sir Robert Heath's advice'; Kenyon, *Stuart constitution*, p. 115; Breslow, *Mirror of England*, pp. 129, 134, 136–8; Hibbard, *Popish plot*, p. 167; Beatty, *Warwick and Holland*, p. 79; Sommerville, *Politics and ideology*, p. 231; Morrill, 'Religious context', p. 162; B. Worden, rev. art., *TLS*, 13 June 1986, p. 635. See also p. 28, n. 98, above. An exception to this overriding pattern of doubt about Charles is Sir Richard Grosvenor, who believed in a plot by evil counsellors carried over from the Jacobean period; Cust and Lake, 'Sir Richard Grosvenor', pp. 46–7.

[213] *CSPV 1636–9*, pp. 124–5. In this context it may be significant that Warwick was a patron of Jeremiah Burroughs, an exponent of resistance theory. Hirst, 'Revisionism revised', p. 98; Hirst, *Authority and conflict*, p. 78; Beatty, *Warwick and Holland*, p. 79. Resistance theory was present among the radical Protestant fringe in Jacobean and Caroline England. Republican ideas were conspicuous by their absence. Sommerville, *Politics and ideology*, pp. 9–11, 44, 57–8, 69ff., 194, 233, 238; Clark, 'Thomas Scott and the growth of urban opposition', p. 18; Fincham and Lake, 'Ecclesiastical policy of King James I', p. 199; Russell, 'Arguments for religious unity', pp. 217ff. See also Russell, 'Career of John Pym', pp. 159ff.; Hibbard, *Popish plot*, pp. 215, 233; Morrill (ed.), *Reactions to the English civil war*, Introduction, pp. 6–7; Morrill, 'Religious context', p. 171 and n; Gardiner, *Speech of Sir Robert Heath*, pp. 7–8; NUL, Ne.C., 15,404, p. 233.

Changing views of Charles encouraged anxiety about the need for reform. They also promoted a sense of the importance of Parliament. Parliament came to be seen not only as a means to such reform, but also as a proper avenue of good counsel. Belief in the traditional principle that England was governed with representation and by consent, when combined with the sense of urgency created by Charles's rule, underlined the symbolic role of the institution, despite its physical absence, during the 1630s. It was belief in the place of Parliament which underlay the contemporary perception of the personal rule as a constitutional aberration: a perception which was – given Charles's eventual resolve not to call Parliament – essentially correct.[214] On a more practical level, the Providence Island Company and similar connections provided a vehicle for association and communication which would otherwise have taken place in, or in closer relation to, Parliament.[215]

There were a number of important and distinctly traditional elements interwoven with the novel political developments of these years. One was the abiding and vital role of ruling-class politics. The network of dissident groupings which grew up in Caroline England enjoyed, directly or indirectly, aristocratic patronage and sanction. Such support and leadership, moreover, were frequently provided for reasons which were essentially unideological. Noblemen such as the earl of Essex, connected to the late Prince Henry but excluded from Charles's court, were jealous of power as well as seeking reform in 1640.[216] Laudianism – in the raising of bishops to high office and the punishments meted out by High Commission – was socially offensive to the aristocracy and encouraged the reaction against episcopacy.[217] The debasement of titles with money transactions since the Jacobean period could only undermine the loyalty of the old nobility.[218] Charles's invasion of

[214] Searle, *Barrington family letters*, p. 211; *CD1629*, pp. 132, 178; *CSPV 1636–9*, pp. 124–6; Green, *Diary of John Rous*, pp. 54 and n, 55; Hirst, *Authority and conflict*, pp. 153, 198; Cust and Lake, 'Sir Richard Grosvenor', pp. 47–8; Russell, *Parliaments*, p. 390; Hibbard, *Popish plot*, pp. 215–16; Reeve, 'Legal status of the Petition of Right', pp. 275–6; E. Cope, 'Public images of Parliament during its absence', *Legislative Studies Quarterly*, vii, 2 (1982).

[215] Pym is clearly a case in point; Newton, *Colonising activities*, pp. 71, 74–5.

[216] Essex was connected to the 'constitutional' opposition of the 1620s: Eliot, Selden, Littleton and Strode. See V. F. Snow, 'Essex and the aristocratic opposition to the early Stuarts', *JMH*, xxxii (1962); Manning, 'The aristocracy and the downfall of Charles I'; Reeve, 'Sir Robert Heath's advice'.

[217] Clarendon, *Rebellion*, vol. i, p. 125; Yule, *Puritans in politics*, p. 87; Mathew, *Age of Charles I*, p. 300; Hill, *Economic problems of the Church*, p. 340.

[218] This is a consistent theme in Clare's correspondence. In 1631 he wrote that if his estate had been better by some thousands, 'the court had befriended me more, and my acquaintance with prisons had been less . . . '; Clare to his son's father-in-law Sir Francis Ashley, 12 Sept. 1631. NUL, Ne.C., 15,405, p. 215. See also ibid., 15,404, p. 260, and 15,405, p. 244; Peck, ' "For a king not to be bountiful were a fault": perspectives on court patronage in early Stuart England', pp. 32–3, 35.

hereditary feudal rights by such means as extending the forest law were opposed by magnates such as Warwick with a stake in the old regime.[219] Warwick and others also had a financial interest, as we have seen, in war with Spain, and therefore in an ecclesiastical policy consistent with it.[220] Broadly personal and social considerations, as well as financial ones, played their part in the aristocratic reaction. The vast majority of Charles's critics were, moreover, conservative and law-abiding men made oppositionist and ideologically aggressive by an innovatory regime. In this struggle there were echoes of traditional dynastic politics. There was the need for, and (as will be seen) an interest in an alternative line of succession. Correspondence and later co-operation with rebel forces in the king's dominions was, likewise, nothing new. Neither was inept kingship, the perennial problem of monarchy, a novel obstacle. It did not require the radicalization of attitudes to monarchy. Such attitudes, when under pressure, could have been appeased at almost any point with concessions by Charles which were significant and sincere. Pym and others wanted to serve, to co-operate, to counsel and to tutor. Their problem was Charles's ideological provocation. It was this, with the poor political quality of his kingship, which rendered that kingship, in their eyes, increasingly irredeemable. Despite the traditional political themes which, on the whole, preserved order and assisted stability, Charles's government remained inherently unstable. It was an inextricable part of the new political context which, in concert with international influences, it had served to create in England.

The European war, from the time of its outbreak, intensified English ideological positions. It was thus a critical factor in English politics. Charles's accession and the dislocating effects of his rule affected an atmosphere already considerably enlivened as the Parliament of 1624 had shown[221] – an atmosphere which could well become highly charged. The polarization of English politics by 1629–30 can be seen as one aspect of the polarization of international politics under the pressure of war.[222] The growth of the English news industry was closely connected to the progress of the war and continually stimulated the national political consciousness. In a Europe divided between Spain and her enemies, English public opinion was definitely anti-

---

[219] One of the royal fiscal initiatives of the personal rule was the fining of landowners for supposedly encroaching on the defunct boundaries of the medieval royal forests. Hirst, *Authority and conflict*, pp. 173–4; Beatty, *Warwick and Holland*, pp. 35–6, 238–42; *DNB*, s.v. Rich, Robert, second earl of Warwick.

[220] Warwick was in financial difficulties after 1631, and while he never had to alienate assets he was in debt to the Providence Island Company; Beatty, *Warwick and Holland*, pp. 89–90, 100.

[221] Adams, 'Foreign policy and the Parliaments of 1621 and 1624', pp. 169, 171.

[222] Parker, *Spain and the Netherlands*, pp. 76, 226.

Spanish.[223] The puritan gentry fervently followed continental events and Dutch and Swedish victories were cause for great rejoicing.[224] Spain was perceived as the international enemy. John Barrington wrote of the fall of Bois-le-Duc to the Dutch in 1629: 'very good news to all that do not love the Spanish faction'.[225] Conversely, Protestant reverses were much mourned. The Treaty of Madrid and Charles's eventual pro-Spanish neutrality were perceived by the puritan gentry as a league against God.[226] To Charles the European drama appeared in a different light. He was influenced, we know, by the idea of an international Calvinist plot which he believed, characteristically, to be largely directed against himself.[227] Charles's suspicion of such a design had its basis in fact, in the connections between English, Dutch, German and, increasingly, Scottish co-religionists.[228] Beyond this, his imagination did nothing to lessen the gulf between his views and those of political puritanism.

Charles's sister Elizabeth, her displaced family and their cause were a crucial link between English politics and the international scene. Elizabeth's influence in England was circumscribed by her financial dependence upon Charles, as well as by her absence on the continent.[229] She was, however, Charles's heir-apparent throughout the 1620s and was extremely popular among the English people. Her popularity was directly related to public disapproval of Charles, to whom she and her children were a threat. Elizabeth, while not a particularly deep personality, was possessed of great charm and strength of character and had an undeniably winning effect upon those who knew her. With a strongly Protestant upbringing, influenced by her brother

---

[223] Zagorin, *Court and the country*, pp. 106ff.; *CSPV 1629–32*, pp. 183–4; Andrews, *Trade, plunder and settlement*, p. 363; AMRE, CPA, 42, fo. 280r.

[224] Searle, *Barrington family letters*, pp. 82–3, 195, 203, 214, 235–6, and passim.

[225] Ibid., pp. 82–3; Breslow, *Mirror of England*, ch. 3.

[226] Searle, *Barrington family letters*, pp. 227, 238, 244; NUL, Ne.C., 15,404, pp. 217–18, 222, 231; Gardiner, *Constitutional documents*, pp. 208–9; Gardiner, *Speech of Sir Robert Heath*, p. 8; Green, *Diary of John Rous*, p. 38; Adams, 'Foreign policy and the Parliaments of 1621 and 1624', p. 147n; Breslow, *Mirror of England*, p. 42.

[227] Hibbard, *Popish plot*, pp. 228, 237, 253n; PRO 31/3/66/fo. 132r; Newton, *Colonising activities*, p. 58 and n.

[228] Newton, *Colonising activities*, pp. 236ff.; AGS, E2562, consulta of (Apr.?) 1630; AMRE, CPA, 42, fo. 274r; Magurn, *Rubens letters*, pp. 342–5; Howard, *War in European history*, p. 45; Cliffe, *Puritan gentry*, p. 117; Sprunger, 'Archbishop Laud's campaign against puritanism at the Hague'; Collinson, 'England and international Calvinism', pp. 208–9; Zagorin, *Court and the country*, pp. 178–9; Yule, *Puritans in politics*, p. 96; Beatty, *Warwick and Holland*, p. 89.

[229] Adams, 'Spain or the Netherlands?', p. 91. The Dutch republic awarded the exiled Frederick a monthly allowance on condition that he also obtained aid from England. He and Elizabeth were receiving over £20,000 per annum from Charles by the early 1630s. Their circumstances were, however, very straitened. Parker, *Thirty Years War*, p. 63; Alexander, *Charles I's Lord Treasurer*, pp. 160, 247.

Henry (of whom she was fond) and by Frederick, she always remained committed to the Protestant cause.[230] With Henry's premature death, much of the loyalty and Protestant expectation he had generated in England was projected on to Elizabeth and her family. During the 1620s the Palatine and Protestant causes became virtually inseparable in the English mind.[231] This, combined with Elizabeth's attractive personality and her arguably tragic circumstances, created a powerful emotional following for the family in England. The image of Elizabeth and Frederick contrasted sharply with the courts of Charles and Henrietta Maria – havens for Catholicism – as well as with the rise of Arminianism.[232] The Palatines had important connections among the English puritan gentry and the war lobby in Parliament. They associated these groups with the international 'front' which their own Protestant servants were seeking to create.[233]

By 1628 there were definite hopes among puritan elements that Elizabeth's line would succeed to the English throne. Their popularity could only increase as disillusionment with Charles set in. It is possible to see in the strength of the Palatine interest something of a barometer of Charles's public standing. From the 1620s onwards it was possible that Parliament, in its discontent, might appeal to the Palatines' influence in England and seek to promote it, even developing a vested interest in the succession of one of their line.[234] The idea of deposing Charles in favour of his nephew, Charles Lewis, was raised by some of Pym's following in 1641.[235] Charles's efforts to re-establish the Palatines in their own hereditary dominions surely derived in part from fear of this reversionary claim to his throne.[236] He was afraid of his

---

[230] Elizabeth had been considered as a bride for Gustavus Adolphus; Hibbard, *Popish plot*, p. 253. She seems to have remained consistently Protestant in sentiment throughout her life. *DNB*, s.v. Elizabeth, queen of Bohemia; Mathew, *Age of Charles I*, pp. 55, 71; see also SP84/139/fos. 27r–28r.

[231] Adams, 'Foreign policy and the Parliaments of 1621 and 1624', p. 147; Hibbard, *Popish plot*, pp. 25–6. This perception was essentially accurate by the end of the decade; Parker, *Thirty Years War*, p. 81.

[232] AGS, E2043, exp. 54; *CSPV 1629–32*, p. 295; Green, *Diary of John Rous*, pp. 19, 38; NUL, Ne.C., 15,405, p. 66; Collinson, 'England and international Calvinism', pp. 207–8; Russell, 'Arguments for religious unity', p. 217; see also Cliffe, *Puritan gentry*, p. 205.

[233] Hibbard, *Popish plot*, pp. 32, 80, 255, 289; Parker, *Spain and the Netherlands*, pp. 76, 266; Parker, *Thirty Years War*, pp. 63–4; NUL, Ne.C., 15,404, pp. 243–4, and 15,405, pp. 60–1; Birch, i, p. 440; Adams, 'Spain or the Netherlands?', p. 91; SP81/35/fo. 157r–v; see also p. 215, n. 201, above.

[234] In 1628 it was rumoured in England that Christian of Denmark and Elizabeth of Bohemia had caused Charles to agree to the Petition of Right. Green, *Diary of John Rous*, p. 18; Breslow, *Mirror of England*, pp. 37–40; see also *CSPV 1629–32*, pp. 67, 70, 75, 295; Laud, *Works*, i, pp. 185ff.; SP77/19/fo. 355r–v; Russell, 'The nature of a Parliament', p. 410.

[235] Wedgwood, 'The Elector Palatine and the civil war', p. 6; Hibbard, *Popish plot*, pp. 151, 167, 177, 207–8.

[236] *CSPV 1629–32*, p. 431. The cost of subsidizing the Palatines would also have been an incentive; see p. 221, n. 229, above.

sister's coming to England and wished to prevent it, as he told Sir Henry Vane, because of the risk of discord: her influence could stir up opposition against him.[237] Charles's insecurity vis-à-vis the Palatines may have been compounded by the fact that Elizabeth had been particularly close to Henry, in whose shadow Charles had lived all his life. Charles's fear of Elizabeth's influence was shared by Weston and Laud who sought to stand well with her.[238] In May 1629 Henrietta Maria miscarried of a son, but the following year gave birth to the prince of Wales. The event created considerable unhappiness in strongly Protestant circles in England. Laud was overjoyed.[239] That Charles failed to make the occasion a matter of public rejoicing suggests his estrangement from, even fear of, his own people.[240] At the court of Spain, the news of the prince's birth was cause for celebration. A Palatine succession in England would mean re-escalation of the Anglo-Spanish war, a war which was damaging to Spain at sea. Olivares wanted an alliance with England against the Dutch and had an increasing stake in the survival of the Caroline regime.[241] Charles's willingness to make peace with Spain on the basis of undertakings, rather than real concessions, in favour of the Palatines was probably influenced by the recent assurance afforded by the birth of an heir. The Treaty of Madrid was a bitter blow to the Palatines and further alienated Charles's critics in England.[242] The king's anxiety about his line was eased but not ended by the prince's birth. The Palatines continued to be a political presence and a potential dynastic threat.

Elizabeth's attitude to the notion of her family's succession in England is difficult to discern. Charles and his sister had a real affection for one another. Elizabeth was deeply grieved by her brother's eventual death. During the

---

[237] SP81/36/fo. 142r, Vane's notes of conference with Charles, *c*. May/June 1630(?); see also *CSPV 1629–32*, p. 349. James had refused to allow Elizabeth to reside in England in 1621. Charles sought to keep Charles Lewis out of England in 1639. Adams, 'Spain or the Netherlands?', p. 91; Hibbard, *Popish plot*, pp. 132–3. Charles invited Elizabeth to England after Frederick died in 1632, but this was probably a gesture he could not avoid and by then he was assured of the succession. He may also have suspected that Elizabeth would refuse, as indeed she did. She had little to gain, and could lose what independence she had, by leaving the Hague. Mathew, *Age of Charles I*, p. 82; Laud, *Works*, iii, p. 216 and n. Charles's fear of the Palatines was probably compounded by the fact that some of their supporters were (just conceivably) potential republicans. Hibbard, *Popish plot*, p. 208; Reeve, 'Viscount Dorchester', p. 142n.

[238] Laud, *Works*, iii, p. 211, vii, pp. 40–1; AMRE, CPA, 43, fo. 338r; Hibbard, *Popish plot*, p. 87; Alexander, *Charles I's Lord Treasurer*, p. 247.

[239] *CSPV 1629–32*, pp. 331, 349–50; Birch, i, pp. 355–6; Laud, *Works*, iii, p. 103; Larkin, *Stuart royal proclamations*, ii, pp. 273–4; Green, *Diary of John Rous*, pp. 53–4; Newdigate (ed.), *Poems of Ben Jonson*, p. 174.

[240] SP94/34/fo. 239r; *CSPV 1629–32*, p. 349.

[241] AGS, E2043, exp. 54; *CSPV 1629–32*, pp. 364, 404; Reade, *Sidelights on the Thirty Years War*, iii, p. 430; Larkin, *Stuart royal proclamations*, ii, p. 273. See also chapter 7, below.

[242] SP84/141/fo. 307v; SP81/35/fos. 172r, 174–5; Gardiner, *Constitutional documents*, pp. 208–9.

1620s, however, jealousies were said to have arisen between them over the English succession.[243] Elizabeth's first priority was the restoration of her husband to his patrimony in Germany. After Frederick's death, she was interested in a marriage between her son, Charles Lewis, and Charles's daughter Mary,[244] apparently as a means of obtaining English support for the family in Germany. Yet she seems to have been interested as well in the general prospects for her children in England. She would not have countenanced her brother's deposition and disavowed her son when he dallied with Parliament in the 1640s.[245] Whatever her aims, it was not in her interests to discourage her own and her family's popularity in England. She could therefore never release her brother from the residual pressure this placed upon him. What can be termed the 'Palatine factor' was critical in English politics during this era. Charles's relationship to his sister was another dimension of his alienation from large sections of the English people.

As the personal rule took shape, a regime reliant upon pro-Spanish neutrality, trade and war profiteering came to protect an English Church whose Laudian innovations were essentially a new departure from Jacobean orthodoxy. This protection was proffered against the danger of a fourth Caroline Parliament. The fusion of interests involved – religious and cultural, financial[246] and (largely as a consequence) constitutional – was innovatory in each part, and as a whole. This coalescence was intolerable to a more traditional alignment of forces whose thinking (among its leadership) had become dangerously stimulated, thus taking the 'new counsels' issue to new extremes. Despite the penchant for the *pax Hispanica* within Charles's political court, his government can legitimately be characterized as nationalistic. Europe was at war, and those who wanted war rather than isolation desired the more intense involvement with the European scene. The conflict between these nationalist and internationalist hopes was one about the basic orientation of the state. The conspiracy theories which in England traditionally served to explain political disagreement, and which were also rife in Europe during this period, had disturbing realities behind them.[247]

The dislocation of English politics did not of necessity involve a timetable for collapse. The inclination of Warwick and his colleagues to go to the New World in 1638 might signal to the speculative historian an alternative future

---

[243] *CSPV 1623–5*, p. 163; *CSPV 1629–32*, p. 431; Hibbard, *Popish plot*, p. 132; *DNB*, s.v. Elizabeth, queen of Bohemia. See also Reeve, 'Viscount Dorchester', p. 24.

[244] Mary was eventually married to William, prince of Orange, the two reigning jointly in England 1689–94.

[245] Hibbard, *Popish plot*, pp. 32, 176–7, 253n; *CSPV 1629–32*, pp. 75, 349, 431; *DNB*, s.v. Elizabeth, queen of Bohemia.

[246] On the novelty of the Caroline balance of forces in the City and the alliance between government, concessionaires and customs farmers see Ashton, *City and the court*, p. 149.

[247] Reeve, 'Sir Robert Heath's advice'; Parker, *Thirty Years War*, pp. 47–8, 220.

and a Caroline survival. Yet the advent of the Scottish prayer book crisis in 1637–8, which led eventually to the summoning of the Long Parliament, was more than simple caprice. There was an inherent vulnerability about Charles's government which derived from the non-parliamentary context – and the absence of national crisis – required for its survival, at least for a generation. Fundamental to that context, which created new boundaries for political and ideological activity, was the fact of a breakdown in the external management of the state in relation to domestic politics. That breakdown, apparent in 1629, would be confirmed in 1631–2. Predicated upon the divisiveness of Westonian and Laudian policy, it had been doubly likely when European war made views of English and international affairs increasingly inseparable. It became, moreover, a self-perpetuating affliction. Laud spoke in 1631 of the peace and plenty which Charles had already provided. Clarendon would look back on an island kingdom, a haven of peace in a sea of war.[248] Charles's enemies, however, were not impressed by the outbreak of peace in England.

All was not well. The Venetian ambassador Soranzo wrote at the beginning of 1630 of 'the serious inconveniences which result from the king being out of sympathy with his people'. The kingdom, he concluded, was enfeebled.[249] The following year Sir Edward Stanhope wished that Wentworth might give leadership to 'this discontented state'.[250] The Suffolk puritan John Carter was one of a number who predicted 'dreadful divisions' in England.[251] Winthrop and D'Ewes contemplated the merits of emigration as a means of escaping what might be in store for the country.[252] In March 1631 Laud preached at Paul's Cross on the sixth anniversary of the king's coronation. His praise of Charles and his rule was betrayed by the anxious and defensive tone which permeated the sermon. The king and his son, the perpetuation of his line, were a blessing upon the kingdom which had not the wit or the piety to appreciate it. Some of Charles's subjects had sunk so low as to oppose his rule:

and the age is so bad, that they will not believe he is so good beyond them. And some, for they are but some, are so waspishly set to sting, that nothing can please their ears, unless it sharpen their edge against authority. But take heed: for if this fault be not amended, justice may seize upon them that are guilty, God knows how soon: and the king's 'judgement' that God hath given him, may pull out their stings, that can employ their tongues in nothing but to wound him and his government.

He felt the need to pray for the king: 'I hope I shall offend none by praying for the king.'[253]

---

[248] Clarendon, *Rebellion*, vol. i, pp. 84, 93–4; Laud, *Works*, i, pp. 210–11.
[249] *CSPV 1629–32*, p. 289.   [250] Zagorin, 'Sir Edward Stanhope's advice', p. 319.
[251] Collinson, *Religion of Protestants*, p. 283.
[252] Ibid.; Cliffe, *Puritan gentry*, p. 203.   [253] Laud, *Works*, i, pp. 185ff.

7

Foreign policy

The foreign policy and domestic government of any sovereign state can never be divorced and understood in isolation. Together they constitute the broader subject of national policy. This is particularly true, as we have seen, of Caroline England. Charles's policies came to form an overall pattern which politically and ideologically, had its internal logic. This chapter examines the way in which English policy interacted with the international scene and, to this end, treats English foreign policy as a subject in itself. This was a momentous period of the Thirty Years War. The recovery of Protestant fortunes, after terrible reverses at the hands of the Habsburgs, meant that by 1632 the balance of forces could be said to be even. English policy exemplified the tension between interventionist and isolationist policies in Europe at this time.[1] England's withdrawal from the war was critical in the reorientation of Protestant alliances and the erection of Richelieu's new anti-Habsburg coalition.

How was English foreign policy formulated during this era? One, and frequently both, Secretaries of State conducted diplomatic correspondence under the oversight of the king and the Council's committee for foreign affairs,[2] which consistently reviewed despatches. Yet with the political eclipse of the Council, the roles of individual ministers were more important than conciliar deliberation. Conflict over policy led to secret and competing lines of diplomatic communication. Thus the distinction between official and unofficial channels is often difficult to draw. As Secretary, Dorchester was responsible for the royal foreign correspondence. In addition, he operated a system of diplomatic and military patronage among Charles's subjects serving in the Protestant countries of northern Europe. It complemented, and competed with, the influence of Weston in relation to the pro-Habsburg states. This divided foreign service reflected differences over policy as well as personal influence. The Dorchester and Weston connections were essentially pro- and anti-war interests. Appointees tended to share the views of their

---

[1] Parker, *Thirty Years War*, pp. 48, 132.   [2] *APC 1628–9*, p. 273.

patrons, and acted as sources of information about international affairs. Foreign service politics were an extension of those at court and came to reflect the declining influence of the war lobby. Dorchester and Elizabeth of Bohemia suffered a significant political defeat in failing to have Roe appointed ambassador to the Hague. He was similarly passed over, in favour of Vane, for the crucial mission to Germany in 1631.[3]

Charles spent a considerable amount of the time he allowed to government in pondering foreign policy. His role in major decisions is usually clear. Despite his belief that diplomacy was a worthy activity for kings, he showed no more aptitude for politics abroad than at home. His inability to inspire trust was an obvious disadvantage. He showed his lack of perception in seeking independence (and irresponsibility) in the international arena, failing to serve his ends by refusing to link them to wider causes such as that of European Protestantism. He doubled up on policies, out of insecurity and indecision, spinning a web of initiatives often too complicated to succeed. Recognizing kingship but misunderstanding power, he saw Louis XIII and Philip IV as brother sovereigns, not realizing the importance of ministers such as Richelieu and Olivares.[4] Perhaps above all, in an age when 'reputation' was highly valued,[5] Charles, so concerned with his honour, suffered the distinct loss of standing which comes with spectacular failure.

What were the stages by which the foreign policy of the personal rule emerged? Europe was at war and England's withdrawal from that war, more than any other policy, defined her political orientation during these years. The withdrawal came about in three successive and interrelated stages. The first began in the autumn of 1628 when Charles became interested in the possibility of a negotiated settlement with Spain. This, with the lack of any guarantee that it would be accomplished, caused him to hedge his bets for another whole year. The second stage emerged towards the end of 1629 when Charles increasingly embraced the idea of peace with Spain. He was encouraged in this by the continuing recalcitrance of the imprisoned members of Parliament, Cottington's mission to Madrid[6] and the progressive revival of trade which relieved his immediate financial need. The third stage, dis-

---

[3] Certain officers in Sir Charles Morgan's force and diplomats such as Averie (agent to Denmark), Sanderson (agent to Sweden) and Anstruther (recipient of various appointments in Germany) were protégés of Dorchester. Besides the use of more prominent figures such as Porter, Cottington and Rubens, Weston employed men such as Taylor in Germany, Gerbier in Brussels and Hopton in Madrid. Reeve, 'Viscount Dorchester', pp. 272–3, 331; AGS, E2043, exp. 172. For a similar situation after Dorchester's death in 1632, see Young, *Servility and service*, ch. 14.

[4] SP94/34/fos. 250r, 251v; Mathew, *Age of Charles I*, pp. 46, 52, 67; Parker, *Thirty Years War*, pp. 225–6; Elliott, *Count-duke of Olivares*, pp. 361–2.

[5] Elliott, 'A question of reputation', pp. 477–8; Elliott, *Count-duke of Olivares*, p. 82.

[6] See p. 247, n. 110, below.

tinguishable after the making of peace with Spain, was one of equivocation and of a partial return to war during 1631. Charles sanctioned Hamilton's expedition to aid Gustavus, and discussed with the Swedes a possible military alliance to restore the Palatinate. This final stage was terminated when the talks proved abortive and led, in 1632, to the pro-Spanish neutrality of the personal rule. Charles never again went to war in Europe. An interest in peace, and, by 1630, a formal commitment to it, was evident at each stage of this transitional period. Charles's objection to Parliament and disillusionment with war fed off one another and encouraged his preference for Hispanophile, Westonian and Laudian policies. The personal rule, with its foreign policy, was the result of as many negative as positive responses on his part.

To what extent was Caroline foreign policy innovatory in English terms? Charles's approach to European affairs had its Jacobean antecedents. James had been enamoured of Spain and had hoped for a Spanish match. He had even contemplated an Anglo-Spanish partition of the United Provinced.[7] Yet he had always sought to mediate and pacify in the European struggle. He had, moreover, remained committed to the Protestant world as his sponsorship of the Synod of Dort attested. Charles abandoned that commitment.[8] He became a covert participant in the Spanish war effort against the Dutch, and his diplomacy was soon pro-Habsburg in principle. He was also prepared to negotiate with the papacy.[9] Finally, he officially sanctioned a religious movement in England which rejected international Calvinism and favoured appeasement of the *pax Hispanica*. This was a novel policy, but it was by no means exclusively or even predominantly ideological. It combined a genuine Hispanophile sentiment with Charles's pragmatism and English economic interest. To a large extent the conflict over English foreign policy was between confessional politics and reason of state. It was that conflict which did so much to destabilize and paralyse the political life of Europe during this era.[10] Yet for all its material and purely dynastic aims, Charles's foreign policy remained offensive to the parliamentary classes in religious terms. Its Arminian and Catholic dimension was undeniable.

Charles's foreign policy, as it became established, was the expression of a constitutional breakdown which rendered effective war or diplomacy impossible. For England to enlist, browbeat or vanquish other states so as to achieve the restoration of the Palatinate needed the active or available co-operation of the political nation in Parliament. Without this, Charles

[7] Adams, 'Spain or the Netherlands?', pp. 88–9; Lockyer, *Buckingham*, p. 173.
[8] Adams, 'Spain or the Netherlands?', p. 90.
[9] Ibid., pp. 100–1; Hibbard, *Popish plot*.
[10] Parker, *Thirty Years War*, pp. 219–21, 223, 226.

could only be partially successful. He could guard his coasts and merchant shipping, escort the Flanders convoys and obtain a certain degree of Spanish goodwill. But while entering into dialogue about a possible German settlement, in a climate of war he could not extract real concessions without the capacity to fight. Since a Habsburg military alliance was unacceptable to the English Parliament, once Charles had rejected Protestant war or negotiation from strength, he could cut no ice. Yet a critical question remains. How far is it true to say that Caroline England, when not bedevilled by disunity, was capable of fighting effectively?

By the standards of the great continental monarchies at this time, England was not a particularly wealthy nation.[11] It does not follow simply from this, however, that she could make no impression upon the course of a European war. The Dutch republic, demographically and geographically smaller, was rapidly becoming a first-rate power through commerce and command of the seas. Dutch wealth became such that the land forces of the republic could be kept under arms throughout the year, an achievement almost unique in early modern Europe.[12] The revolutionary increase in the scale of war (and the fact that it was becoming a global affair), together with the international inflation known as the price revolution, made all states subject to a sharply rising cost of warfare, on land and sea, in the early seventeenth century. England, despite the feat of supporting numerous armies during the 1640s,[13] could not in the normal course of events sustain a long war on land. The principal English element, like that of the more powerful Dutch, was the sea.[14]

English entry into the European war in 1625 immediately involved a number of difficulties. James had run up a significant royal debt which war would probably compound.[15] As against the cost of war, the value of parliamentary subsidies was being eroded by under-assessment and inflation.[16] War with Spain disrupted England's Iberian and Mediterranean trade and affected customs revenues. Finally, there was always the risk and uncertainty

---

[11] Clay, *Economic expansion and social change*, ii, p. 251.

[12] Howard, *War in European history*, p. 55; L. J. Reeve, 'The politics of war finance in early Stuart England: a comparative European view' (unpublished article).

[13] The success of the Long Parliament in funding the English and Scottish armies (the indemnifications for which totalled £1,100,000) during the emergency of 1640–1 is a case in point; Fletcher, *Outbreak of the English civil war*, pp. 23, 29, 40, 87. See also Parker, *Spain and the Netherlands*, p. 100; G. Parker, *The military revolution. Military innovation and the rise of the West, 1500–1800* (Cambridge, 1988), p. 24 and passim.

[14] Parker, *Spain and the Netherlands*, pp. 86–7; Parker, *Europe in crisis*, pp. 66ff.; AMRE, CPA, 43, fo. 188v.

[15] This debt was of the order of at least one year's income. Russell, 'Parliament and the king's finances', p. 102; Hirst, *Authority and conflict*, pp. 109, 124.

[16] Moreover, the greater the number of subsidies granted the less they yielded. Russell, *Parliaments*, pp. 49–53, 398, 418; *CSPD 1628–9*, p. 482; Thomas, 'Financial and administrative developments', pp. 117, 143.

of war, with no guarantee of great plunder and every possibility of loss. An English war effort was, however, financially and strategically quite feasible. This was recognized by Parliament in 1624 when a grant of three subsidies and three fifteenths was made subject to the money's being spent for four specific purposes: the defence of Ireland, the guarding of the English coasts, the fitting out of the fleet and the provision of assistance to the Dutch and other friends and allies of England. The grant was also conditional, the subsidy act implied, upon James's entering into open war against Spain.[17] The act thus sought to institutionalize the strategy of war by diversion at the expense of James's desire for an expensive land campaign in the Palatinate. The latter strategy had little to commend it. It was born of James's wish to avoid a wholesale confessional war. Anglo-Dutch action against Spain in the Netherlands and at sea was ideologically acceptable to Parliament. It was also well suited to a conflict in which total victory was elusive and in which economic pressure and logistics were frequently decisive. Effective war at sea deprived Spain of resources while increasing those of the attacker. England had no great traffic to protect and the great volume of Spanish war trade and treasure was distinctly vulnerable.[18] This strategy was also economical. Beyond the use of the royal fleet the war could be privatized, tapping gentry wealth at no cost to the crown. The English government, moreover, took a share of prizes won by ships carrying its letters of marque.[19]

The cost of war by diversion was not prohibitive for England. It was generally estimated that to master Spain at sea would cost £200,000 per annum during wartime. Part or all of such a sum could be raised by private sub-

[17] Adams, 'Foreign policy and the Parliaments of 1621 and 1624', pp. 165ff.
[18] This vulnerability was perceived not only by the English Parliament and the Dutch, but by Richelieu, who urged a union of Anglo-Dutch sea power, and by the Spaniards themselves. Reade, *Sidelights on the Thirty Years War*, iii, pp. 468–9; Magurn, *Rubens letters*, pp. 335, 342–5; *CSPV 1628–9*, pp. 516, 518–19, 557, 590; *CSPV 1629–32*, p. 235; Thompson, 'Origins of the politics of the parliamentary middle-group', pp. 80–1; Adams, 'Spain or the Netherlands?', p. 83; Russell, *Parliaments*, pp. 163, 188, 293–4, 299–300. Sir Michael Howard has pointed to the difficulty in mounting a successful attack on the Spanish treasure fleets. The loss of the plate fleet in 1628 was the first occasion on which Spanish American silver had fallen into enemy hands. Yet the financial and military catastrophe this involved for Spain suggests that such a blow, if only delivered once, was worth the seeking. This was in addition to the constant effect of attacks on Spanish trade. Howard, *War in European history*, pp. 43–5; Elliott, *Imperial Spain*, p. 335; Elliott, *Count-duke of Olivares*, pp. 362–5. See also Parker, *Thirty Years War*, pp. 222–3; Andrews, *Trade, plunder and settlement*, p. 363; Israel, *Dutch republic*; J. S. Kepler, 'The value of ships gained and lost by the English shipping industry during the wars with Spain and France, 1624–1630', *Mariner's Mirror*, lix (1973), p. 220n; J. P. Cooper, 'Sea power', in *NCMH*, iv, pp. 234 and n, 235 and n.
[19] Howard, *War in European history*, pp. 49–50; Kepler, 'Value of ships', p. 218; *CSPV 1629–32*, pp. 69, 123, 142, 178, 235; Thomas, 'Financial and administrative developments', p. 117.

scription to a West India company, regulated by statute, to make war in the name of the crown.[20] To assist the Dutch on land to the extent that England did after 1624 would raise the cost to about £300,000, or something slightly in excess of four parliamentary subsidies per annum.[21] This was certainly not beyond the capacity of the nation. The grant for war in 1624, intended as an initial supply only, was worth £300,000. In 1625 the low vote of two subsidies was directly related to suspicion of Buckingham's intentions, as well as to the belief that the crown had reneged upon an agreement to declare war against Spain.[22] Four subsidies were lost in 1626 when Charles dissolved Parliament to save Buckingham.[23] Five subsidies were made available after the passing of the Petition of Right in 1628. An unknown supply was lost with the abrupt termination of the 1629 session.[24] Despite reservations in some quarters about the desirability of annual subsidies,[25] this record is ample evidence of a parliamentary preparedness to support a popular war which was reasonably well managed. As Coryton, supported by the Commons, made clear in 1629, there was no question about the willingness to supply.[26] The West Indian war strategy – with the idea of plundering an eldorado that

---

[20] The navy could actually be fitted out for significantly less than this sum. Dietz, *English public finance 1558–1641*, ii, p. 216; Hirst, *Authority and conflict*, p. 130; Russell, 'Parliament and the king's finances', p. 103; Russell, *Parliaments*, pp. 293–4, 299–300; Rushworth, *Historical collections*, i, p. 473.

[21] This estimate assumes that the six British regiments already in Dutch service (13,000 men) would continue to be paid by the republic. In 1624 four further regiments were added by the English government. A year later Sir John Coke reported to Parliament that £99,000 (which presumably included some establishment expenses) had been spent on the regiments in the Low Countries. By comparison, the cost of hiring Mansfeld to mount an expedition to the Palatinate – an initiative of which Parliament did not approve – was agreed on as £20,000 per month (or £240,000 per annum). Mansfeld's force, however, was slightly larger than the additional regiments in Dutch service and included cavalry, and as a mercenary he needed to make a profit. The cost of guarding the English coasts was negligible compared with that of supporting troops and fitting out ships. There was no reason why Ireland could not essentially meet the cost of its own defence as was largely done during the 1620s. Adams, 'Spain or the Netherlands?', p. 85; Adams, 'Foreign policy and the Parliaments of 1621 and 1624', p. 170; Lockyer, *Buckingham*, pp. 192, 210, 247; Dietz, *English public finance 1558–1641*, ii, pp. 216–22; T. W. Moody, F. X. Martin and F. J. Byrne (eds.), *A new history of Ireland* (Oxford, 1976), iii, pp. 233–5; Reeve, 'Viscount Dorchester', pp. 239–40; Reeve, 'The politics of war finance'.

[22] Almost certainly, James's demand for a higher sum in 1624 was at least partly aimed at avoiding war altogether. Adams, 'Spain or the Netherlands?', pp. 97, 99; Adams, 'Foreign policy and the Parliaments of 1621 and 1624', pp. 160, 167–9; Russell, *Parliaments*, p. 226; Lockyer, *Buckingham*, p. 245; G. L. Harriss, 'Medieval doctrines in the debates on supply, 1610–1629', in Sharpe (ed.), *Faction and Parliament*, pp. 94–5; Gardiner, *History*, v, pp. 196–7, and vi, p. 6.

[23] Russell, 'Parliament and the king's finances', p. 103; Russell, *Parliaments*, p. 304.

[24] CD1629, p. 261.

[25] Russell, *Parliaments*, pp. 226–7, 426.

[26] CD1629, p. 261. See also ibid., p. 178; *CSPV 1628–9*, p. 537; *CSPV 1629–32*, pp. 183–4; *CSPV 1636–9*, pp. 124–5; AGS, E2043, exp. 209.

supported Antichrist – was easily made popular in the country.[27] The level of supply in the 1620s was impressive given Charles's military failures, and success was more likely to improve rather than reduce that response. The idea, increasingly prevalent, that Parliaments should be annual could only beg the question of a consistent, if reorganized, supply in time of war.[28] Credit was almost always available to the crown, given any degree of rational financial management.[29] All warfare during the early modern period involved anticipatory saving or the contraction of debt. War funding on credit and post-war debts were the norm. Virtually all the European states engaged in the Thirty Years War were technically spending beyond their means.[30]

The Anglo-Dutch sea war against Spain in the 1620s was not without its military and political effect. The Dutch West India Company's capture of the New Spain silver fleet in 1628 was a near-crippling blow to the war effort of Spain. The receipts of the army of Flanders fell dramatically and the republic could command (and eventually reject) excellent terms for a truce.[31] The running war at sea was very damaging to Spain and the constant English attacks came to cause considerable alarm. English privateers, at no cost to the crown, took Iberian prizes worth at least £200,000.[32] Besides the fact of plunder, the loss of English trade was a most serious handicap to Spain. With the Dutch systematically excluded from commerce with the peninsula after 1624, trade with England and the Hanseatic League was the lifeline for vital commodities. The lack of materials for shipbuilding in particular made Spain

---

[27] Jones, *Britain and Europe*, p. 46; Craven, 'The earl of Warwick, a speculator in piracy', p. 465.

[28] Sommerville, *Politics and ideology*, p. 104; Russell, *Parliaments*, pp. 226–7, 426.

[29] The decline of Charles's credit was linked to his unnecessarily exorbitant war expenditure in the 1620s. Ashton, *Crown and the money market*, pp. 135, 163; *CD1628*, iii, p. 213.

[30] Parker, *Spain and the Netherlands*, p. 100; Parker, *Thirty Years War*, pp. 112, 222–3; J. R. Hale, *War and society in Renaissance Europe 1450–1620* (London, 1985), p. 244; Reeve, 'The politics of war finance'.

[31] In 1629, in seeking a truce, Spain offered the United Provinces their sovereignty, freedom of worship, their war gains in the Netherlands and the East and West Indies, and free trade in places where they then traded – humiliating terms for the Spanish monarchy in view of its political, economic and military investment in the Dutch conflict. Parker, *Europe in crisis*, pp. 191–2; Parker, *Army of Flanders*, pp. 256, 295; Elliott, *Count-duke of Olivares*, pp. 350–4, 358, 362–5, 372, 378; Israel, *Dutch republic*, pp. 226–7, 236–8; Reeve, 'Viscount Dorchester', p. 294n.

[32] The total may have been considerably more; J. C. Appleby, 'English privateering during the Spanish and French wars, 1625–1630' (unpublished University of Hull PhD thesis, 1983), i, pp. 298–300, 341. (I am grateful to Dr Appleby for making this material available to me.) See also Andrews, *Trade, plunder and settlement*, pp. 362 and n, 363; AGS, E2562, Council of State, 8 Mar. 1630 (n.s.); Birch, i, p. 443; *CSPV 1629–32*, pp. 69, 123, 133, 142, 178, 235, 267; Laud, *Works*, iv, p. 635; Thomas, 'Financial and administrative developments', p. 117; Young, *Servility and service*, pp. 154–6; Kepler, 'Value of ships'; Magurn, *Rubens letters*, pp. 343–4; Reade, *Sidelights on the Thirty Years War*, iii, p. 493.

doubly anxious for peace with Charles by 1630.[33] In the context of Spanish vulnerability in the late 1620s, England enjoyed a definite political leverage while she remained in a state of war. Charles, as will be seen, failed to exploit this advantage and to negotiate from strength in conjunction with his allies the Dutch. While the English ability to fight did not imply the need for continual war, it could be a significant force in international politics. That ability, moreover, cannot be denied by appeal to the consensual and therefore supposedly inadequate nature of parliamentary war finance.[34] Even amid the strategic and financial mismanagement of the Buckingham era, it was obvious that an Anglo-Dutch (not to mention an Anglo-Swedish) alliance had teeth.

England's capacity to make war was very largely dissipated during the 1620s. An incompetent and over-sanguine gambler, Buckingham had failed miserably, spending a royal fortune beyond the basic need to fulfil the purposes outlined in the subsidy act of 1624. The hiring of Mansfeld, which arguably violated the act, had been James's decision.[35] Yet under the Treaty of the Hague (1625), which insofar as it concerned England was Buckingham's work, Charles had been bound to provide Denmark with a subsidy of £30,000 per month to wage war in Germany.[36] The duke had also entered into the French war – a grave strategic error – thus diverting valuable resources and spending the equivalent of three parliamentary subsidies on the Rhé expedition alone. His mismanagement of policy lost the government at least four subsidies, as we have seen, in 1625 and 1626. The remonstrance of 1628 accused him correctly of wasting over a million pounds of the kingdom's treasure.[37] While it is difficult to calculate the extent of English war expenditure between 1624 and 1630, the sum total was somewhere in the vicinity of one-quarter of the entire value of Spanish treasure imports from

[33] *CSPV 1629–32*, pp. 279–80, 333; Israel, *Dutch republic*, pp. 204–9; Israel, 'Politics of international trade rivalry'; Elliott, *Count-duke of Olivares*, pp. 357, 394, 403.

[34] The error of such an argument is a failure to distinguish between the cost of a land campaign in Germany and other strategic options such as war by diversion. Adams, 'Foreign policy and the Parliaments of 1621 and 1624', p. 150 and n; Russell, *Parliaments*, pp. 186, 189; Thomas, 'Financial and administrative developments', p. 116; Dietz, *English public finance 1558–1641*, ii, p. 246. See also Hale, *War and society*, pp. 251–2.

[35] Adams, 'Spain or the Netherlands?', p. 97.

[36] Lockyer, *Buckingham*, pp. 278–9; Reeve, 'Viscount Dorchester', p. 19; Parker, *Thirty Years War*, p. 77.

[37] *CD1628*, iv, pp. 148, 171, 212, 315; *CSPD 1627–8*, p. 86; NUL, Ne.C., 15,404, pp. 208–9; Rushworth, *Historical collections*, i, pp. 474–5; *DNB*, s.v. Coke, Sir Edward; Russell, 'Parliament and the king's finances', p. 105; Sommerville, *Politics and ideology*, pp. 236–7; Lockyer, *Buckingham*, p. 469; T. Cogswell, 'Foreign policy and Parliament: the case of La Rochelle, 1625–6', *EHR*, xcix (1984), pp. 247–8.

the New World during this period.[38] Charles's view that Parliament had refused to finance a war it had advocated cannot be justified.[39] The war which Buckingham was seeking to fight was not that of which Parliament had approved and agreed to support. The grant of five subsidies in 1628, moreover, made clear that Parliament did not wish Charles to be left in the lurch. Charles would never admit, and probably never perceived, that war by diversion had not been properly pursued.[40] Finally, his religious policy led to a disastrous breach with Parliament in 1629. The cost of war was a necessary but not sufficient cause of his failure. Ideological and political factors, in the forms of Charles, the duke and Laudianism, were greater obstacles to the war effort than its fiscal requirements. The military and strategic options available to the crown in the 1620s were thus complicated and became the subject of political conflict. The fact that these options involved attitudes to the European war at a time when it was escalating in turn facilitated the importation of international influences which intensified English politics.

Prior to the 1629 parliamentary session, Charles was in two minds about war. The collapse of his third Parliament could only act as an incentive to peace. Yet his resolve to fulfil his commitments – to his uncle and his sister – was slow to disappear. It was not until early 1630 that he committed himself to peace. During the interim period of a year the case in King's Bench, with all its attendant difficulties, moved to a hard-fought conclusion. Eliot's political revolt clearly encouraged Charles's interest in the Treaty of Madrid.[41] Those, such as Dorchester, who wished to continue the war were seeking to repair the constitutional breakdown. Given the power of the religious issue, this presented an enormously difficult task.

Dorchester saw the peace with France as a means to better deploying English power in the general war. The pressing need in the spring of 1629 was to prevent the capitulation of Denmark. Christian was arguably the greatest loser in the failure of English parliamentary supply. Weston's financial control and desire for economy made action more difficult.[42] Dorchester was the English minister most closely associated with the Danish ambassadors.

---

[38] Calculated on the basis of four ducats to one pound sterling, the rate of exchange then current. Adams, 'Foreign policy and the Parliaments of 1621 and 1624', p. 169; Gardiner, *History*, v, p. 347; Dietz, *English public finance 1558–1641*, ii, p. 246 and ch. x; Russell, *Parliaments*, pp. 72–3; Elliott, *Imperial Spain*, p. 184; Reeve, 'Viscount Dorchester', p. 221n.

[39] SP16/141/80; Cust, 'Charles I, the Privy Council, and the forced loan', p. 233; *CD1629*, p. 48; *CJ*, i, p. 927.

[40] Gardiner, *History*, vii, pp. 172–3.

[41] PRO 31/3/66/fo. 140v; Reeve, 'Arguments in King's Bench', p. 285; see also chapter 5, above.

[42] Weston had partly disbanded the force returning from La Rochelle; Gardiner, *History*, vi, p. 372.

Their king acknowledged his favour and urged him to continue it. During 1629 he was the leading English advocate of aid to Denmark and was important in keeping alive Charles's interest in the war.[43] The Danish representatives had encouraged an end to the Anglo-French war to facilitate English aid to their country and diversionary action by France in Italy against the Habsburgs. Playing for time in the talks at Lübeck, Christian would be forced into a losing peace in the absence of English assistance. Charles had held out hopes to him but the fruitless ending of the Parliament was a cruel blow.[44] Olivares still harboured his design of a Habsburg naval presence in the Baltic which would sever the Dutch economic lifeline.[45] While Christian wished to continue the war, he feared the conquest of his kingdom and the loss to Protestantism of the Baltic and Scandinavia.[46] Dorchester, sharing the sense of common danger, wrote of Charles's resolve to help his uncle once he had settled his government in England. Ships were sent to the Elbe and arrangements for reinforcements of men progressed.[47] The idea of recalling Parliament had not, apparently, been entirely abandoned and the interest in supporting the war was real. Charles had no guarantees from Spain at this point and keenly felt his commitment to his own, his family's and perhaps still his dead favourite's honour in the European conflict.

At the end of May 1629 Christian made peace with the emperor. For the Danish king this was a holding measure forced upon him by the military situation and dissent among his ministers. He understood the English situation which had dashed his hopes of resistance, but he was bitter at the result of the war. Under the Peace of Lübeck, he was bound never again to interfere in the affairs of the Empire. Some of his troops remained mobilized, however, and he still harboured the notion of fighting again if aid came from England and France. There were religious and political problems for Danish policy. Christian would not compromise the Protestant cause by responding to French overtures to join the Catholic League; and just as the Danish treaty was a blow to English and Dutch morale, Charles's apparent interest in negotiations with Spain sapped the confidence of the Danes. The Peace of Lübeck was one part of a Habsburg effort to divide the allies of the Hague by

---

[43] SP103/2/fo. 63r; SP75/9/fos. 199r, 201r, 215r–v, 217r, 258r, SP75/10/fos. 19r–20r.
[44] SP75/9/fos. 205r–v, 207r–v, 330r–331r, SP75/10/fos. 19r–20r, 23r, 25r–29r, 53r–v, 58r–v, 64r; SP103/2/fos. 74r–75v, 76v–77v, 88r–90r, 111r–112v, 119r–120r; *CSPV 1628–9*, pp. 527–9.
[45] Elliott, *Count-duke of Olivares*, pp. 332–4, 352, 354–5, 360–1; Parker, *Thirty Years War*, p. 79.
[46] SP75/10/fos. 100r–103r.
[47] SP75/10/fos. 93r–v, 139r–140v; SP78/85/fo. 238r–v; SP84/139/fos. 149r–150v; SP104/170, p. 26; *CSPD 1628–9*, p. 556; *CSPV 1629–32*, pp. 43–4; PRO 47th Deputy Keeper's report, Appx, p. 50.

diplomacy, and was complemented by Spain's negotiations with England.[48] Weston was delighted at Christian's ending of hostilities, opposed as he was to war spending.[49] Dorchester recognized the renewed imperial persecution of German Protestantism,[50] and while awaiting the effects of the Peace of Lübeck believed it could be turned to advantage.[51]

In late June 1629 Roe left on his mission to the United Provinces and the Baltic. His main purposes were to promote the idea of a northern Protestant league and to mediate peace between Poland and Sweden. The latter would help free Gustavus Adolphus to engage in the German war and would facilitate the opening of the eastern trade.[52] Dorchester enlisted Charles's support for the mission which was based upon proposals by Roe. The two men intended it as a means of defending the Baltic and sustaining the Protestant powers, while further committing England to the war. Unlike Roe, with his residual objection to alliance with Catholic powers, Dorchester also advocated alliance with France. Even without a commitment to England, French action in Italy would assist the revival of the northern war. Charles saw Roe's mission as a less positive venture. He approved of the notion of a northern league but was reluctant to make specific financial and diplomatic commitments. His eventual refusal to support Gustavus's German campaign reflected Weston's counsel as well as Charles's political problems and personal preferences. Without the authority to make substantial and binding commitments to the Dutch, the Danes and the Swedes, Roe was sceptical about the value of his mission. He did, however, obtain an undertaking from Charles that he would not begin to treat with Spain without the consent of his friends and allies.[53]

Roe's departure from England was delayed until after the Peace of Lübeck. Roe blamed Weston, who apparently withheld the necessary funds for the mission. The Treasurer feared the northern policy and worked against it. Roe

---

[48] SP75/10/fos. 177r–178r, 191r–193v, 203r–v, 239r–244r; SP80/8/fo. 88r; SP84/139/ fos. 211r–212v; PRO 31/3/66/fo. 123r; SP103/2/fos. 121r–123v; _CSPV 1628–9_, pp. 539, 541; _CSPV 1629–32_, pp. 117, 119–20, 122; Parker, _Europe in crisis_, p. 189; Parker, _Thirty Years War_, pp. 79–80; Alcalá-Zamora, _España, Flandes_, p. 526.

[49] _CSPV 1629–32_, p. 120; SP84/139/fo. 158r–v.

[50] In the spring of 1629 Ferdinand signed the Edict of Restitution by which in the Empire, save for the Imperial Free Cities, all Church property acquired by Protestants since 1552 was intended to be recovered, and by which non-Lutheran Protestants were supposed to be deprived of all political rights. Parker, _Europe in crisis_, pp. 216–18; Parker, _Thirty Years War_, pp. 97–9.

[51] SP96/3/fos. 45r–46r; SP97/14/fos. 329r–330r.

[52] SP84/138/fos. 204–5, SP84/139/fo. 158r–v; SP88/5/fos. 42r–48r.

[53] SP75/10/fos. 164r–165r, SP75/11/fo. 49r–v; SP95/3/fo. 21r; SP84/139/fos. 27r–28r, 199r–v; SP81/35/fos. 179r, 266r–267v; SP16/174/101; SP88/5/fos. 60r–61v; _CSPV 1629–32_, pp. 111–13, 122; J. K. Federowicz, _England's Baltic trade in the seventeenth century_ (Cambridge, 1980), p. 188.

was aware of the conflicting aims of his mission and that of Vane to the Dutch republic to facilitate the Spanish negotiations.[54] Weston's financial regime, with Charles's sense of rectitude, did not ease the resolution of an Anglo-Danish dispute over England's financial commitment under the Hague agreement.[55] Yet Dorchester's lobbying and Roe's mission sustained Charles's interest in the northern theatre. Christian of Denmark had recently refused an imperial alliance. Charles stated the reality of his intentions towards his uncle, and Dorchester encouraged the alliance on the basis of affinity, religion and reason of state. The Secretary knew the danger posed by the imperial threat to the Baltic and promoted the coalition of the two kings.[56] He and Roe worked hard to resolve the financial dispute but a final settlement seems to have eluded them.[57]

Dorchester and Roe had high hopes of Swedish participation in the war. Intervention by Gustavus in Germany had been looked for since 1624, when England, the Dutch and the German Protestants had invited him to lead an allied army. He had already agreed to fight for Frederick's restoration. But Christian of Denmark, not wanting to be eclipsed, had rashly assumed the military leadership of the Protestant cause. Gustavus had returned to the Polish war. In September 1629 Richelieu's envoy Charnacé, together with Roe, ended hostilities between Poland and Sweden with the armistice of Altmark. The Swedish crown, for the duration of the six-year truce, was granted the major share of the shipping tolls at the Polish and Prussian ports. This was a valuable source of support for Swedish action in Germany. The negotiation made possible the long-awaited intervention, and Roe encouraged Gustavus to undertake it and fight for Protestantism, considering the Swedish king 'elect of God for this great work'.[58] The ambassador, for his role in facilitating the German campaign, was honoured by Sweden. Oxenstierna, the Swedish Chancellor, called Roe the '*auctor* and *impulsor*' and Gustavus, when victorious at Breitenfeld in 1631, was reported to have sent Roe a gift of copper worth £2,500. In 1629 Roe offered him English aid. The Swedish king apparently preferred an English (and Protestant) alliance despite the overtures of France. Roe saw this as the best opportunity of the war for England and the Protestant cause. Charles, however, refused to be com-

---

54 Melbourne Hall, Coke Mss, bundle 37, newsletter of 5 June 1629; *CSPV 1629–32*, p. 130; see also SP75/11/fo. 49v. On Vane's negotiations see below.

55 SP88/5/fos. 42r–48r.

56 SP75/10/fos. 249r–250r, 253r–254v, 258r–262v, 282r–283v, 290r, 313r–314r, 315r, 323r–324r, 325r–326r.

57 SP75/11/fos. 218r–220v, 284, 290r–v.

58 SP95/3/fo. 51r, Roe to Sanderson, 16 Aug. 1630. See also Parker, *Thirty Years War*, pp. 122–3; M. Roberts, *Gustavus Adolphus: a history of Sweden 1611–1632* (2 vols., London, 1953–8), ii, pp. 397–9, 417–18; Federowicz, *England's Baltic trade*, pp. 188–206.

mitted. In 1629 he allowed Gustavus to levy two British regiments. But in the spring of 1630 he refused the Swedish request for financial support. His decision paved the way for Franco-Swedish domination of German affairs for the next two decades at the expense of English and Palatine interests.[59] Charles, in the autumn of 1629, had not abandoned the war option, but his thinking had started to swing in favour of peace. Six months later he had surrendered to such a peace policy, encouraged by his own experience of war, political dissent, customs revenues and above all by the tempting approaches of Spain.[60]

Charles's negotiations with Spain, which led to the Treaty of Madrid, were for him an attempt to achieve the principal object of the Spanish war, a Palatine restoration, by peaceful means. They combined his dynastic and familial concerns with his ideological outlook. The wealthier and greater part of the lands of the banished Frederick, the Lower or Rhine Palatinate, had been in Spanish hands since the invasion of 1620. It was a valuable, but not indispensable, link between the Spanish territories in Italy and the Netherlands.[61] The overall direction of the Habsburg dealings with England increasingly came from Spain. Spanish influence in Vienna was also greatly strengthened by the Swedish victories of 1631. Olivares knew that Ferdinand would accept Spanish direction of a settlement in the Palatinate, given certain concessions by Frederick such as toleration of Catholicism.[62] It was unlikely,

---

[59] On Anglo-Swedish relations in 1624–30 and the background to Swedish intervention see SP75/11/fos. 30r–v, 49r–v, 51r–52r, 59r, 85r–86r; SP78/85/fos. 30–1; SP88/5/fos. 156v, 186–7, 190–1; SP88/6/fos. 101–2, 181r–182r; SP88/7/fo. 267r–v; SP95/3/fo. 93r; *CSPV 1629–32*, pp. 373, 379; Birch, ii, pp. 143–4; Searle, *Barrington family letters*, p. 102 and n; Parker, *Europe in crisis*, pp. 214–15; Parker, *Thirty Years War*, pp. 74, 122–3; Trevor-Roper, *Archbishop Laud*, p. 128; Gardiner, *History*, vii, pp. 102–3; Mathew, *Age of Charles I*, p. 78; E. A. Beller, 'The Thirty Years War', in *NCMH*, iv, p. 321. See also AMRE, CPA, 43, fo. 295r; Elliott, *Count-duke of Olivares*, pp. 369, 399.

[60] AMRE, CPA, 43, fos. 187v–189v and 44, fo. 67v; *CSPV 1629–32*, p. 251; Gardiner, *History*, vii, pp. 172–3. See also *CSPV 1629–32*, pp. 289; PRO 31/3/66/fos. 251ff.; AGS, E2043, exp. 209, and E2562, Council of State, 2 Apr. 1630 (n.s.); Elliott, *Count-duke of Olivares*, p. 205.

[61] The route through the Rhine Palatinate, while utilized by Spain, was not the sole available avenue to the Netherlands. Until the Protestant victories of 1631 and the French invasion of Lorraine in 1632–3 cut all the military corridors of the army of Flanders, an alternative route was available through Alsace and Lorraine, Alsace being more important to Spain than the Palatinate. The five key Spanish garrisons in the Lower Palatinate were in Baccarat, Crasena, Alsenz, Frankenthal and Appeneins. Parker, *Army of Flanders*, pp. 54–5, 73–4, 76–7; Parker, *Thirty Years War*, pp. 132, 230–1; SP80/8/fo. 120v; PRO 31/3/66/fo. 144v; Cooper, 'Fall of the Stuart monarchy', pp. 549–50.

[62] AGS, E2519, exp. 140, and E2562, voto of Olivares, Nov. 1631, Hopton to Philip IV, 1631/2; SP80/7/fos. 58r, 66v, 170r; L. J. Reeve, 'Quiroga's paper of 1631: a missing link in Anglo-Spanish diplomacy during the Thirty Years War', *EHR*, ci, 401 (Oct. 1986), p. 922; R. Bireley, *Religion and politics in the age of the Counterreformation* (Chapel Hill, 1981), pp. 169–77, 186; Adams, 'Spain or the Netherlands?', p. 100.

however, that Spain, save *in extremis*, would allow England significant concessions in Germany without comparable advantages in return. Besides relief from effective Anglo-Dutch attack, such advantages might, in theory, consist of use of the 'English road' to the Spanish Netherlands, English rejection of anti-Habsburg alliances at a critical point or military action by Charles against France or the United Provinces. Of these options, exploitation of the 'English road' was of dubious value,[63] and an anti-French or anti-Dutch alliance was well-nigh impossible in the English political context. Charles's best chance at the end of the 1620s lay in negotiation, while still in a state of hostilities, in alliance with the Dutch (who were extracting concessions comparable to those he sought).[64] Frederick and Elizabeth saw this, as did Olivares who responded with typical directness. As part of his diplomatic offensive designed to divide the enemy powers and win peace and breathing space, the count-duke set out to make peace with England the means of destroying the Anglo-Dutch alliance. He would seek to make the dissolution of that alliance the one irreducible condition for peace between England and Spain.[65]

Madrid was under enormous and increasing pressure. A pair of crushing defeats in 1628 and 1629 – the loss of the silver fleet and of Bois-le-Duc, the gateway to the Spanish Netherlands – was accompanied by impending escalation of the Mantuan war, the prospect of Swedish action in Germany and the *rapprochement* between England and France.[66] Olivares was confirmed in his worst fears that Spain was continuing to decline.[67] Despite the loss of English trade and the destructive English attacks at sea,[68] the principal threat to Spain at this point was the Dutch. Dutch victories had rendered Flanders ripe for revolution and encouraged the Spanish Council of State to seek immediate agreement for a truce. Olivares was, as ever, reluctant to

---

[63] This was not an active military contribution to the Spanish cause and was only a potential bargaining point between the Swedish victory at Breitenfeld (1631) and the Habsburg victory at Nördlingen (1634) when the Spanish land corridors to Flanders were thoroughly blocked; Parker, *Army of Flanders*, pp. 73–4. I am grateful to Simon Adams for discussion of this point. See also Parker, *Thirty Years War*, pp. 140–1.

[64] See p. 232, n. 31, above.

[65] *CSPD 1629–31*, pp. 326–7; SP84/141/fos. 307r–311r; SP103/5/fo. 400r; AGS, E2519, exp. 54; Elliott, *Count-duke of Olivares*, p. 325.

[66] Elliott, *Count-duke of Olivares*, pp. 357–8, 362–7, 369, 377–9, 387–8, 399; Wedgwood, *Thirty Years War*, p. 248; Parker, *Army of Flanders*, pp. 256–7; Parker, *Thirty Years War*, pp. 105, 108; Parker, *Europe in crisis*, pp. 190–2, 201; Kossman, 'The Low Countries', p. 378; R. A. Stradling, 'Olivares and the origins of the Franco-Spanish war, 1627–1635', *EHR*, ci, 398 (Jan. 1986); AGS, E2562, Council of State, 2 Apr. 1630 (n.s.); PRO 31/3/66 fos. 258r–v, 260, 265v–266v; Magurn, Rubens letters, pp. 235–7; *CSPV 1628–9*, p. 420; *CSPV 1629–32*, pp. 3–4, 15, 69–70, 117, 229, 270–2; Reeve, 'Viscount Dorcester', p. 280.

[67] I am grateful to John Elliott for this point. See also Elliott, *Count-duke of Olivares*, pp. 368, 389, 394–5, 406.

[68] See p. 232, n. 32 and p. 233, n. 33, above.

compromise in the Netherlands. His main aim in northern Europe was to isolate the Dutch.[69] He also nursed the hope that England, by diplomacy or war, would assist in bringing them to a satisfactory peace and even in returning them to Spanish rule. This reflected his optimism, about England and about Charles himself, which had its roots in the Jacobean marriage negotiations.[70] The count-duke's belief in the good disposition of the young English king was not unjustified. Olivares saw too that England could be a significant power. Yet, unlike Richelieu (who had had personal experience of Calvinist politics), he did not perceive the importance of English puritanism. This critical flaw in Olivares' mental picture of Caroline England was typical of a mind which embraced sometimes ambiguous but grand designs.[71]

Olivares' global vision, founded upon his belief in the unity of the House of Habsburg, included the notion that the German question could be used to enlist England against the Dutch. Spanish policy had always been open-minded about Frederick's possible restoration. The partial obstacle here was Maximilian, duke of Bavaria, who had held the Upper Palatinate and the electoral title (of which Frederick had been deprived) since 1623 and showed no willingness to part with either.[72] The duke, as head of the Catholic League, controlled the major army in the service of the emperor and was not a figure whom Spain could afford readily to offend. Maximilian and Lamormaini, Jesuit confessor to Ferdinand, were the leading advocates of a confessional war against Protestantism in Germany in alliance with France. Olivares' Habsburg and increasingly anti-French policy ran counter to this design. The fact remained, however, that Maximilian might well prove valuable to Spain if the League could be persuaded to fight the Dutch. If this were achieved, and Bavaria were to become more useful than England to Spain, the chances of Frederick's restoration, even in part, would be very significantly diminished. Maximilian, however, essentially out of a sense of self-preservation, studiously preserved his neutrality in relation to the war in the Low Countries. By 1629 Olivares had come to consider the League an unreliable

---

[69] I am grateful to John Elliott for this point. See also Elliott, *Count-duke of Olivares*, pp. 359, 366, 385, 387–9, 391; Parker, *Thirty Years War*, pp. 103–4.

[70] Elliott, *Richelieu and Olivares*, p. 128; Lockyer, *Buckingham*, ch. 5; Elliott, *Count-duke of Olivares*, pp. 210, 357.

[71] Elliott, *Count-duke of Olivares*, pp. 293–5, 332. This was despite his awareness of pro- and anti-Habsburg factions within Charles's government. Magurn, *Rubens letters*, p. 313 and passim; Alcalá-Zamora, *España, Flandes*, pp. 263–4.

[72] Spain had opposed the bestowal of the title on Maximilian. The Upper Palatinate was sold to him in 1628; Parker, *Thirty Years War*, pp. 67, 93. See also Bireley, *Religion and politics*, p. 245; Parker, *Europe in crisis*, p. 290; Elliott, *Count-duke of Olivares*, pp. 331–2, 361–2, 369, 385, 401; Elliott, 'A question of reputation?', p. 479; SP94/34/fos. 159r–160r.

ally.[73] Here lay the origins of the count-duke's desire not only to have peace with England but to enlist Charles in the Habsburg cause.

The English response to Spanish policy reflected Charles's own attitudes as well as the conflict within his government. The king sought to achieve the ends of the war by diplomacy as part of a *rapprochement* with Spain. Weston also wanted peace, but was sceptical about the chances of Spanish concessions and prepared to abandon the Palatines.[74] The negotiations were generally unpopular in England and were opposed by a majority in the Council, where Dorchester, Holland and Pembroke were the leading opponents.[75] Charles's Spanish treaty was prejudicial to England's relations with the whole of the Protestant world and ultimately with France. It failed to achieve anything for the Palatines or the Protestant cause, and promoted rather than limited Habsburg hegemony.

The seasoned diplomats Dorchester and Roe understood perfectly the tactics of Olivares. Just as Charles's dealings with Spain had encouraged the Danes to sign at Lübeck, separate Spanish overtures to England could destroy the Anglo-Dutch alliance of Southampton of 1625.[76] Dorchester wrote to Elizabeth of Bohemia of his confidence that the Palatine cause would revive, if 'it be not undermined by the artifice of enemies, in parting and separating of friends; which if it should take place, would prove our common ruin'. If England and the Dutch were undivided

and our affairs be conducted jointly and unitedly, we may both, by God's blessing, promise ourselves good issue. But if out of a peaceably [*sic*] disposition we strive [to see] who should take the enemy by the hand first, and thereby grow to separation, the devil cannot do us a greater mischief.[77]

Dorchester wrote to the English diplomat Sir Isaac Wake that while the European scene was in transformation, and other states (France, Sweden and the United Provinces) readied themselves for war, 'our designs abroad only tend for the present to pacification'.[78] Dorchester's tactical sense was fused

---

[73] Elliott, *Count-duke of Olivares*, pp. 391, 395; Alcalá-Zamora, *España, Flandes*, pp. 246–7, 286, 288; Parker, *Thirty Years War*, pp. 104–5; Gardiner, *History*, vii, pp. 180–1; Bireley, *Religion and politics*, pp. 6, 177; Lonchay, *Correspondance de la cour d'Espagne*, ii, p. 467n; Reade, *Sidelights on the Thirty Years War*, iii, pp. xxvii, 477; SP94/35/fos. 252r–253v.

[74] *CSPV 1629–32*, pp. 178, 331–2; Melbourne Hall, Coke Mss, bundle 37, newsletter of 5 June 1629.

[75] *CSPV 1629–32*, p. 250; PRO 31/3/66/fo. 208r; Magurn, *Rubens letters*, p. 352.

[76] Under the Treaty of Southampton, England and the United Provinces established an offensive and defensive alliance emphasizing naval co-operation against Spain; Gardiner, *History*, vi, p. 6.

[77] SP81/35/fo. 218r–v, Dorchester to Elizabeth, 24 Oct. 1629. See also SP75/10/fos. 253r–254v, 258r–262v, Roe's negotiations with Denmark, Aug. 1629.

[78] SP92/18/fo. 92r–v, Dorchester to Wake, 4 Mar. 1630; SP92/18/fo. 19v, Dorchester to Wake, 8 Jan. 1630.

with the language of militant Calvinism. Spain was the natural enemy of England and true religion. Charles, he wrote, was tempted to settle with Philip, but Dorchester believed the attack should be pressed home. He urged Sir Henry Vane (then at the Hague) to make no mistake. Despite the loss of the silver fleet, the Spaniard still might have a lot of fight left in him:

this blow he hath received, unless it be pursued with the like good success, will weaken him nothing but be rather like a blood-letting to a strong body, which is a cause of health . . .

Dorchester commended the Dutch war effort in the West Indies 'where in truth the life blood of the Spaniard lies'.[79] The religious conviction which lay at the root of this approach to international affairs was shared, in varying degrees, by the vast majority of the English political nation. Charles's hearkening to the overtures of Spain would further offend this body of opinion and deepen the distrust in which, among many, he was coming to be held.

In the spring of 1629, Elizabeth of Bohemia wrote to Charles, and Frederick to Dorchester, of what they said was their confidence that England would make no peace with Spain without their full restitution, as Charles had promised.[80] Their anxiety was not unjustified. Charles had become interested in peace. Among the influences turning him to Spain was his personal hatred of the French, a passion which was now as strong as ever. His honour had been wounded by the treatment of the Huguenots[81] and he had no faith in the French commitment to the Palatines or the general war. As Richelieu saw clearly, Charles cared nothing for the overtures of France and wished to see the outcome of his treaty with Spain. He had great hopes of Olivares and pondered the possibility of an alliance with Spain against France.[82]

Early in 1629, Philip IV issued powers for the conclusion of separate truce agreements with England and with the Dutch. Rubens was chosen as the Spanish envoy to England because, as a painter, he could establish a personal rapport with Charles. He left Madrid in April, having been briefed by Olivares, and travelled via Brussels. He arrived in London in June and lodged with his friend Gerbier.[83] Charles had sent Gerbier to meet him at Margate,

---

[79] SP84/139/fo. 96r–v, Dorchester to Vane, 10 Apr. 1629; Reeve, 'Viscount Dorchester', pp. 282, 292–3; Magurn, *Rubens letters*, pp. 342–5.

[80] SP81/35/fos. 172r, 174–175r.

[81] Charles may not have abandoned the idea of giving further aid to the Huguenots; Reade, *Sidelights on the Thirty Years War*, iii, p. 446.

[82] Ibid., iii, pp. xlvi, 447, 468; Magurn, *Rubens letters*, pp. 333–5, 366; AGS, E2519, exp. 11–13; SP92/14/fo. 223r; SP84/139/fos. 60r–62r; Avenel, *Lettres de Richelieu*, iii, pp. 477–8; Lonchay, *Correspondance de la cour d'Espagne*, ii, pp. 453–4.

[83] Lonchay, *Correspondance de la cour d'Espagne*, ii, pp. 445 and n, 446, 450; A. J. Loomie, 'Olivares, the English Catholics and the peace of 1630', *Revue Belge de Philologie et*

and to say that if he were commissioned to arrange an Anglo-Spanish war against France he must not discuss it with anyone but Charles. The king wished to keep such a secret to himself.[84] Rubens, in fact, had no such commission. He was empowered only to negotiate the badly needed armistice with England. He was not authorized to deal with anything relating to the United Provinces as long as Kesselaer still negotiated, on Philip's behalf, with the victorious Dutch at Roosendaal.[85] Olivares, as well as wanting to split the alliance, desired an end to English harassment at sea and the resumption of trade. To make matters worse, the diversion of ships to Italy was leaving the Spanish coast virtually defenceless.[86] Rubens was instructed to obtain as long a cessation of hostilities as he could and, whatever happened, to keep talking.[87]

Olivares was well aware that in terms of his hopes of England, once he had a truce he was halfway home. Having obtained some relief, Spain could spin out the treaty and play for advantage. On the other hand, it was increasingly clear to the count-duke and to Philip that if the Anglo-Dutch alliance remained unbroken and in a state of war with Spain, the sole resort for a very seriously over-extended Spanish monarchy was a military alliance with the Empire and the Catholic League, a highly dubious possibility.[88] By the autumn, Alvise Mocenigo, the Venetian ambassador in Madrid, could write:

I know well enough that the Dutch and English have never had a better opportunity of scoring off their enemies, and if they persist courageously with their demands they will subject the wishes of the Spaniards to their own. The confusion and disorder of the government here is excessive.[89]

Unlike the Dutch, the war party in England and all in Madrid, Charles did not perceive the margin of leverage which he possessed while he remained in a state of hostilities. The precise extent of that leverage cannot be known for it was never allowed to be tested. Yet clearly, if it could be sustained and the

---

d'Histoire, xlvii, 4 (1969), p. 1157n; Elliott, *Count-duke of Olivares*, pp. 366, 368; Israel, *Dutch republic*, pp. 226–7; Melbourne Hall, Coke Mss, bundle 37, newsletter of 5 June 1629.

[84] Reade, *Sidelights on the Thirty Years War*, iii, pp. xlv–xlvi, 437.

[85] Lonchay, *Correspondance de la cour d'Espagne*, ii, p. 446; Israel, *Dutch republic*, p. 227; Reade, *Sidelights on the Thirty Years War*, iii, p. 435.

[86] Reade, *Sidelights on the Thirty Years War*, iii, pp. 477, 493; *CSPV 1629–32*, pp. 45, 70, 123, 133, 229, 267, 280, 332–3, 405–6; SP94/34/fos. 159r–160r.

[87] Lonchay, *Correspondance de la cour d'Espagne*, ii, p. 450; Reade, *Sidelights on the Thirty Years War*, iii, pp. 450, 452.

[88] Elliott, *Count-duke of Olivares*, p. 369; Archives Générales du Royaume (AGR), Brussels, Secrétaire d'Etat et de Guerre (SEG), liasse 208, fo. 31r–v, Philip IV to Infanta Isabella, 22 Aug. 1629 (n.s.) (I am grateful to Simon Adams for bringing this document to my attention); Lonchay, *Correspondance de la cour d'Espagne*, vi, 307; see also Reade, *Sidelights on the Thirty Years War*, iii, pp. 450–1.

[89] *CSPV 1629–32*, p. 229. See also ibid., pp. 133, 209.

alliance with the Dutch maintained, it was considerable. Once it was surrendered, Charles's difficulty in providing a substantial quid pro quo with which to obtain concessions from Spain would become a much greater liability. Charles, however, in briefly attempting to hold out for concessions, was more concerned with honour than with tactics. Above all, he dreaded a collapse in the talks which would force him to adopt policies he wished to avoid:[90] the recalling of Parliament, the renewal of Protestant war and dealings with France and the Dutch. He came to look upon the Anglo-Spanish treaty more and more as a means to personal security and salvation.

Rubens came to London bearing personal letters from Olivares to Charles, Weston and Cottington.[91] The morning after his arrival he was interviewed by the king at Greenwich. While Charles preferred an understanding with Spain to one with France, he was unwilling to agree to an armistice without an undertaking about the Palatinate or without reference to his allies. Under the Treaty of the Hague, England and the Dutch were bound to treat in consultation. Yet Charles's sense of honour and obligation was to prove no stronger than his desire to be on good terms once again with Spain and to believe in her government.[92] Rubens had no authority for such an agreement as Charles proposed or for discussion of the interests of the Dutch. Weston and Cottington smoothed the way to an understanding. The Treasurer presented Rubens with a statement of Charles's terms which was forwarded to Spain. Charles would agree to a truce if Philip guaranteed to restore the territories in Spanish hands, that is the Lower Palatinate, and to do his best to intercede with the emperor and Bavaria for Frederick's full restitution. Charles gave his word that he would make no alliance with France prejudicial to Spain during the Spanish negotiations.[93]

By opening negotiations with Spain in this way, Charles was in breach of his treaty obligations to the Dutch. He also broke the undertaking he made to Roe that he would not begin to treat with Spain without the consent of his allies.[94] Rubens having referred the Palatine question to Madrid, Charles was

---

[90]   Reade, *Sidelights on the Thirty Years War*, iii, p. 469.
[91]   To which Weston and Cottington replied in very gracious terms. AGS, E2519, exp. 25–6; see also Melbourne Hall, Coke Mss, bundle 37, newsletter of 5 June 1629.
[92]   Melbourne Hall, Coke Mss, bundle 37, newsletter of 5 June 1629; AGS, E2519, exp. 23; Lockyer, *Buckingham*, p. 279; Reade, *Sidelights on the Thirty Years War*, iii, pp. 445–7.
[93]   AGS, E2519, exp. 23, statement of English terms in Weston's hand, French, deciphered, exp. 24, Spanish translation; Magurn, *Rubens letters*, pp. 299–301, 303–6, 306–7, 308–10, 310–12. See also Reade, *Sidelights on the Thirty Years War*, iii, pp. 444–5.
[94]   While the Dutch ambassador in England responded favourably to Charles's idea of English mediation between Spain and the Dutch, this was after Charles had undertaken not to ally with France against Spain pending a Spanish treaty, and when he and Rubens had agreed upon the procedure for an Anglo-Spanish armistice. These understandings were reached without the participation or consent of the Dutch, who objected to Charles's talks with Rubens. The States General never agreed to participate in the Treaty of Madrid. Denmark

willing to send Cottington to Spain to negotiate a treaty if Philip's guarantee arrived before his departure.[95] Rubens prevaricated and Charles agreed that Cottington would go and would negotiate on the basis of the stated English conditions. The matter was rammed through the Council in the third week of July when, by prior arrangement, Weston proposed that Cottington be sent and Charles immediately declared his approval. There was no dissent expressed. To Cottington's mind, this was a miraculous coup.[96] Weston and the Spaniards worked progressively to end hostilities by opening trade without an official armistice. English merchants were given a vested interest in peace with Spain and Charles was given the incentive of customs revenues. The reopening of Anglo-Iberian commerce broke down the last remnant of the stoppage of trade which had affected England since the end of the parliamentary session.[97] Charles thus became vulnerable to Spanish diplomatic manipulation and was committed by degrees to peace with Spain. He still entertained the thought, moreover, of an alliance with Spain against France and perhaps (as Rubens and Cottington advocated) even against the United Provinces.[98]

The reaction in Madrid to the discussions in London was cautiously optimistic and moderated the general mood of desperation. The Council of State observed on 10 August that if the talks with the Dutch went well this would weaken the English bargaining position. Cottington's coming was taken as a good sign of England's desire for peace.[99] Olivares appeared to be getting his breathing space. The count-duke's tactic of dividing the Anglo-Dutch alliance meant that he needed to lure Charles with hopeful words. A junta of the Council, meeting on 18 October, resolved that no undertakings should be made by Spain to England. Philip should make peace with Charles and consider any further English proposals.[100] While seeking peace and hoping for an English alliance, it was necessary for Spain to consider what would certainly be a renewed emergency if the (now increasingly separate)

---

may have forfeited Charles's consideration by capitulating on 28 May, although in 1628 he had issued an authority to treat with Spain to the Danish resident in London. SP84/139/ fos. 60r–62r; SP94/34/fo. 21r; *CSPV 1629–32*, p. 149; Magurn, *Rubens letters*, pp. 299–301, 306–7, 308–10; Parker, *Europe in crisis*, p. 189; Israel, *Dutch republic*, p. 300.

[95] Magurn, *Rubens letters*, pp. 314–15.

[96] Ibid., pp. 324–6, 333–5, 338–42; *CSPV 1629–32*, pp. 148–9.

[97] *CSPV 1629–32*, pp. 16, 45, 57, 70, 251, 267, 279–80, 290, 332–3, 405–6, 493; Gardiner, *History*, vii, p. 168; NUL, Ne.C., 15,404, p. 223; Birch, i, pp. 426, 453; AGS, E2517, fos. 58, 108, and E2519, exp. 29; PRO 31/3/66/fo. 258r–v; Supple, *Commercial crisis*, p. 110.

[98] Rubens and Cottington may well have been motivated by fear of the failure of the treaty and the personal repercussions for them. Magurn, *Rubens letters*, pp. 324–6, 333–5, 342–5, 353.

[99] AGS, E2519, exp. 17.

[100] Ibid., exp. 29; Reade, *Sidelights on the Thirty Years War*, iii, p. 478.

talks with London and the Hague both collapsed. With Charles's desire to insist upon the restoration of the Palatinate, and with the chance that he might yet show solidarity with the Dutch, that outcome could by no means be discounted. A second Protestant West India company in England was a terrifying possibility of which Rubens made Olivares aware.[101] The emperor and Maximilian of Bavaria were informed of the dealings with Charles. They were asked to send envoys to Madrid to participate in a general Anglo-Habsburg settlement with Cottington. While Philip considered an Anglo-Spanish alliance the proper price of concessions, he also professed to see the justice of Charles's claims. As Olivares saw matters, if Spain were to risk a continuation of the war in the north – a war in the interests of German Catholicism insofar as it was for Frederick's continued exclusion – then Ferdinand and Maximilian should bear their fair share of the burden and conclude an offensive and defensive alliance with Spain. The count-duke sought to pressure the emperor and Bavaria as those who should accept responsibility for, and justify, refusal of Charles's demands.[102] Olivares was in fact caught between Scylla and Charybdis. Desperate for peace with England and unable to withstand any joint Anglo-Dutch terms, he could hardly relinquish real assets in Germany, perhaps alienating the allies of Spain, in the course of making peace with England alone – unless, that is, Charles made some positive contribution to the Habsburg cause. With Spain at the wall in Flanders, a war beginning in Italy and no certainty of wholehearted help from the Empire, the count-duke was hopeful and fearful of Charles. The diplomatic game in which England was now a player was very much an open competition. Others were to play it more skilfully than Charles.

International influences, in conjunction with Charles himself, were having a profound effect upon English politics. Rubens' mission took Olivares' designs and the directly divisive power of the European conflict into the heart of political circles in London. There these wider forces played upon existing political divisions. The secret negotiations between Charles and Rubens represented, as Rubens understood, the growing influence of the pro-Spanish ministers at court and Charles's emerging desire for an alignment with Spain.[103] Weston deliberately excluded Dorchester and Holland from these negotiations.[104] As advocates of the French alliance and the Protestant cause

---

[101] *CSPV 1628–9*, pp. 516, 518–19, 557, 590; *CSPV 1629–32*, p. 133; Magurn, *Rubens letters*, pp. 335, 342–5; Israel, *Dutch republic*, p. 227.

[102] AGS, E2519, exp. 1, 29; Archives Générales du Royaume (AGR), Brussels, Secrétaire d'Etat de Guerre (SEG), liasse 208, fo. 31r–v (I am grateful to Simon Adams for this reference); Reade, *Sidelights on the Thirty Years War*, iii, pp. 451–2; Alcalá-Zamora, *España, Flandes*, pp. 264–5; Elliott, *Count-duke of Olivares*, p. 369.

[103] AGS, E2519, exp. 10; Magurn, *Rubens letters*, pp. 303–6, 310–14, 324–30, 342–7.

[104] Magurn, *Rubens letters*, pp. 312–14; Birch, ii, p. 65.

they might well have been able, once admitted to the discussions, to destroy an Anglo-Spanish agreement with the majority of the Council opposed to one.[105] The Spanish negotiations ignited fierce factional strife over English policy. The Hispanophile clique was in a definite minority.[106] The pro-war group at court, especially Dorchester, Holland and the French, Venetian and Dutch ambassadors, worked tirelessly to discredit the dealings with Rubens. The French ambassador Chateauneuf had orders from Richelieu to prevent the conclusion of peace between England and Spain. The Venetian ambassador Contarini, a professional anti-Habsburg lobbyist, was considered by Rubens the greatest firebrand in Europe. This group advocated a French alliance and a Parliament for the renewal of the war against Spain. Weston and Cottington feared the Spanish negotiations would be their ruin. They thought Charles had gone too far by undertaking not to ally with France while negotiating with Spain, but could not prevent the king confirming his promise to Rubens. Weston, surrounded by enemies, did not wish to be deprived of Cottington's services by his mission to Spain for longer than was strictly necessary. The Treasurer wrote to Olivares to this effect. In these circumstances, Rubens believed it was all he could do to open negotiations and cursed the day he came to England.[107] His presence and dealings in London, following hard upon the collapse of the last Parliament, increased suspicion of Weston's (and Charles's) designs as well as the Treasurer's fear of the war lobby. English politics thus fell victim to foreign influences and conflicts.[108] Yet those influences also found a reflection in native perceptions of correct English policy abroad as well as at home.[109] It is possible to discern in Rubens' talks the emerging polarization of English high politics and the remaking of power relationships at court under Charles. The king, when facing key decisions, was inclined to exclude those who did not share his views. This weakened his government and largely delivered him into the hands of partisans with whom he felt secure.

In late 1629 Cottington went to Madrid to negotiate a peace.[110] He seems to have received no detailed instructions, beyond Charles's stated terms, except to uphold his king's reputation. Yet he professed to serve Olivares and

---

[105] Magurn, *Rubens letters*, p. 352.
[106] Melbourne Hall, Coke Mss, bundle 37, newsletter of 5 June 1629.
[107] Magurn, *Rubens letters*, pp. 303–6, 312–14, 324–6, 327–30, 333–5, 338–42, 352–3; *CSPV 1629–32*, pp. 118, 136, 148; PRO 31/3/66/fos. 134v–135v; SP77/19/fos. 329r–333r; AGS, E2519, exp. 25–6; Avenel, *Lettres de Richelieu*, iii, pp. 420–1; Reade, *Sidelights on the Thirty Years War*, iii, pp. 441, 443–5; Knowler, *Strafford letters*, i, p. 51.
[108] I am grateful to Sir Geoffrey Elton for this point.
[109] Reeve, 'Viscount Dorchester', pp. 286–7. See also chapter 6, above.
[110] Cottington left England, after delays, at the beginning of November and arrived in Madrid on 1 January. SP94/34/fos. 100r, 104r, 106r, 148r; *CSPV 1629–32*, p. 267. Olivares was the only senior Spanish minister who already knew Cottington personally; Elliott, *Count-duke of Olivares*, p. 394.

Philip as well as Charles.[111] This attitude, while rooted in his cultural preferences, was dictated, as will be seen, by the circumstances of his mission. It was also worthy of Charles's positive view of a settlement with Spain. Coloma, who went to London to reciprocate Cottington's embassy, found Charles even better disposed to peace with Spain, and to its benefits, than James had been.[112] Charles was optimistic about the Spanish attitude to the Palatines and was prepared to sacrifice the Dutch to an Anglo-Spanish agreement. As Cottington's talks evolved, Charles preferred to surrender his position rather than risk the rupture of the treaty.[113] Weston and Cottington were deeply committed to the success of the negotiation, upon which their very political survival depended. The conflict within the English government continued as the treaty progressed. The king, Coloma and Weston held confidential discussions. The Treasurer told the ambassador of Charles's desire for the friendship of Spain, urging him to keep this from Dorchester, and asked him to communicate it secretly to the count-duke.[114] Weston, and through him the king, maintained a correspondence with Cottington in Spain distinct from that of the Secretary. Dorchester was disadvantaged in this situation but caused Weston anxiety by opposing compromise and seeking to break the treaty.[115] Dorchester was deeply suspicious of Spain and sought to place the full burden of proof upon the Spanish intentions. He wished to end the talks quickly, protect the Dutch alliance and continue the war. He wrote to Cottington in Spain: 'The labour of the Spaniards is to divide and separate us, which peace or war will turn to their advantage if they can bring it to effect.'[116]

Despite Coloma's presence in England, the real negotiation of the Treaty of Madrid took place in Spain. Don Carlos did, however, play a role in receiving confidences and building Charles's hopes.[117] Charles's attitude, especially his

---

[111] Magurn, *Rubens letters*, pp. 324–6, 342–5; AGS, E2562, 'prima conferencia' on treaty with England, 14 Feb. 1630 (n.s.).

[112] AGS, E2519, exp. 77. Coloma had been Spanish ambassador in England between Gondomar's departure in 1623 and September 1624. I am grateful to Albert Loomie for advice on this point. See also Elliott, *Count-duke of Olivares*, p. 214.

[113] AGS, E2519, exp. 70; SP94/34/fos. 110r–111r, 129r–v.

[114] AGS, E2519, exp. 71, Coloma to Olivares, 7 Apr. 1630. See also ibid., exp. 77, and E2562, Coloma to Infanta, 5 Dec. 1630 (n.s.); Magurn, *Rubens letters*, pp. 324–6, 342–5; Birch, i, p. 51.

[115] AGS, E2519, exp. 114; SP77/19/fos. 329r–333r, 359r–v. Dorchester also worked against the pro-Spanish and anti-French intervention of Savoy in the negotiations. Charles was prepared to assist Savoy against France if necessary. Reeve, 'Viscount Dorchester', p. 287; AGS, E2519, exp. 99, and E2562, memo to Rozas of 28 Aug. 1630 (n.s.); Elliott, *Count-duke of Olivares*, pp. 399–400.

[116] SP94/34/fo. 138r, Dorchester to Cottington, 10 Jan. 1630.

[117] PRO 31/3/66/fo. 241v; Lonchay, *Correspondance de la cour d'Espagne*, ii, p. 501; *CSPV 1629–32*, p. 269; AGS, E2519, exp. 71, 77; Archivo del Duque del Infantado, Madrid, Palafox Mss, leg. 94, fo. 137 (I am grateful to John Elliott for this reference).

disregard for the Dutch, played right into the hands of Olivares. Desperately needing a settlement with England and in the Netherlands, and unable to pressure the Dutch without help (not forthcoming) from the emperor and Bavaria,[118] the count-duke clearly aimed to draw Charles into a state of peace with Spain without making significant concessions. An Anglo-Dutch front united and giving no quarter without political satisfaction could threaten, at this moment, to bring about the downfall of Spain. England, despite the failures and miscalculations of the last half-decade, still had real power while in a state of war. At peace she had none, and would immediately become vulnerable to Spanish bartering of the destiny of the Palatines in exchange for some positive contribution to the Habsburg cause.

Cottington made clear to Olivares, before he ever left England, how dependent he and his mission would be upon the count-duke's trust and goodwill. Given the opposition to the treaty in England, Cottington believed that its failure would be his nemesis. He accepted the mission since he was ordered to do so and (he said) out of obligation to Olivares. Just as he had worked with Rubens to open negotiations, he would work with the government in Madrid to secure an agreement. His statement that he would speak as a Spanish councillor as much as an English ambassador was, whatever else, the inspiration of necessity.[119] Cottington's situation and Charles's desire for a settlement together profoundly affected the outcome. The result was a treaty favourable to Spain which accommodated Charles in the general form rather than the substance of the agreement. It was, within a pro-Spanish framework, a compromise. Before that agreement could be reached, however, the obstacle of Charles's stated terms for a settlement had to be overcome.

In late January 1630 Cottington had preliminary discussions with Philip and Olivares in Madrid. With the ambassador's hands tied by Charles, the Palatinate was the obvious stumbling-block. Philip stated his intention of having the Palatines fully restored. Olivares inquired about the re-opening of Anglo-Spanish trade, but Cottington stated that Charles needed some prior satisfaction. Olivares professed that in exchange for the Palatinate Spain required peace in the north, that is a settlement with the Dutch, by Charles's mediation. Cottington opined somewhat rashly that the Dutch were resolved to treat only in consultation with Charles.[120] Olivares appeared troubled at

---

[118] Lonchay, *Correspondance de la cour d'Espagne*, vi, p. 307; Elliott, *Count-duke of Olivares*, p. 352.

[119] Magurn, *Rubens letters*, pp. 324–6, 342–5; *CSPV 1629–32*, p. 364.

[120] This was the position under the Treaty of Southampton, but the alliance was being progressively undermined by the separate talks in Spain and the Netherlands. Ultimately the Dutch resolved to treat without England (see below, p. 262). Cottington's antipathy to the Dutch underlines the difficulty of his mission in which, initially, he had to express solidarity with the alliance. Reeve, 'Viscount Dorchester', p. 286; Reade, *Sidelights on the Thirty Years War*, iii, p. 496.

this. Cottington correctly identified the issue in his despatch as the crux of the matter. He grew sceptical of the prospects of success and suggested his recall.[121] Cottington may simply have wished to avoid compounding his failure. He may also have been encouraging Charles to soften his stance. The king's response was positive. Charles was delighted at Philip's willingness to consider the restoration of the entire Palatinate. In this the Spanish king had exceeded his expectations. Charles also wished to acquit himself of the Dutch alliance. He ordered Cottington to persevere.[122] Dorchester added a statement on what he saw as the insincerity of the Spaniards. He favoured renewal of the war and awaited the failure of negotiations.[123] Olivares protested that his intentions in Germany were sincere but argued that peace should precede restitution. When the emperor and the duke of Bavaria refused to treat in Madrid Cottington considered his mission aborted.[124] Dorchester's statement of the English position was, politically and diplomatically, difficult to fault. It was Spain which had seized the Palatinate, and promises made to the king's father concerning restitution had been broken. James had had no alternative but war. The cause of war must needs be the cause of peace and thus peace should be preceded by the lifting of the imperial ban placed upon Frederick, by a Spanish undertaking to restore at least the Lower Palatinate within a limited time and to intercede for full restitution and by the authorization of Charles to mediate with the Dutch according to the last Spanish terms offered them. This would achieve peace. The only alternative was continuation of the war. For England to make peace upon lesser conditions while retaining the war option would achieve nothing but separation from her allies. The attitude of Austria and Bavaria was only to be expected. This being the position, Dorchester informed Cottington that his recall was imminent and expected the treaty to break.[125]

At this point, in early April 1630, Charles made a fatal error. He had assured Frederick that he would not end hostilities without restitution.[126] With Olivares' tactics becoming clear, he faced two choices. He could either join with the Dutch to extract better terms or continue the war, or allow him-

---

[121] For Cottington's account of these discussions see SP94/34/fos. 159r–164v.
[122] SP94/34/fos. 169r–170v.
[123] SP94/34/fos. 190r–192v.
[124] AGS, E2519, exp. 64; SP94/34/fos. 180r–184v, 198r–v; Lonchay, *Correspondance de la cour d'Espagne*, ii, p. 510.
[125] Dorchester's draft implies that he desired the restitution of the Lower Palatinate and the lifting of the ban to be conditions of peace and security for full restitution, and that Charles wanted a general undertaking and a time limit for the return of the Lower Palatinate to be substituted. Frederick was declared an outlaw under the laws of the Empire in 1621. SP94/34/fos. 204r–207r; AGS, E2562, paper of Charles for Olivares, 20 Mar. 1630 (n.s.?); Parker, *Europe in crisis*, p. 181; Parker, *Thirty Years War*, p. 65.
[126] SP81/36/fo. 17r–v.

self to be drawn into further negotiations which implied unrealistic expectations. Spain was in no position to dictate to England. She had, however, ample scope for diplomatic manipulation if Charles could not temper his desire for an immediate and independent settlement. Charles weakened. Encouraged by Weston and Coloma he was both unwilling to accept his position and unable to recognize the alternative for what it was. He abhorred the prospect of recalling Parliament and had an unwarranted belief in the Spaniards' intention of giving him satisfaction. In sanctioning Dorchester's statement of policy he had modified his demands, but even without insistence upon actual restitution the English terms were sufficient to rupture negotiations. Charles now wrote to Cottington that he trusted in Philip's intentions, that the ambassador should remain in Madrid and that he desired to hear further propositions to judge whether they were worthy of peace.[127] He thus continued to sacrifice his position, further opened the door to Spanish manipulation and saved Cottington from failure.

There are two accounts of what then occurred in Madrid. One, Cottington's official report to Dorchester, is clearly deficient and was intended to give as little offence as possible to the English war lobby. The other can be reconstructed from the Spanish archival sources and tells a rather different and fuller story. According to Cottington's account, written on 14 May, the ambassador delivered an ultimatum. He stated the English terms – including 'assurance of immediate and effectual offices for the restoration of the Palatinate' – and threatened to leave. Olivares replied that his departure would be taken as a new declaration of war. Cottington, having thus played his last card towards securing immediate concessions, qualified his demands. He wanted a general promise from Philip of his best endeavours for Frederick and an undertaking that Spain would immediately institute proceedings to advance his restitution. The Spaniards, Cottington wrote, had agreed to these terms. They were resolved that England would not be authorized to mediate with the Dutch until Charles's peace with Spain was concluded.[128] This account of proceedings, essentially true as far as it went, arouses suspicion. In the first place, it is too momentous and simple. Cottington was seeking to portray a situation in which the Spaniards had responded to English insistence. This, to a degree, they had done if Cottington's account is to be trusted. It is unlikely, however, that sheer insistence would have produced this response without a fuller agreement, inspired by an element of reciprocity, having evolved. The talks in Madrid were part of a most complicated and critical diplomatic conjuncture. Secondly, from what we already know,

---

[127] SP94/34/fos. 207r, 212r–214r; SP84/141/fo. 186r; PRO 31/3/66/fos. 265v–266v; AGS, E2519, exp. 70–1, 73, 77. See also ibid., exp. 46.

[128] SP94/34/fos. 232r–235r.

Cottington's account almost certainly exaggerated his own and the count-duke's preparedness to risk a rupture of the treaty. Finally, when compared with the external evidence of the Spanish documentary record, the ambassador's report makes a number of highly significant omissions.

On 23 April Cottington's reply to a Spanish paper reflected the principle thus far underlying the English terms: Frederick's satisfaction should precede the making of peace. Three days later the ambassador made an overture along different lines. He was clearly acting upon Charles's letter of the 7th which introduced a flexibility – and a willingness to compromise – into the English position. Cottington proposed to Olivares that if Philip undertook to do his best for the banished elector and to return the Rhine Palatinate (given that the emperor lifted the ban at Philip's intercession), then Charles would reciprocate the king of Spain's generosity as it deserved. Cottington, now free to act, had done what he knew was required for an agreement. He had sought to persuade Charles of the merits of such an offer before ever having left England. His proposal transformed the stalemate into an explosion of initiatives. Olivares advised Philip that under certain circumstances it might well be reasonable to restore the Rhine Palatinate. The count-duke was still enamoured of the idea that Charles might bring the Dutch to satisfactory terms. Within two weeks of having made his proposal of reciprocity, Cottington took the opportunity to suggest an Anglo-Spanish alliance against the Dutch. On 10 May Olivares and the count of Oñate were authorized to listen to this proposal. The following day the count-duke's secretary Rozas replied to Cottington that Philip would perform what was asked with regard to Frederick once the Anglo-Spanish peace had been concluded. Surprisingly, Cottington did not report this immediately to London. Two days later, on the 13th, he was told by Olivares that Philip was prepared to ally with Charles against the Dutch.[129] It was only then that Cottington, on the 14th, wrote to Dorchester that the critical breakthrough in the treaty had been achieved. His report made no reference to three essential aspects of the agreement which was now in the making. He did not inform the Secretary (and through him the war lobby) that he had actually acceded to a deferral of effective Spanish action until after the making of peace, that he had offered the Spanish government some form of quid pro quo and that he had successfully proposed an alliance against the Dutch. Dorchester would have sought to raise strenuous objections to all these measures. Cottington's account and his supposed ultimatum could well have been a version of an encounter with the count-duke prior to the breakthrough. It is difficult to believe that that account,

---

[129] AGS, E2519, exp. 45, 54, 80–1, 86, and E2562, Cottington's response of 3 May 1630 (n.s.), Hopton to Philip IV, 1631/2; SP94/34/fos. 212r–214r; Magurn, *Rubens letters*, pp. 343–4; Gardiner, *History*, vii, p. 172; Loomie, 'Spanish faction', p. 39n.

under the circumstances, was not dramatized for the conciliar audience in England. Certainly it was not the whole story.

What, exactly, were the outlines of the new agreement? Charles would be empowered to mediate with the Dutch and to bring them to a settlement acceptable to Spain. He would not receive this authority until after the Anglo-Spanish peace was concluded. In treating with the Dutch he was to make a public declaration that his alliance with them was dissolved. Cottington's proposal of an alliance against the Dutch was obviously an integral part of the agreement. The prospective Spanish undertakings about German concessions did not, however, depend at this point upon Charles's making war on the Dutch. In 1630 Olivares held to his view that successful mediation by England would be sufficient recompense for Spain. Yet armed intervention by Charles was coming to be seen as a logical recourse in Madrid in the event of the failure of diplomacy. Cottington's proposal of alliance would eventually take the form of the famous Cottington Treaty of 1631. In time that alliance would become an inextricable part of the Spanish terms for the restoration of the Palatinate. Meanwhile the Anglo-Spanish peace treaty could go ahead. Olivares decided to bypass a formal truce in favour of the conclusive peace with England, on Spanish terms, now within his grasp. On 15 May, the day after Cottington had penned his report, Philip wrote personally to Charles. He stated that he would support Frederick's claims at the approaching imperial Diet. He added that if the imperial ban declaring Frederick an outlaw were revoked (an important caveat which preserved Spain's freedom of action), then he, Philip, would return the fortresses by which Spain controlled the Rhine Palatinate. The hand of Olivares is clearly discernible behind the linking of potential settlements in Germany and the Netherlands which ran through the dealings with England. Before Cottington left Madrid he was given to understand by the count-duke what the two men already knew: that Spanish concessions would depend upon Charles's assistance in procuring a satisfactory settlement in the Netherlands.[130] Olivares carefully preserved his options with regard to the German Catholics, advising Philip that the emperor and the League be assured that he would make no agreement with Charles save on more beneficial terms than before the war with England. Spain, in other words, would extract some significant advantage in return for

---

[130] Almost certainly Olivares nursed the hope of Dutch recognition of Spanish sovereignty once again. SP94/34/fos. 159r–164r, SP94/35/fos. 6r–10v; SP80/7/fo. 64r–v; SP84/140/fo. 223r; AGS, E2519, exp. 49, 61, 63, 74, 87, 89, 93–4, 101, 132, unnumbered, E2562, Olivares to Cottington, May 1630 (n.s.?), Coloma to Infanta, 5 Dec. 1630 (n.s.), Olivares in Council of State, 13 July 1630 (n.s.), Oñate in Council of State, 30 July 1630 (n.s.), consultas of 6 May, 30 July, 4 Nov. 1630 (n.s.), Council of State, 7, 9 Jan. 1632 (n.s.), undated consultas; Lonchay, *Correspondance de la cour d'Espagne*, ii, p. 534; Israel, *Dutch republic*, pp. 10–11; Gardiner, *History*, vii, pp. 172–3; Elliott, 'A question of reputation?', p. 479; Elliott, *Count-duke of Olivares*, pp. 372–3, 403–5; Reeve, 'Quiroga's paper'.

the concessions sought by Charles. Until then, as Olivares told Philip, any Spanish undertakings should not be felt to be binding.[131] Above all, the count-duke had achieved the desperately needed breakthrough by the second week of May. For Spain it came none too soon. Word had just arrived that the list of military disasters had lengthened with the loss in February of Pernambuco in Brazil to Dutch West India Company forces.[132]

Charles had allowed English interests to be manoeuvred into a position in which Madrid could now call the tune. He does not appear, at least at this point, to have realized that this was so. His hopes had been raised. Dorchester's protests were to little or no avail. Charles immediately sent an envoy, Sir Robert Anstruther, to the imperial Diet at Regensburg to test the Spanish overtures. The emperor was beset by difficulties: conflict over the religious issue in the Empire, the threat of Swedish invasion and the need to enlist imperial support for the Habsburg wars in Italy and the Netherlands. With Charles's virtual commitment to peace with Spain, Ferdinand's attitude could only be uncompromising with no offer of an English quid pro quo.[133] Nevertheless, Charles, Weston, Cottington and the Spaniards all desired to conclude the treaty in Madrid. Charles's political court had closed ranks with Spain.[134]

The Anglo-Spanish treaty of peace was essentially a reaffirmation of that which had ended the Elizabethan War in 1604. On the three most contentious issues in which that treaty had favoured England, Spain was prepared to give way in 1630. England was still permitted to provide military aid to the United Provinces, English ships were allowed to enter West Indian waters and all mention of the English Catholics was omitted from the articles. Olivares had no desire to jeopardize peace with England by standing on such matters particularly after Gustavus landed in north Germany in July.[135] With the treaty now drawn up, Cottington attempted to have its ratification made conditional upon Charles's further consideration and approval. This the

---

[131] AGS, E2519, exp. 52, 86; Loomie, 'Peace of 1630', pp. 1163–4.
[132] SP84/141/fos. 215r–216r; Israel, *Dutch republic*, pp. 202–3. The winter of 1629–30 also saw Dutch expulsion of the Spanish garrisons from north-west Germany and the collapse of the river blockade against the republic; Parker, *Thirty Years War*, p. 102.
[133] SP94/34/fos. 204r–207r, 239r–240r, 249r–250r; AGS, E2519, exp. 49; Reeve, 'Viscount Dorchester', pp. 298–300; Bireley, *Religion and politics*, pp. 113–14.
[134] AGS, E2519, exp. 81, and E2562, consulta of 3 Dec. 1630(?) (n.s.), Coloma to Infanta, 5 Dec. 1630 (n.s.).
[135] AGS, E2519, exp. 89–90, 96, 102–3, and E2562, Council of State, 26 July 1630 (n.s.), voto of Oñate in consulta of 30 July 1630 (n.s.); SP94/34/fos. 249r–250r, 265v, SP94/35/fos. 6r–10v, 20r–21r, 39r–41v, 71r–75r; Loomie, 'Peace of 1630'; Adams, 'Spain or the Netherlands?', pp. 99–100; Parker, *Thirty Years War*, p. 123; Parker, *Army of Flanders*, p. 257; Elliott, *Count-duke of Olivares*, p. 403.

Spaniards apparently disallowed.[136] Cottington dutifully insisted that the continuation of peace was conditional upon the restoration of the Palatinate, but no real concessions were obtained by the treaty. Philip presented Charles with a written assurance of his best endeavours for Frederick and with an authority to mediate with the Dutch. Spain offered the banished elector a yearly pension until such time as he might be restored. The articles of the Treaty of Madrid were signed on 5 November, when the peace was proclaimed in England, and Coloma swore to it in Philip's name on 7 December. Weston's anxiety was not relieved until that very day. In Madrid, Olivares expressed his admiration and gratitude to Cottington (and eventually to Weston) in pecuniary form.[137] The count-duke does not seem to have realized the critical influence they could bring to bear until the deed was almost done.

The treaty was a triumph for the peace party in England and for Spanish diplomatic professionalism. The immediate casualties were the Palatines. Frederick protested bitterly at Charles's ending of the war despite his assurances. Dorchester wrote to Elizabeth describing England as 'this wicked land'.[138] In the longer term the casualty in England was the standing of Charles's government. The Treaty of Madrid was blasphemy to the puritan gentry.[139] The Grand Remonstrance would describe it as the means

whereby the [elector] Palatine's cause was deserted and left to chargeable and hopeless treaties, which for the most part were managed by those who might justly be suspected to be no friends to that cause.[140]

It was a fair conclusion. Yet the religious fervour which inspired it contributed, perhaps ironically, to the failure it condemned. Charles's conclusion of peace with Spain signified eloquently the constitutional breakdown of English foreign policy. His inclination to peace was an essential part of that breakdown and revealed how much it derived from his rule. In espousing peace he was repelled by dissent in Parliament and the courts; the religious issue was sure to arise in the new Parliament required to continue the war; the debts of the Buckingham era remained and royal solvency was still fragile at

---

[136] AGS, E2519, exp. 104. Cottington was accused of upsetting an established agreement and seeking to gain time. He was probably attempting to evade responsibility for the negotiation.
[137] See p. 186, n. 79, above. See also AGS, E2519, exp. 114, and E2562, consultas of 26 July 1630, 25 Jan. 1631 (n.s.), Coloma to Infanta, 5 Dec. 1630 (n.s.); SP94/34/fos. 232r–235r, SP94/35/fos. 79v–80v; SP80/8/fos. 58r, 77v; SP81/36/fo. 127r–v; SP84/143/fos. 94r–95r; *CSPV 1629–32*, pp. 131, 438, 456; Birch, ii, pp. 91–2; Reade, *Sidelights on the Thirty Years War*, iii, p. 519; Larkin, *Stuart royal proclamations*, ii, pp. 306–7; Lonchay, *Correspondance de la cour d'Espagne*, ii, p. 554; Gardiner, *History*, vii, pp. 175–6; Alcalá-Zamora, *España, Flandes*, pp. 266–7.
[138] SP84/141/fos. 307r–311r, SP84/142/fos. 28r–29r; SP81/36/fos. 113r–v, 127r–v; Reeve, 'Viscount Dorchester', pp. 292–3.
[139] Searle, *Barrington family letters*, pp. 227, 238, 244; Breslow, *Mirror of England*, p. 42.
[140] Gardiner, *Constitutional documents*, pp. 208–9.

best; finally, there was the attraction of Spain, increased for Charles by its being (to his mind) a means of escape from all he feared and detested: the French, the Dutch, the political puritans, the recalcitrant common lawyers and the amorphous and apparently menacing conspiracies against him at home and abroad. Weston, Cottington and Laud had earned an indefinite reprieve from the Parliament which they dreaded.[141] Olivares, in his hour of desperate need, had all but extinguished the Caroline crusade. But the citadel had also been surrendered from within. A nation's, like an individual's, capacity to fight is not only physical but spiritual also. Ideologically divided and politically dislocated, England in 1630 had lost that capacity.

The Treaty of Madrid was the linchpin of a whole diplomatic edifice which served to make England a non-combatant satellite of Spain. In late 1630 secret proposals were made to Charles for Anglo-Spanish naval co-operation to the detriment of the Dutch. He told Coloma of his eagerness to implement them, which indeed he soon did. When Dutch and Spanish vessels found themselves together in the same English port, the stronger force was obliged to wait at least two tides before pursuing the weaker. This greatly hindered Dutch attacks and assisted Spanish supplies for the war in Flanders to escape unmolested. Dutch prizes taken from Spain were sequestered in English ports and Charles's government was able to suspend Admiralty judgements against Spanish shipping. Dunkirk privateers were allowed to shelter and refit in English and Scottish ports. These measures were a reversal of the pattern by which the Dutch had enjoyed such privileges in England. This was a particular handicap to the West India Company ships, which needed the haven provided by England en route to the Netherlands. At sea the English navy protected the Spanish convoys. The availability of the English carrying trade, with the safety given by neutral vessels, complemented these arrangements.[142] Before leaving Spain, Cottington was given permission to negotiate for the coining in London of a proportion of the silver sent by the 'English road' to pay the army of Flanders. It was public knowledge in England that he had returned in the spring of 1631 with a load of bullion, thus personally inaugurating this mutually advantageous Anglo-Spanish arrangement.[143] As it happened, these agreements were of greater practical consequence than the notorious Cottington Treaty which they accompanied.

On 2 January 1631 Olivares and Cottington signed articles of alliance for

---

[141] AGS, E2562, Coloma to Infanta, 5 Dec. 1630 (n.s.).
[142] AGS, E2519, exp. 94, 114, 131, and E2562, consulta of 4 Nov. 1630 (n.s.); SP94/35/fos. 6r–10v, 39r–41v, 71r–75r, 219r–v, 311v–312v; *CSPV 1629–32*, pp. 426, 438, 461, 467, 484, 491, 502–3, 506, 541, 551; Loomie, 'Spanish faction', p. 38; Jones, *Britain and Europe*, p. 23; Reeve, 'Viscount Dorchester', p. 298; see also chapter 6, above.
[143] Green, *Diary of John Rous*, p. 59; *CSPV 1629–32*, pp. 458–9, 471, 480–1, 490–1; Birch, ii, pp. 100, 103; Gardiner, *History*, vii, p. 177; see also p. 207, n. 166, above.

joint Anglo-Spanish action for the conquest of the United Provinces. The treaty made provision for the partition of those provinces and the ceding of certain areas (to be agreed upon) to England. The English war effort would be subsidized by Spain. The practice of the Roman religion was to be freely allowed in those territories under English control. No similar guarantee was inserted for Protestantism under the government of Spain. The articles needed ratification by Philip and Charles, but the agreement was destined never to be concluded. In England in 1629, Cottington and Rubens had suggested to Charles that such an alliance would be appropriate compensation for a Palatine restoration. While Charles believed that Frederick and Elizabeth should be restored by right, and harboured the hope that this might be so achieved, he hated the Dutch and certainly treasured the notion of laying them low. Clearly he authorized Cottington to hold discussions along these lines and to formulate a possible agreement. From Olivares' point of view, an Anglo-Spanish alliance against the Dutch would be ideal. The fall of Bois-le-Duc in September 1629 recommended it more urgently. The count-duke may well have been encouraged to believe in the efficacy of such an enterprise by the successful conclusion of the peace treaty with the aid of the Spanish faction in England.[144]

Charles, to be sure, would have contemplated the articles of the Cottington Treaty with a mixture of glee and frustration. Militating against the satisfying notion of an Anglo-Spanish victory over the Dutch were two very powerful and virtually insuperable factors. One was the sheer authority, the economic and military power of the Dutch, which implied an enormous risk in open English action against them. (Charles's fear of the Dutch was well founded.) The other was the fact of English Protestantism. Given the essential dependence of English war finance upon parliamentary subsidies, this always stood between Charles and full alliance with the Spain of Philip IV. It would require another two decades of intensified Anglo-Dutch rivalry, the significant growth of English power and the political complications of revolution in England before an English government was prepared to engage in war against the United Provinces. Cottington, in this sense, was ahead of his time. Another consideration might have undermined concerted action by England and Spain against the Dutch. Olivares was aware of the danger of replacing Dutch with enhanced English power in the critical areas adjacent to Spanish Flanders. An article of the Cottington Treaty would oblige England not to

---

[144] Bodl. Lib., Ms Clarendon 5, fos. 38r–39r, 44r, 56r; AGS, E2519, exp. 114, 139, and E2562, Council of State, 7 Jan. 1632 (n.s.); *CSPV 1629–32*, p. 500; Magurn, *Rubens letters*, pp. 343–4; Alcalà-Zamora, *España, Flandes*, p. 265; Elliott, *Count-duke of Olivares*, pp. 403–5; Gardiner, *History*, vii, pp. 176–7; M. J. Havran, *Caroline courtier: the life of Lord Cottington* (London, 1973), pp. 96ff.; Reeve, 'Viscount Dorchester', p. 318.

interfere with the sea approaches to Antwerp and Holland. The realities of power politics and of international strategy could well intrude upon another of Olivares' treasured schemes.[145]

The Treaty of Madrid, Philip's undertaking to Charles, the Cottington Treaty and the Anglo-Spanish naval and financial agreements together constituted a diplomatic package the achievement of which was, under the circumstances, a recognizable coup. Cottington's career was boosted by his mission which caused Charles to grant him a peerage. The episode had a positive effect upon the king, pandering to his desire to damage the Dutch and keeping alive his hopes of a German settlement freely recognizing Frederick's rights.[146] The reorientation of English foreign policy after 1630 was clear. Favour to Spain was also evident in the generous rights to levy troops in England and Ireland, the obstruction of French and Dutch fishing in English waters and the low customs rates on Spanish goods re-exported from England.[147] In January 1631 Coloma reported the pleasure of his English friends at the safe arrival of one of the Atlantic treasure fleets.[148] In April the Venetian ambassador in England, Giovanni Soranzo, wrote: 'there is no doubt that they aim here at giving an advantage to the Spaniards in everything possible . . . '[149] In October Charles's envoy in Madrid, Sir Arthur Hopton, described his master's foreign policy as pro-Habsburg.[150] Dorchester complained to Soranzo of the way in which England was spoken of abroad 'as if it were altogether, so he put it, corrupted by the Spaniards . . . as if they [the English] meant to join with them in making war on the States'.[151] The actual Cottington Treaty was apparently kept secret from all in England save Charles and his closest Hispanophile confidants. Yet an alliance such as it outlined was but the logical extension of the arrangements already being implemented. The treaty, while never ratified, represents the complete division of Charles's government on questions of foreign policy. Against the English tradition of Protestant war, which saw the Dutch as endangered

---

[145] Bodl. Lib., Ms Clarendon 5, fo. 39r; AGS, E2562, consulta on treaty with England, 4 Nov. 1630 (n.s.), voto of Olivares, Nov. 1631; Magurn, *Rubens letters*, pp. 343–4; *CSPV 1629–32*, p. 522; SP84/140/fo. 225r; Archivo del Duque del Infantado, Madrid, Palafox Mss, leg. 94, fo. 136v (I am grateful to John Elliott for this reference); Reade, *Sidelights on the Thirty Years War*, iii, p. 496; Israel, *Dutch republic*, p. 398; Alcalá-Zamora, *España, Flandes*, pp. 265n, 292, 347; Jones, *Britain and Europe*, ch. 4; Elliott, *Count-duke of Olivares*, pp. 293–5, 332.

[146] AGS, E2519, exp. 114; Gardiner, *History*, vii, pp. 177–8.

[147] AGS, E2519, exp. 131, and E2562, consulta of 15 Mar. 1631 (n.s.); *CSPV 1629–32*, p. 530; Loomie, 'Spanish faction', pp. 42, 48; Kepler, 'Fiscal aspects of the English carrying trade', pp. 265, 279.

[148] AGS, E2562, Coloma to Philip IV, 2 Feb. 1631 (n.s.).

[149] *CSPV 1629–32*, p. 493.

[150] SP94/35/fo. 309r–v, Hopton to Weston, 23 Oct. 1631.

[151] *CSPV 1629–32*, p. 530, Soranzo to the Doge and Senate, 22 July 1631.

co-religionists and Elizabeth and Frederick as martyrs, there was a new approach to policy, patronized by Charles, concerned with the emerging menace of France and the Dutch, the relevance of Flanders to England's security and the growing importance of English trade to southern Europe – an approach which had, during this period, its own cultural milieu. The ascendancy of such counsel in England served the interests of an embattled Spain. To disconnect English policy from the common effort of the Protestant world was a significant achievement.[152]

As Olivares had intended, his policy towards England had a destructive effect upon Anglo-Dutch relations. The Treaty of Madrid and Charles's alignment with Spain brought Anglo-Dutch rivalry to the verge of open hostility and poisoned Anglo-Dutch relations for years to come.[153] Dorchester felt this keenly, having spent years as ambassador at the Hague promoting an alliance he considered vital to England and based upon common interests.[154] He strove to preserve it despite the effect of Charles's negotiations with Spain. Olivares, seeking to isolate the Dutch by drawing England out of her alliance with the bait of the Palatinate, also sought to remove Dutch power from the German question and to keep that issue out of the talks in the Netherlands.[155] As well as seeking to divide her enemies, Spain wished to divide the Dutch among themselves, to take the edge off their resolve for war and to promote the Dutch movement for peace.[156] Charles's attitude facilitated the ends of Spain. He sought to dissolve the Dutch alliance by mediating peace in the Netherlands; and he refused, as we have seen, to sanction the creation of an English West India company.[157] His treaty with Spain, while it encouraged the development of pro- and anti-Dutch parties in England, divided the Dutch on the issue of the English alliance, underlining existing divisions in Dutch politics.[158] Charles thus lessened the chances of his own satisfaction by forfeiting the advantages to England of Dutch power, and of Dutch goodwill towards the Palatines,[159] and furthering Spanish policy.

---

[152] AGS, E2519, exp. 134, and E2562, Council of State, 8 Mar. 1630 (n.s.); Magurn, *Rubens letters*, pp. 333–5, 342–5; HMC, 7th report, Appx, p. 548; Reeve, 'Viscount Dorchester', pp. 286, 319; Alcalá-Zamora, *España, Flandes*, pp. 344–7; P. Haskell, 'Sir Francis Windebank and the personal rule of Charles I' (unpublished Southampton University PhD thesis, 1975), ch. 6; Reade, *Sidelights on the Thirty Years War*, iii, p. 447.

[153] *CSPV 1629–32*, pp. 492–7; C. V. Wedgwood, *The king's peace 1637–41* (London, 1955), pp. 117–18; Jones, *Britain and Europe*, p. 23.

[154] SP92/13/fos. 228r–229r, SP92/16/fo. 208r; SP84/137/fos. 255r–256r, SP84/142/fo. 207r; SP81/35/fo. 218r–v.

[155] SP84/140/fos. 180r–181r, SP84/141/fos. 74r–78r.

[156] SP84/140/fos. 66r–69v, 86r–87r; PRO 31/3/66/fo. 261; Magurn, *Rubens letters*, pp. 342–5.

[157] Magurn, *Rubens letters*, pp. 342–5; SP84/141/fos. 98r–99r.

[158] SP84/142/fos. 14r–20v, SP84/144/fos. 56r–57r; AGS, E2519, exp. 49; Israel, *Dutch republic*, ch. 4 (v).

[159] SP84/140/fos. 36r–40r.

The spectacular military victories of 1628 and 1629, which had placed the United Provinces in such a commanding position over Spain, had caused Charles, Weston and Cottington the deepest regret.[160] The king and those most influential with him were utterly out of sympathy with the course of the war in Flanders. This attitude, and the prospect of peace with Spain, governed the instructions Charles issued to Vane when sending him on a mission to the United Provinces in October 1629. Vane was to investigate the attitude of the Dutch to a possible treaty with Spain by English mediation. His instructions were pure Charles. They exhibit that blend of unctuous rectitude, devious literalness, selfishness, pure ignorance, clear ideological preference and rationalization of betrayal which rendered so many of Charles's political endeavours positively destructive. The king believed, perhaps rightly, that the current Dutch talks with Spain freed him of the Treaty of Southampton and that he dealt with the Dutch by condescension. This belief was, however, without regard to his own breach of faith in dealing with Rubens.[161] Charles told Vane that if the Dutch continued to treat separately he would consider himself freed of obligation towards them. Otherwise he would treat by common consent and would include the interests of the Palatines, obtaining a satisfactory settlement or resuming the war.[162] Vane left for the Hague at the same time as Cottington for Spain. The Anglo-Dutch alliance was certainly not beyond repair. Charles, however, broke an undertaking to the Dutch ambassador Joachimi that the republic would be consulted before Cottington's departure.[163] His intentions, moreover, were definitely deleterious to Dutch interests. If the Dutch did not treat for peace on Charles's terms they would be abandoned. Effectively they would be given no alternative. He did not wish to be obliged by alliance to continue the war or to solicit their consent to his negotiations. Charles, moreover, was clearly not averse to the idea of an active alliance against them.[164] The drafts of Vane's instructions reflect Dorchester's efforts to persuade the king of the value of the Dutch alliance, but to no avail.[165]

Charles's choice of envoy was indicative. Vane sought favour and had an

[160] Magurn, *Rubens letters*, pp. 342–5.
[161] There is a *prima facie* case for a Dutch, as well as an English, breach of faith. The prince of Orange responded positively to Spanish overtures of May 1629 by July. No notice was given to Charles (who had begun talks with Rubens in June) of this exchange. Before September the prince told the English representatives in the republic that the Dutch were entitled to treat alone since Charles had done so. Israel, *Dutch republic*, p. 227 and n; SP84/140/ fos. 36r–40r.
[162] SP84/140/fos. 101r–105v, 107r–121v; SP104/170, pp. 42–8, instructions for Vane going to the United Provinces, 18 Oct. 1629.
[163] *CSPV 1629–32*, p. 162.
[164] Ibid., pp. 161–3; Magurn, *Rubens letters*, pp. 334, 341–5; SP78/85/fo. 238r–v; PRO 31/3/66/fos. 176r, 239r–v; Bodl. Lib., Ms Clarendon 5, fos. 38r–39r, 44r, 56r.
[165] Reeve, 'Viscount Dorchester', pp. 295–6.

essentially pragmatic approach to foreign policy. He was also an ally of Weston and at the Hague was distrustful and unsympathetic towards the Dutch.[166] In England Dorchester continued to counsel Charles to remain committed to the Dutch and the Palatine cause in war.[167] The king did not understand the political value of military pressure upon Spain when after grievous defeats she was attempting to fight in both northern and southern Europe.[168] On the contrary, with a treaty now being formulated in Madrid, in July 1630 Charles instructed Vane to press the States to a resolution. He also offered a few strategic reflections remarkable for muddled thinking and their distance from reality. He announced the end of any attempt to pursue the strategy of war by diversion against Spain, regardless of the fact that this had never been properly done. Buckingham or Charles, however, could not be the cause of failure, 'for experience hath shown us that to beat the king of Spain until he bring the emperor to reason is not the next [sic] way to gain our desires.'[169] Charles complained of the understandable neutrality of France and the Dutch towards the German conflict. If his Spanish negotiations failed, he was confident of retaking the Palatinate by arms.[170] This was, however, highly dubious, added to which Charles had just refused the Swedish request for aid. Above all, it was not necessary to abandon the Dutch to treat with Spain. Charles's attitude combined political ineptitude and self-preoccupation with an antipathy to recalling Parliament, a strong belief in Spain and a fear that the Dutch would obstruct a settlement. He was both ignorant of, and here averse to, the merits of staying with the strength in diplomacy and war.

In view of Charles's attitude it was unlikely that the States General, in such a powerful position, would place their interests in his hands. The prince of Orange, Frederick Henry, wished well to the Palatines. He believed that Charles could capitalize on the Dutch victories in negotiating their restoration. He also believed, however, that Charles had broken the Anglo-Dutch alliance and suspected (as did the Dutch generally) the nature of the Anglo-Spanish agreement. Charles, as Frederick Henry understood, was acting as an agent of Spanish policy, and Vane (the prince told the Venetian resident) was practically the ambassador of Spain.[171] Vane's mission served to promote dis-

---

166 Vane was also connected to Cottington and Arundel. He had supported the idea of a Spanish marriage. SP84/141/fos. 34r–37v, 70r–v, 74r–78r, 142r–143v, 192r–197r, 210r–211v, SP84/142/fos. 32r–33r, 83r, 146r–147r, SP84/143/fo. 38v; *DNB*, s.v. Vane, Sir Henry, the elder; *CSPD 1625–49*, p. 336; Birch, ii, pp. 94, 101; *CSPV 1629–32*, p. 141; see also p. 182, n. 56, above.
167 SP84/141/fos. 98r–99r.
168 Israel, *Dutch republic*, p. 174; Parker, *Army of Flanders*, pp. 256–7.
169 SP84/141/fo. 286r–v.   170 SP84/141/fos. 284r–286v.
171 SP84/140/fos. 36r–40r, 215r–216r, SP84/142/fos. 14r–20v, 32r–33r; *CSPV 1629–32*, pp. 161–3, 382, 401–2, 433, 513–14; Gardiner, *History*, vii, p. 176.

cussion within the republic but otherwise had no positive impact on Dutch views.[172] Eager to conclude the Treaty of Madrid, in September 1630 Charles gave the Dutch an ultimatum: delay on their part would terminate his negotiations with them.[173] The States General made no reply before England concluded peace with Spain and saw the Treaty of Madrid as extremely damaging to Dutch and particularly English interests. Disillusioned with England and wooed once more by Richelieu, the Dutch had concluded a new subsidy treaty with France in June 1630 and agreed in May 1631 to contribute (as France had begun to do) to the Swedish campaign. The States General's answer to Charles was a foregone conclusion. They preferred to treat without England. This they did, despite the continuation of the war, throughout the 1630s. Spanish influence caused Anglo-Dutch relations to worsen steadily and inflamed existing commercial and naval rivalry. Dorchester worked to favour Dutch shipping, but Charles and Weston settled into their policy of pro-Habsburg neutrality, which brought England and the Dutch to the brink of war. The Anglo-Dutch alliance was dissolved and the strategy of Olivares had succeeded.[174] With his peace policy, Charles had forfeited his position in the anti-Habsburg camp to France and Richelieu had seized the chance to erect his own coalition.

While the face of European affairs had altered dramatically, and Charles had turned from war to diplomacy, the political disorders in England had given way to greater calm. The king enjoyed the absence of national crisis as well as his domestic life.[175] Yet he considered his honour engaged in the Palatine cause. While he had great hopes of Spain, his search for a peaceful settlement had still produced nothing by late 1630, and the case for war, his stated alternative, was strong. Dorchester advocated the war, and Frederick called for continued negotiations in Germany as well as aid to Gustavus.[176] Vane equivocated but sought to warn Charles against the dangers of just such a policy in 'this difficult after-game',

---

[172] Israel, *Dutch republic*, pp. 237–8, 300.   [173] SP84/142/fos. 66r–67v.

[174] If independent English and Dutch negotiations had not broken the Treaty of Southampton, as both parties held they had, the conclusion of the Treaty of Madrid and the Dutch refusal of mediation and resolution to treat separately would have done so and freed Charles of obligation to the United Provinces. Under the Treaty of Compiègne (1624) French subsidies were paid to the Dutch but were temporarily suspended with a slump in Franco-Dutch relations during the late 1620s. The Franco-Swedish Treaty of Bärwalde was concluded in January 1631 (see below). See also SP77/20/fos. 27r–35v; SP78/87/fos. 182r–185r, 362r–v; SP84/140/fo. 225r, SP84/141/fos. 291r–292r, SP84/142/fos. 100v, 231r–232r, 236r–239r, 242r–243v, SP84/143/fos. 81, 101r–v, SP84/144/fos. 61r–67r; PRO 31/3/66/fo. 272r–v; CSPV 1629–32, pp. 438–9, 445, 466–7, 487, 525; Israel, *Dutch republic*, pp. 224–5, 236–49; Alcalá-Zamora, *España, Flandes*, pp. 299–300, 306, 308–10; Parker, *Thirty Years War*, pp. xxxii, 124; Wedgwood, *Thirty Years War*, p. 291; Birch, ii, pp. 175–6. See also p. 256, n. 142 and p. 259, n. 153, above.

[175] See chapters 5 and 6, above.

[176] SP16/173/49; SP84/142/fos. 253r–254r, SP84/143/fo. 29r–v.

which ... will either render you more glorious or more unfortunate than any of your predecessors, whether God dispose your heart to peace or war ... half ways will neither settle your government at home nor keep friends abroad ... [177]

Having failed in war and thus far in peace Charles was unable to choose between them. Fearing the implications of war and of failure he adopted, during 1631, an equivocal position which involved a partial return to participation in the European war. But with events on the continent ripening for a Palatine restoration by arms, or on the basis of negotiation from strength, Charles would not recommit himself to the war. The failure of this equivocal policy, which involved trying to play both sides in the German conflict, caused him to be eclipsed by French and Swedish initiatives and led to England's complete withdrawal from the Thirty Years War.

In the process of making peace, which Charles had come to prefer to war, he had definitely reduced his military options. Glad to be rid of the Dutch, he detested and suspected the French and had refused financial aid to the Swedes. Charles thus found himself distanced from all the major anti-Habsburg powers. He did sanction, as we have seen, British levies for Gustavus, hoping by this limited contribution to keep the goodwill of the Swedish king. He also entertained, briefly, French overtures for an alliance against Spain and the emperor. Such an alliance was an unlikely and dubious proposition from the English point of view, given Charles's commitment to Spain and Richelieu's nationalistic – and Catholic – ambitions in the international sphere, particularly in Germany. Charles, however, out of pragmatism and insecurity, negotiated with France during the winter of 1630–1. These dealings came to nothing. It is difficult to believe that either party was completely serious and that there was not a strong element of cynicism on both sides. These dealings were part of the tangled web of Anglo-French relations during this period, a subject in itself.

The Anglo-French war had left ill will between the two nations and paved the way for French leadership against the Habsburgs.[178] With the end of the conflict, the possibility of an Anglo-French alliance was secondary to that of an alignment between England and Spain. The French alliance solicited by Chateauneuf in England in 1629 was prevented by Charles's undertaking that pending a Spanish treaty he would not ally with France against Spain. Richelieu had essentially offered an alliance to prevent an Anglo-Spanish agreement. With France engaged in Italy, it was most unlikely that he would have made any commitment to English ends in Germany. The French cultivation of Bavaria and the cardinal's reluctance to declare openly against Spain were also obstacles to an Anglo-French alliance. Richelieu, however,

---

[177] SP84/143/fo. 38v, draft of Vane to Charles, *c.* late 1630.
[178] *CSPV 1629–32*, pp. 251–2, 310, 464, 470.

continued to court England during 1629 and 1630. His overriding intention
was to divide London and Madrid. He was also interested in exploiting any
available English resources in the battle against the Habsburgs.[179]

During this period, Anglo-French relations were affected by struggles of
faction and personality. These conflicts involved the competing interests of
England, France and Spain as well as those of certain individuals. In 1629 and
1630 the major foreign interests in English politics were those of France and
Spain as those two nations competed for England's favour. In 1631 international politics were complicated by Richelieu's crucial victory over his
domestic opponents: the French queen mother and Louis XIII's brother,
Gaston of Orléans.[180] Both fled abroad, exporting the division in French
politics just as French influence was increasing in Europe. In England, as we
have seen, Henrietta Maria was a natural, while politically limited, focus of
French interests. Around her and the ambassador Chateauneuf gathered
those sympathetic to France and to Richelieu and antipathetic to Spain. Their
principal political opponent was of course Weston. Chateauneuf failed to
achieve an Anglo-French commercial agreement and later in France, as
Keeper of the Seals, was jealous of Fontenay, his successor as ambassador,
who became associated with Weston.[181] The Treasurer, wanting peace at
home and abroad, did not want England to become involved in the developing Franco-Spanish conflict by lapsing into war with France. He entered into
a correspondence with Richelieu in 1629 and 1630 which the cardinal seems
to have treated with suitable suspicion. Weston found it as convenient to
humour French overtures of alliance as Richelieu to make them. It was in the
latter's interest to minimize Anglo-Spanish conspiracy.[182]

Yet Weston could not prevent England from being significantly drawn into
the escalating Franco-Spanish contest. Charles's Spanish treaty had linked
him to the international enemies of Richelieu, particularly Marie de' Medici
who was deeply involved in Spanish intrigues. This caused Charles to be
caught in a cross-fire of political conspiracy. Olivares wished to turn England

---

179 Avenel, *Lettres de Richelieu*, iii, p. 432–3, 447, 503–7, 671–3; AMRE, CPA, 44, fos. 70r–v,
     75r–76v, 92r; Magurn, *Rubens letters*, pp. 304, 315–16, 346–7; PRO 31/3/66/fos. 148r–v,
     158r–v; SP78/84/fos. 124, 158v, 231, SP78/86/fo. 4; SP84/141/fos. 171–173r; SP92/18/
     fos. 140r–142v; *CSPV 1629–32*, pp. 324–5, 330–2.
180 Parker, *Europe in crisis*, pp. 205–6.
181 AMRE, CPA, 44, fos. 296r–v, 303r; SP16/193/51; SP78/86/fo. 359r–v, SP78/89/fos.
     338r–340r, SP78/90/fo. 128r–130r; PRO 31/3/67/fos. 16r–18v, 20r–v, 23r–25r, 32r, 35r;
     CSPV 1629–32, pp. 141–3, 311, 314–15, 585; Magurn, *Rubens letters*, p. 486n; Gardiner,
     History, vii, pp. 184–6; Hibbard, *Popish plot*, p. 32; Alexander, *Charles I's Lord Treasurer*,
     p. 156. On Henrietta Maria's circle see also chapter 6, above.
182 AMRE, CPA, 43, fos. 47r, 338r–v, and 44, fos. 44r, 70r–v, 75r–76v, 292r; Avenel, *Lettres
     de Richelieu*, iii, pp. 503–7, 671–3; Reeve, 'Viscount Dorchester', p. 315n; Gardiner,
     History, vii, pp. 184, 186, 217–19.

against France and to foment revolution against the Richelieu regime in favour of the queen mother's party. He sought to have Charles intervene in her favour, if necessary by force. He promoted jealousy between England and France as he had between England and the Dutch. Anglo-French relations were strained during 1631, particularly after the queen mother fled to the Spanish Netherlands. Richelieu feared Anglo-Spanish action against him. He built up his naval forces, causing England to do the same. The cardinal also conspired to have Marie de' Medici seek refuge with her daughter and thus foil Spain by causing division in England, now virtually a Spanish political satellite. Charles disavowed the idea of the queen mother's coming, fearing the expense as well as the political implications of harbouring such a refugee.[183] Dorchester lamented 'the interest France and Spain take upon them to monopolize in the affections of this court ... to what presumption are those two nations grown, to think they can part and divide the world?'[184] Partisan sentiments, however, had roots at home and in the mind of the king himself.

Overtures were made to Charles by Richelieu in August 1630 for an alliance to retake the Lower Palatinate from Spain. The dealings which followed were the work of Henrietta Maria's circle in England – Montagu, Dorchester and Holland – and of Chateauneuf in France, who sought an agreement at the expense of his enemies Weston and Fontenay.[185] Richelieu wanted Charles to break off negotiations with Spain. Charles, however, wished to see the result of his treaty and would not withdraw Cottington. He listened to the terms being offered by France. Louis and Richelieu wanted Charles to join in supporting Gustavus and the Dutch and suggested Anglo-French action in Germany at some future time. France would supposedly intercede with Bavaria for Frederick and garrison the Lower Palatinate if restored by Spain. These terms implied not only financial commitment and likely involvement in war, but also that English and Palatine interests be drawn into the French sphere of influence. Charles, discouraged by Weston, was noncommittal. England would join France to aid Gustavus when the Swedish power of restoration was demonstrated.

The likelihood of these talks producing an agreement was minimal.

---

183 Marie de' Medici actually went to England in 1638. SP78/87/fos. 453r–v, 486r, SP78/89/fos. 227r, 336r, 357r–358r, SP78/90/fos. 27r–28v, 128r–130r, 187r–189v, 206r, 236r–238r, 240r–241r; SP84/143/fo. 186r–v; SP94/35/fo. 263; SP77/20/fos. 55r–57r, 168r, 169r–171v, 214r–215r, 326r–328r, 401r; PRO 31/3/67/fos. 22r, 24r; *CSPV 1629–32*, pp. 484, 492, 500, 528–9, 536 , 542, 581–2; SP16/190/18, SP16/193/44; AGS, E2519, exp. 133; Searle, *Barrington family letters*, pp. 133–4; Birch, ii, pp. 10–11, 122–3; Magurn, *Rubens letters*, pp. 334, 343–4; Green, *Letters of Henrietta Maria*, pp. 12–13; Gardiner, *History*, vii, pp. 186–7; Reeve, 'Viscount Dorchester', p. 307.
184 SP78/90/fos. 17r–18r, Dorchester to Wake, 10 Aug. 1631.
185 Reeve, 'Viscount Dorchester', pp. 302–3, 308–10, 312–13.

Charles's preference, crystal clear, was for a peaceful settlement by agreement with Spain, not a warlike undertaking with France. His conclusion of the Treaty of Madrid in the midst of the Anglo-French talks underlined this point. Charles confided the French terms to Coloma who reported them to Madrid. Neither did Charles promote goodwill by appointing Sir Isaac Wake – known for being anti-French – as ambassador to France. The contrast with Cottington's appointment to Spain was striking. The French would have preferred Montagu, an opponent of Weston, who coveted the post.

Richelieu had failed to prevent the Treaty of Madrid. This had been his principal aim in dealing with England in 1630 and 1631. Beyond his fears of overt or covert Anglo-Spanish action against him, he would probably not have refused English aid in the new war he was promoting in Germany. The extent to which he would honour any commitment to the Protestant Palatines was very dubious. He did not wish them to have any stake or involvement in French politics.[186] Within the context of his anti-Habsburg ambitions, the cardinal was seeking a role as protector of Bavaria and the German Catholics not readily reconcilable with the promotion of Frederick's restoration. On 13 January 1631 Richelieu concluded the Treaty of Bärwalde with Sweden. He undertook to finance for five years what was effectively a Swedish war on the emperor. The treaty made no reference to the Palatines and provided for the neutrality of Bavaria and the territories of the Catholic League – a potential obstacle to Frederick's full restoration. It was open to any German ruler who wished to ally against the emperor: an invitation to the German Protestants.[187] A new phase of the Thirty Years War had begun.

Charles may have just sensed that this was so. In characteristic fashion he did not wish to neglect entirely the chance to be associated, however ineffectively, with the Swedish intervention. He had allowed the adventurous young Hamilton to levy English and Scottish volunteers to serve Gustavus and the Palatine cause under the marquis's command. With difficulty a force of 7,000 men was raised, which sailed for the Baltic in July of 1631. The financial

---

186 Richelieu, in Louis's name, forbade Madame de Rohan to marry her daughter to the eldest son of Frederick of Bohemia unless, apparently, the daughter left France; SP78/89/fo. 100r. On the Anglo-French negotiations in 1630–1 see AMRE, CPA, 44, fos. 236r–237r, 257r–258r, 290r; AGS, E2519, exp. 120–1, and E2562, Coloma to Philip IV, 2 Feb. 1631 (n.s.), consulta of 15 Mar. 1631 (n.s.); Avenel, *Lettres de Richelieu*, iv, pp. 40–1; Magurn, *Rubens letters*, p. 346; Reeve, 'Viscount Dorchester', pp. 309–12, 314–16.

187 Richelieu concluded the Swedish alliance immediately upon hearing that the Mantuan war had been ended by an agreement at Regensburg. The Treaty of Bärwalde was officially an alliance for 'the restitution of the suppressed Estates of the Empire'. It provided for respect for Catholic worship in conquered areas where it already existed. SP78/88/fos. 155–6; SP84/143/fos. 97–8; Parker, *Europe in crisis*, pp. 218–19; Parker, *Thirty Years War*, pp. 119–20, 124–5, 128; Wedgwood, *Thirty Years War*, pp. 278–9; Gardiner, *History*, vii, p. 179. When Gustavus intervened in Germany after 1630 he had Russian as well as French and Dutch support; Parker, *Thirty Years War*, p. 80.

support for the expedition was grossly inadequate. Charles had provided a modest sum of between £20,000 and £40,000, which could really only gather and launch the force.[188] Hamilton's men would effectively be dependent upon Gustavus for the indefinite future. Strictly speaking, Charles was not responsible internationally for the consequences of the expedition, since Hamilton was arguably acting as a private individual. Yet Charles fancied that this qualified recommitment to the war would prompt Habsburg concessions while serving to restrain the Swedish king. For Charles was also offering his services as an arbitrator and peacemaker in the German conflict.[189] His policy during 1631 was thus thoroughly equivocal. He was, however, insufficiently involved to affect the outcome of events, particularly when Swedish victories greatly altered the situation and escalated the German war. Gustavus wished to restore Frederick and looked to England, but Charles's refusal of aid in 1630 had forced him to ally with the French whom he distrusted. He continued to solicit and obviously would have preferred an English alliance.[190] Charles was urged on by Hamilton, Dorchester and Roe. Weston was horrified at the possible revival of a war policy and desperately worked against it.[191] The potential Anglo-Swedish alliance became the subject of a political battle in England during the winter of 1631–2: a contest which would confirm the orientation of the Caroline regime.

Hamilton's contribution to the continental war was less than distinguished. Gustavus sent him, in the autumn of 1631, to guard the fortresses at the mouth of the Oder in Silesia while the Swedes engaged the army of the League. Hamilton's force was then involved in the blockade of Magdeburg before it was abandoned by the enemy. By the end of 1631, however, that force had almost ceased to exist. Ill provided for, the men fell mass-victims to famine and disease. Estimates of their able number at that time went as low

---

[188] SRO, Hamilton Mss, nos. 123–4, 141, 145–7, 158, 206, 9255, 9273, 9277, 9320, 9322, 9337, 9360, 9631, 10444–53, 10464–7; *CSPV 1629–32*, pp. 414–15, 537–8, 550–1; Birch, ii, pp. 87–8, 100, 102; Searle, *Barrington family letters*, pp. 197, 217; SP84/143/fo. 217r; BL, Harl. Ms 6988, fo. 89r–v; Gardiner, *History*, vii, pp. 174–5, 178 and n, 181–3; Parker, *Thirty Years War*, pp. 195–6; *DNB*, s.v. Hamilton, James, third marquis and first duke of Hamilton; Clarendon, *Rebellion*, vol. iv, p. 491.

[189] SP75/12/fos. 204r–209v, Charles's instructions to Vane for his mission to Denmark, Sweden and Germany, Sept. 1631. See also SP80/7/fos. 217r, 218r–v, 234v, 280r–v; SP81/36/ fos. 214r–215r; Gardiner, *History*, vii, pp. 175, 178; Reeve, 'Quiroga's paper', p. 922; Reeve, 'Viscount Dorchester', pp. 326–7.

[190] SP84/144/fos. 31v, 77r–v; SP88/5/fos. 186–7; SP95/3/fos. 60r–61r, 81r, 128r–v; SP75/11/ fos. 262v–263r, 272r; SP78/90/fo. 221v; SRO, Hamilton Mss, nos. 9256–7, 9298, 10445.

[191] Weston attempted unsuccessfully to smear Hamilton with treason. Gardiner, *History*, vii, pp. 182–3; Reeve, 'Viscount Dorchester', pp. 302, 322–3; Alexander, *Charles I's Lord Treasurer*, pp. 180–1; *CSPV 1629–32*, pp. 537–8; SRO, Hamilton Mss, nos. 209, 231–2, 242, 267.

as 500.[192] In England, perusing the dispatches and newsbooks, Dorchester put the best face on this unhappy story, placing it in the context of the revival of a long forlorn Protestant cause. His cool diplomatic exterior gave way to the passionate voice of Calvinist war, in which England had her chance to play a role. Hamilton, Dorchester believed, was in a 'way of virtue and glory'. He wrote to the marquis that this contribution justified the losses,

which sickness and other casualties (not unusual to our English troops before they are accustomed to the discommodities of the field) have . . . occasioned. But your Excellency I know looks forward and upon the new work whereunto you are called . . . the siege of Magdeburg . . . where you may have the honour to revenge the rape committed on that maiden city and withall recover to your side a passage of much importance . . . [193]

Dorchester wished to remedy any flagging on the marquis's part, but Charles did not share his religious enthusiasm. The king, moreover, was affected by the sufferings of his men.[194] As Hamilton's force dwindled and as negotiations with Gustavus – and with the Habsburgs – proved abortive, England's withdrawal from the Thirty Years War was completed.

Hamilton's expedition was a symbolic, but not a politically effective, commitment to the war. It was sufficient neither to gain a stake in a German settlement established by Sweden nor to intimidate the Habsburgs into concessions. Anstruther was nevertheless sent to Vienna in March 1631, on the basis of Charles's hopes, renewed by Cottington's return from Spain. Anstruther's instructions stated clearly Charles's preference for peace over war. While Anstruther was a protégé of Dorchester and supported the war, he was also a specialist in German affairs and a dutiful envoy who followed instructions. He was on a hopeless mission, making his dangerous way across a war-torn Germany which rendered his negotiations futile. The emperor faced not only the advance of Gustavus, but also a powerful and disaffected Bavaria supported by France. Maximilian was now the strongest political and military force in the Empire, increasingly suspicious of Habsburg diplomacy and designs. Yet in the wake of the Franco-Swedish alliance of Bärwalde, he urgently needed an arrangement with Cardinal Richelieu. In May 1631 he concluded a secret alliance for the mutual defence of France and

---

[192] SP81/37/fo. 176v; SP95/3/fos. 148r–149r, 167r–v; *DNB*, s.v. Hamilton, James, third marquis and first duke of Hamilton; Parker, *Thirty Years War*, pp. 202–3; Gardiner, *History*, vii, pp. 190–1; SRO, Hamilton Mss, nos. 233, 9245–6, 9248, 9250, 9355–8, 9361–2, 9368, 10454, 10457–9.

[193] SP95/3/fos. 148r–149r, Dorchester to Hamilton, 13 Nov. 1631. The brutal sacking of Magdeburg and the accompanying slaughter, in May 1631, was without parallel in the Thirty Years War. Wedgwood, *Thirty Years War*, pp. 286–91; Parker, *Thirty Years War*, p. 125.

[194] AGS, E2519, exp. 139; Gardiner, *History*, vii, p. 191.

Bavaria, the Treaty of Fontainebleau, which placed the electoral title and the Upper Palatinate under French protection in the interests of Maximilian and his heirs.[195] French ambitions in Germany had become a potent threat to the Habsburgs.

Moreover, Ferdinand's intention to uphold the imperial Edict of Restitution implied a deepening religious war in Germany. The Swedish advance was fanning the flames of such a conflict with each new day. Gustavus had raised the banner of Protestantism and increasingly recognized only friend or foe.[196] In Madrid this appeared a highly dangerous development and a threat to the overall imperial interests of Spain. Olivares did not relish the prospect of diverting precious forces from Flanders to fight the Swedes in a conflict which was serving to advance heresy and the ends of the anti-Habsburg powers. Gustavus was threatening the political existence of Catholic Germany and the safety of the imperial patrimonial provinces. The ending of the Mantuan war with the Peace of Cherasco (in April 1631) enabled a transfer of Spanish troops and resources away from Italy. Yet Spain was once again preoccupied with two conflicts. Olivares wanted a negotiated settlement in Germany to consolidate the Spanish position in the north. His principal aim in early 1631 was to recover stability in Flanders and to strengthen the Infanta's regime against the expected Dutch assault. This strategy, and the need to defuse the German religious war, involved a political effort to win over or remove Lamormaini. The emperor's confessor was the most powerful hawk in Vienna and was clearly in collusion with Bavaria.[197] In this complex and potentially explosive situation, Spain could afford less than ever to satisfy Charles without some notable advantage in return. The restoration of the Calvinist Frederick to his title and lands in such a strategically vital region would be naked provocation of both Maximilian and Richelieu. It might also offer a prize hostage to fortune as the destiny of the Empire – and of German Catholicism – evolved. Yet it was the earnest hope of Olivares that affairs in Germany and the Netherlands might be managed together for the advancement of Habsburg interests: England and Spain might solve the eternal problem of the Dutch. Philip wrote to the Infanta in

---

[195] In 1623 Maximilian was invested with the electoral title for life only. SP80/7/fos. 180r–183v, 221r–229r, 271r–v, SP80/8/fos. 5r–6v, 38r–39v, 58v; SP94/35/fos. 292r–293r; SP103/10/fos. 181–189; Magurn, *Rubens letters*, pp. 343–4; Reeve, 'Quiroga's paper', pp. 916, 921; Reeve, 'Viscount Dorchester', pp. 329–30; Gardiner, *History*, vii, p. 179; Parker, *Thirty Years War*, pp. 119–20; Bireley, *Religion and politics*, pp. 4, 160.

[196] Bireley, *Religion and politics*, pp. 25, 166–7, 171; Parker, *Thirty Years War*, pp. 113–16, 118, 127–8. On the Edict see p. 236, n. 50, above.

[197] AGS, E2562, voto of Olivares, Nov. 1631; Bireley, *Religion and politics*, pp. 160–5, 166–7, 178–82, 184; Israel, *Dutch republic*, pp. 181, 184–5, 237–8; Elliott, *Count-duke of Olivares*, p. 405; Elliott, *Richelieu and Olivares*, pp. 113, 117–18, 120; Parker, *Thirty Years War*, p. 109.

May that if Charles could perform such a service, Spain would deliver the Lower Palatinate to Frederick. Olivares continued to write to Charles and Cottington during the summer of 1631. By the autumn, England's failure to act was becoming a sore point in Madrid.[198] And while Habsburg anxiety grew with the Swedish advance, Hamilton's role did not facilitate Charles's negotiations. The presence of English troops with the Swedish army was resented in both Spain and Vienna.[199]

In late August it was clear that dramatic developments were approaching in Germany. The imperial Diet at Frankfurt was nearing deadlock, with the Saxon delegates insisting upon the suspension of the Edict of Restitution, the exclusive exercise of Protestantism in cities where then practised and the year 1620 as the touchstone for settling all questions of Catholic ecclesiastical property.[200] As the outlook for political compromise deteriorated, the military situation was hotting up. The army of the League under Tilly, desperately short of provisions, faced the prospect of confronting Gustavus. Trapped between the two forces were the lands of the Lutheran elector, John George of Saxony. In August he refused to allow Tilly to enter his territory, nor would he disband his army as the general requested. The Catholic forces entered Saxony on 25 August and started to lay waste the land. John George reluctantly committed treason against the emperor and immediately allied with Sweden. In Vienna word arrived from Tilly that unless he received money and supplies he would be forced to retreat to the gates of the capital. John George's defection was virtually inevitable in the event of his coming under Catholic attack.[201]

In this emergency, the Spanish ministers in Vienna made some startling revelations to Anstruther.[202] The English ambassador, as instructed, had been seeking a lifting of the imperial ban and the restoration of at least the Lower Palatinate on the basis of the peace made with Spain and the undertaking given by Philip to Charles in favour of Frederick. This reflected Charles's belief that the war with Spain was a struggle justified by right which would be properly ended in fair exchange for Frederick's restitution. There was, however, no incentive for Spain to act for England in the Empire until

[198] Philip also asked Scaglia to discover Charles's views on possible intervention in France. Lonchay, *Correspondance de la cour d'Espagne*, ii, pp. 576–7, 579; SP80/8/fos. 44r–49v; AGS, E2519, exp. 131, and E2562, voto of Olivares, Nov. 1631; Parker, *Thirty Years War*, pp. 108–9.

[199] SP94/35/fos. 199r–v, 252r–253v, 262r–263v, 272r–273r; AGS, E2519, exp. 136, and E2562, voto of Olivares, Nov. 1631; *CSPV 1629–32*, pp. 537–8.

[200] Bireley, *Religion and politics*, pp. 167–8.

[201] The alliance between Sweden and Saxony was signed on 1 September. Ibid., p. 168; Wedgwood, *Thirty Years War*, pp. 279ff., 293–4; Parker, *Thirty Years War*, pp. 115–16, 118, 123, 125–6; SP80/8/fo. 25v.

[202] This episode is discussed at greater length in Reeve, 'Quiroga's paper'.

England herself had been of service in the Netherlands. Accordingly, the Spanish diplomats in Vienna prevaricated throughout the summer. They did not, moreover, reveal to Anstruther the basis of Cottington's agreement. To do so would have been to alert the English war lobby, the Dutch and the whole Protestant international to the progress of an initiative critical for Spanish foreign policy. In the highly threatening circumstances of August, however, the Spaniards put their cards on the table. The promises of their king were conditional, they told Anstruther, upon the contents of a paper given to Cottington in Spain. Anstruther was directed to Diego de Quiroga, a Spanish Capuchin and confessor to the queen of Hungary (sister of Philip IV). Quiroga was the personal political agent of Olivares at the imperial court, placed there by the count-duke to counteract the influence of Lamormaini and to act for Spain in high-level dealings within the Empire. Quiroga enlightened Anstruther to the full, providing him with a summary of the paper given to Cottington by Olivares. The text of the latter document, taken by Cottington to England, seems to have been suitably ambiguous, but Quiroga's paper – like the understanding reached in Madrid – was absolutely clear. In exchange for real concessions Charles was required to assist Spain, if necessary by force of arms, in bringing the Dutch to satisfactory terms. Alternatively, he could bring about a general peace in Germany including the Dutch upon terms acceptable to Spain.[203] Anstruther and Dorchester were utterly surprised. The conditions made known to Cottington were obviously kept from those English ministers opposed to negotiations with the Habsburgs. The interests of Spanish diplomacy and of Charles's political court had marched together in this conspiracy.[204]

Charles promptly disavowed and rejected the official Spanish position as Quiroga had stated it. He even claimed never to have read the paper taken to England by Cottington and brought to his knowledge. This is scarcely credible. What is clear is that Charles, characteristically wilful and imperceptive, chose to believe that he could obtain satisfaction simply on the basis of peace with Spain. In this, we know, he was encouraged by Weston who feared a return to war.[205] Cottington may well have been obtuse in his debriefing out of a desire not to colour the apparent success of his mission. But the fact

---

[203] The apparent ambiguity of the paper given to Cottington was doubtless to preserve the honour of both England and Spain in the form of the peace. For the text of Quiroga's paper see Reeve, 'Quiroga's paper'. See also AGS, E2520, Council of State, 7 Jan. 1632 (n.s.), and E2562, Council of State, 20 Nov. 1631 (n.s.), voto of Olivares, Nov. 1631, Hopton to Philip IV, 1631–2; Elliott, *Count-duke of Olivares*, pp. 394–5, 398, 403, 424, 458, 467; Reeve, 'Viscount Dorchester', p. 329.

[204] Reeve, 'Viscount Dorchester', p. 327; Reeve, 'Quiroga's paper', pp. 920–2.

[205] Reeve, 'Quiroga's paper', p. 921; Reeve, 'Viscount Dorchester', p. 327; Magurn, *Rubens letters*, pp. 343–4; *CSPV 1629–32*, p. 537; SP80/8/fo. 77v; AGS, E2519, exp. 141, and E2562, Council of State, 20 Nov. 1631 (n.s.).

remains that Charles, while aware of the arrangements made against the Dutch and their obvious relevance to his own ambitions, chose to separate the two against all political sense and every source of contrary advice. Now that combination of royal naivety, rectitude, fear and ideological preference was confronted by reality. Yet even Quiroga's unadorned statement did not cause Charles to shed his illusions. It did, however, encourage his preparedness to equivocate in the European war. He promptly set about exploring dealings with Sweden.[206]

On 7 September, at Breitenfeld near Leipzig, Gustavus inflicted a shattering defeat upon the army of the League under Tilly. The League treasury was captured in the Catholic retreat. Central and South Germany lay open to the conqueror from the north. Alsace, the key to the 'Spanish road' to Flanders, was also endangered. By the spring Gustavus would be in Munich. Breitenfeld halted the advance of the Counter-Reformation and redressed the balance of power between Protestant and Catholic. The victory also escalated the war. It thus made a Palatine restoration virtually impossible during any foreseeable future failing a substantial English commitment to the war.[207] Yet Breitenfeld had dramatically increased the options for Charles if he wished to pursue them. Of this the Spaniards became all too aware in the weeks after the Swedish victory. Scaglia went to England in September as the official envoy of Philip IV. His brief was apparently to negotiate along the lines of Cottington's agreement.[208] He endeavoured to extract from England a definite commitment to war with the Dutch. Charles told the abbé that whilst his sympathies were with Spain in the Low Countries, he feared the Dutch and was reluctant to declare openly against them. The king, Weston and Cottington favoured the idea of English troops being allowed to serve the emperor, and Scaglia obtained permission to levy in England. Charles also told the abbé that he felt no commitment to Gustavus's aims in Germany. It was obvious, however, that he wished to see the outcome of the Swedish king's campaign, and Scaglia's negotiations were soon defunct. The abbé

---

[206]   AGS, E2519, exp. 141; SP75/12/fos. 204r–209v; SP80/8/fos. 110r–111r; *CSPV 1629–32*, p. 543; Reeve, 'Viscount Dorchester', p. 327.

[207]   The threat to the Habsburg lands renewed the political ascendancy of Spain in Vienna, and the Rhine Palatinate remained occupied by Spanish troops. Parker, *Thirty Years War*, pp. 126–7, 129; Parker, *Army of Flanders*, p. 257; Parker, *Europe in crisis*, p. 224; Wedgwood, *Thirty Years War*, pp. 295–303, 319; Howard, *War in European history*, p. 58; Bireley, *Religion and politics*, pp. 169–77, 186; Elliott, *Count-duke of Olivares*, p. 430; HMC, 7th report, Appx, p. 547.

[208]   The Spanish agent Necolalde had been holding inconclusive talks on the Palatine question since the summer. On Scaglia's arrival his negotiations took precedence. AGS, E2519, exp. 124, 132, and E2562, Council of State, 20 Nov. 1631 (n.s.); *CSPV 1629–32*, pp. 531, 549; Birch, ii, p. 129; Reeve, 'Quiroga's paper', p. 921n.

observed how Charles could not bring himself to terminate the talks with Spain.[209]

Hearing in Madrid that Charles rejected Quiroga's statement and that Scaglia's talks had proved fruitless, and contemplating the news of the Swedish victory at Breitenfeld, Olivares drafted a long and troubled opinion for his king on the possible options for Spain in Europe. The count-duke found this a problem, as he said, of the greatest difficulty. He was attempting to integrate diplomatic propriety and Spanish honour with the compound problem of Anglo-German politics, with military disaster and with the religious dimension of the German war. Olivares' first priority was still the Netherlands, inseparable to his mind from the German question. What he still wanted from Charles was a satisfactory settlement with the Dutch, which end (he realized) would probably involve England in war. (The Dutch had already once refused Charles's diplomatic mediation, and Olivares had never wished for a truce.) Charles's fear of the Dutch could be overcome if his declaration of war were sufficient to frighten them into submission. Olivares also felt the need for an English alliance with the emperor. Yet the Anglo-Spanish league against the Dutch was his basic price for the restoration of the entire Palatinate. English assistance against the Dutch would outweigh the competing factor of Bavarian interests. The count-duke would have preferred a compromise, by which England might be satisfied with the Lower Palatinate, leaving room for Maximilian's compensation. The duke still deserved consideration as an hereditary Catholic prince, and the danger of his defection to save his lands was all too real. Olivares' concern for Bavaria was encouraged by the hardening of his attitude towards Charles. He now saw the English king as an opportunist, perceiving Charles's new equivocation in the German war. The count-duke wished to separate the English and Saxon from the Swedish heretics. This would avert the restoration of Frederick by arms and the ruin of Christianity. Olivares' verdict, amidst his vexation, made one thing fully clear. The Protestant revolution in Germany had underlined his resolve not to compromise with Charles. Philip endorsed this position.[210]

As winter came and Gustavus marched southwards, celebrating Christmas

---

[209] Scaglia was reported to be on intimate terms with the Spanish faction. *CSPV 1629–32*, p. 549; AGS, E2519, exp. 139, 141, E2562, Council of State, 20 Nov. 1631 (n.s.); AMRE, CPA, 44, fo. 341r; Lonchay, *Correspondance de la cour d'Espagne*, ii, p. 590; Gardiner, *History*, vii, p. 190.

[210] AGS, E2562, voto of Olivares, Nov. 1631; Lonchay, *Correspondance de la cour d'Espagne*, ii, p. 604. See also AGS, E2562, voto of Olivares on despatches of Necolalde, 11 Sept. 1631 (n.s.), consulta of Olivares, 22 Dec. 1631 (n.s.), Council of State, 9 Jan. 1632 (n.s.), Hopton to Philip IV, 1631/2; Reeve, 'Viscount Dorchester', p. 327; Parker, *Thirty Years War*, pp. 56–7, 119; Wedgwood, *Thirty Years War*, pp. 314ff.; Elliott, *Count-duke of Olivares*, p. 391; Bireley, *Religion and politics*, pp. 6, 245; Alcalá-Zamora, *España, Flandes*, p. 292; BL, Add. Ms 24,909, fo. 237v.

in triumph at Mainz, Olivares could not afford to cease soliciting Charles. The count-duke's designs were not fully anchored in reality. He dreamt of a naval armada sent by Charles to deliver the *coup de grâce* to the Dutch and of English procurement of a negotiated settlement in Germany. The Habsburgs needed help badly, but even if that help were not forthcoming, Charles's breaking off of talks with Spain could spell disaster. A significant commitment by England to Gustavus stood every chance of having Frederick restored. An Anglo-Swedish alliance now appeared imminent. Olivares was terrified that Charles would call Parliament and turn again to war.[211] A Capuchin, Alexandre d'Alès, arrived in England from Vienna to keep the negotiation alive.[212] Such efforts were not to be entirely without success. The bankruptcy of Charles's equivocation was becoming apparent but the battle within his mind was not yet over. There was no doubt, however, that he was being forced to the logic of a war policy if he wished to fulfil his coveted dynastic aim.

[211] Hopton to Weston, 17 Jan. 1632, SP94/36/fo. 14r. See also AGS, E2519, exp. 140, E2520, Council of State, 7 Jan. 1632 (n.s.), and E2562, consulta of Olivares, 22 Dec. 1631 (n.s.), Council of State, 7, 9 Jan. 1632 (n.s.), Hopton to Philip IV, 1631/2; Bireley, *Religion and politics*, p. 169.
[212] Lonchay, *Correspondance de la cour d'Espagne*, ii, p. 596; Gardiner, *History*, vii, p. 190; *CSPV 1629–32*, pp. 559, 567, 572, 277–8, 592.

8

Decision

Protestant Europe was euphoric with joy at the victory of Breitenfeld. As Gustavus struck south through Germany during the autumn of 1631, it was clear that a revolutionary change of affairs was at hand. The following months would present Charles with the best opportunity to achieve his international goal. In early October, Elizabeth implored her brother to take advantage of this precious conjunction of circumstances:

I only beseech you to give me leave to say freely to you that if this opportunity be neglected, we may be in despair of ever recovering anything, for by treaty it will never be done, as you may easily see by the delays they have already made, and let not yourself be deceived . . . if they give you good words now, it will be only to gain time and keep you from assisting so that the king of Sweden may be disheartened to do anything for us . . . so as we shall never have anything but live to be a burden to you and a grief and affliction to ourselves and posterity . . . [1]

Elizabeth and Frederick enlisted Dorchester's support, and the Secretary worked to further their interests at court.[2] For those in England interested in the Palatine and Protestant causes, the war option appeared more attractive every day. Its advocates urged it on Charles, as Dorchester wrote, 'diverse ways with no small earnestness'.[3] The king was now utterly in two minds. He joyfully knighted the messenger, John Caswell, sent by Gustavus to announce his victory. Caswell brought a letter from the Swedish king, pointing to the great opportunity to free Bohemia and encouraging English aid.[4] Charles had just sent Vane to negotiate with Gustavus, but did not authorize the ambassador to form an alliance in the field without his approval. Vane was preferred above Roe, who spoke too strongly in favour of war. His appointment indicated that Charles had not abandoned all hope of a negotiated settlement. Dorchester managed to alter Vane's instructions to refer solely to a war

---

[1] SP81/37/fo. 77r–v.
[2] Reeve, 'Viscount Dorchester', pp. 6–7; SP80/8/fo. 79r; SP81/37/fos. 65r–v, 71r–72r, 79r, 81r–83r, 108r; *CSPV 1629–32*, p. 558.
[3] SP80/8/fo. 79r, Dorchester to Anstruther, 16 Oct. 1631.
[4] SP95/3/fo. 128r–v; Searle, *Barrington family letters*, p. 212; Birch, ii, pp. 129–30, 138.

policy.[5] On 7 November the Secretary wrote to Elizabeth, restating Charles's commitment to her family and outlining his policy. If the English ambassador in Vienna, having pressed the talks to an issue, got no satisfaction then Charles would ally with Sweden for the prosecution of the war, including the interests of the Palatines in the agreement.[6] The continuing failure of dealings with Spain could only erode Weston's position. He had secured Vane's appointment, however, and his power remained considerable. Working against the Treasurer at court during the autumn and winter, Dorchester represented a growing preparedness to go to war felt in the Council and the country.[7]

The Protestant war lobby had to contend not only with Weston and Charles's indecision. French diplomacy was also a complicating factor. England's failure to engage during the winter of 1630–1 had allowed French and Swedish policy to dominate German affairs. While Richelieu's new ally Gustavus espoused the interests of Sweden and of Protestantism, the cardinal had somewhat different aims. He sought to extend French influence in Germany, and to build a French-led alliance which would subdue the House of Austria while not endangering German Catholicism. The religious conflict between the emperor and Gustavus cut across these aims. By unleashing Sweden in Germany the cardinal got more than the satellite he bargained for: in 1631 and 1632 the tide of Swedish success brought Richelieu's policy to the verge of collapse. The Protestant threat to French arbitration of German affairs could be even greater if Sweden were able to restore Frederick by force. Richelieu therefore sought an agreement with Charles for a Palatine restoration in late 1631. But the French had no real concern for the exiled Protestant prince, and suspicion of their designs was growing fast in England, even with Dorchester.[8] With an Anglo-French agreement, the complications of French policy in Germany would bring trouble for England. As Wake wrote from France, '*Domus divisa non stabit* . . . these people here can hardly

---

[5] SP75/12/fos. 204r–209v; SP16/203/108, SP16/204/107, SP16/533/61; SP80/8/fos. 77r–79r; SP81/37/fo. 123r; SP95/3/fo. 132r; *CSPV 1629–32*, p. 555; *DNB*, s.v. Vane, Sir Henry, the elder; Gardiner, *History*, vii, p. 175; Alexander, *Charles I's Lord Treasurer*, p. 174; Birch, ii, pp. 123, 140, 153–4, 161; SRO, Hamilton Mss, no. 187; Reeve, 'Viscount Dorchester', p. 332.

[6] SP81/37/fos. 110r–111r.

[7] *CSPV 1629–32*, pp. 555, 588, 592; SP94/35/fos. 329r–v, 331v–333r, 335r–336r; SP80/8/fos. 77r–79r; SP75/12/fos. 210r, 252r–253v; SP81/37/fos. 104r–106v, 108r, 167r–168r, SP81/38/fos. 19r–20r; SP16/203/108, SP16/204/72, SP16/204/107, SP16/211/18, SP16/533/61; Gardiner, *History*, vii, pp. 188, 196.

[8] AGS, E2519, exp. 141; SP78/89/fos. 357r–358r, SP78/90/343r–344r, 345r–v, 472r–473v, 474r–475r, 476r–478r; SP78/91/fos. 24r–27r, 39r–44v; SP81/37/fos. 157r–158r, 233r–236r; *CSPV 1629–32*, pp. 575, 588; Wedgwood, *Thirty Years War*, p. 284; Elliott, *Richelieu and Olivares*, pp. 119, 124, 155; Howard, *War in European history*, p. 62; Bireley, *Religion and politics*, p. 185; Gardiner, *History*, vii, p. 179.

play two games so contrary.' With the religious dimension of the war intensifying, Richelieu's investments lay on both sides.[9]

It was Gustavus who, predictably, formulated the dilemma for Charles. Sweden's program in Germany included Frederick's eventual restoration to the Palatinate.[10] Gustavus saw this as part of an ultimate and satisfactory settlement of Germany. The Swedish king, however, had a definite view of the nature of that settlement and no intention of countenancing the elector's unconditional restoration. Full of the pride of victory, and imbued with what has been called an 'inexorable' political realism,[11] Gustavus was aware that for the indefinite future he needed neither Frederick nor England enough to be forced into concessions he saw as unreasonable. With or without Frederick, he wanted to secure the resources, strategic position and political solidarity of the Palatinate for Sweden and her aims. He also wished to eliminate any independent English influence in Germany, rightly seeing Charles as unreliable (although thinking him preferable to the French). Finally, he wanted the Anglo-Palatine interest to bear its share of the cost of the war in proportion to its resources and in the light of its likely rewards. He would, therefore, treat Frederick with respect for his royal rank and political potential. But he would also insist upon alliances, with Charles and with the elector, which involved real military assistance and subordinated their interests to his. Gustavus's interlocking priorities were the rights of Lutheranism, the cause of German Protestantism and the enhancement of Swedish as well as of his own personal power.[12]

In November 1631 the Swedish forces were approaching the Palatinate, and Gustavus was interested in an English alliance and a Palatine restoration. In mid-November, Vane wrote from the Swedish camp that if Charles gave Gustavus substantial support in money and men the Swedish king would commit himself to fight for Frederick's restoration. Gustavus also wanted Frederick to join him in Germany. The elector asked for military aid from Charles and permission to leave the Hague. This appeared to be and was indeed his best chance for salvation. Without English resources, however, he was essentially powerless. The Swedish alliances in Germany did not mention him, and his ultimate fate might depend upon an immediate English commitment. Without it, he could not influence Gustavus, would be excluded from

---

[9] SP78/91/fos. 40v–41r, Wake to Dorchester, 30 Jan. 1632; AGS, E2519, exp. 141, and E2562, Council of State, 20 Nov. 1631 (n.s.); see also SP75/12/fo. 213r.

[10] Frederick's restoration to the crown of Bohemia seems to have become a separate question. Gustavus, in the end, apparently countenanced the idea of the crown's being given to Wallenstein; Roberts, *Gustavus Adolphus*, ii, pp. 421–2, 575, 610–11, 616–17, 679–80, 749–51.

[11] Ibid., pp. 617–18.

[12] Ibid., pp. 610–18; Rushworth, *Historical collections*, ii, p. 169.

any negotiations and exposed to French designs. Vane told Charles that, if he were to opt for war, it was now or never. He awaited further instructions.[13]

Gustavus was now more than any man the arbiter of Germany. He was advancing on Heidelberg, the Palatine capital, at the beginning of December. It was only a tactical consideration (the opportunity to cross the Rhine and make for Mainz) which caused him to delay his liberation of the Palatinate. Yet he had the electorate in his grasp and he needed it.[14] The League army, Maximilian's main political weapon, was shattered and Ferdinand in Vienna, now terribly vulnerable, was willing to negotiate. The English aid demanded by Gustavus involved a sum of approximately £200,000. This was the minimum commitment which would purchase his political recognition of Frederick and guarantee the Palatines the backing of Swedish power. Given such help from Charles, Gustavus would restore the elector by arms, or insist upon his restoration in dealing with the Habsburgs.[15] Gustavus's demands were not unreasonable and he was to prove flexible in negotiating the level of English commitment.[16] Charles had no choice but to consider calling a Parliament, the only means to the necessary financial supply. The kind of sum required, by the same token, was well within the capacity of the nation to provide. Parliament (as has been noted) in 1624 awarded £300,000 to launch the Spanish war, and in 1628 granted five subsidies (£275,000) despite suspicion of Buckingham's designs.[17] Now, by contrast, the tide of Protestant victory was high and the Palatinate was there for the taking. There was tremendous popular enthusiasm in England at this point and the willingness to give.[18] The Venetian ambassador considered that a collection for

[13] SP81/37/fos. 104r–106v, 108r, 118r–124v, 138r–142v, 143r–147v, 164r–165v, 175r–176v, 179r, 183r–184v, 187r–188v, 220r–v, 222r–223r, 228r–230r; Wedgwood, *Thirty Years War*, pp. 303–6; *CSPV 1629–32*, pp. 575, 577.

[14] Gustavus's grand strategy involved the destruction of Bavaria, the focus of Catholic opposition, followed by an attack on Vienna from the west. The Rhine was central to this strategy. It would cut off Spanish access from Flanders and Lorraine, integrate the Swedish conquests, forestall French encroachment and provide logistic support. Mainz stood at the critical confluence of the Main and Rhine. Its occupation closed the Rhine to Spanish troops. Dutch victories the following summer forced Spanish reinforcements from Flanders for the Palatinate to turn back. AGS, E2562, Council of State, 9 Jan. 1632 (n.s.); *CSPV 1629–32*, pp. 573–4; Alcalá-Zamora, *España, Flandes*, pp. 293–6; Wedgwood, *Thirty Years War*, pp. 305–6; Parker, *Europe in crisis*, pp. 222–4, 229; Parker, *Thirty Years War*, pp. 129–30; Roberts, *Gustavus Adolphus*, ii, pp. 538–58, 611, 616, 674–6; Parker, *Army of Flanders*, pp. 54–5.

[15] £200,000 was the sum Gustavus mentioned to Vane, which included support for at least 10,000 more men in the spring. SP81/37/fos. 120r, 175r–176v, 179r; Gardiner, *History*, vii, p. 193.

[16] SP81/38/fo. 40v and see below, pp. 286–8.

[17] Adams, 'Foreign policy and the Parliaments of 1621 and 1624', pp. 168–9; Thomas, 'Financial and administrative developments', p. 117.

[18] *CSPV 1629–32*, p. 574; Birch, ii, pp. 157, 160, 166, 174; Searle, *Barrington family letters*, pp. 189, 195, 197, 203, 210–11, 214, 218, 230, 233–40, 244, 247; NUL, Ne.C., 15,404,

Elizabeth of Bohemia in the churches would easily provide for her cause.[19] The debate within the government in December 1631 as to the wisdom of calling a Parliament was conducted on the basis of the projected Swedish alliance and in the context of this highly charged atmosphere. Vane warned from Germany 'that every day, if not every hour, alters the face of affairs'.[20]

The form of decision made during the winter of 1631–2 against holding a Parliament was a turning point in the history of Charles's reign. It signified the establishment of an era of government without reference to Parliament which might be ended only by physical necessity. It was not in itself a decision neatly made. It involved the attitudes of a number of competing individuals and their reactions to wider circumstances. Yet the role of one actor, Charles himself, was absolutely paramount and the final outcome was his choice. He came within a hair's breadth of holding a Parliament and recommitting England to the war. He had everything to gain: popularity again at home, influence abroad and a satisfactory solution to the perennial English problem of the Palatinate. With all this at stake, why were events allowed to take another course with the confirmation of a non-parliamentary regime?

By the end of November, the advocates of war were making further headway with Charles. The king was reported to be deeply undecided.[21] On the 29th, Dorchester wrote to the English envoys in Madrid and Vienna with a final ultimatum. He accused the Spaniards, in Charles's name, of duplicity and delays.[22] On the arrival of Vane's despatch with the Swedish terms the political battle reached its height. There were lengthy debates in Council, in Charles's presence, as to whether a Parliament should be called. There was very strong conciliar support for Frederick and for war.[23] Weston and Laud, afraid to speak publicly and doubtless terrified of the outcome, sought to win over Charles in private.[24] The Treasurer attempted to take out political insurance, including likely activists such as Barrington in the bill for shrievalty. Dorchester, Holland and Pembroke worked against him, having Sir Thomas spared appointment as a sheriff and thus still eligible to sit in the

p. 278; SP16/203/108; Green, *Diary of John Rous*, pp. 66–7; Parker, *Thirty Years War*, pp. 131–2; Reeve, 'Viscount Dorchester', pp. 218, 332; Gardiner, *History*, vii, pp. 189–90, 197, 207; Breslow, *Mirror of England*, pp. 39–40, 125, 128–38; Grosart, *Letter book of Sir John Eliot*, p. 196.

19 *CSPV 1629–32*, p. 574.
20 SP81/37/fo. 136r, Vane to Dorchester, 20 Nov. 1631.
21 *CSPV 1629–32*, p. 567.
22 SP80/8/fos. 110r–111r; SP94/35/fos. 337r–338v.
23 *CSPV 1629–32*, pp. 538, 567, 573–4, 588, 592; SP16/204/80; Searle, *Barrington family letters*, p. 247; AGS, E2519, exp. 141, and E2562, Council of State, 20 Nov. 1631 (n.s.).
24 *CSPV 1629–32*, pp. 574–5, 588, 592; Laud, *Works*, vii, pp. 42–3; Birch, ii, p. 137; Knowler, *Strafford letters*, i, p. 59; Reeve, 'Viscount Dorchester', pp. 217–18; Supple, *Commercial crisis*, pp. 216–18.

House of Commons.[25] Rumours of a Parliament, which had been circulating since August, now intensified.[26] Charles had been making preparations, seeking to buy off his legal critics. In October William Noy had been appointed Attorney-General and in December Edward Littleton was made Recorder of London. In the City it was rumoured that Selden, now free on bail, would become the king's solicitor.[27] A court pundit ventured to say that 'Noy and Selden are come on our side, and the rest of the rebels would be glad of worse conditions'.[28] At least one 'rebel', however, remained recalcitrant and played a key role in Charles's final decision.

The king had clearly helped to raise expectations that a Parliament would be called. This served to refocus attention upon Eliot who consequently became the subject of Charles's renewed scorn. Eliot was informed of political events and could command great support in the country. A new Parliament might not be pacified without his release. Indeed, he was assured of a seat and seems to have been working on a speech.[29] When the recall of Parliament became a definite possibility, Eliot and Selden received overtures from those at court who feared criticism in the Commons.[30] This was too much for Charles in whom it triggered a rapid response. He felt threatened and insulted by such solicitation of a defiant subject, and pressured and pre-empted by the general climate of expectation. On 21 December he addressed the Council in shrill and defensive terms. He had, he said, heard of frequent visits to Eliot, jollity and feasting, not befitting the circumstances of a prisoner in the Tower. He was resolved that since no other lodging there would satisfy Eliot but the king's own bedchamber, that the prisoner should be removed to more miserable quarters and be seen only on private business.[31] Eliot was put under close restraint and his communications restricted and watched.[32] The idea of him renewing his political credit, having defied Charles's regal auth-

---

[25] Sheriffs acted as returning officers and could not be returned to Parliament. The third earl of Pembroke had been succeeded by his brother Philip, the Lord Chamberlain. Searle, *Barrington family letters*, pp. 214, 217–18 and n; Birch, ii, p. 140; Russell, *Crisis of Parliaments*, p. 303.

[26] PRO, C115, M35, 8386, Pory to Slego, 17 Dec. 1631; *CSPV 1629–32*, pp. 538, 545, 567; SP16/203/108, SP16/204/80, 107; SP77/21/fo. 9r–v; Searle, *Barrington family letters*, pp. 211, 217; Birch, ii, p. 144; Gardiner, *History*, vii, p. 191.

[27] Knowler, *Strafford letters*, i, p. 58; Birch, ii, pp. 137, 161–2; Gardiner, *History*, vii, pp. 220–1.

[28] SP16/203/108.

[29] Grosart, *Letter book of Sir John Eliot*, pp. 196–7, 206, 218–21; Birch, ii, p. 158; Hulme, *Life of Sir John Eliot*, p. 381 and n.

[30] PRO, C115, M35, 8386, Pory to Slego, 17 Dec. 1631; Birch, ii, pp. 152–3; SP16/203/108; Gardiner, *History*, vii, p. 191.

[31] PRO, C115, M35, 8387, Pory to Slego, 24 Dec. 1631. Whether Eliot was actually visited in the Tower is irrelevant. What mattered was Charles's belief that he was; Gardiner, *History*, vii, p. 191.

[32] Grosart, *Letter book of Sir John Eliot*, pp. 211–12.

ority, was intolerable to the king. Charles's unwillingness to free him, out of contempt and fear of his influence (there was also the memory of Buckingham's death), was apparently a critical element of the king's ill-disposition towards calling a Parliament at this time. Eliot was a threat not only in his personal capacity. He also represented, to Charles, the spectre of parliamentary power. The king's speech to Council continued:

by the discourses of many concerning a Parliament he was now offended and his proclamation violated, and therefore wished all men to be wary how they displeased him in that kind, adding further, that he would never be urged by necessity or against his will to summon one.[33]

The proclamation of 27 March 1629[34] had held out the prospect of another Parliament, given an improvement in political conditions. Now a measure of order and stability had been regained and the case for a Parliament, in the light of the opportunity in Germany, was virtually irrefutable. Charles, however, could not see matters in terms of reason of state, even when he obviously stood to gain and otherwise had much to lose. The political innocence – and the inadequacy – of his personality here appear clearly. With a limited perception of his personal interests and monarchical role, and encouraged by those about him who stood to lose by a Parliament, he acted to compound, not lessen, his difficulties and to minimize his chances of achieving his goal. As in the past, a pattern of fear asserted itself in his mind, weaving personal and ideological themes into a single whole. There was his animosity towards Eliot and sense of constitutional threat. There was also religion. The Palatine issue was in England a religious issue, and might spill over into discussion of Laudianism. (Charles, nonetheless, by restoring the Palatines stood to win inestimable religious prestige which could well ease his way at home.) Finally, there was foreign policy. Parliament, like the Palatines, would recognize the failure of diplomacy and call for a new war with Spain and a commitment to the Protestant cause.[35] Charles had just threatened to abandon Frederick altogether if he so much as stirred to activate the issue any further.[36] Despite his definite interest in the possibility of a Parliament, which had peaked in early December, Charles's personality and preferences – with a policy of intransigence – had reasserted themselves. If he had not made his final decision when he addressed Council on 21 December, condemning Eliot and

---

[33] PRO, C115, M35, 8387, Pory to Slego, 24 Dec. 1631. This speech may have been partly intended to encourage the customs farmers to advance money to Charles, for the Swedish campaign, by dispelling fears of parliamentary inquiry. But the scheme was an anti-parliamentary initiative and Charles's emotional involvement in the speech is clear. Ibid. and see below, p. 282.

[34] See chapter 4, above.

[35] PRO, C115, M35, 8387, Pory to Slego, 24 Dec. 1631; SP81/37/fos. 104r–106v.

[36] *CSPV 1629–32*, pp. 570, 572.

all who spoke of a Parliament, he was rapidly doing so. By then he and Weston were exploring a scheme to borrow money from the customs farmers, so as to fund a Swedish treaty without recourse to Parliament. (The scheme would fail and was partly designed, it seems, to placate the public desire for Charles to act in support of his sister.)[37] By the end of the month the king had stated that the very suggestion of a Parliament was derogatory to his authority and (he added out of pique and a misreading of his experience) equally remote from giving him satisfaction.[38] It is conceivable, while unlikely, that at this point he had not utterly rejected the idea. The possibility of another Parliament was never explicitly excluded but to all intents and purposes Charles had set his mind against it.

Despite the king's relapse into constitutional intransigence, he still harboured the hope of reaching an agreement with Sweden. Dorchester and the war lobby still pushed their line. Of those ideologically committed to international Protestantism, only the Secretary remained in close proximity to the king. Dorchester's growing suspicion of France would have enhanced his credibility with Charles. As events in Germany unfolded he brought all his diplomatic abilities to bear on the king. In early December the Secretary wrote to Elizabeth of Bohemia of a meeting with Charles. Dorchester, clutching correspondence from the Palatines, went into the picture gallery at Whitehall, finding Charles, as he wrote, 'seriously employed':

In the midst of his antique pictures . . . placing and removing his emperors' heads and putting them in right order. Which work being ended, I besought him that now he had done disposing his emperors, he would think of supporting of kings (the king of Bohemia and the king of Sweden) whose interests began to be joined each with other and both with his majesty['s] . . . [39]

It was an uphill struggle for Dorchester to detach Charles from his introverted world. Yet the Secretary informed Elizabeth of the deep distrust in England of the Habsburg treaty, whereas 'on the other side there are strong and fair invitations' and 'the apt and proper opportunity of action'.[40] He gave Elizabeth an expectation of good resolutions.[41]

Promoted by Dorchester, the dealings with Gustavus went ahead. Charles resented the size of the initial Swedish demands but by the third week of December it appeared that Gustavus was willing to negotiate. His impatience

---

[37] While no money was raised (the farmers surely feared reprisals) the government announced that it had obtained £100,000 for the Swedish war effort: a deliberate attempt to mislead. Ibid., pp. 579, 582, 602; PRO, C115, M35, 8387, Pory to Slego, 24 Dec. 1631.

[38] *CSPV 1629–32*, p. 574. Charles may also have spoken this way out of fear of the strength of the war lobby's case.

[39] SP81/37/fos. 167r–168r, Dorchester to Elizabeth, 2 Dec. 1631.

[40] Ibid.

[41] Ibid.

probably encouraged the English response.[42] At Christmas Charles expressed his delight at fresh news of the progress of Swedish arms.[43] By the end of the month he had authorized Dorchester to act. On the last day of 1631, the Secretary wrote to Vane with an offer of terms. Charles was prepared to provide £5,000 a month with reasonable reimbursement of charges in the recovery of the Palatinate, or £10,000 a month for the duration of the war, in return for the full restitution of Frederick and his heirs to their hereditary lands and electoral title.[44] Vane should inform Gustavus of the certainty of supply upon these conditions. Dorchester concluded: '... the importance of this main business you have ... and the opportunity not to be hazarded makes me as much wish these letters in your hand and an answer in due time as ever anything passed my pen ...'[45] Frederick was finally allowed to join Gustavus in Germany.[46] Dorchester wished to bring Charles to a financial commitment to give England a stake in the German question. The English offer was not unreasonable and could form the basis for negotiation. The treaty was eventually ruptured not by the question of Charles's level of commitment but principally by his refusal to break with Spain.[47] He was, however, seeking to finance that treaty without parliamentary supply. And he intended to make no alliance, with Sweden against Spain for example, which implied open war and recourse to Parliament. The capacity of the Anglo-Swedish negotiations to bring about an agreement was thus very limited.

The conflict raged at court. Dorchester not only wished to commit England to the war but also to escalate it. His target was Bavaria. Maximilian was an obstacle to Frederick's restoration and as head of the League a great enemy of Protestantism. Dorchester saw the danger that Richelieu might intercede to protect Bavaria and save the duchy from Swedish invasion.[48] Above all, he feared French sacrifice of Palatine interests by such an agreement. He seems to have suspected correctly, however, that France would not fight for Bavaria as she was obliged to do by treaty. Consequently, he sought to use English diplomacy to ensure the destruction of Maximilian's

[42] SP81/37/fos. 120r, 124r–v, 156r–v, 175r–176v, 179r, 233r–236v.
[43] Birch, ii, pp. 157–8; *CSPV 1629–32*, p. 589.
[44] SP81/37/fos. 256v, 282r.   [45] SP81/37/fos. 256v–257v.
[46] SP81/37/fo. 256r, SP81/38/fos. 15r, 34r–35r; *CSPV 1629–32*, pp. 570, 573, 577, 579. When Frederick left the Hague for Germany, the Dutch government gave him an allowance of £5,000 per month. *CSPV 1629–32*, pp. 573, 588; Birch, ii, pp. 136, 138.
[47] Roberts, *Gustavus Adolphus*, ii, p. 612; and see below.
[48] The cardinal attempted such intercession unsuccessfully during the winter of 1631–2. Bireley, *Religion and politics*, pp. 176–7. In the spring of 1632 Tilly forfeited the protective neutrality granted the Catholic League under the Treaty of Bärwalde by attacking Swedish forces in the ecclesiastical principality of Bamberg, a member of the League. Maximilian countenanced the act by joining Tilly's forces at Ingolstadt. Gustavus thus had his justification for invading Bavaria. Parker, *Thirty Years War*, pp. 128–9; Wedgwood, *Thirty Years War*, pp. 314, 317–18.

dominions at the hands of the king of Sweden. In pushing this policy he could play upon Charles's Francophobia. The Secretary wrote to Vane on 6 January with further instructions on the Anglo-Swedish treaty:

to reinforce a point I have already expressed in my despatch . . . be careful to comprehend clearly both the lower and higher Palatinate together with the electoral dignity . . . and that further you do not only dissuade and hinder that king [Gustavus] from any accommodation with the duke of Bavaria, but also incite him all you may to pursue and assail the duke and his dominions.[49]

It was factors other than England's wishes which eventually inspired Gustavus's invasion of Bavaria. Yet Dorchester was making life difficult for those in England who wished to avoid the war. When Frederick left the Hague for Germany at the beginning of 1632 he thanked Dorchester for his help and entrusted him with the affairs of his family and with his interests.[50] Yet fate soon removed the Secretary from the scene. He fell ill of a fever in the depth of winter and died in February. His death, as contemporaries observed, was a significant event in the shaping of English policy. It facilitated the work of the peace lobby and allowed them to monopolize Charles's ear once again. The Treasurer was once more riding high.[51]

Weston met opposition in Council but could rely on the coincidence of his aims with Charles's prejudices. He worked on the king to ensure that there would indeed be no Parliament. He took advantage of Dorchester's final illness in January to seize control of the correspondence with Germany, enabling him to halt the progress of the treaty and finally scuttle it. Having little sympathy for the Palatines, he encouraged Charles to believe, naively, that Gustavus would naturally hand over the Palatinate to Frederick.[52] The Treasurer, aided by Cottington, also toiled to keep the talks with the Habsburgs alive and to play upon Charles's hopes, against all reason, of a peaceful resolution. Weston still argued that Charles was entitled to concessions on the basis of Philip's promise at the time of the Anglo-Spanish peace. Charles wrote to Philip in February along these lines. His painful reluctance to break off the dialogue with Spain was clearly linked to his rejec-

---

[49] SP81/38/fo. 16r. See also SP81/37/fos. 157r–158r, 187r–188v, 233r–236r, 282r, SP81/38/fos. 19r–22v; SP75/12/fo. 207v; *CSPV 1629–32*, pp. 591, 602; Bireley, *Religion and politics*, p. 177.

[50] SP81/38/fo. 31r.

[51] Dorchester died on 15 February 1632. SP81/37/fos. 110r, 167v, SP81/38/fos. 16r, 80r–v; SP16/211/74; *CSPV 1629–32*, p. 593; Gardiner, *History*, vii, p. 194; Mathew, *Age of Charles I*, p. 80.

[52] SP81/37/fo. 256r, SP81/38/fo. 55r, 57r, 59r (these three last from Weston to Vane, *c*. Jan. 1632, in the hand of Weston's secretary), 70r–v, 80r–v, 85r–86v; SP16/203/108; *CSPV 1629–32*, pp. 575, 588, 590, 592, 598, 602, 630, 636; AGS, E2562, summary of despatch of Necolalde, 5 Mar. 1632 (n.s.); Searle, *Barrington family letters*, p. 247; Gardiner, *History*, vii, p. 196.

tion of the idea of calling a Parliament. Yet his desire for the friendship of Spain remained sincere. Cottington wrote to Olivares of Charles's extreme goodwill, but the problem remained his refusal to act against the Dutch. Weston and Cottington nonetheless strove to convince Scaglia that some kind of solution was still possible.[53] Madrid had a vested interest in reciprocating and keeping the line to London open. Necolalde and Scaglia had felt the tide of English opinion running against them since October. Yet they worked away, understanding that an Anglo-Swedish alliance could well force Spain into concessions. Olivares intended that Scaglia should seek a settlement to the last. The Capuchin sent to England from Vienna sought to discredit Anstruther's reports and to raise hopes of an agreement with the emperor.[54] And the Infanta's government in Brussels, seeing the Swedish threat to the Rhine and the Palatinate, in January offered to hand over the vital fortress of Frankenthal to Vane. This was an offer which apparently impressed Charles. It was surely a ploy to stave off the likely capture of Frankenthal by Sweden and perhaps to prevent an alliance between Charles and Gustavus.[55] In Madrid Olivares, despite his fear of such an alliance, by this time was aware that all was not well in England. He knew that Charles was weak at home and needed customs revenues and this reinforced his resolve to obtain a quid pro quo. Charles's dealings with Spain were thus ineffectual without a stake in the

[53] *CSPV 1629–32*, pp. 567, 572, 588, 592, 628–9; SP16/203/108; SP80/8/fos. 110r–111r, 149r–150v; SP81/38/fos. 55r, 57r, 59r, 85r–86v; SP94/35/fos. 337r–338v, 357r; AGS, E2519, exp. 142, and E2562, summary of Charles to Philip IV, 16 Feb. 1632 (n.s.), of Scaglia (to Olivares?), 5, 7, 12 Mar. 1632 (n.s.), summary of despatch of Necolalde, 18 Mar. 1632 (n.s.), summary of letters of Scaglia, Necolalde, Charles and Cottington, Feb.–Mar. 1632, summary of Cottington to Olivares, *c.* Feb./Mar. 1632.

[54] *CSPV 1629–32*, pp. 567, 572, 592; AGS, E2519, exp. 140–1, and E2562, Council of State, 20 Nov. 1631 (n.s.), consulta of Olivares, 22 Dec. 1631 (n.s.), summary of letter of Scaglia to Philip IV, 29 Feb. 1632 (n.s.).

[55] Frankenthal was the most important Spanish garrison in the Lower Palatinate. It was surrendered on deposit to the Infanta Isabella by James I in 1623, pending a peace conference. England held that there was a treaty obligation to return it. By the beginning of 1632 it was threatened by the Swedish forces on the Rhine: the military context of the Infanta's offer which reached London in January but which was revoked in Brussels the same month. It is most unlikely that such an offer would have been made, even as a ploy, without authorization from Madrid, particularly given Olivares' policy of no compromise and pan-European concerns. The Brussels government may have responded to the emergency of its own accord. The offer was disclosed to Gerbier in Brussels by Coloma, a distinguished veteran of the army of Flanders. The offer anticipated the Spanish instructions for Necolalde of October 1632, which authorized the offer of Frankenthal on deposit in return for a defensive Anglo-Spanish league. Necolalde was instructed to do everything possible to avoid such a concession without prior agreement with the emperor and Bavaria. SP77/21/fos. 23r, 32r–34r; SP81/38/fos. 19r–22v; *CSPV 1629–32*, pp. 402, 580, 583–4, 594; Birch, ii, pp. 163–5; Parker, *Thirty Years War*, p. 65; Alcalá-Zamora, *España, Flandes*, p. 295; Elliott, *Count-duke of Olivares*, p. 348; Archivo del Duque de Medinaceli, Seville, leg. 86, instructions for Necolalde of 18 Oct. 1632 (n.s.) (I am grateful to John Elliott for this reference). See also p. 278, n. 14, above, and below, p. 287, and n. 59.

European conflict. The count-duke, despite the emergency, stuck to his guns.[56]

In Germany Vane was engaged in his invidious mission. Weston, his political ally and master, had a vested interest in protracting and ultimately destroying the dealings with Sweden. He wished to avoid war and to discover the intentions of France. Charles wanted to test his own proposal for a limited commitment but to go no further. Vane, therefore, while entering into discussions, sought to complicate them and to prevaricate, hedging on the side of peace. The ambassador was caught between the strategy of his mission on the one hand and the commanding position of the king of Sweden on the other. In England, the Treasurer and his circle (and probably the king) were critical of the extent to which Vane gave ear to the Swedes. Charles was doubtless frustrated at the eventual failure to reach an agreement on his terms. On the other side, Vane was virtually destined to fall out with Gustavus. The Swedish king did not trust him, knowing him to be Weston's protégé, and finally told him to his face that he seemed more the friend of Spain than of Germany. Besides his suspicion of Vane and the power of his negotiating position, Gustavus had grown arrogant with success and was preoccupied with the war. He treated Vane and Hamilton with a brusqueness which they resented. This was a volatile combination. The king and the ambassador quarrelled violently on at least one occasion. Gustavus would have preferred to deal with Roe, and, entrusted to him, the mission just might have produced an agreement.[57]

Gustavus's attitude to England, and to the Palatines, was essentially fixed in principle but negotiable in detail. In addition to a commitment to the war and his wider aims, he insisted on absolute authority to conduct hostilities and negotiate a peace. He also wanted toleration for Lutheranism in the Palatinate. All his German alliances had been built upon terms at least as rigorous as these.[58] Charles's hesitation had also allowed French power to enter the calculation of forces in Vane's discussions with Gustavus. Richelieu, who had an army on the frontiers, wanted to protect his satellite Bavaria against his ally Sweden. Gustavus, however, ranked the Protestant above the anti-Habsburg cause and wanted no meddling by France in the German war.

---

[56] SP94/36/fo. 14r; AGS, E2562, Council of State, 22 Apr. 1632 (n.s.). See also ibid., Hopton to Philip IV, 1631–2, Council of State, 7, 9 Jan. 1632 (n.s.).

[57] SP16/203/108, SP16/204/107; SP81/38/fos. 19r–22v, 39r–41r, 55r, 57r, 59r, 70r–v, 76r–77r, 85r–86v, 92r–94r, 119r–121r; SP95/3/fo. 187r–v; SP103/18/fo. 218r, SP103/69/ fos. 58r, 62r, 64r–v, 101r–v; *CSPD 1631–33*, pp. 388–9; *CSPV 1629–32*, pp. 588, 590, 595, 605, 608, 620, 626; Rushworth, *Historical collections*, ii, p. 166; Roberts, *Gustavus Adolphus*, ii, pp. 609–18; Parker, *Europe in crisis*, p. 228; Gardiner, *History*, vii, pp. 206–7; *DNB*, s.v. Vane, Sir Henry, the elder.

[58] SP81/38/fos. 39r–41r, 76r–77r, 92r–94r; SP95/3/fo. 187r–v; Roberts, *Gustavus Adolphus*, ii, pp. 503, 526–7, 612–13, 625, 649.

He rightly saw Bavaria as the centre of Catholic resistance. It was also a major segment of still unravaged territory. He needed to quarter his troops and provide for further war. Richelieu might intervene to protect Maximilian but Gustavus was prepared to risk war with France. In January 1632 he was exploring a contingency plan to be activated if there were a Franco-Swedish conflict: the making of peace with the Habsburgs by English mediation, with the Spanish surrender of Frankenthal to Vane. The English ambassador rejected this impractical notion and called it an unreasonable requirement of England.[59]

The Anglo-Swedish treaty effectively broke down in March. Gustavus decided that he wanted an English contribution of 10,000 men for his war effort. He also wanted English naval protection in the Baltic, where his coastal position and communications with Sweden might be subject to Spanish attack. Vane, however, wished to discuss a purely financial arrangement. He suggested a sum of 40,000 rixdollars (approximately £10,000) per month to help support the war, an offer which Charles subsequently confirmed. Gustavus accepted it. Such a level of contribution was slightly in excess of what he had sought from Charles in 1629. He still wished to insist, however, on naval aid. Here was the sticking point. Vane said that Charles would take no such risk of hostilities with Spain. The ambassador, moreover, was not fully co-operative in these talks which were more difficult than they might otherwise have been.[60] In the English Privy Council there was

[59] This was less a lapse of judgement by Gustavus than evidence of the fluidity of Swedish policy when his power was at its height. The idea was triggered in his mind by the Infanta's offer to hand over Frankenthal to Vane. Gustavus envisaged the possible withdrawal of Spanish forces from the Empire by this means. Madrid and Vienna, however, could not so easily be divided, as Vane pointed out. He probably suspected that Spain would not make such concessions without reciprocation by England. His rejection of this overture may have angered Weston. SP77/21/fo. 23r; SP81/37/fos. 179r, 183r–184v, 187r–188v, 243r–244r, 246v–248r, SP81/38/fos. 19r–22r, 24r–25v, 27r–28r, 39r–41r; *CSPD 1631–33*, pp. 388–9; Bireley, *Religion and politics*, pp. 176–7; Roberts, *Gustavus Adolphus*, ii, pp. 586–7, 591, 594; Wedgwood, *Thirty Years War*, p. 318; and see also p. 285, n. 55, above.

[60] Vane, for example, would not immediately offer English financial assistance, despite being authorized to do so. He may also have delayed objecting to the idea of naval aid until after the financial contribution was agreed upon. Sir James Spence wrote from Swedish headquarters, apparently to Roe, implying that Vane had been unhelpful. SP81/38/fos. 92r–94r, 119r–121r; SP95/3/fo. 187r–v; SP103/18/fo. 218r, SP103/69/fos. 58r–v, 62r; Gardiner, *History*, vii, p. 196; Roberts, *Gustavus Adolphus*, ii, p. 212 and n. Parallel talks between Frederick and the Swedes were inconclusive. Gustavus insisted on the subordination of Palatine to Swedish and Protestant interests for the duration of the war. Frederick objected to this. He was, however, no necessary obstacle to an Anglo-Swedish agreement. Dependent upon Charles, he could not bargain independently with Gustavus or reject terms acceptable to England. With Charles squandering a golden opportunity, there was no Anglo-Swedish agreement nor conquest of the Palatinate with which Frederick had to come to terms. His expectations were unrealistic to the end. SP103/69/fo. 100r; Rushworth, *Historical collections*, ii, pp. 166, 171–2, 174–5; Roberts, *Gustavus Adolphus*, ii, pp. 613ff.; SRO, Hamilton Mss, no. 147.

apparently still strong support for the Swedish alliance. Charles, however, was unimpressed. He was not prepared to entertain a general alliance with Sweden implying a new war with Spain and the disturbance of his domestic political quiet. He would offer nothing more than the financial contribution under a league of friendship and assistance, without further political commitment.[61] The treaty had reached a dead end. Vane continued to follow Gustavus's camp but could reach no agreement. Talks were abandoned in the summer and Charles recalled his envoy.[62] In fact the treaty had died by the spring, with Dorchester gone and, above all, with Charles decided against a Parliament and open war. Cottington praised Vane for having saved Charles's money and honour, 'and yourself from any kind of blame, as I understand it'.[63] Weston had triumphed.

In March, Gustavus had invaded Bavaria. He routed Tilly's forces, ravaged and plundered the duchy and entered Munich in triumph in May. France did not fight for Bavaria. Richelieu preferred to sacrifice Maximilian rather than destroy the anti-Habsburg cause by fighting the powerful Swede. Gustavus allowed Frederick to enter Munich at his side. But he would not rank Palatine dynastic interests with the military needs of German Protestantism and Swedish power. Nevertheless in England there were paeans of praise. Sir Thomas Roe wrote that the king of Sweden fought battles and took towns as fast as they were read of in the book of Joshua, 'whose example indeed he is'.[64] Sir Thomas Barrington thanked God for the progress of Gustavus: 'That brave king tutors the king of Bohemia in his discipline for war exquisitely . . . '[65]

At court there were those who received the news more coolly. The Treasurer and the peace lobby spoke of Gustavus's arrogance and ambition and the danger of Swedish domination of German affairs. In June Laud was successful in having Windebank appointed, rather than Roe, to the vacant Secretaryship of State.[66] During the summer the king's resolve against calling

[61] SP103/69/fos. 64r–v, 101r–v; *CSPV 1629–32*, pp. 605–6; Gardiner, *History*, vii, pp. 196–7.
[62] Charles allowed Hamilton, who wished to return to court, to come home at approximately the same time. The marquis was frustrated by Gustavus's refusal to allow him to levy forces in Germany and obtain another independent command. SP81/38/fo. 334v–335v; SRO, Hamilton Mss, nos. 160–1, 271, 9364–5, 9367; *CSPV 1629–32*, p. 644; Rushworth, *Historical collections*, ii, pp. 166–75; Gardiner, *History*, vii, p. 205; Roberts, *Gustavus Adolphus*, ii, pp. 614–15.
[63] Cottington to Vane, 29 Sept. 1632, quoted in Gardiner, *History*, vii, p. 206.
[64] Roe to Horwood, 28 May 1632, quoted in Gardiner, *History*, vii, p. 197. See also Parker, *Thirty Years War*, pp. 128–9; Roberts, *Gustavus Adolphus*, ii, pp. 694ff.
[65] Sir Thomas Barrington to Lady Barrington, Apr. 1632, Searle, *Barrington family letters*, pp. 235–6.
[66] SP81/38/fos. 85r–86v; *CSPD 1631–33*, pp. 388–9; Laud, *Works*, iii, p. 215, and vii, p. 144; Birch, ii, p. 169; Roberts, *Gustavus Adolphus*, ii, p. 614 and n; Gardiner, *History*, vii, p. 200; Trevor-Roper, *Archbishop Laud*, pp. 127–8; R. Cant, 'The embassy of the earl of Leicester to Denmark in 1632', *EHR*, liv (1939), p. 255; Federowicz, *England's Baltic trade*, p. 206.

Parliament was reported to be stronger than ever. Among his ministers Weston was supreme and growing in power.[67] This state of affairs was reflected in the sending of the earl of Leicester to Denmark in September, when Charles's talks with Sweden were broken off. This was a peace mission, most unlikely to succeed and supposedly aimed at furthering the interests of the Palatines. Leicester's instructions referred to the danger of Swedish hegemony, the abiding power of the Habsburg and Catholic states and the likelihood of a long European war. This combination of strategic sense, anti-Protestant bias and unwarranted optimism suggests the joint inspiration of Weston and the king. Leicester asked Christian IV to consider allying with the Catholic states – while offering no such initiative on England's part – or joining with Charles to intervene and bring about a peace. Christian could make no positive response to an overture so ill-conceived. He was sorry for the plight of the Palatines but said that Charles must help them himself.[68] Weston's policy was now dangerously at variance with English public opinion. In October it was necessary to silence the press and prevent it from publishing news of the Swedish successes. Information, of course, found its way through and could only damage Charles.[69]

Gustavus was killed at Lützen in the first week of November: welcome news to the advocates of peace.[70] After his death, Charles sent Frederick a small amount of money, hoping that his brother-in-law might lead the German cause.[71] The displaced elector, however, died twelve days after the king of Sweden, and the episode was but a coda to Charles's last involvement with the Protestant cause.[72] The pacific foreign policy of Charles's regime had already been established. The deaths of Dorchester, Frederick and Gustavus marked the end of an era in the history of Anglo-continental Protestantism –

---

[67] *CSPV 1629–32*, pp. 610, 623, 626, 628, 630, 636–7.

[68] Cant, 'The earl of Leicester's embassy'; Roberts, *Gustavus Adolphus*, ii, pp. 655ff. Weston also allowed his son Jerome to go on embassy to France and Italy, supposedly to promote the German cause (leaving on 2 August). The Treasurer was surely humouring Charles's incurable optimism and desire to leave no option, however illogically, unexplored. Weston also sought to protect himself against hostile English Protestant opinion. He may also have been reaching out to Richelieu to ensure stable relations in the wake of the Swedish attack on Bavaria. His statement to his son that Charles's offer to Gustavus was likely to be accepted was no doubt to give credibility to his embassy. It was incompatible with the deterioration (which Weston had successfully promoted) of the Anglo-Swedish treaty. Gardiner misinterpreted this document, which he admitted was a copy and possibly corrupt. *CSPV 1629–32*, pp. 588, 590, 595–7, 606, 613, 643–4; Birch, ii, p. 167; Rushworth, *Historical collections*, ii, p. 170; Gardiner, *History*, vii, pp. 196–9, 204 and n, 205.

[69] Gardiner, *History*, vii, p. 206; F. J. Levy, 'How information spread amongst the gentry, 1550–1640', *JBS*, xxi, 2 (1982), pp. 23–4.

[70] Gardiner, *History*, vii, p. 208; Parker, *Europe in crisis*, pp. 228–9.

[71] The sum was £16,000. Gardiner, *History*, vii, p. 207.

[72] Parker, *Thirty Years War*, p. 131; Wedgwood, *Thirty Years War*, p. 332.

an era in which Charles had never been at home. In November 1632 there died also Sir John Eliot in the Tower. His passing was less of a milestone than a painful reminder of the political failures which created the personal rule.[73]

The chance to restore the Palatines which was presented to Charles in 1631 was never to be bettered. The reality and the excellence of that opportunity throw Charles's rejection of it into very sharp relief. Clearly he made a decision about the basic nature of his regime. He had been turning against the alternative over a period of time, drifting away from the need to achieve parliamentary co-operation. But during the winter of 1631–2 he was tested and his choice was clear. When forced to choose between achieving his aim in the international sphere – a cherished goal – and the definitive rejection of Parliament and war, he chose the latter. It was a positive as well as a negative choice. Charles had a preference for unaccountable kingship under God and for friendship with Spain. These ideas were inextricably linked in his mind. He felt committed to both in principle; a new Parliament would call for war with Spain;[74] and any general war would require parliamentary supply. Charles's decision was not, of course, an active one but it was a decision nonetheless. England resounded with his refusal to the extent that public news itself became an indictment. Most of Europe was aware that he was so much in dispute with his people that he would not act to restore his family to their patrimony.[75] Charles's government was unmistakably premised upon an isolationist foreign policy wedded to Spain;[76] and it was marked by a preference for non-parliamentary government, not least in the interests of an exclusive clique about the king. Charles, at home and abroad, had come to preside over an island kingdom.

So it might have remained, save for the irresistible force of necessity. In

---

[73] For Charles's refusal to release Eliot's body from the Tower for burial see Hulme, *Life of Sir John Eliot*, p. 392. His death was held against Charles's government in the Grand Remonstrance; Gardiner, *Constitutional documents*, p. 210.

[74] Gardiner, *Constitutional documents*, pp. 208–9, 253–4; Adams, 'Spain or the Netherlands?', p. 101; Fletcher, *Outbreak of the English civil war*, p. 64.

[75] SP94/36/fo. 14r; PRO 31/3/66/fo. 132r; *CSPV 1629–32*, pp. 204, 572, 574; Magurn, *Rubens letters*, pp. 342–5.

[76] Charles's next major international endeavour was the first maritime treaty of 1634 for Anglo-Spanish naval co-operation against the Dutch. This inspired the Ship Money project in England. Charles could not extract concessions from Spain without an actual break with the Dutch, which the Spaniards knew to be unlikely. Despite the opportunity presented by French entry into the war in 1635, Charles stayed at peace with Spain. The Anglo-Spanish discussions were revived in 1637 and on the eve of the English civil war. By that time Charles was solely concerned with his survival and was seeking Spanish aid against the Scots. On the failure of the war party in England in 1637 see Hibbard, *Popish plot*, pp. 72ff. See also ibid., pp. 104ff.; Adams, 'Spain or the Netherlands?', pp. 84, 86, 100–1; Sharpe, 'Personal rule of Charles I', p. 69; Gardiner, *History*, vii, pp. 215, 349, 351–9, 366–72, 380, 382–4; Loomie, 'Spanish faction', pp. 39–42; Alcalá-Zamora, *España, Flandes*, pp. 510–13; and see p. 239, n. 63, above.

1631 and 1632 Charles could ignore that force for it was visited upon his sister, not upon him. In 1640 the necessity was his and could not be ignored. He could not, as on that earlier occasion, indulge his prejudices, conceding nothing. 1632 in fact saw a double disaster for Charles. There was a lost opportunity to achieve success, but also a damaging failure. Public confidence in Charles was further undermined.[77] The breakdown between domestic and foreign policy under his rule was compounded. And the Caroline political court, with a critical victory over the Council, was confirmed in its provocative monopoly of access to royal power. Weston's next close call would come with an attack upon him by Laud, and Laud could only be threatened by Charles's necessity.

[77] SP16/204/107; Breslow, *Mirror of England*, p. 137; and see p. 218, nn. 212–13 and p. 282, n. 37, above.

9

The anatomy of a political transition

The most satisfying historical explanation must always combine analysis of the particular and the general, the wide canvas and the immediate detail of events. It must also incorporate understanding of various aspects of human life: the personal, political, economic and social as well as the intellectual and religious. As I trust I have shown, only such a liberal historical approach can be expected to comprehend the complexities involved in the emergence of Charles's regime. At this point one might ask whether the making of that regime was a revolutionary or more evolutionary development. The question, however, is misplaced and the answer could legitimately (and unhelpfully) be 'neither' or 'both'. This period saw a most complicated re-orientation of English politics as the implications of Charles's rule began to be worked out. What can be said is that the year 1629, traditionally assumed to have marked a sudden departure, did no such thing. It is also true, however, that Charles's attitudes were eventually decisive.

This study has rested on the assumption that English developments during this period can only be understood within their international context. The Thirty Years War arguably constituted the cataclysmic end of the Renaissance world.[1] The prevailing European climate was one of war, with all that that implied. England could not avoid its effects. The emergence of Charles's personal rule was a European event. It was so in the sense of being an inextricable part of the whole, but also in the sense that English events sometimes had a critical impact upon European affairs. Most notably, the fate of the Palatinate, with which England was intimately concerned, was a matter of vital significance for all the great powers. On a general level, England's withdrawal from the war was an essential ingredient of the remaking of the anti-Habsburg cause, of the rise of French power, of the new influence of Lutheranism and even of the decline of confessional politics in favour of

[1] H. R. Trevor-Roper, *Renaissance essays* (London, 1986), p. vi.

292

reason of state.[2] English events were always subject to foreign influences and vice versa. The workings of Spanish foreign policy illustrate this well.

In the English context, the pattern of change which we can term a new politics radically transformed national political life during these years. This dislocation of the habits of a traditional society rendered it politically unstable and distinctly vulnerable to crisis. That Charles bore a direct responsibility for this was perceived, indirectly, at the time. The years after 1625, and particularly after 1629, acquired an immediate notoriety.[3] The years of personal rule have an abiding place in English political culture, not shared by other lengthy periods without a Parliament (such as that between 1614 and 1621), which ultimately derives from this political transformation and the trauma it engendered. The new politics created a 'credibility gap' between the rhetoric and ideology of consensus and the fact of conflict and dislocation. In attempting to come to terms with this problem men were hampered by not yet having a language to describe it.[4] This in turn worsened the dangerous shortage of trust and reason among the political elite. Specifically, each of the principal elements of the new politics represented a problem which only time would solve. In dealing with the dilemma of the constitutional fiction, men did not resort to the fallacy of equating innocence with virtue. Charles's supposed innocence was increasingly seen as malignant. It took many years, however, for him to be perceived as personally malicious and an impossible obstacle to good government while he lived. This realization (unpopular as it was), and its effect upon traditional attitudes to kingship, was part of the creation of a more modern and more free mental world. The breakdown between the internal and external workings of the state could only be repaired by the re-establishment of ideological harmony, by fiscal reform and by the emergence of a wealthier nation. The evils of political polarization, exclusive government, subversion and conspiracy theory were rendered less relevant when the political court was shattered by the attack of the Long Parliament, when new divisions arose over the religious issue, and when a royalist party was created and circumstances were altered by civil war. Those evils never reappeared in early modern England in such dangerous combination.

The story of the damaging impact of Charles's rule provides a powerful argument against the theory that England was on a high road to civil war from the beginning of the century or even earlier in time. Moreover, the crisis of the Long Parliament involved a number of elements novel in Caroline politics: the distinct reality of a popish plot,[5] a crisis in the relationships between different parts of a multiple kingdom, the failure of projected

---

[2] Parker, *Thirty Years War*, p. 219.   [3] Gardiner, *Constitutional documents*, pp. 208ff.
[4] I am grateful to David Underdown for this point.   [5] See Hibbard, *Popish plot*.

Spanish aid to England as a political satellite,[6] the emerging politicization of the localities,[7] and a 'rescue operation'[8] attempted by a whole political nation. It is important, however, to see the Caroline period as a whole and to recognize the links between the two crises: between that which produced the personal rule and that which led, eventually, to civil war. They are causally and inextricably connected. The fears of Charles's critics were confirmed and deepened during the 1630s and in a real sense it was the climate of the new politics, considerably exacerbated, which created the crisis of the Long Parliament. There was the same inability to fight a war, the same insidious political polarization and the same troubled development of political ideas under the pressure of events. Among those ideas, theories of Charles's irresponsibility were explored,[9] the notion of a conspiracy against the godly commonwealth was very much extended[10] and the theory of treason was developed, in ways that Eliot had anticipated in 1629, in attempting to justify the proceedings against the earl of Strafford.[11] Over one hundred members of the Long Parliament had sat in the 1620s[12] and the Providence Island connection provided experienced leadership. Yet Charles, while maintaining his belief in a Calvinist conspiracy against him,[13] was the crucial link between the political experiences of the 1620s and the early 1640s.

A word about the role of ideology is in season here. Ideology, as a subjective structure of thought through which observations are filtered, can indeed become a driving force in politics. As we have seen, it did so at points during this period. Ideological animosities also played their role in the civil war to the extent that the divisions they created may have gone sufficiently deep to give the misleading impression, in many cases, of pure caprice.[14] There is nothing inherently or necessarily noble in such a spectacle. Human values are the casualty when the ideological battle lines are drawn. This is not to deny the beneficial influence of principle in the political world. Yet men with any

---

[6] Elliott, 'The year of the three ambassadors'.
[7] Fletcher, 'National and local awareness in the county communities', pp. 163–4, 173–4.
[8] Russell, 'The nature of a Parliament', pp. 135, 149.
[9] Morrill, 'Religious context', p. 171 and n.
[10] Hibbard, *Popish plot*, pp. 214–16, 226, 232ff.; Gardiner, *Constitutional documents*, pp. 202ff.; Reeve, 'Legal status of the Petition of Right', pp. 275–7.
[11] Wentworth became earl of Strafford in 1640. The Commons supposed his treason to have involved attempting the alteration of government and to have constituted an offence against the state; C. Russell, 'The theory of treason in the trial of Strafford', *EHR*, lxxx, 314 (Jan. 1965). On Eliot's Three Resolutions see chapter 3 above.
[12] Zagorin, *Court and the country*, p. 80.
[13] Hibbard, *Popish plot*, pp. 228, 234, 237.
[14] Russell, *Parliaments*, Appendix. Understanding of the relative influence of ideological and non-ideological factors can only be achieved to any degree, of course, by study of each individual case.

political sophistication are neither solely concerned with principle nor with self-interest. They are usually concerned with getting their personal interests and principles aligned to promote and protect them both. This can involve rationalization or ideological inspiration or a combination of the two. Eliot is a classic example of this last. Neither should it be forgotten that the requisite power to put principles into practice has its own eternal attraction. Weston and (probably less so) Laud no doubt felt the pull of power for its own sake. Above all, ideology cannot remain of paramount importance for an indefinite period without falling foul of human nature or the unavoidable dictates of circumstances. The parliamentary war effort in the 1640s depended significantly upon imports of Spanish silver.[15] John Gauden, who had been chaplain to the earl of Warwick, eventually ghost-wrote the classic of royalist propaganda, *Eikon Basilike*.[16]

The critical estimate of Charles's kingship presented here might reflect favourably on the government of his father. Considered in retrospect, James's political sagacity is striking. Three men who acted contrary to his advice at critical points came to miserable ends. He warned Frederick against accepting the crown of Bohemia and against the German war.[17] He warned Buckingham against the promotion of Laud.[18] And he opposed Charles's desire for parliamentary war finance in 1624, a course which would provoke the religious issue and raise the political temperature in England.[19] It is idle to speculate about how James would have dealt with the political difficulties which beset his son. We do, however, know that there was no civil war in England under James.

Is there no way in which Charles's political reputation can be redeemed? It is possible to ponder certain positive aspects of the personal rule: commerce and prosperity, enhancement of the navy, efforts at administrative reform, the search for order and uniformity, a lack of sympathy with confessional strife and a nation at peace rather than at war. Yet peace abroad was far from being the necessary concomitant of peace and political stability at home. Charles insulted and undermined the workings of English national life, creating a political desert he wished to call peace but which others would not. There was nothing inherently evil about his policies save for the natural reservation one feels towards the autocrat, the war-profiteer and the dogmatist in religion. His faithlessness and inhuman streak are in no way appealing. He clearly loved family life, religious piety and artistic merit. But these

---

[15] Kepler, 'Fiscal aspects of the English carrying trade', pp. 270ff.
[16] Newton, *Colonising activities*, p. 78; Hirst, *Authority and conflict*, p. 287.
[17] Lockyer, *Buckingham*, pp. 79–80.
[18] Collinson, 'Jacobean religious settlement', pp. 50–1.
[19] Lockyer, *Buckingham*, p. 174; Fincham and Lake, 'Ecclesiastical policy of King James I', pp. 198ff.

qualities were flawed when coupled with his capacity for political destruction, particularly in a king in his time and place. He was fundamentally
imperceptive in believing, however unconsciously, that he could shape reality
absolutely to his personal ends. The Venetian diplomat Soranzo wrote with
great perspicacity that Charles's nature was such as to oblige no one in word
or in deed.[20] That ruler who makes no concessions in a potentially divided
society, in a world at war, stands to inherit the wind. Charles's regime was
never really stable for it did not rest, like those of Elizabeth I and of his
father,[21] upon a foundation of consent.

[20] Soranzo to the Doge and Senate, 2 July 1630; *CSPV 1629–32*, p. 373.
[21] Collinson, *Religion of Protestants*, pp. viii–ix, 20, 282–3, and passim; G. R. Elton, *The Parliament of England 1559–1581* (Cambridge, 1986), pp. 377–9.

BIBLIOGRAPHY

I MANUSCRIPT SOURCES

Great Britain
Bodleian Library, Oxford:
 Clarendon State Papers
 Rawlinson Ms C197 (instructions for Wentworth as Lord President of the North, 18 June 1629)
 Tanner Ms 71 (letters and papers 1629–33)
British Library, London:
 Additional Ms 22,959 (diary of John Rous 1625–43)
 Additional Ms 24,909 (collection of Padre Diego de Quiroga's papers, 1629–46, including letters of Olivares and Philip IV)
 Harleian Ms 1584 (state papers 1623–8)
 Harleian Ms 6988 (royal letters 1625–48)
 Harleian Ms 7000 (state papers 1620–31)
Cambridge University Library:
 Ms Mm, 6.63.4 (draft of Littleton's argument in King's Bench in 1629)
Melbourne Hall, Derbyshire:
 Coke Manuscripts (state papers of the Elizabethan, Jacobean and Caroline periods). This collection was acquired in July 1987 by the British Library, where it will eventually be available to researchers.
Nottingham University Library:
 Newcastle Manuscripts, Ne.C., 15,404–5 (letter books of the Holles family, c. 1615–37)
Public Record Office, Chancery Lane, London:
 C115, M, N, Chancery Master's exhibits, Duchess of Norfolk deeds (seventeenth-century newsletters)
 KB29/278 (King's Bench controlment roll, Hilary Term, 1629)
 PC2/39, 40 (Privy Council registers 1628–30, 1630–1)
 PRO 31/3 (Baschet's transcripts from French archives)
 SP16 (state papers, domestic, Charles I)
 SP39 (sign manual, Charles I)
 SP45/10 (printed proclamations, Charles I)
 SP63 (state papers relating to Ireland)
 SP75 (state papers relating to Denmark)
 SP77 (state papers relating to Flanders)
 SP78 (state papers relating to France)

297

SP80 (state papers relating to the Holy Roman Empire)
SP81 (state papers relating to the German states)
SP84 (state papers relating to the United Provinces)
SP88 (state papers relating to Poland)
SP92 (state papers relating to Savoy)
SP94 (state papers relating to Spain)
SP95 (state papers relating to Sweden)
SP96 (state papers relating to Switzerland)
SP97 (state papers relating to Turkey)
SP99 (state papers relating to Venice)
SP101 (newsletters)
SP103 (treaty papers)
SP104/170 (*inter alia*, letter book of Dorchester as Secretary of State)
SP105/95 (letter book of Sir Dudley Carleton, later Viscount Dorchester, 1616–18)
Scottish Record Office, Edinburgh:
  Hamilton Manuscripts (family and state papers). (I have cited these documents by
  the old catalogue numbers. They are currently being re-numbered by the SRO
  which is also producing a list for conversion from the old references to the new.)

Belgium
Archives Générales du Royaume, Brussels:
  Secrétaire d'Etat et de Guerre, liasse 208 (file on Rubens' negotiations in 1628–9)

France
Archives du Ministère des Relations Extérieures, Paris:
  Correspondance Politique, Angleterre, vols. 42–4 (state papers relating to England,
  1627–32)

Spain
Archivo General de Simancas:
  Sección Estado, Inglaterra, leg. E2517, E2519–20, E2562 (state papers relating
  to England, 1628–35)
  Sección Estado, Flandes, leg. E2042–3 (state papers relating to Flanders,
  1628–9)
Archivo del Duque del Infantado, Madrid:
  Palafox Mss, leg. 94, fos. 133–8 (Coloma's instructions for Necolalde, 26 May
  1631 (n.s.))
Archivo del Duque de Medinaceli, Seville:
  leg. 86, instructions for Necolalde, 18 Oct. 1632 (n.s.)

II PRINTED PRIMARY SOURCES

Acts of the Privy Council (of England)
Barrington family letters 1628–1632, ed. A. Searle (Camden Society, London, 1983)
Birch, T. (ed.), *The court and times of Charles I*, 2 vols. (London, 1848)
The autobiography of Sir John Bramston of Skreens, ed. Lord Braybrooke (Camden
  Society, London, 1845)
Calendar of state papers, colonial
Calendar of state papers, domestic
Calendar of state papers, domestic, addenda 1625–44
Calendar of state papers, Venetian

The poems of Thomas Carew, ed. R. Dunlap (Oxford, 1949)
Calendar of the Clarendon state papers, ed. O. Ogle, W. H. Bliss and W. D. Macray, 3 vols. (Oxford, 1869–76)
Clarendon, Edward Hyde, earl of, *History of the rebellion and civil wars in England*, ed. W. D. Macray, 6 vols. (Oxford, 1888)
Cobbett, W., Howell, T. B. *et al.* (eds.), *State trials*, 34 vols. (London, 1809–28)
Keeler, M. F., Cole, M. J. and Bidwell, W. D. (eds.), *The Commons debates in 1628*, 4 vols. (New Haven and London, 1977)
Notestein, W., and Relf, F. H. (eds.), *The Commons debates for 1629* (Minneapolis, 1921)
Commons' journals
The works of the Right Reverend father in God John Cosin, Lord Bishop of Durham, ed. J. Samson, 5 vols. (Oxford, 1843–55)
Correspondence of John Cosin, ed. G. Ornsby, 2 vols. (London, 1869)
The autobiography and correspondence of Sir Simonds D'Ewes during the reigns of James I and Charles I, ed. J. O. Halliwell, 2 vols. (London, 1845)
The letter book of Sir John Eliot, 1625–1632, ed. A. B. Grosart (London, 1882)
The letters of Elizabeth queen of Bohemia, ed. L. M. Baker (London, 1953)
Elton, G. R. (ed.), *The Tudor constitution*, 2nd edn (Cambridge, 1982)
Gardiner, S. R. (ed.), *Parliamentary debates in 1610* (Camden Society, London, 1862)
  The constitutional documents of the puritan revolution 1625–1660, 3rd edn, revised (Oxford, 1906, repr. 1979)
Hacket, J., *Scrinia reserata*, 2 pts (1693)
Speech of Sir Robert Heath ... in the case of Alexander Leighton in the Star Chamber, 4 June 1630, ed. S. R. Gardiner (Camden Society Miscellany VII; London, 1875)
Letters of Queen Henrietta Maria, ed. M. A. E. Green (London, 1857)
Letters of Henrietta Maria, 1628–1666, ed. H. Ferrero (Turin, 1881)
Historical Manuscripts Commission, Buccleuch Mss
Historical Manuscripts Commission, 4th report
Historical Manuscripts Commission, 7th report
Historical Manuscripts Commission, 11th report
The poems of Ben Jonson, ed. B. H. Newdigate (Oxford, 1936)
Kenyon, J. P. (ed.), *The Stuart constitution*, 2nd edn (Cambridge, 1986)
Laud, W., *Works*, ed. W. Scott and J. Bliss, 7 vols. (Oxford, 1847–60)
Lismore papers, ed. A. B. Grosart, 10 vols. (London, 1886–8)
Lonchay, H., and Cuvelier, J. (eds.), *Correspondance de la cour d'Espagne sur les affaires des Pays-Bas au XVIIe siècle*, 6 vols. (Brussels, 1923–7)
Lords' journals
Keeler, M. F. *et al.* (eds.), *Lords proceedings 1628* (New Haven, 1983)
Public Record Office, 47th Deputy Keeper's report (1886)
Lettres, instructions diplomatiques et papiers d'état du Cardinal de Richelieu, ed. D. L. M. Avenel, 8 vols. (Paris, 1853–77)
The diary of John Rous, ed. M. A. E. Green (Camden Society, London, 1856)
The letters of Sir Peter Paul Rubens, ed. R. S. Magurn (Cambridge, Mass., 1955)
Rushworth, J. (ed.), *Historical collections*, 8 vols. (1659–1701)
Rymer, T., and Sanderson, R. (eds.), *Foedera*, 20 vols. (1704–32)
The earl of Strafford's letters and despatches ... , ed. W. Knowler, 2 vols. (London, 1739)
Stuart royal proclamations, ed. J. F. Larkin, vol. ii (Oxford, 1983)
Whitelocke, B., *Memorials of English affairs*, 4 vols. (Oxford, 1853)

III SECONDARY SOURCES

Adams, S. L., 'Foreign policy and the Parliaments of 1621 and 1624', in K. M. Sharpe (ed.), *Faction and Parliament, essays on early Stuart history* (Oxford, 1978)
  'Spain or the Netherlands? The dilemmas of early Stuart foreign policy', in H. Tomlinson (ed.), *Before the English civil war* (London, 1983)
  'Eliza enthroned? The court and its politics', in C. Haigh (ed.), *The reign of Elizabeth* (London, 1985)
Alcalá-Zamora y Queipo de Llano, J., *España, Flandes y el mar del norte (1618–1639)* (Barcelona, 1975)
Alexander, M. C., *Charles I's Lord Treasurer* (Chapel Hill, 1975)
Allan, D. G. C., 'The rising in the west, 1628–1631', *EcHR*, v (1952)
Andrews, K. R., *Trade, plunder and settlement* (Cambridge, 1984)
Appleby, J. C., 'An association for the West Indies? English plans for a West India Company, 1621–1629', *Journal of Imperial and Commonwealth History*, xv (1987)
Ashton, R., *The crown and the money market 1603–1640* (London, 1960)
  The English civil war (London, 1978)
  The City and the court 1603–1643 (Cambridge, 1979)
Aylmer, G. E., *The king's servants: the civil service of Charles I, 1625–1642* (London and New York, 1961)
  Rebellion or revolution? England 1640–1660 (Oxford, 1986)
Bangs, C., 'The enigma of Arminian politics', *Church History*, xlii (1973)
Barcroft, J. H., *Buckingham and the central administration 1616–1628* (University of Minnesota PhD thesis, 1963; published Ann Arbor, 1964)
Beatty, J., *Warwick and Holland* (Denver, 1965)
Beller, E. A., 'The Thirty Years War', in *NCMH*, iv (Cambridge, 1971)
Bireley, R., *Religion and politics in the age of the Counterreformation* (Chapel Hill, 1981)
Breslow, M. A., *A mirror of England, English puritan views of foreign nations, 1618–1640* (Cambridge, Mass., 1970)
Brown, J. and Elliott, J. H., *A palace for a king* (New Haven and London, 1980)
Calder, I. M., *The activities of the puritan faction of the Church of England* (London, 1957)
Cant, R., 'The embassy of the earl of Leicester to Denmark in 1632', *EHR*, liv (1939)
Carlton, C., *Charles I, the personal monarch* (London, 1983)
Clark, P., 'Thomas Scott and the growth of urban opposition to the early Stuart regime', *HJ*, xxi, 1 (1978)
Clay, C. G. A., *Economic expansion and social change: England 1500–1700*, 2 vols. (Cambridge, 1984)
Cliffe, J. T., *The puritan gentry* (London, 1984)
Cogswell, T., 'Foreign policy and Parliament: the case of La Rochelle, 1625–6', *EHR*, xcix (1984)
  'Prelude to Ré: the Anglo-French struggle over La Rochelle, 1624–1627', *History*, lxxi, 231 (1986)
Coleman, D. C., *The economy of England 1450–1750* (Oxford, 1977)
Collinson, P., *The religion of Protestants* (Oxford, 1982)
  'A comment: concerning the name Puritan', *JEH*, xxi, 4 (1980)
  'The Jacobean religious settlement: the Hampton Court conference', in H. Tomlinson (ed.), *Before the English civil war* (London, 1983)

'England and international Calvinism, 1558–1640', in M. Prestwich (ed.), *International Calvinism 1541–1715* (Oxford, 1985)

Cooper, J. P., 'The fall of the Stuart monarchy', in *NCMH*, iv (Cambridge, 1971)

'Sea power' in *NCMH*, iv (Cambridge, 1971)

(ed.), *The new Cambridge modern history*, vol. iv: *The decline of Spain and the Thirty Years War 1609–48/59* (Cambridge, 1971)

Cope, E., 'Public images of Parliament during its absence', *Legislative Studies Quarterly*, vii, 2 (1982)

Craven, W. F., 'The earl of Warwick, a speculator in piracy', *Hispanic American Historical Review*, x (1930)

Crawford, P., *Denzil Holles, 1598–1680, a study of his political career* (London, 1979)

Cross, C., *Church and people 1450–1660*, 3rd edn (London, 1983)

Cust, R. P., *The forced loan and English politics 1626–1628* (Oxford, 1987)

'Charles I, the Privy Council, and the forced loan', *JBS*, xxiv, 2 (1985)

'News and politics in early seventeenth century England', *P&P*, cxii (1986)

and Lake, P., 'Sir Richard Grosvenor and the rhetoric of magistracy', *BIHR*, cxxx (1981)

Daly, J., *Cosmic harmony and political thinking in early Stuart England* (*TrAPS*, lxix, pt 7; Philadelphia, 1979)

The dictionary of national biography

Dietz, F. C., *English public finance, 1558–1641* (London, 1932)

Donagan, B., 'A courtier's progress: greed and consistency in the life of the earl of Holland', *HJ*, xix (1976)

Elliott, J. H., *Imperial Spain 1496–1716* (Harmondsworth, 1970)

Richelieu and Olivares (Cambridge, 1984)

The count-duke of Olivares (New Haven, 1986)

'England and Europe: a common malady?', in C. Russell (ed.), *The origins of the English civil war*, rev. edn (London, 1980)

'The year of the three ambassadors', in H. Lloyd-Jones, V. Pearl and B. Worden (eds.), *History and imagination: essays in honour of H. R. Trevor-Roper* (London, 1981)

'A question of reputation? Spanish foreign policy in the seventeenth century', rev. art., *JMH*, lv (1983)

'Yet another crisis?', in P. Clark (ed.), *The European crisis of the 1590s* (London, 1985)

Elton, G. R., 'A high road to civil war?', in G. R. Elton, *Studies in Tudor and Stuart politics and government* (3 vols; Cambridge, 1974–83), vol. ii

The Parliament of England 1559–1581 (Cambridge, 1986)

'Tudor government: the points of contact, ii, the Council', *TRHS*, 5th ser., xxv (1975)

'Tudor government: the points of contact, iii, the court', *TRHS*, 5th ser., xxvi (1976)

rev. art., *TLS*, 16 Sept. 1983

Evans, R. J. W., rev. art., *JEH*, xxxiv, 1 (1983)

Federowicz, J. K., *England's Baltic trade in the seventeenth century* (Cambridge, 1980)

Fincham, K. and Lake, P., 'The ecclesiastical policy of King James I', *JBS*, xxiv, 2 (1985)

Fletcher, A., *The outbreak of the English civil war* (London, 1981)

'Factionalism in town and countryside: the significance of puritanism and Arminianism', Studies in Church History, xvi (1979)

'National and local awareness in the county communities', in H. Tomlinson (ed.), Before the English civil war (London, 1983)

Forster, J., Sir John Eliot: a biography, 2 vols. (London, 1864)

Foster, E. R., 'Printing the Petition of Right', HLQ, xxxviii (1974–5)

Fraser, I. H. C., 'The agitation in the Commons, 2 March 1629, and the interrogation of the leaders of the anti-court group', BIHR, xxx (1957)

Fuidge, N. M., 'Queen Elizabeth and the Petition of Right', BIHR, xlviii (1975)

Gardiner, S. R., History of England from the accession of James I to the outbreak of the civil war, 1603–1642, 10 vols. (London, 1883–4)

Grayson, C., 'James I and the religious crisis in the United Provinces', in D. Baker (ed.), Reform and Reformation: England and the continent c. 1500–1750 (Oxford, 1979)

Gregg, P., King Charles I (London, 1981)

Guy, J. A., 'The origins of the Petition of Right reconsidered', HJ, xxv, 2 (1982)

Hale, J. R., War and society in Renaissance Europe 1450–1620 (London, 1985)

Haller, W., The rise of puritanism (New York, 1957)

Harriss, G. L., 'Medieval doctrines in the debates on supply, 1610–1629', in K. M. Sharpe (ed.), Faction and Parliament, essays on early Stuart history (Oxford, 1978)

Havran, M. J., Caroline courtier: the life of Lord Cottington (London, 1973)

'Parliament and Catholicism in England, 1626–1629', Catholic Historical Review, xliv (1958)

Hervey, M. F. S., The life, correspondence and collections of Thomas Howard, earl of Arundel (Cambridge, 1921)

Hibbard, C. M., Charles I and the popish plot (Chapel Hill, 1983)

Hill, C., Economic problems of the Church from Archbishop Whitgift to the Long Parliament (Oxford, 1956)

Antichrist in seventeenth century England (Oxford, 1971)

'Parliament and people in seventeenth century England', P&P, xcii (1981)

Hirst, D., Authority and conflict, England 1603–1658 (London, 1986)

'Court, country, and politics before 1629', in K. M. Sharpe (ed.), Faction and Parliament, essays on early Stuart history (Oxford, 1978)

Holdsworth, W. S., A history of English law, 13 vols. (London, 1922–52)

Howard, M., War in European history (Oxford, 1976)

Howarth, D., Lord Arundel and his circle (London, 1985)

Hoyle, D., 'A Commons' investigation of Arminianism and popery in Cambridge on the eve of the civil war', HJ, xxix, 2 (1986)

Hughes, A., 'Thomas Dugard and his circle in the 1630s – a "Parliamentary–puritan" connexion?', HJ, xxix, 4 (1986)

Hulme, H., The life of Sir John Eliot (London, 1957)

Hutton, W., William Laud (1896)

Huxley, G., Endymion Porter: the life of a courtier, 1587–1649 (London, 1959)

Israel, J. I., The Dutch republic and the Hispanic world 1606–1661 (Oxford, 1982)

'The politics of international trade rivalry during the Thirty Years War: Gabriel de Roy and Olivares' mercantilist projects, 1621–1645', International History Review, viii, 4 (Nov. 1986)

Jones, J. R., Britain and Europe during the seventeenth century (London, 1966)

Kendall, R. T., Calvin and English Calvinism to 1649 (Oxford, 1979)

Kenyon, J. P., The history men (London, 1983)

Kepler, J. S., 'Fiscal aspects of the English carrying trade during the Thirty Years War', *EcHR*, ser. 2, xxv (1972)
  'The value of ships gained and lost by the English shipping industry during the wars with Spain and France, 1624–1630', *Mariner's Mirror*, lix (1973)
Kossman, E. H., 'The Low Countries', in *NCMH*, iv (Cambridge, 1971)
Lake, P. G., 'Calvinism and the English Church, 1570–1635', *P&P*, cxiv (1987)
Lambert, S., 'Procedure in the House of Commons in the early Stuart period', *EHR*, xcv (1980)
Lee, M., *The road to revolution: Scotland under Charles I, 1625–37* (Urbana, 1985)
Leonard, H. H., 'Distraint of knighthood: the last phase, 1625–1641', *History*, lxiii (1978)
Levy, F. J., 'How information spread amongst the gentry, 1550–1640', *JBS*, xxi, 2 (1982)
Lindley, K. J., 'Riot prevention and control in early Stuart London', *TRHS*, 5th ser., xxxiii (1983)
Lockyer, R., *Buckingham, the life and political career of George Villiers, first duke of Buckingham 1592–1628* (London, 1981)
Loomie, A. J., 'Olivares, the English Catholics and the peace of 1630', *Revue Belge de Philologie et d'Histoire*, xlvii, 4 (1969)
  'Canon Henry Taylor, Spanish Habsburg diplomat', *Recusant History*, xvii, 3 (May 1985)
  'The Spanish faction at the court of Charles I, 1630–38', *BIHR*, lix, 139 (1986)
McGee, J. S., 'William Laud and the outward face of religion', in R. L. DeMolen (ed.), *Leaders of the Reformation* (London, 1984)
Maclear, J. F., 'The influence of the puritan clergy on the House of Commons, 1625–29', *Church History*, xiv (1945)
Maitland, F. W., *The constitutional history of England* (Cambridge, 1908, repr. 1968)
Maltby, W. S., *The black legend: the development of anti-Spanish sentiment, 1558–1660* (Durham, N.C., 1971)
Manning, B., 'The aristocracy and the downfall of Charles I', in B. Manning (ed.), *Politics, religion and the English civil war* (London, 1973)
Mathew, D., *The social structure of Caroline England* (Oxford, 1948)
  The age of Charles I (London, 1951)
  Scotland under Charles I (London, 1955)
Mattingley, G., *Renaissance diplomacy* (London, 1955)
Millar, O., 'Strafford and Van Dyck', in R. Ollard and P. Tudor-Craig (eds.), *For Veronica Wedgwood these studies in seventeenth century history* (London, 1986)
Mitchison, R., *Lordship to patronage, Scotland 1603–1745* (London, 1983)
Moody, T. W., Martin, F. X. and Byrne, F. J. (eds.), *A new history of Ireland*, vol. iii (Oxford, 1976)
Morrill, J. S., *The revolt of the provinces*, 2nd edn (London, 1980)
  'The religious context of the English civil war', *TRHS*, 5th ser., xxxiv (1984)
  (ed.), *Reactions to the English civil war 1642–1649* (London, 1982)
Mosse, G. L., 'Changes in religious thought', in *NCMH*, iv (Cambridge, 1971)
Mousnier, R., 'The exponents and critics of absolutism', in *NCMH*, iv (Cambridge 1971)
Namier, L. B., 'Human nature in politics', in F. Stern (ed.), *The varieties of history* (London, 1970)

New Cambridge modern history, vol. iv, *see* Cooper, J. P. (ed.)

Newton, A. P., *The colonising activities of the English puritans* (New Haven, 1914)

O'Farrell, B., *Politician, patron, poet: William Herbert, third earl of Pembroke, 1580–1630* (UCLA PhD thesis, 1966; published Ann Arbor, 1985)

Ollard, R., *The image of the king: Charles I and Charles II* (New York, 1979)
    and Tudor-Craig, P. (eds.), *For Veronica Wedgwood these studies in seventeenth century history* (London, 1986)

Parker, D., *The making of French absolutism* (London, 1983)

Parker, G., *The army of Flanders and the Spanish road 1567–1659* (Cambridge, 1972)
    Spain and the Netherlands 1559–1659 (London, 1979)
    Europe in crisis 1598–1648 (London, 1981)
    The Thirty Years War (London, 1984)
    The military revolution. Military innovation and the rise of the West, 1500–1800 (Cambridge, 1988)

Parry, G., *The golden age restor'd* (Manchester, 1981)

Peck, L. L., *Northampton: patronage and policy at the court of James I* (London, 1982)
    ' "For a king not to be bountiful were a fault": perspectives on court patronage in early Stuart England', *JBS*, xxv (1986)

Prawdin, M., *Marie de Rohan, duchesse de Chevreuse* (London, 1971)

Quintrell, B. W., 'The making of Charles I's Book of Orders', *EHR*, xcv (July 1980)

Rabb, T. K. and Hirst, D., 'Revisionism revised: two perspectives on early Stuart parliamentary history', *P&P*, xcii (1981)

Ranke, L. von, *A history of England principally in the seventeenth century*, 6 vols. (Oxford, 1875)

Reade, H. G. R., *Sidelights on the Thirty Years War*, 3 vols. (London, 1924)

Reeve, L. J., 'Sir Thomas Roe's prophecy of 1629', *BIHR*, lvi, 133 (1983)
    'The legal status of the Petition of Right', *HJ*, xxix, 2 (1986)
    'The arguments in King's Bench in 1629 concerning the imprisonment of John Selden and other members of the House of Commons', *JBS*, xxv, 3 (July 1986)
    'Quiroga's paper of 1631: a missing link in Anglo-Spanish diplomacy during the Thirty Years War', *EHR*, ci, 401 (Oct. 1986)
    'Sir Robert Heath's advice for Charles I in 1629', *BIHR*, lix, 2 (1986)
    'The politics of war finance in early Stuart England: a comparative European view' (unpublished article)

Richards, J., ' "His nowe Majestie" and the English monarchy: the kingship of Charles I before 1640', *P&P*, cxiii (1986)

Roberts, C., *Schemes and undertakings* (Columbus, 1985)

Roberts, M., *Gustavus Adolphus: a history of Sweden 1611–1632*, 2 vols. (London, 1953–8)

Russell, C., *The crisis of Parliaments, English history 1509–1660* (Oxford, 1971)
    Parliaments and English politics 1621–1629 (Oxford, 1979)
    'The theory of treason in the trial of Strafford', *EHR*, lxxx, 314 (Jan. 1965)
    'Arguments for religious unity in England, 1530–1650', *JEH*, xviii, 2 (1967)
    'Parliamentary history in perspective, 1604–1629', *History*, lxi (1976)
    'The parliamentary career of John Pym, 1621–9', in P. Clark, A. G. R. Smith and N. Tyacke (eds.), *The English commonwealth 1547–1640* (Leicester, 1979)
    'Parliament and the king's finances', in C. Russell (ed.), *The origins of the English civil war*, rev. edn (London, 1980)

'The nature of a Parliament in early Stuart England', in H. Tomlinson (ed.), *Before the English civil war* (London, 1983)

'The British problem and the English civil war', *History*, lxxii (1987)

(ed.), *The origins of the English civil war*, rev. edn (London, 1980)

Salmon, J. H. M., *The French religious wars in English political thought* (Oxford, 1959, repr. 1981)

Renaissance and revolt. Essays in the intellectual and social history of early modern France (Cambridge, 1987)

Schreiber, R. E., *The first Carlisle* (*TrAPS*, lxxiv, pt 7; Philadelphia, 1984)

Schwartz, H., 'Arminianism and the English Parliament, 1624–1629', *JBS*, xii (1973)

Scott, W. R., *The constitution and finance of English, Scottish and Irish joint-stock companies to 1720*, 3 vols. (Cambridge, 1910–12)

Sharpe, K. M., *Sir Robert Cotton, 1586–1631* (Oxford, 1979)

'The earl of Arundel, his circle and the opposition to the duke of Buckingham, 1618–1628', in K. M. Sharpe (ed.), *Faction and Parliament, essays on early Stuart history* (Oxford, 1978)

'The personal rule of Charles I', in H. Tomlinson (ed.), *Before the English civil war* (London, 1983)

'Crown, Parliament and locality: government and communication in early Stuart England', *EHR*, ci, 399 (Apr. 1986)

'The image of virtue: the court and household of Charles I, 1625–1642', in D. Starkey *et al.*, *The English court from the Wars of the Roses to the civil war* (London, 1987)

(ed.), *Faction and Parliament, essays on early Stuart history* (Oxford, 1978)

Slack, P., 'Books of orders: the making of English social policy, 1577–1631', *TRHS*, 5th ser., xxx (1980)

Smuts, R. M., *The culture of absolutism at the court of Charles I* (Princeton University PhD thesis, 1976; published Ann Arbor, 1985)

'The puritan followers of Henrietta Maria in the 1630s', *EHR*, xciii (1978)

Snow, V. F., 'Essex and the aristocratic opposition to the early Stuarts', *JMH*, xxxii (1962)

Sommerville, J. P., *Politics and ideology in England 1603–1640* (London, 1986)

'The royal supremacy and episcopacy *jure divino*, 1603–1640', *JEH*, xxxiv, 4 (1983)

Sprunger, K. L., 'Archbishop Laud's campaign against puritanism at the Hague', *Church History*, xliv (1975)

Starkey, D. 'Court and government', in C. Coleman and D. Starkey (eds.), *Revolution reassessed* (Oxford, 1986)

Stradling, R. A., 'Olivares and the origins of the Franco-Spanish war, 1627–1635', *EHR*, ci, 398 (Jan. 1986)

Supple, B., *Commercial crisis and change in England 1600–1642* (Cambridge, 1959)

Swales, R. J. W., 'The Ship Money levy of 1628', *BIHR*, 1, 122 (1977)

Tapié, V.-L., *France in the age of Louis XIII and Richelieu* (Cambridge, 1984)

Taylor, H., 'Trade, neutrality and the "English Road" 1630–1648', *EcHR*, ser. 2, xxv (1972)

Thomas, D., 'Financial and administrative developments', in H. Tomlinson (ed.), *Before the English civil war* (London, 1983)

Thompson, C., 'The origins of the politics of the parliamentary middle-group, 1625–1629', *TRHS*, 5th ser., xxii (1972)

'The divided leadership of the House of Commons in 1629', in K. M. Sharpe (ed.), *Faction and Parliament, essays on early Stuart history* (Oxford, 1978)

Tomlinson, H. (ed.), *Before the English civil war* (London, 1983)

Trevor-Roper, H. R., *Archbishop Laud, 1573–1645*, 2nd edn (London, 1962)
  Renaissance essays (London, 1986)
  Catholics, Anglicans and puritans (London, 1987)
  'Spain and Europe 1598–1621', in *NCMH*, iv (Cambridge, 1971)

Tuck, R., ' "The ancient law of freedom": John Selden and the civil war', in J. S. Morrill (ed.), *Reactions to the English civil war 1642–1649* (London, 1982)

Tudor-Craig, P., 'Charles I and Little Gidding', in R. Ollard and P. Tudor-Craig (eds.), *For Veronica Wedgwood these studies in seventeenth century history* (London, 1986)

Tyacke, N., *Anti-Calvinists* (Oxford, 1987)
  'Puritanism, Arminianism and counter-revolution', in C. Russell (ed.), *The origins of the English civil war*, rev. edn (London, 1980)
  'Arminianism and English culture', *Britain and the Netherlands*, vii (1981)
  and White, P., 'Debate. The rise of Arminianism reconsidered', *P&P*, cxv (1987)

Venn, J. and J. A., *Alumni Cantabrigiensis*, Part I, 4 vols. (Cambridge, 1922–7)

Walter, J., 'Grain riots and popular attitudes to the law: Maldon and the crisis of 1629', in J. Brewer and J. Styles (eds.), *An ungovernable people* (London, 1980)
  and Wrightson, K., 'Dearth and the social order in early modern England', *P&P*, lxxi (May 1976)

Wedgwood, C. V., *The Thirty Years War* (London, 1981)
  The king's peace 1637–41 (London, 1955)
  Thomas Wentworth, first earl of Strafford 1593–1641: a revaluation (London, 1961)
  'The Elector Palatine and the civil war', *History Today*, iv (Jan. 1954)

Welsby, P., *George Abbot: the unwanted archbishop* (London, 1962)

White, P., 'The rise of Arminianism reconsidered', *P&P*, ci (1983)

White, S. D., *Sir Edward Coke and 'the grievances of the commonwealth', 1621–1628* (Chapel Hill, 1979)

Woolrych, A., 'The English revolution: an introduction', in E. W. Ives (ed.), *The English revolution 1600–1660* (London, 1968)

Worden, B., rev. art., *London Review of Books*, 19 Apr.–2 May 1984
  rev. art., *TLS*, 13 June 1986

Young, M. B., *Servility and service: the life and work of Sir John Coke* (Royal Historical Society, London, 1986)

Yule, G., *Puritans in politics* (Appleford, 1981)

Zagorin, P., *The court and the country* (London, 1969)
  'Sir Edward Stanhope's advice to Thomas Wentworth . . . ', *HJ*, vii, 2 (1964)
  'Did Strafford change sides?', *EHR*, ci (1986)

Zaller, R., 'The concept of opposition in early Stuart England', *Albion*, xii (1980)

IV THESES

Adams, S. L., 'The Protestant cause: religious alliance with the West European Calvinist communities as a political issue in England, 1585–1630' (Oxford University D.Phil. thesis, 1973)

Appleby, J. C., 'English privateering during the Spanish and French wars, 1625–1630' (University of Hull PhD thesis, 1983)

Cust, R. P., 'The forced loan and English politics 1626–1628' (London University PhD thesis, 1984)

Haskell, P., 'Sir Francis Windebank and the personal rule of Charles I' (Southampton University PhD thesis, 1975)

Reeve, L. J., 'The Secretaryship of State of Viscount Dorchester 1628–1632' (Cambridge University PhD thesis, 1984)

Tyacke, N., 'Arminianism in England: religion and politics 1604–1640' (Oxford University D.Phil. thesis, 1968)

INDEX

Cambridge Studies in Early Modern British History

Titles in the series